EDMUND
HILLARY
A Biography

EDMUND
HILLARY
A Biography

MICHAEL GILL

Vertebrate Publishing, Sheffield
www.v-publishing.co.uk

Edmund Hillary – A Biography
Michael Gill

First published in New Zealand in 2017 by Potton & Burton.
First published in Great Britain in 2019 by Vertebrate Publishing.
This paperback edition first published in 2020.

 VERTEBRATE PUBLISHING
Omega Court, 352 Cemetery Road, Sheffield S11 8FT, United Kingdom.
www.v-publishing.co.uk

Front cover: Edmund Hillary on the 1953 British Everest expedition. Photo: Alf Gregory.
Photography © individual photographers.

Lines from 'Abel Janszoon Tasman and the Discovery of New Zealand' by Allen Curnow,
which forms the narrated component of Douglas Lilburn's Landfall in Unknown Seas
© Tim Curnow, reproduced with permission.

This book is a work of non-fiction. The author has stated to the publishers that,
except in such minor respects not affecting the substantial accuracy of the work,
the contents of the book are true.

A CIP catalogue record for this book is available from the British Library.

ISBN: 978-1-911342-96-0 (Hardback)
ISBN: 978-1-839810-25-1 (Paperback)
ISBN: 978-1-911342-97-7 (Ebook)

10 9 8 7 6 5 4 3 2 1

Edited by Jane Parkin.
Cover and internal design by Lisa Noble, Paperminx.

Vertebrate Publishing is committed to printing on paper from sustainable sources.

Printed and bound in Scotland by Bell & Bain Ltd.

Contents

Ed Hillary on the 1953 British Everest expedition. ALF GREGORY

Introduction

⟫◆⟪

I was 15 years old when Edmund Hillary made the first ascent of Mount Everest with Tenzing Norgay on 29 May 1953. I had placed a bet that the attempt would fail. Nine previous efforts had come to nothing – why should a tenth fare any better? Even when I was proved wrong, I still had no understanding of why 1953 was different. I came closer seven years later when Ed invited me to spend nine months in the Himalayas on his Silver Hut expedition of 1960–61. This was an expedition that began with a yeti hunt but moved on to the more serious business of studying high-altitude physiology in a laboratory on a high snowfield in the heart of the Everest region. We went on to test ourselves – disastrously – with an oxygenless attempt on Mount Makalu, fifth-highest peak in the world. I learnt that oxygen was a key player in the high-altitude game.

My qualifications for the expedition were that I had climbed widely in New Zealand, had a degree in physiology and was halfway through a medical degree. During the three months before the expedition, Ed and his wife Louise generously invited me to join them on a trip to the home of the sponsors in Chicago, and to London where I worked in Dr Griffith Pugh's physiology laboratory. I met famous Everesters whose books I had read: Eric Shipton, John Hunt, George Lowe, Mike Ward, James Morris. Ed and Louise took me with them to Chamonix in the French Alps. They were great fun. During the years that followed Ed invited me on more than a dozen expeditions. It was a friendship that lasted until Louise's death in 1975 and continued in an attenuated form through to Ed's death in 2008. He shaped my life, as he did so many others.

What makes me believe that I have something new to say about Edmund Hillary? He writes his own story in his autobiographies. He always preferred his own version of his life. As he said to journalist Pat Booth who published the unauthorised *Life of a Legend* in 1991, 'I write my own books!'

The idea that I might write a biography came in 2009, a year after Ed's death. I was writing a book about his aid work in Nepal between 1961 and 2003. He had bequeathed his papers and photos to the Auckland Museum, and for my research I read this large archive. There were surprises. There was a thick diary written by Ed's father Percy describing his excitement when he went to war in 1915 and his horror when he experienced the reality of Gallipoli. Percy is clearly the father of the son who becomes a conscientious objector in the war that starts in 1939. Ed teaches Radiant Living and for a year in 1940–41 he runs a Young Citizens' session on national radio each Sunday. When finally he enters the Air Force, his life of adventure begins. In Box 24 of the archive, 1965, there is an unpublished novel, *Call Not to the Gods*, under the nom de plume Gary Sankar.

More than this I had access to private letters between Louise and Ed which were held by Peter and Sarah Hillary. Ed always acknowledged the central importance of Louise in their shared life but without much detail. In the archive she enters Ed's life as a lively 21-year-old in a ski club hut on Mount Ruapehu. On his way to Everest in 1953 he is meeting her for a weekend in Sydney, and he writes to her throughout the expedition. Three months after the famous climb, they marry and enjoy an extended honeymoon as part of a lecture tour through the UK, Europe and USA. Through the rest of the decade Louise is at home raising three children, but in 1961 after a trek into Everest country she joins him as a full partner in bringing education and health to the Sherpas. The wrenching tragedy of the plane crash of 31 March 1975 is all there in the files.

As I read through the archive I became immersed in the life of Ed Hillary. Like him I am a New Zealander, born in Auckland. New Zealand is small, and in the days before air travel it was a long way from the rest of the world. Though I am 18 years younger than Ed, the social and physical environment he grew up in is recognisably mine.

There are many biographies of famous men. This is mine, and it reflects how I saw Edmund Hillary during the time I knew him. It is not the complete story. The years after 1980 are too recent for me to attempt to cover them satisfactorily – the years of Ed's marriage to June Lady Hillary will have their own biographer. One of the fascinations of Ed's life is the way he handled his fame and came to be recognised as the person who best represented the 'essence and spirit' of New Zealand. It has been a privilege to have entered his remarkable life through those old letters and photos, as well as my own memories and those of others who knew him.

– Michael Gill
Auckland, 2017

Edmund Raymond Hillary (b.1836), father of Percival Augustus Hillary (b.1885), and grandfather of Edmund Percival Hillary (b.1919). JOHN HILLARY COLLECTION

CHAPTER 1

A pioneering heritage

⟫✦⟪

It is not absolutely certain that Sir William Hillary (born 1771) was a forebear of Sir Edmund Hillary (born 1919) but, had he been asked, Ed would almost certainly have approved of the baronet's life of adventure. William married Frances Disney Fytche, said to be the richest heiress in Essex, against her father's wishes. He spent the whole of her £20,000 inheritance raising a private army to fight against Napoleon, earning a hereditary baronetcy in 1805. Three years later, to put a few miles and a little water between himself and his creditors (and apparently his wife), and to bury quietly the murkier details surrounding his elopement and marriage, he fled to the Isle of Man. Here he married again and embarked on the work for which he became most famous. The principal port of the isle was poorly protected and its fishing fleet vulnerable to storms from the east. Dismayed by the sight of wrecks and dead sailors washing ashore, Sir William established a fleet of lifeboats manned by volunteers to rescue crew from distressed vessels. The organisation would later become the Royal National Lifeboat Institution.

The Hillarys of Dargaville

We are on surer ground genealogically when we come in 1884 to Edmund Raymond Hillary of Dargaville, grandfather of the Edmund who climbed Mt Everest. Edmund senior was born in Lancashire in 1836 and trained as a watchmaker. A need for adventure led him to India where he made a good living working for maharajahs on their

11

collections of clockwork birds and animals. In 1881 he was in Wales, then on 3 December 1884, when he re-enters the record at age 48, he was in Dargaville, marrying a 28-year-old Irish woman by the name of Annie Clementina Fleming, always known as Ida.

There is no record of where Edmund arrived in New Zealand, but it was probably Auckland, where inquiries in the early 1880s would have shown that the formerly rich southern goldfields were in decline, whereas Dargaville to the north was on the rise, lifted by its kauri timber and gum trade. From Auckland immigrants travelling north went by rail to the southern reaches of the Kaipara Harbour, described as the largest enclosed harbour in the southern hemisphere. Embarked on a steamer, they moved north down a tidal river through mangroves before emerging on to an expanse of storm-swept water, land-locked except where the powerful tidal stream poured through the narrow harbour entrance between bare sandhills. On the beaches were skeletons of ships that had missed the navigable channel winding between breakers pounding the shoals of the bar. Once past the intimidating entrance, the steamer entered the tidal waters of the broad Northern Wairoa River with its main town of Dargaville on the west bank. Kauri timber was in demand in New Zealand and beyond, and was in evidence everywhere as rafts of logs coming down the outgoing tide, and as huge stacks of sawn timber in riverside mills or being loaded on to ships crowding the wharves.

Edmund set up shop in a main street that had the makeshift look of a set for a western movie. His two-storey house on the Dargaville waterfront was substantial; he became secretary of the Dargaville Town Board and kept racehorses. His wife Ida, born in 1856, had come to New Zealand at the age of eight and had worked as a governess until her marriage. She had a warm personality and like her husband was a storyteller. Four children were born to the Hillarys: Percival Augustus, future father of Edmund Percival; John, Leila and Clarice. For 20 years the family prospered and the four children grew up strong, healthy, independent, and as well educated as the times allowed.

But by 1905 Dargaville was past its peak. The great forests of kauri disappeared as all but the most inaccessible trees were felled and dragged and floated to the mills. Where once there had been stands of the most majestic trees on Earth, their trunks rising like the pillars of a cathedral, now there were only their burnt-over remnants. The timber

Annie Clementina Fleming, always known as Ida, married Edmund Raymond Hillary in 1884 when she was 28 and he 48. HILLARY FAMILY COLLECTION

trade had brought wealth to the north, as the goldfields had to the south, but it came at a price. The gum, too, that poor man's gold, had almost run out.

The Hillary family fortune declined along with that of the rest of the community. Edmund had owned and betted on horses, and lost heavily. His Leorina was an 'also ran' in the Auckland Cups of 1889 and 1890, and his Bravo was a non-paying third in the much humbler Matakohe Cup of 1892. The big house had to be sold. Family lore has it that in his late sixties Edmund took to his bed in a fit of depression that lasted through to his death in 1928 at the age of 92. The story is plausible. A streak of depression runs through the Hillary family and, besides, he had a younger wife to take over. To Ida fell the task of earning money and raising the children. She did what work she could – dressmaking, painting pictures for sale – but she must have been hard-pressed. The children completed eight years of their compulsory primary schooling, though not all the way through to the legally

13

Percy in best dress pre-war, age c.28. HILLARY FAMILY COLLECTION

required age of 15. Somehow, as people did, they got by. Ida too was long-lived, dying in 1952 at age 95, a year short of seeing her grandson climb Mount Everest.

Percival Augustus, the eldest of Edmund and Ida's four offspring, grew into an energetic and resourceful youth. In 1898, at the age of 13, he began a lifelong connection with journalism when he became a copy boy for the *Wairoa Bell*, an entry-level job delivering telegraphs and as general factotum. He learned photography, and after proving his writing skills became a reporter. Three years later, inspired by tales and photographs of the heroic British fighting the Boers, he volunteered for war in South Africa but was too young. The glories of battle would have to wait until the Great War in 1915 at Gallipoli.

By 1911 Percy was printing and publishing the *Wairoa Bell* on behalf of its locally based proprietor, and three years later, in April 1914 and at the age of 29, he left the *Wairoa Bell* to buy its rival, the *North Auckland Times*. All he needed was a wife, and he knew who she would be: Gertrude Clark, one of a perceptibly superior family of 11 siblings who lived 10 kilometres downstream at Whakahara on the other side of the Wairoa.

The Clarks of Whakahara

By North Auckland standards, the Clarks were landed gentry. Gertrude's grandparents, Charles and Dinah Clark, had arrived in New Zealand from Yorkshire in 1843, 40 years before Edmund Raymond Hillary, and just three years after the beginning of systematic British colonisation and the signing of a treaty with Māori at Waitangi. The Clarks made their landfall in Nelson at the northern tip of the South Island, but found no opportunities for advancement there. Forming a friendship with a family by the name of Paton, they decided to move into the timber trade, first in Auckland, then in the northern Wairoa at a settlement called Paradise, upriver from Dargaville.

The Clarks became well known on the Wairoa River, and Dinah was described as a clever businesswoman. Those early days in timber set them up financially, and in 1860 they were able to purchase a small farm downriver on a low hill known to Māori as Whakahara. Charles built a raft – standard technology for timber workers – on to which he loaded all their possessions, including livestock, before setting off on the outgoing tide. On sloping ground overlooking the broad expanse of

The Clark homestead at Whakahara on the banks of the Northern Wairoa branch of the Kaipara Harbour. Dargaville and the school at Te Kopuru are on the opposite bank of the tidal river. HILLARY MUSEUM COLLECTION

the river they built their homestead of pitsawn local timber, and filled it with mahogany and Venetian glass imported from England, as well as local kauri furniture. In time they established a fine garden. In front of the house Charles added a one-roomed store selling basic items such as flour, tea, sugar, oatmeal, tinned meats and hardware to passing timber workers and gumdiggers. To these amenities they added a post office and a butchery, and the service of a cutter as transport across and around the Kaipara Harbour. Church services were held in the big dining room, and the home became a centre of hospitality for early settlers and travellers on the river.

Despite their isolation, Dinah kept in touch with political developments. Among the 31,872 signatures to the suffragettes' 1893 petition to Parliament – from a quarter of New Zealand's women of voting age – were 211 from rural Northland, one of them that of Dinah Clark of Whakahara, then in her seventies. The petition became law that same year, making New Zealand the first country in the world to give women the vote.

Charles and Dinah had four children. The youngest, George, married a local seamstress, Harriet Wooderson, and took over the working of the Whakahara farm and store. Between 1882 and 1900, Harriet gave birth to 11 healthy children, spaced on average 18 months apart. She might well have delivered many more had not George been killed in 1901 by a kick from a horse. The family held together despite the tragedy, kept their store in business, and maintained their position as the sort of pioneers others might try to emulate.

Gertrude, born in 1892, was the eighth of George and Harriet's children. She and her siblings were at first educated by a succession of governesses, young women who quickly gave up the isolation of Whakahara in favour of the bright lights of Auckland. By building a schoolhouse on their property, the Clarks were able to persuade the government to pay the salary of a primary school teacher. But secondary schools were in short supply, the nearest being at Te Kopuru, south of Dargaville, on the other side of the river. Gertrude later described what getting to school entailed:

> When I was twelve years old I was determined to go to High School but this meant crossing the wide and oft-times treacherous tidal river, a distance of half a mile. My mother conferred with her older children, my father having died earlier, and it was decided that the daily journey would be too much for a girl. This I would not agree to.
>
> For two years my brother and I set off in a small rowing boat. Sometimes it was very rough, and the mill hands on the opposite side of the river would come out, and stand along the river bank watching our progress, especially when we reached the sand bank in the centre of the river where the waves broke in all directions and our frail barque was greatly in danger of being capsized.
>
> On some nights when there was a storm and the waves were racing down the river with the out-going tide, we would have to row across very strongly to land at our house. Sometimes we would be swept down-river before we could get the boat ashore. We would grab hold of a mangrove as we swept past and sopping wet would wade ashore, tie up the boat for the night and wearily trudge home.

Gertrude Clark, age 23. Signed: 'From Gertie 1915'. HILLARY FAMILY COLLECTION

> However, even with these vicissitudes, I passed my
> Candidates Examination as a teacher. It was a great life indeed.[1]

It might have been a great life but the future lay in Auckland, not Whakahara. George Clark had understood this, and before his death had set up a business in the Auckland suburb of Mt Eden, selling china from a shop with a small attached house. When the shop failed, the house came into use as accommodation for various members of the family. Later Harriet, as matriarch, bought a section nearby at 20 Herbert Road, and despatched Mabel, her eldest and most able daughter, to supervise the building of a substantial house and manage it as the family centre for a growing tribe of siblings, cousins and other more distant family members – including, eventually, Gertrude's son Edmund. Artistic Helen made a sign in beaten copper for the veranda announcing that this was 'The New Whakahara'.

In 1907, 15-year-old Gertrude was still at Te Kopuru but now as a trainee teacher rather than a pupil. Soon she was moving south to Herbert Road to complete her teacher training, and from there went to Te Awamutu Primary School in the Waikato. Photographs of the time show Gertrude as a slim, elegantly dressed, rather dreamy-looking young woman. She had acquired her values from her grandparents and parents. She had a powerful belief in the importance of education and aspired to the social values of the English middle class that existed in New Zealand in rudimentary form. She believed it was important to mix with the right people, difficult though that might be in such an unformed society. She kept a journal in which she copied poetry, and she believed strongly in books and the people who wrote them. Traditional Christianity was an integral part of her upbringing.

How and where she met Percival Augustus Hillary, seven years older than her and living in Dargaville, some 10 kilometres north of little Te Kopuru, is not recorded. But he was a lively young man with good prospects in the newspaper industry. In the archive is a postcard from Percy, who is smartly dressed and striking a pose between two friends in the whitest of shirts. He writes:

> Dear Gertie, These are three friends of mine, one of whom
> you know, and thinking it might interest you to see the
> postcard, I am sending it to you. Yours, Percy.[2]

Percy Hillary c.1913 poses (centre) and writes to Gertie, 'These are three friends of mine, one of whom you know, and thinking it might interest you ...'
HILLARY FAMILY COLLECTION

Gertie wrote in the front of her notebook:

> Gertie Clark is my name
> Single is my station
> Happy be the little man
> That makes the alteration.

But by the second half of 1914 a much bigger alteration was afoot, and on 4 August Britain announced that the nation – surely to be joined by its empire – had declared war on Germany.

Like most Pākehā New Zealanders, Percy had been raised in the belief that Britain and its far-flung empire represented all that was great and good in the world. She might suffer the occasional setback

20

but always triumphed over enemies, whether in Europe, India, New Zealand or any other part of the globe. For a Pākehā schoolchild in the early twentieth century, it was a British navigator, Captain Cook, who in 1769 had discovered New Zealand and drawn its map. There might have been a distant awareness that Māori navigators had somehow sailed their outrigger canoes to make landfall on the undiscovered islands they called Aotearoa some 600 years earlier, but the magnitude of that achievement went untaught.

So when war was declared on Germany, Percy wanted his share of the excitement and glory from what would surely be a quick and splendid victory. Along with others from Dargaville, he went to Auckland to volunteer. He was accepted into the 15th North Auckland Infantry.

Percy kept a record of his war experience in a diary – a thick sheaf of handwritten papers in a confident, round hand, and a surprise find in the Hillary archive. Ed must have known of the diary's existence, but he made almost no mention of his father's searing Gallipoli experience. In his two autobiographies, Ed uses three almost identical sentences to describe the most important event in his father's life:

> When World War One erupted my father was quick to volunteer for what he regarded as a worthy cause. He went overseas as a sergeant, served with the Australian and New Zealand Army Corps in the grim Gallipoli campaign, was shot through the nose and laid low with severe dysentery. He was finally invalided home more than a little disillusioned about noble causes.[3]

Gallipoli, and Percy's account of it, deserve more space than this. Percy is recognisably the father of Edmund. He is hard-working, competitive, alert for adventure. He likes to express himself in writing. The diary shows a more vivid personality than the dour person portrayed by Ed. Percy describes a year that will change him forever and create a family climate that will profoundly influence his first son, born five years later. And he sketches briefly two more steps in the relationship between himself and Gertrude Clark that will be so important to him for the rest of his life.

Lance-corporal Hillary (one stripe) with Gertrude in 1914 before he departs New Zealand. At Gallipoli he became a sergeant. HILLARY FAMILY COLLECTION

CHAPTER 2

Percy goes to Gallipoli

==—⧫—==

Ed Hillary lived a life of adventure and risk, but his father Percy entered an arena of vastly greater risk when he went to Gallipoli in 1914. Of 13,977 New Zealand soldiers who took part, 2,799 died and 5,212 were wounded.[1] Ed is often quoted as saying, 'It is not the mountain we conquer but ourselves,' but it is unlikely that Percy ever said, 'It is not Gallipoli we conquer but ourselves.' Indeed, there is no record of Percy saying anything about Gallipoli outside the 45,800-word diary he wrote at the time.[2] I have edited this down to 4,100 words, all of them Percy's. They show with rare eloquence the pre-Gallipoli bravado and the in-Gallipoli horror. He might not have talked to his sons and daughter about these events, but they were there beneath the surface for the rest of his life.

Percy joined the New Zealand volunteer army on 20 October 1914, and for two months was in a training camp at Trentham, outside Wellington. In November, he escaped briefly to act as best man at the wedding of his sister Leila. It was also a chance to spend time with Gertie Clark, who joined the train at Te Awamutu en route to Auckland. 'The wedding went off beautifully. At 9pm, Miss Clark and I left again for our southern destinations, she for Te Awamutu to continue her teaching, me for Wellington.'

That might have been the end of it, but Gertie had other ideas. When she discovered that the troops were to leave Wellington on

SS *Willochra*, she took the train south for the farewell parade in mid-December. Percy describes the day:

> This morning we marched up the streets of Wellington
> through crowds of cheering well-wishers. Girls were allowed
> to fall in with their soldier-boys and march beside them,
> taking this last opportunity of talking with their departing
> sweethearts.
>
> To my surprise Gertie was there and joined me having
> come all the way from Te Awamutu. She was accompanied by
> the two Misses Atkinson and we walked along having a great
> old chat. I was to meet her afterwards at the wharf where
> the *Willochra* was tied up. The wharf was crowded with men
> and women densely packed together. I couldn't see the girls.
> I stood on a crane on the wharf till at 6pm someone told me
> the *Willochra* was leaving. So I waited till the ship was 10 feet
> out from the wharf then ran to get on (ahem!) but couldn't, so
> I told those on board that I would get a launch and come out.
>
> Then I turned to take a car to the Atkinsons where Gertie
> is staying. As I was setting off a picket who had been left
> ashore to pick up stragglers caught me and made me fall in to
> join a boat going in half an hour. I went quietly but when they
> were busy I stole into a right-of-way, ran down it and then to
> the tramline where I caught a car and thus neatly escaped.
>
> I met Gertie near the Atkinsons and we all had tea up at
> their house. Afterwards Gertie and I went out to the pictures
> and took a taxi home, having a jolly evening together. I might
> get into trouble and even lose my lance-corporal's stripe but
> I don't care a pin now that I have seen Gertie and had the
> evening with her. In the end I caught a small steamer across
> to the *Willochra* and slipped on board. Thus I escaped scot free
> from any punishment.

Cruise ship to Egypt and sightseeing in Cairo
The four months before the landing at Gallipoli were full of excitement
and pleasurable anticipation:

> The whole wide world now seems before us, full of
> strangeness and adventure, and while misgivings trouble our

hearts at leaving our people and our native land, yet the old exploring, adventuring spirit of our nation draws us irresistibly to contemplate the future with delight and expectant elation. A spirit of comradeship exists everywhere.

In Colombo, Percy records his first impressions of Asia:

The beaches here are fringed with palms and the seething, swarming, confused chattering of swarthy Hindoos, makes us realise that we are in the East, the land of patience and impatience, of riches and poverty, of silence and uproar, of vivid attraction and awful repulsion, of stately pride and grovelling beggardom. All is animation, the Hindoos shouting their wares and the guards warning them away. I am in my glory and revel in scenes like this.

As the ship enters the Suez Canal he notes:

The shores here are bleak hills and arid desert. Last night we passed a monument on the spot where Moses and the Israelites crossed the Red Sea into Arabia. There is great excitement on board. We are going to Cairo to camp beside other New Zealand Forces. What grand sport! What a time I shall have! I'll get all the leave I possibly can and explore the pyramids, sphinxes, temples and all the wonderful historical works of this ancient race of highly-civilised architects and sculptors. I'll bring home cases of mummies and old Egyptian ornaments, weapons, etc.

Percy did not bring home an Egyptian mummy but for three months he and his mates rode camels to the pyramids, skirmished with the Australians, and enjoyed the sights and smells of oriental bazaars. But by April Percy is noting that: 'The Dardanelles bombardment is a most important event and is followed by us with keenest interest for we believe our movements are influenced by its success. We hope to go to Turkey to help take Constantinople, thence through the Balkan states and Austria into Germany, but this is only our wish. We don't know where we will go.'

Two weeks later, they are preparing to depart:

25

You should have seen the cleaning and polishing of rifles and the careful sharpening of bayonets. Everyone has suddenly become most attentive and minutely particular regarding their 'best friend', their rifle. There is severe work ahead and the prospect of it acted like a tonic on the men, even those who are lazy and neglectful.

From the deck of our troopship we enjoy the sight of a mass of shipping, a forest of masts and funnels, like being in a leafless forest. It is said that 200,000 troops are taking part in this action. I am glad I have spent two educative months in Egypt but I rejoice in being at sea again and am now looking forward to exploring new cities and countries.

I have become very philosophic. It is brave, strong work this soldiering, benefitting and improving the very weakest of characters.

On 24 April he writes:

For two days we were at sea, crossing the blue Mediterranean to Lemnos where we have been at anchor in this splendid harbour. There are dozens of warships, cruisers, destroyers and other war-craft and scores of troop transports. Everybody is on the tip-toe of expectation and excitement and speculating on our probable movements. Tomorrow at 1.30am on April 25th, we up anchor and set sail for a future none of us can guess.

Gallipoli – the reality

From 25 April, the day of the landings on Gallipoli, a month of diary is missing. None of the forces who landed on the Gallipoli peninsula captured the ground they had hoped for. To the south, the British and French never broke out of their beachheads. Twenty-five kilometres north at Anzac Cove, the Australian and New Zealand (ANZAC) troops established forward posts high on the inhospitably steep cliffs and gullies above the beach where they landed, but they could not break through the Turkish trenches defending the highest ground. Within days of the landing, fighting was deadlocked between the corpse-strewn trenches of the Turks and the ANZACs.

Landing in Anzac Cove at Gallipoli, April 1915. ALEXANDER TURNBULL LIBRARY, WELLINGTON, PACOLL-4318

25 May – in the trenches on Walkers Ridge. 'On Sunday at dark we moved quietly off to a new position, no smoking or talking permitted. We filed silently past sleeping men in their dug-outs, past rows of hobbled mules with Indians beside them, then up a darksome gully enclosed by towering sandstone cliffs. From the tops comes the roar of rapidly-fired rifles and the hysterical clattering of machine guns, with a continuous circle of light from the rifle flashes edging the dark cliff-top. Further we went till right underneath the savage activity, then we climbed up a steep, zigzag road that led into the trenches where the men were fighting. Here, about halfway up, we lay down on the hard ground in our greatcoats with our equipment on and our rifles beside us ready loaded.

'We dropped straight away into sound sleep but were awakened an hour later in alarm – the Turks were threatening our left flank. Hurriedly we jumped up, seized our rifles and fell in, waiting for the order to march off to support our comrades in the firing line. The rifle

The steep slopes behind Anzac Cove which were the scene of bitter fighting between ANZAC soldiers and the Turks. AUSTRALIAN WAR MEMORIAL, C01621

fire was now thunderous and seemed to spell death and danger for those above us, making our pulses beat the faster, but suddenly it all eased – the danger was past for the time.

'On Monday an armistice was observed for nine hours – arranged by the German general – whilst the Turks buried their dead, six and seven deep. It was so unreal, the silence and peace, the oppressive stillness, that we really welcomed the sound of the rifle reports again when hostilities recommenced. It may sound a strange thing to say but it is true, that the stealthy quietness made us uneasy.'

27 May – Anzac Cove. 'Today I was told that I was transferred to a new platoon and that I was to be a sergeant. The weather here is clear, a most healthy and delightful climate. I go in for a swim every day – it is hot during the middle of the day, and the sea, but 100 yards away, is beautifully calm and cool. How we revel in it, although stray bullets hit the water near about us frequently, sometimes claiming a victim.

'The atmosphere gives magnificent effects upon the Grecian isles scattered across the sea within our view. The sea is everywhere blue but the further isles are of a far deeper blue, whilst those bordering the horizon seem painted with solid cobalt. They stand on the sea like blue pieces cut from card whilst the sky and the sea effects defy description. Alas, in sad contrast, huge shells are humming over us, exploding with thunders, whilst bullets whistle and sing their death song.'

31 May – Anzac Cove. 'Anzac Cove is the name of this place where we have been for five long weeks now. Yesterday, whilst we were road-making in our little gully, Lieutenant Simpson of our 15th Company was shot dead through the heart by a stray bullet. It was hard, for he had not seen a Turk or fired a shot. He was a young Auckland solicitor. Every day men are being shot dead or wounded all about us and right beside us for although we are not in the trenches, we get shelled and fired at by the enemy all the time.'

4 June – Quinn's Post. 'Two days ago we crossed over a hill to Shrapnel Gully where we cut ourselves dugouts and settled down. This is a more dangerous place than before; we had four men wounded and one killed before lunch. Yesterday at 10.30am we set off to occupy a trench at Quinn's Post. The Turkish trenches are only 25 feet away from ours and we hear the Turks talking away and see them at their loopholes, through which they shoot at anything. No 3 trench is the most fearful place, the Turks throwing bombs which burst terrifically, shaking the ground and throwing up clouds of dust, blowing off an arm or leg. They are horrible, awful things and all night and day the Turks throw them over. A few landed nearby, but did no harm to us. An overcoat thrown over a bomb makes it almost harmless and by this means we lost only two killed and four wounded. Of course, we fired bombs back at them, and rifles blazed all night too. I had charge of a portion of the trench and didn't have a wink of sleep all night, having to watch things and keep the men awake.

'Today Captain Algie called for 100 men and two NCOs from Auckland Company to attack and capture Turkish trenches. I gave my name in as one of the volunteer sergeants and so did two others of the fifteenth company. It probably will be somewhat dangerous, so I am writing this before we march off tonight. I felt it was my duty to volunteer though I was anything but happy at the thought of the job in front of us. We are in for it now, however. We intend to get the trenches and hang on to them.'

5 June – Quinn's Post. 'After the most awful 12 hours that could be imagined by even Dante himself, I am indeed lucky to be alive to tell the tale of horror upon horrors through which we passed. At 10.30pm last night we left our bivouacs and silently in single file marched along the track, then up the hill through big communication trenches to the entrance to the fire trenches. It was a glorious night, starry, brilliantly starry, the soft faint light emanating from these "eyes of heaven" giving a gentle radiance, which made all objects most mysterious. After a few minutes' waiting, a fierce rifle fire broke out on every side, the continuous rattle and crackle filling the air with deafening sound, whilst the machine guns, soon joined in with their spiteful, crackling, running reports. The volume of sound swelled greater still as our howitzers thundered their whistling hells [*sic*] and our Japanese mortars threw their fearsome bombs into the enemy's trenches. Accompanied by tremendous explosions, huge clouds of dirt were blown into the air. The cruel hand bombs, which burst with awful violence and terrible effect, were freely thrown and put the finishing touch to the infernal orchestra. The Canterbury volunteers now charged the enemy's trenches and took them, capturing 80 prisoners, of which one escaped on the way along the trenches.

'Meanwhile the Australians had taken the machine gun opposite Courtney's Post, which was most deadly if left alone. Then 20 Aucklanders were sent as reinforcements to the Canterbury men and I was one of them. We went along a trench that ran up, curving through heaps of sandbags, till the blazing cliff top was reached where we crept one after another through a small curved tunnel in which our rifles, shovels and sandbags got jammed to our alarm and impatient dismay. Emerging from the mouth of the tunnel we climbed over the sandbag parapet and ran swiftly across the ground intervening between our own and the Turks' trenches, getting safely over this dangerous area and jumping into the latter like a shot. We then proceeded to make the trench stronger for defence and till daylight the Turks troubled us only with rifle fire so we felt fairly safe.

'However we had reckoned without our host for their second

trench back was at exact bomb-throwing distance. When daylight broke it showed our trench but little fitted for defence, it being a miserable place to convert to our use – there being dead Turks buried in the earth parapet, which we needed to move to be able to fire. We had thus no bomb proof shelter and our trench was crowded with men – twice too many. All along our front, these hand bombs, like black cricket balls, or innocent-looking jam tins, began to fly through the air, bursting within a second of landing with a deafening thunder and fearful results. The men not injured were stunned or dazed with shock. Like rain they came and our men began to thin rapidly, men falling dead all along, others writhing, groaning in fearful agony, yet others running with fearful gashed-open wounds to the entrance to a wee tunnel along which they had to crawl to reach our trenches in the rear.

'Reinforcements filled their places and we kept up rifle fire but this was useless against their bombs. These brutal, cruel murderous missiles poured on us, and we tried to erect bomb proof shelters and get bombs to throw back. But it seemed useless, for our men were falling like leaves and a stream of wounded flowed endlessly back to our rear. I saw men writhing in death agony with wounds too fearful to mention, others with injuries nearly as gruesome, stumbling along the trench, dragging their poor, bloody bodies past us, frantically trying to escape another thunder-bomb. Poor fellows! Some of them had better been hit again than survive as they were. The bottom of the trench was red, the world swam about us and death held our hands, ready at any moment to pull us across the Rubicon. The incessant, thunderous bursting of bombs was a fitting death chant to prepare our hopeless, desperate spirits for almost any fate, and those who came out unscathed were filled with wonder at the marvel of it. At length the position became untenable and at 8am we retired, and then peace and comparative quiet descended upon the scene. Our loss was heavy, my platoon being reduced from 31 to 14.

'I was in it all and can never forget it. I stayed there fighting and keeping the fellows at it till only a corporal and I were left of the original occupants. At length a bomb burst just above me with fearful effect. I just had time to put an overcoat over my head and so escaped its direct force, but I must have been dazed by the concussion for I hazily remember getting out of the trench and wandering into an Australian's dugout where I lay down for a good while, afterwards going back to my bivouac where I remained. I had previously been covered with dirt dozens of times from nearby explosions. Dozens of our men are suffering in the same way as I – no wounds, just shock from the concussion. I had nightmares all Saturday night, but felt almost all right on Sunday morning. I continued my duties and didn't bother the doctor as I only felt a bit "groggy".

'It was Auckland again who stood all the losses, and our Fifteenth Company which bore the brunt as usual. We sustained practically 80% casualties, an absolutely unheard of percentage, 20% being considered extremely high.'

To England as an invalid

11 June – Anzac Cove. 'Flies! I thought Egypt was bad for flies but I had not then known what I now do. This place, since summer has come, is very hot during the day. The dead have been lying unburied for weeks between the trenches and, although all were interred during the Armistice, scores soon took their places and Colonial and Turk lie side by side in sad neglect between the two posts of entrenched men seeking each other's lives day and night. It is impossible to do anything about these dead. The air is tainted revoltingly, the sun beats like a furnace into our deep, narrow trenches. The flies swarm in millions on the poor, silent forms, and also on us, voraciously swooping on our food, and in our mouths, obliterating with their endless myriads anything left down. They swarm over each other in heaps fighting to get beneath. There is no escape from them. They are a condition to be suffered in loathing, in disgust. As a danger to health they are a menace to us all. Woe to anyone not strong – the bullets of the enemy are safer. Our survival is due to only two things – the natural, outdoor health of the sturdy New Zealanders, and inoculation.'

26 June – Courtney's Post. 'Today a Turkish aeroplane dropped some papers which blew into the Turkish trenches where they tied them on to an old bomb and threw them towards us. They were invitations to us Colonials to come and surrender, "as we are being merely used by England for her own purposes" and were thus practically betrayed. They invited us to surrender and promised us the best of treatment with splendid food. They are sick of the war too.'

2 July – Courtney's Post. 'We are all heartily sick and tired of this trench warfare, awaiting an attack, working at all hours of day and night at navvies' work – digging trenches, roads, tunnels; carrying timber, bags of earth, gravel, stores, water, up these fearfully steep hills and cliffs. The men's tempers and spirits are becoming ragged and grumbling is now continual at every little thing. We have been nine weeks under fire. In the reserve gully we lost men almost every day and we have had no spell. A week away from hostilities would refresh the men but we push on. The men want to finish Turkey off and get the job done. Then, after a couple of weeks in Constantinople, sail for England for a month or so, then off to France – this is their cry.

'For the last three weeks I have had diarrhoea and feel entirely run down and ill with it.'

5 July – Lemnos Hospital. 'Because of my illness Major Craig ordered me away and I am now in hospital. For three months I had splendid health not parading sick once, although all that time was spent in action under most trying conditions. I am one of only 18 men left of our original group of 227 – the race is not always to the fast! Captain Algie has told me to stay away till I am completely better.'

13 August – Malta. 'At last I feel well, though a bit weak, and I have taken to my diary again. On my way here I was given a first-class cabin. There was an electric fan and all sorts of comforts – cupboards, electric lights, and fresh water in plenty to wash in as often as I wished. I have been living like a millionaire: Soup, fish, rissoles and sauce, savoury mince and mashed potatoes, curry and rice, roast meats and vegetables, pie or pudding. There are nurses on board, such nice, obliging girls, anxious for everyone's comfort. Two men died and were buried on the way, the steamer just stopping for a couple of minutes each time.

'When I found I was unable to sleep enclosed by walls I moved onto the deck in the sea breeze. I am afraid I shall advocate the simple, primeval life when I get back – just a roof to keep off the rain; and I think I could eat anything, even grass, after being alive for three months on bully beef and iron biscuits.

'Do you know that the Turks are fighting as fair a fight as could possibly be, not using any of the dirty German tactics and treating the wounded well. At first in the rage and ferocity of those few awful days

Percy after evacuation from Gallipoli, July 1915. HILLARY FAMILY COLLECTION

after landing, terrible things were done – on both sides, our men were equally to blame. Some Colonials captured a German officer with soft-nosed bullets on him that inflict awful wounds. They tied him to a pine tree, lifted bayonets and charged him, just as they reached his chest, dividing and passing to either side of him not having touched him; the officer fainted, was revived and the performance thrice repeated, then finally he was shot dead with his own soft-nosed bullets.

'The Turks brutally bayoneted our wounded and some of our own men replied in kind. But when the savage fever abated many gallant acts were performed. There was a Turk who picked up a wounded Australian calling for help and carried the injured man to his Australian mates. Another brought them water. They bandage up our men well and give them every attention.'

15 September – Bristol. 'We landed at Southampton and were brought here to Bristol through countryside where orchards were glowing brightly with ripening fruit, and the harvests being gathered under thatched barns. Rabbits and pheasants were thick as bees. Our hospital is a beautiful place. The staff is very large and the nurses are so very good, gentle and willing.

'Regarding my own health. I certainly am better than when I left Malta, for I have gained eight pounds in weight during the fortnight after leaving there, which is not so bad. I still lack energy for, as the doctor says, I am in a quiescent state, recuperating after a prolonged physical strain. My digestion too is weak. However, I am having a splendid time, new experience being gained, seeing fresh countries and people, and having a thorough change and rest.'

On 2 February 1916, Percy returned to Auckland. He was suffering from that state of anxiety, exhaustion and depression that became known as shell-shock – later post-traumatic stress disorder – and he was not drafted back into the war. As was almost invariable in Gallipoli veterans, he never spoke of his experiences. One might have thought the average Kiwi bloke would return from the war with a fund of yarns that he would tell for the rest of his life, but this rarely happened. Men had indeed overcome their fears, shown extraordinary courage and risked their lives, but to what end? They had been defeated. Great Britain had been shown to be far from great. Her vaunted army and navy had been grievously in error in planning and execution. When the final evacuation from Gallipoli took place at the end of 1915, almost one-fifth of the 100,000 Allied troops were dead and nearly half had been wounded. Military historian B.H. Liddell Hart wrote, 'Thus the curtain rang down on a sound and far-sighted conception, marred by a chain of errors in execution almost unrivalled in British history.'[3]

Many war veterans returned weak, disillusioned and alienated. Heroism had not been an easy code to follow. At Gallipoli, the usual reward for a conspicuous display of heroism was death. For many there must have been acts of commission or omission that could make them feel ashamed of themselves. Humanity itself, they might have thought, should feel ashamed of perpetrating this vast theatre of insanity on the Turkish peninsula. When Percy passionately advocated pacifism throughout the rest of his life and taught his two sons to be conscientious objectors in the Second World War, he was speaking from the depths of his own bitter experience.

Percy and Gertrude were married at St Matthew-in-the-City in Auckland on 6 February 1916. HILLARY FAMILY COLLECTION

CHAPTER 3

Growing up in Tuakau
and Auckland

Percy's ship arrived in Auckland on 2 February 1916. A week later he had married his Gertie at the church of St Matthew-in-the-City. A week is a short time in which to set up a wedding. Such speed suggests desperation, a need to reach a safe haven – at least on Percy's part. For the rest of his life he would carry the reputation of being a hard, withdrawn man, tough on his children, but the few surviving letters he wrote to Gertie show the softer side of a man who remained in love with his wife and dependent on her – a trait that would be inherited by his son.

Here is Percy, aged 55, away from home and writing to Gertrude in 1940:

> My Dearest, Do you know what today is? The 24th anniversary of our wedding. Heaps of love and happy memories! What a dainty bride you were, sweet, sensitive and charming. And what a wonderful wife you have been, steadfast as a rock, willing and full of constructive action.
>
> I wish I were home instead of miles away. I miss your love and affection and wise counsel. Every daily silence I send you my whole heart full of love and protection, and I also send each of the children thoughts of love, harmony and happiness. And my last thoughts at night are of you … Heaps of love …[1]

For four years between 1916 and 1920, Percy and Gertrude lived in Auckland, possibly with the Clark sisters at Herbert Road in Mt Eden. In May 1916, Percy was discharged from the army as 'medically unfit'. From time to time he found work as a freelance journalist. Gertie, to begin with at least, was teaching, but by 1917 she was pregnant, and on 19 June their first child was born, a daughter, June St Hilaire Hillary.

Two years later, Edmund Percival was born at the Kelvin Private Hospital in Clonbern Road, Remuera. And 15 months after Edmund came Wrexford Fleming. These were grand names that said something about the social aspirations of their parents. Much later in life, Wrexford gave up the struggle of signing his name Wrex and changed his name by deed poll to Rex.

Tuakau, 1920–1934

By 1919 beekeeping has appeared in the Hillary family: this was the occupation given by Percy in the electoral roll for that year. Returned servicemen could learn about bees at a government-run model farm in Ruakura, near Hamilton, and perhaps Percy had taken advantage of this. Whether he kept hives in Auckland is doubtful, but the family's next move opened up the opportunity for bee farming across as much farm and scrub land as he could reach.

As a returned soldier Percy was offered a grant of land, and in 1920 he became the owner of seven acres of flat, fertile land in the small farming town of Tuakau, 60 kilometres south of Auckland. Situated on the banks of the Waikato, the North Island's largest river, Tuakau had begun life in 1840 as a flax-milling centre. In the war of 1863–64 between Māori and colonial forces, an important redoubt covering the river was located on a promontory just south of the town.

By the time of the arrival of the Hillarys in 1920, Tuakau, along with its larger neighbour Pukekohe, had become a prosperous agricultural and farming centre thanks to its fertile, volcanic soils. There were market gardens supplying Auckland with potatoes, onions, cabbages and carrots; there were dairy and poultry farms, orchards, apiaries. Whitebait from the river were canned in a local factory. The road to Auckland was narrow and rough, but Tuakau had an excellent rail link to the big city, only one hour away on the Main Trunk Line. Percy's land was centrally located at one end of what is now the main street, with the railway station a kilometre away at the other end. The

The main street of Tuakau in the 1920s. TUAKAU MUSEUM

house came with two rooms, to which Percy would add home-built extensions that were usable but left incomplete for lack of time and priority in his busy life.

A farm of seven acres was unlikely to make its owner much money, but it provided food for subsistence from its gardens, orchards, chickens and six cows. Surplus milk was sold to the butter factory just across the railway line. Percy got bored with milking six cows by hand twice a day, but eased the tedium by reading from a wooden book-holder hung off the back of his cows. The land was also a base for farming bees, which collected nectar from clover in the surrounding paddocks and from mānuka growing on the steeper land not under cultivation. After purchasing an old van, Percy could buy new hives and locate them further afield wherever there were nectar-bearing flowers.

Soon he was back in his old profession of journalism as founding editor and publisher of the *Tuakau District News*, a weekly, two-page local news-sheet selling for the modest sum of one penny. The paper was owned by Northern Waikato Newspapers Ltd and printed locally, and the *Pukekohe Race Day* was added for punters at the big racetrack nearby. The *District News* was centred on advertising, but included coverage of local social and sports news, especially rugby and tennis. Percy was particularly enthusiastic about rugby and developed a sound technical knowledge of the game which he passed on to his sons. Ed remembered accompanying Percy on Saturday afternoons to watch the winning Te Kohanga team, composed mainly of Māori players and with a fullback described by the *District News* as a genius.

Percy became an important figure in local affairs. He was president of the Tuakau Chamber of Commerce and secretary of the local rugby and tennis clubs. In his *District News* he shaped and reflected local issues through his editorials, which were accompanied by poetry that Gertie had selected from Palgrave's *Golden Treasury of Songs and Lyrics*. Percy's powerful work ethic was not always sustained, and June remembered how there were days when her father would lapse into a depressive lethargy, lying around doing nothing.

As a father, Percy was a good storyteller. The lounge in their small house was a cosy room with an open fire, and June, Ed and Rex would curl up while Percy told them Jimmy Job stories. Jimmy lived in a hollow tree at the bottom of the garden and though each day he'd be in Africa riding cheetahs or finding sacks of diamonds, he slept back home in a hollow tree stump in the Tuakau garden.

The evidence, including that from June and Rex, suggests that Ed had a reasonably happy childhood in Tuakau up to the time he went to secondary school.[2] The children had a loving mother and a caring, though stern, father who was always engaged in interesting projects. They lived in the sort of rural environment that wistful memories are made of: farms all around, fields of hay, farm animals with their warm smells, trees of all shapes and sizes to climb in, the banks of a great river. Ed and Rex would make driftwood rafts and float downriver to a landing where Percy and Gertrude would be waiting with a picnic beside their Overland Tourer. They had beach holidays at the Waikato Heads with Auntie Leila, and other family holidays with Uncle John ('Jack') Hillary at Tatuanui, where he ran a successful country store.

Writing of his years in Tuakau, Ed grudgingly concedes 'my memories of those early years are happy enough',[3] but added later:

> I was a restless, rather lonely child and even in my teens I had few friends. My father was a man of rigid principles and any straying from the path by me was usually severely punished.

Rex, June and Ed, c.1925. HILLARY MUSEUM COLLECTION

> Not that I believe my behaviour was irresponsible, but I had
> a stubborn temperament and would often refuse to admit to
> errors – at times because I didn't think I was to blame. This
> infuriated my father who would take me to the woodshed and
> thump me until his anger or his arm weakened. But I rarely if
> ever gave in.[4]

It is a strong image and one that has been used by documentary film-
makers to summarise Ed's childhood: a looming adult male with a
wooden slat in one hand, leading a very small boy out to a woodshed
for an apparently sadistic beating. There can be no doubting Ed's sense
of injustice but he was also aware that his father had good qualities. In
Two Generations, published in 1984, he qualified the image:

> And yet, strangely enough I had a considerable respect for my
> father. I admired his moral courage – he would battle fiercely
> against society or the powers-that-be on a matter of principle
> and he also had the ability to make his children laugh – and
> there was nothing I enjoyed more in life than laughing.[5]

In 1991 Ed was still trying to soften the image he had created when he wrote to script writer and film-maker Tom Scott:

> … my father was not as big a bastard as you make him appear. Although I argued with him a great deal I had quite an admiration and respect for him too. He was a man of principle with very determined views – and such people are always troublesome to their kids – or so say I …
>
> Can't we somehow build in my father's good points – his tremendous work ethic; his courage and refusal to give way to oppression; his constant concern for the underdog; his strong principles which maybe I inherited – although I must have been a sore trial to him at times …
>
> He was very strongly Labour oriented. I can remember him almost raving during the depression days.
>
> He worked like mad – harder than I ever worked and I work pretty hard.
>
> He was a great vege gardener …[6]

Rex's memories of the encounters in the woodshed were less harrowing:

> We had a strict father, no denying that, he'd cart us over to the woodshed and give us a damn good hiding. In those days benzene containers came in crates made of wooden slats and Percy would give us a whack with them but they were so wide it didn't hurt. He wasn't really angry with us. You know, Ed and I were reasonably clued up. We knew that if we started crying and really put on a performance we wouldn't get that much, so once we were on the way to the shed we started bawling – it helped! Yeah, he was a strict man but he had blind spots that let us get away with things.[7]

Of his mother Ed wrote: '[She] had a more gentle disposition, although strongly principled too, and we relied on her for the warmth and affection that all families need.'[8] She kept up the social habits she had learnt at Whakahara with visiting cards printed for herself and Percy: 'Mrs P. Augustus Hillary of St Hilaire, Tuakau, will be at home at 2pm on Tuesdays'. And she was ambitious for her three children.

The junior classes of Tuakau School in the 1920s. School motto reads: SERVICE THE MASTER KEY OF LIFE. TUAKAU MUSEUM

She wanted them to have a level of education that would take them into social strata higher than those available in Tuakau.

At the age of five, Ed entered Tuakau Primary School, expecting to spend eight years there before passing the Certificate of Proficiency, the entrance qualification for high school. There were eight grades in three classrooms. Movement up the grades was erratic, depending on the motivation of pupil, parents and teacher. Gertrude, a teacher herself, was a powerfully motivated parent. June used to say, 'Ed was brainy, Rex was the good-looking one, and I was the girl.'[9] She was being too modest: she was 'brainy' as well, and at the age of 10 won a scholarship to the private Diocesan School for Girls in Auckland.

But it was Ed more than the others who was coached at home. He was the eldest son and liked reading and writing, skills which Gertrude admired. The results of her hot-house treatment were spectacular. At age 10 he passed Standards 3 and 4 in the same year, coming second in class. In his last year he passed both Standards 5 and 6, and became the youngest pupil in the school to achieve the Certificate of Proficiency. In his school report for 1930, Ed was first in class with uniformly excellent results. His teacher was enthusiastic:

This is to certify that while under my tuition at the Tuakau School, Edmund Hillary proved to be an intelligent pupil whose work was always of a high standard.

His character was in all respects excellent, while his manner and general bearing clearly indicated a sound home training.

Edmund thoroughly deserves his place in class. He has worked well all term.

Well done, Edmund![10]

As Ed used to say ruefully in later years, 'I was the child genius of Tuakau Primary School.'

But Ed's academic success came at a cost. He was not just the smallest and youngest in his class, he was socially more than two years behind his scholastically undemanding peers, some of them large and pubescent as they entered their teens. Ed remembers gratefully 'a very big Maori girl who was like a mother to me and if anyone laid a hand on me she'd give them a backhander that would make them lay off'.[11] Despite the occasional protector, Ed was lonely.

I had almost no friends at school. My mother's attitude didn't help. She was so kind in many ways, but had the philosophy that you can judge people by the company they keep and she didn't feel my classmates had too much to offer.[12]

… As a consequence I was permitted to play no games after school but had to return immediately home to the safety of the family circle. This attitude by my mother, who was so generous and kind in other ways, greatly irked me and I never knew if it was related to the substantial proportion of Maori pupils we had in the school.[13]

Rex, however, remembered playing with other children, including a Catholic family of seven next door: 'We were fairly religious and went to the Anglican church in Tuakau. But Dad didn't like us mixing too closely with Catholics.'[14] Anti-Catholic feeling, imported from the old country, was alive and well in 1920s New Zealand.

Some of the better memories of Tuakau were of the movies that arrived during the 1920s. They were shown in the War Memorial Hall, a grand brick building, its entrance flanked by Grecian pillars and a bronze plaque with the names of the 32 young men whose lives little Tuakau had given to Gallipoli and Flanders. Romance movies were shown on Tuesdays and westerns on Saturdays; Gertie and June sat upstairs, Ed and Rex down. In front of the screen a pianist played a sound accompaniment and later a gramophone was added to play songs (repetitively) before the film began. Two songs, 'There's a Bridle Hanging on the Wall' and 'Red River Valley', later became part of Ed's repertoire on special occasions, preferably around a camp fire, and sung *con spirito*.

At Auckland Grammar School

In 1931, Ed had his entrance ticket to high school. There were two options: the first at Pukekohe just eight kilometres away but with a patchy scholastic record; the second at Auckland Grammar School, the city's premier school, the Eton of colonial society. It had been founded by Governor Sir George Grey in 1869, and since then had been educating the sons of Auckland's elite. Its 900 pupils were taught by the best teachers the city could find. For Gertrude, insistent that her clever eldest son have the best education available, there could be no hesitation, and 11-year-old Ed was duly enrolled at Grammar, an arduous daily train journey away.

The school day began with a bike ride to the Tuakau Railway Station to catch the 7 a.m. train, an hour on the train and then a walk to reach school by 8.30 a.m. He was placed in Form 3D, lowest of the 'academic' forms which included Latin and French in their curriculum. In the first week he was humiliated by the gym instructor whose job it was to turn slouching, evasive boys into straight-backed, muscular young men. The school system had its sprinkling of sadistic masters and this gym instructor seems to have been one of them. Humiliation was the path to improvement. He fulminated at Ed that his shoulders were round, his back not straight, his ribs flared unnaturally. Ed wrote, 'I developed a feeling of inferiority about my physique that has remained with me to this day … a solid conviction about how appalling I looked.'[15]

Discipline at boys' schools of the time depended on corporal punishment with the cane for the most minor infringements. Schools, like the military, believed that without stern discipline, mayhem would ensue. Ed, along with large numbers of his fellow pupils, was beaten frequently.

He continued to be a reader, and when not distracted by horseplay on the daily train journey, read avidly at the rate of a book a day. Edgar Rice Burroughs (*A Princess of Mars*, *Tarzan*), Henry Rider Haggard (*King Solomon's Mines*), John Buchan (*The Thirty-Nine Steps*) were favourites: 'In my imagination I constantly re-enacted heroic episodes, and I was always the hero. I died dramatically on a score of battlefields and rescued a hundred lovely maidens.'[16]

Here Allan Quartermain watches his companion Sir Henry Curtis overcome the giant African chief Twala in single-handed combat:

> Again Twala struck out with a savage yell, and again the sharp knife rebounded, and Sir Henry went staggering back. Once more Twala came on, and as he came our great Englishman gathered himself together, and swinging the big axe round his head with both hands, hit at him with all his force. There was a shriek of excitement from a thousand throats, and, behold! Twala's head seemed to spring from his shoulders: then it fell and came rolling and bounding along the ground …[17]

And here is Captain Carter's first encounter with the Princess of Mars:

> … she turned and her eyes met mine. Her face was oval and beautiful in the extreme … her eyes large and lustrous and her head surmounted by a mass of coal black, waving hair … Her skin was of a light reddish copper colour, against which the crimson glow of her cheeks and the ruby of her beautifully molded lips shone … She was as destitute of clothes as the green Martians who accompanied her; indeed, save for her highly wrought ornaments she was entirely naked …[18]

This is not Henry James, but such tales fired Ed's imagination and fed later into his natural gift for storytelling – and his own unpublished novel. They were also an escape from the misery of feeling physically inadequate in comparison with his peers.

A slight respite was his promotion from Form 3D to 3B at the end of the first term on the basis of a report which classed him as 'satisfactory' in all subjects, with a fourth place in history as his best.

The next year in Form 4B passed without E.P. Hillary leaving any trace, though his term reports record that he was top of his class in mathematics.

Ed's third year at Grammar saw the beginning of a more physically assertive Hillary. He grew like the proverbial weed, 10cm in 1933 and a further 12cm in 1934. From being one of the smallest in the class he had become the tallest, with a rangy build toughened by the work he did for Percy in the weekends. The train too had become a second home, full of rough adventure with the other schoolboy commuters joining at stations along the way:

> The train became the most important part of my life … and I learned to excel. Leaping off while it was gaining speed, holding onto the handrails, running furiously alongside and then leaping tigerishly aboard at the last desperate moment … The horseplay and battles, the broken windows and smashed seats … I learned how to fight in the train, how to hurl my opponent into the corner of the seat and lie on him so he couldn't use any superior skill at boxing or wrestling. I learned how to push all the glass out of the broken window so the guard wouldn't see it. I learned how to collect 'Schoolboys Only' stickers and place them on a choice carriage on the 4.20 express and then travel home in uncrowded comfort …
>
> I started getting boxing lessons and rather favoured my skill with a long straight left. I persuaded one of the younger boys to spar with me and duly pranced around him and showed off my primitive skill. A couple of days later I was approached by the guard on the train – the boy's parents had complained that their son was being bullied – he was coming home with his arms black and blue. A bully? Me? There was nothing I despised more … yet I realized the accusation was justified …[19]

Ed added a couple of modest disclaimers. Of the horseplay in the carriages he said, 'nothing vicious about it – merely violent, youthful energy a little misdirected'. And of his boxing: 'I wasn't really a good fighter as I lacked the necessary "killer instinct".'[20] This may have been true, in part, but he wasn't shy about defending himself, and it is clear that the newly grown Ed Hillary was not a person to be messed with.

He was strong, tall, had a long reach and didn't like being pushed around. He went on to learn wrestling and ju-jitsu. Several years later, he was still boxing at a local Auckland gym in his spare time. He tells how Vic Calteaux, New Zealand welterweight champion, came to the gym and asked for sparring partners. Ed, taller and heavier, volunteered but forgot that sparring is about getting fit, not punching your partner in the head.

> We pranced around the ring for a while, largely shadow boxing, when I noticed his guard was rather slack so reached out and thumped him rather firmly on the nose. Calteaux's temper was never particularly well controlled and he set about me in furious fashion and duly lowered me to the canvas with a terrific hook to the solar plexus. I was helped from the ring by my concerned instructor who muttered, 'Why didn't you stick to sparring?'[21]

But Ed was still not making much headway academically, partly because of the wasted hours travelling to school. Gertrude, who was in regular contact with her schoolteacher sisters at Herbert Road, knew that the time had come for all three children to move closer to good schools in Auckland. In mid-1934, the Hillarys moved to a rented house at number 298 on Remuera Road, a long ridge whose sunny northern slopes, with views of Auckland Harbour and the Hauraki Gulf, accommodate some of the city's best real estate. It was the road on which Ed would live for the rest of his life.

Two years later in 1936, at a cost of £2025, Percy and Gertrude bought their final home at 730 Remuera Road, a kilometre beyond the terminus of the electric tram which linked them to Auckland Grammar, Auckland University and the city centre. The house at number 298 has long gone, but number 730 still stands, a handsome, two-storey house with tall tiled gables. Not long after this move, Percy and Gertrude bought a beach property with two desirable adjoining sections at Ōrewa, 40 kilometres north of Auckland. These were the accoutrements of success. Ed remembered the family being endlessly short of money at this time, but New Zealand, along with the rest of the world, had been sunk for most of the decade in a disastrous depression, and Percy was thriving, mainly on the bees. He could recognise an opportunity when he saw it; he was intelligent and worked hard – and he skilfully disguised the extent of his success from his equally hard-working sons who were contributing their unpaid labour to the bee business.

In 1934 Ed sat the matriculation exam that would qualify him for entry into Auckland University. He passed in seven subjects: English, history, French, arithmetic, algebra and geometry, chemistry and drawing. 'It was one of the great moments of my life when I read in the New Zealand Herald that I had passed matriculation,' he told the school assembly on a visit in 2003.[22] Staying on for the Sixth Form, he earned his only mention in the school magazine in five years. In the account of his rugby team's successes, it was noted that 'E P Hillary dominated the lineouts.' A good lineout forward had to be tall, with a long reach, but also light enough to jump higher than the opposition. An added skill was using an elbow skilfully enough to wrong-hand the opposition yet unobtrusively enough not to be penalised for rough play. Ten years later, when playing rugby in the Air Force, Ed was still dominating lineouts.

A seminal event in Ed's life took place in the early spring of 1935, when he saw his first mountain and touched snow for the first time. Ski runs had been established on the northern slopes of Ruapehu, a 9180ft occasionally eruptive volcano in the central North Island, and each year a group of Auckland Grammar senior pupils spent 10 days on the mountain.

The trip needed money, so Ed approached the thrifty Percy. The honey crop from the summer of 1935 had been a good one. Ed and Rex had worked hard with the hives in weekends and holidays for nothing, not even pocket money. Percy thought hard and finally agreed to pay. August was the time of year when bees needed almost no attention.

The train from Auckland arrived at National Park station at midnight. The boys stepped out into a brilliant night with snow on the ground. 'As our bus carried us steadily upwards ... its headlights sparked into life a fairyland of glistening snow and stunted pines and frozen streams ... I was in a strange and exciting new world ... For ten glorious days we skied and played ...'[23] There was no suggestion that anyone should climb to the summit, where there was the risk of avalanche or falls on ice or rock, but the experience of a mountain world found a place in Ed's imagination that would remain for the rest of his life.

A studio portrait of Ed in 1938. HILLARY FAMILY COLLECTION

CHAPTER 4

'The most uncertain and miserable years of my life'

———⋙◆⋘———

With his schooldays at an end, Ed had to think about his future. Regrettably, Rider Haggard provided no answers. Prompted no doubt by Gertrude and perhaps also by his elder sister June, who was already passing units for her Bachelor of Science degree at Auckland University, he followed in her footsteps, studying the subjects he was best at: maths and science. For Ed it was like being back in his first year at Grammar. He was 16, with few social skills and no academic ambitions. Why was he at university? To become a teacher, perhaps? If he had thought of joining the profession, he never mentioned it.

His one escape was the University Tramping Club, a haven for eccentrics and intelligent misfits[1] who enjoyed the outdoors and burning up energy on the network of tracks in the forests that covered the Waitakere Ranges between Auckland and its west coast. On a Friday evening they took the train north, got off at Swanson station and climbed in the dark a steep track to the club hut called Onuku. There were gorges and waterfalls to be clambered down, their wet walls covered in ferns and moss. There were wild black-sand beaches pounded by a hazardous surf whose rips and holes could drown the unwary. It was a coast Ed grew to love.

Racing around the Waitakeres, however, was getting him no closer to a vocation. At the end of 1936 he failed all his papers, and in 1937 he failed again. His heart wasn't in it. Quite simply, he was lost.

In 1938 he left university and took a job as a law clerk in the office of Wiseman Brothers, Barristers and Solicitors, Queen Street, Auckland. Aunt Clarice, sister of Percy and now living in California, wrote approvingly:

> Dear Edmund, I hear you are in an office going for the law. I am glad, always thought your dad had the makings of a lawyer. More than likely you have it too. The profession may be crowded but there is always room for an exceptional man in any profession. Do you like the work? That I think is particularly important …[2]

But there is no further mention of the law, except for a letter of reference:

> This is to certify that E.P. Hillary was employed by us as a Law Clerk from 14th February to 26th August 1938, and that he proved to be a most willing and intelligent worker besides being absolutely trustworthy and reliable. Mr. Hillary resigned from his position in this Office to go into his Father's business and we were very sorry to lose his services. J.S. Wiseman.[3]

For someone who loved the outdoors and dreamed of adventure, such an outcome was unsurprising. There was not much adventure in the office of the Wiseman brothers – but nor was there anything on the horizon to take its place.

One wonders how different life might have been for Ed had he started at Grammar one year older than average, rather than two years younger. He would have started in the Third Form in 1934 when the family moved to Auckland, so there would not have been three years dominated by those long train journeys. He would have been one of the biggest in his class rather than the smallest, and with his strength and combativeness no one would have risked taking him on physically. He would have looked down on his peers both literally and figuratively. He would have been in demand as a lineout forward in a succession of rugby teams, culminating in the 1st Fifteen in his last year, perhaps even in his fourth year, and that would have given him the status that excelling at rugby can bestow in a New Zealand boys'

Rex, Gertrude, Percy, June and Ed in front of their house at 730 Remuera Road, c.1936. HILLARY FAMILY COLLECTION

school. He had the intellectual ability to pass exams and would always have been in a top form. With a final year in the Upper Sixth he might have developed the maturity to look around and find a vocation. He would have lost some of his shyness, found friends and got to know their sisters. Ed says that he saw himself as physically unattractive, but in reality he was tall and good-looking with a considerable presence. Given confidence and a sense of direction he would have obtained a degree, a job and a wife. He would have a role in the small city of Auckland. He would not have had the decade of uncertainty, inadequacy and searching that lay ahead as he left the law office.

He would probably not have made the first ascent of Mt Everest.

The Hillary brothers as beekeepers

In 1938 Rex too was at a loose end. He had failed his Certificate of Proficiency at Tuakau Primary in 1932 by one mark, though by 1933 his report notes that 'Rex is now putting more effort into his work.' In 1934 he was at Auckland Grammar in Form M3C: 'Results generally very satisfactory. 1st in class, 1st in maths, 1st in French.' But in 1935 and 1936 Rex was out of school, working for his father, and when he reappears in 1937 he is in Form 4U at King's College and, at 16 and a half, a year older than the class average. His form master reports: 'He should exert himself to do better.'

By the spring of 1938, the Hillary brothers had abandoned the higher education their mother had hoped for and were hard at work beekeeping, an occupation which, apart from a two-year interlude in the Air Force, would provide Ed with his modest – very modest – income up to 1953. In his 1975 autobiography, he writes:

> It was a good life … of open air and sun and hard physical work … We had 1600 hives of bees spread around the pleasant dairy land south of Auckland, occupying small corners on fifty different farms. We were constantly on the move from site to site – especially when all 1600 hives decided to swarm at once. We never knew what our crop would be … but all through the exciting months of honey flow the dream of a bumper crop would drive us on through long hard hours of labour; manhandling thousands of ninety pound boxes of honey comb for extracting … and grimacing at our daily ration of beestings … In the summer we worked seven days from dawn until dark … We accepted cheerfully that this was the right thing to do …[4]

This is about as much as he ever wrote about bees, despite their central role in the formative years from his teens through to the age of 33. He doesn't mention his imagination being stirred by the extraordinary life of the bees, their specialised roles, their devotion and obedience to their matriarchal queen whose unceasing egg-laying sustained her hive.

It was Gertrude who learnt about queens and how to breed and sell them. At the height of her success she was dispatching them not only around New Zealand but also to Australia, California, England,

The Hillary honey van provided necessary transport to check hives, feed bees and collect honey comb from sites around South Auckland. HILLARY MUSEUM COLLECTION

even Egypt. Her daughter June remembers packaging each queen in a tiny basket for the journey abroad, along with worker bees who would attend to her majesty and feed her royal jelly. For a while Gertrude was said to be earning more money than the honey gatherers. Though June helped, in the late 1930s she was busy with her university studies, achieving the success that had eluded her two younger brothers. Science and maths were her best subjects, and her BSc was taken with a major in botany. Later she became a psychologist.

Percy was always on the lookout for better ways of managing his bees. He was largely self-taught, using his questioning mind to garner information from the New Zealand Beekeepers' Association, its members and his own hard-won experience. In 1937 he began his own quarterly journal, the *N. Z. Honeybee, a Journal Devoted to the Interests of Beekeepers*, and he worked with the government to improve overseas marketing. He was lucky that he had two extremely hard-working sons who did the heavy lifting in his bee business without complaining too much about his frugality. From a distance one can only marvel at Percy's strength of will that kept his two sons in such a submissive role.

Radiant Living

Part of that strength came from the ethical convictions that had grown out of Percy's war experiences and the economic failures of the 1930s. Political systems were in crisis and inquiring people were searching for something better. Into this spiritual vacuum, in September 1938, stepped a charismatic evangelist, Dr Herbert Sutcliffe, with his School of Radiant Living.

Sutcliffe was born in 1886 in Lincolnshire, England, where he trained as a telegraph engineer and sang in the cathedral choir. After emigrating to Australia, he became interested in the psychology of Freud and Jung. He then moved to New York, where he gained a doctorate in divinity through the Divine Science Church which followed a path of alternative spirituality.

From these sources, he developed a philosophy which he called Radiant Living, a holistic, quasi-religious faith centred on the need to keep in balance the threefold nature of human beings: body, mind and spirit. The body was kept radiant through a wholesome diet and exercise, and the mind and spirit through teachings and meditation. There were Buddhist overtones to the belief that humans are condemned to suffering owing to their fear, hate and feelings of inferiority. He was a charismatic speaker, dressed in a Masonic-style royal-blue gown, and was known to turn cartwheels on stage in his sixties. He was lively and entertaining and, according to Rex, attractive to some of his more susceptible female disciples.

A strong thread of moral seriousness ran through the Hillary family, much of it not answered by traditional Christianity. With war in Europe looming, they were ripe for conversion, and all five of them joined the cause with enthusiasm. Percy was briefly a vice-president, Rex a teacher; June led communal singing and Gertrude was the first Auckland secretary. Ed became more closely involved than any of them. Sutcliffe wrote later:

> For five years, from 1938 to 1943, the Hillary family was closely associated with the Auckland School of Radiant Living. I am glad to have on record the many times they testified to the fact that Radiant Living came into their lives bringing harmony and understanding to each member of the family and the family as a whole just when it was most needed.

> Father Percy Hillary was so appreciative that he requested
> me to take Edmund with me on lecture campaigns because he
> could not think of anything better for Edmund's future.[5]

Sutcliffe's claim that Radiant Living brought harmony to the family could easily be true, particularly for Ed who in 1938 was a troubled 19-year-old. The processes of education that were meant to have helped him towards finding answers about the nature of the world and his place in it had failed him. He later described himself as 'academically mediocre and emotionally unsure; Victorian in outlook; but physically strong and with a mind crammed full of dreams, ambitions, loyalties, spiritual searching ... plus a basic set of principles pounded into me by my parents'.[6] Radiant Living came to fill this void. He began to read about philosophies and religions. He became an Associated Teacher of Radiant Living. With developing confidence he began to speak in public. His writing skills grew. From feeling himself a failure he became a leader, of sorts. The School of Radiant Living was his high school and his university.

In 1941 he sat the exams, passing all subjects (apart from PE) in exceptional fashion:

- Health   98%
- Everyday psychology   98%
- Psycho-cosmology   100%
- Letters to Students   100%
- Physical exercises   91%
- Lecturing Ability   100%

Percy observed Ed as a speaker at a meeting in 1940:

> We had a wonderful meeting at School last night, 105 present.
> Miss Sutherland was radiant with the baton and Edmund
> was excellent. Mr. Dunningham gave a splendid address, most
> comprehensive, with inspiring ideals, and aims for the future.
> Love offering £2-18-6.[7]

Gertrude kept a notebook with scraps of poetry and quotations. She wrote of spirituality, God, right thought, the life force, worthy purpose and the desire to serve:

Herbert Sutcliffe, founder of Radiant Living, with Ed who had become his secretary.

The radiance you express will be in accordance with the ideal you tenaciously hold.

Prayer: To ask earnestly and reverently as in worship; to make known one's desires to God. And what is prayer but the expansion of oneself into the living ether.

Love is divine emotion. I surround my child with infinite love and wisdom.[8]

But flashes of wit are slipped in as well:

Her face is her fortune and it runs into a nice figure.

Slips that passed in the type.

She gave her husband a look that spoke volumes which would be read to him later.[9]

Conscientious objection and a glimpse of two mountaineers

Meanwhile, on 1 September 1939, the German invasion of Poland had triggered the Second World War. When New Zealand's call for volunteers for the armed forces was less successful than expected, the government, in June 1940, introduced conscription for males between the ages of 21 and 40. The Hillarys were conflicted. Ed had briefly volunteered for the Air Force but soon withdrew and declared himself a conscientious objector, as did Rex. Percy was an uncompromising pacifist and he was hard to ignore, as was the moral argument against killing. But the arguments in favour of joining the battle against evil were at least as strong, and most of the country's young men accepted their conscription and went off to Greece, Crete, the Battle of Britain, North Africa, Italy and the rest of it. Conscientious objectors were likely to be subjected to the humiliation of being handed the white feather of cowardice, and once conscription had been enacted in June 1940 they could be held for the duration of the war in one of the country's seven detention camps. Of the years between 1939 and 1943 Ed wrote, 'I was very restless and unhappy and the first few years of the war were the most uncertain and miserable of my life.'[10]

As an early escape from his inner turmoil, Ed, then aged 20, persuaded Percy to give him time off over the Christmas period of 1939–40. His destination was the high mountains in the Hermitage–Mt Cook area of New Zealand's Southern Alps. He was accompanied by 'an older friend' who was a tramper rather than a climber, and they had no clear plan apart from making their first crossing of Cook Strait and getting close to big mountains. It was to be another intense and unforgettable experience on Ed's mountain journey, and he described it in almost identical words in his autobiographies of 1955, 1975 and 1999:

> We arrived in the early afternoon. It was a perfect day and the
> great peaks seemed to tower over our heads. I looked on them
> with a growing feeling of excitement – the great walls, the
> hanging glaciers, and the avalanche-strewn slopes ... Sitting
> in the lounge that evening I felt restless and excited. And then
> the hum of voices hushed, and I looked up to see two young
> men coming into the room. They were fit and tanned; they
> had an unmistakable air of competence about them. I could

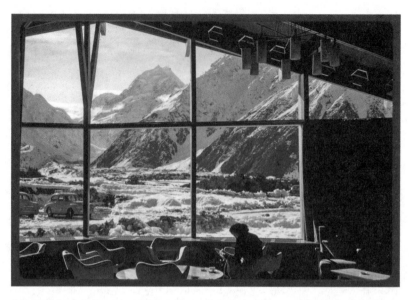

Mt Cook and the Hooker Valley seen through the window of The Hermitage Hotel.
HILLARY MUSEUM COLLECTION

hear a whisper going round the room: 'They've just climbed Mount Cook.' And soon they were the centre of an admiring group with all the pretty girls fluttering around like moths in the flame … I heard one of them say 'I was pretty tired when we got to the icecap but Harry was like a tiger and almost dragged me to the top.'

I retreated to a corner of the lounge, filled with an immense sense of futility at the dull and mundane nature of my existence. Here were chaps who were really getting some excitement out of life. Tomorrow I must climb something. My companion agreed to give it a try and suggested we take a guide.

Fate was kind to us and next morning was fine … we'd tackle Ollivier, a small peak on the Sealy range above the Hermitage … I climbed up the steep narrow track with a feeling of freedom and exhilaration … we swam in the cold clear water of the Sealy lakes while our guide lit a fire and boiled a billy. A thousand feet of snow stretched between us

and the crest of the range ... This was real mountaineering
... We reached the crest of the ridge and looked over into
a magnificent valley of great glaciers and fine peaks ... In a
few minutes I was climbing onto the summit of my first real
mountain. I returned to the Hermitage after the happiest day
I had ever spent.[11]

Ollivier is a modest summit in a small range of low peaks, but it was
a start. Perhaps more inspirational was the sight of those two tanned
heroes who had just climbed Mt Cook. But 1940 was wartime, and it
would be five years before Ed went to the Hermitage–Mt Cook area
again.

Ed attained the age of conscription in July 1940, but a year passed
with no military call-up for him or for Rex, who was 15 months
younger. In July 1941, with the bees in hibernation, both brothers were
working for Radiant Living, Rex in Christchurch and Ed in Hastings
where he was secretary to Dr Sutcliffe. In a letter to Gertrude, Ed
shows that he remained committed to his position as a conscientious
objector:

> Dear Mum,
> I was very pleased to hear that Rex has returned [from
> Christchurch]. He will be invaluable with the feeding of the
> bees ... In regard to my coming home: - When I am called
> up I will put in two objections to service. One will be on the
> grounds of Conscientious Objection and the other will be that
> it is detrimental to the Public interest – because of the bees.
> Therefore if I do not succeed in the C.O. I hope to succeed in
> the Honey one. To do this I will have to be working the bees
> to show that I am necessary. So it looks like I will be home
> for good. Ask Dad what he thinks about it anyway. He may
> have some ideas on the matter. As regards the Doctor, I think
> he will be very sorry to lose me. In fact I'm sure he will be. He
> has given me some great help in regard to my attitude to the
> C.O. question ...[12]

Eventually Ed was called up and his objection was sustained on the
grounds that his work as a bee farmer was in the national interest. Rex,
as the second conscientious objector in the family, was not so lucky and

on 19 May 1942 he was placed in the Strathmore Detention Centre. Disciples of Radiant Living – and various other beliefs – did not have the same immunity from conscription as Quakers or Christadelphians. Ed felt guilty that he was free while Rex was in prison. In 1944 he was writing to Gertrude, 'I think it is most necessary to take every possible channel and means to get Rex out of camp. It's a most abnormal life for him, especially at his particular age'[13] – but there was not much they could do and Rex was not released until early 1946.

Ed might not have been conscripted, but at home his speaking skills were put to public use, as shown in a letter revealing that in 1940–41 he had been conducting his own national radio programme for a full year:

> 26 June 1941. Letter from J. N. Gordon, Production Supervisor for National Commercial Broadcasting Service, 1ZB.
> This is to certify that MR. EDMUND HILLARY for something over twelve months has been conducting the 'Young Citizens' Session' at 1ZB every Sunday morning. The session has been handled entirely by Mr. Hillary, and incorporates various Youth Organisations in Auckland, and invites co-operation and comment from Youth in general. Mr. Hillary can be commended upon the work and initiative put into these sessions.[14]

Equally surprising is this undated 1600-word address:

> Dominion Reconstruction Conference. Youth: Mr. Edmund Hillary.
> I consider it a great privilege to have been chosen as the opening youth speaker this afternoon … I noticed when I came this afternoon that some of you seemed very tense so I would suggest that we all have a try at just relaxing and taking a few deep breaths …
>
> During the last war people looked to the future and said: 'There is a new and better dawn coming.' But the dawn that followed the last war was one of sorrow and sadness, overcast and depressing. The dawn that must follow the darkness of this war depends on **our** efforts …

The attributes of youth for success are enthusiasm, energy, courage, ability and vision. Youth goes forward despite difficulties in the path, and has the courage of its convictions. Youth supplies the driving force ...

Now, the spiritual side of life: youth is rather wary of this and associates it with repression but that is a misconception ... Everything we do is in accord with or working with spiritual forces ... The spiritual, God, is with us here and now, with us everywhere ...

Also I think youth can serve its greatest purpose by using the power of prayer. The great scientist Einstein tells us that if 3% of the people in the world knew how to pray effectively, the present war could not have happened. Three out of every hundred people could have prevented this catastrophe! Let us all as young people determine to play our part by using the dynamic power of spiritualised thought to uplift the world. Material things are not everything – but the greatest blessings we can achieve are the blessings which are mental and spiritual ...

There is a great work for us to do. If we look forward we can see a world of happiness and harmony, a world in which the people live in brotherhood and understanding, in which there is no fierce competition, no selfishness, because individuals are free from these qualities. Let us not wait but go forward now; let us endeavour to enthuse others with these ideals. We must act now. As Mr. Winston Churchill says: 'Let's go to it.'[15]

In 1942, Ed briefly became less conscientious, as he explained for the first and only time in *View from the Summit* (1999):

When I was about 22 years old I had my first notable relationship with a member of the opposite sex, and indeed the only one until my marriage 12 years later. How I met her, or even her full name, I don't now remember. She was a couple of years younger than me, slim, pretty with beautiful auburn hair. I could never understand why she bothered with me. We had a warm relationship and it was certainly a new experience for me. I was still working hard for my father and

63

Rex, unknown, June and Ed at Ōrewa beach north of Auckland where Percy had bought a bach. HILLARY FAMILY COLLECTION

receiving very little pay in return, but whatever I did obtain I hoarded carefully – it wasn't very much. Finally I bought her the cheapest of engagement rings which she seemed to prize greatly.

Then my chance came! ... My father and mother were invited to Australia ... and would be away for a month. We had completed the extracting of honey from our apiaries but I knew of a small group of hives that still had honey in place. On the departure of my parents, I removed the boxes of honey, extracted it, and filled a number of four-gallon tins. I then put an advertisement in the paper and, as sugar was short in those days, I had a rush of replies. For the first time in my life I had £25 in my pocket, a vast sum of money to me. I spent it carefully, but did take my girlfriend on a weekend holiday to Lake Taupo – we stayed in separate rooms of course.

I was naïve to think my actions would not be discovered by my father on his return from Australia. He made me give back all the money I had not spent and then paid me nothing for some months … My romance faded, largely due to lack of money I suspect …[16]

By 1943, a hard-fought world war was turning in favour of the Allies. Radiant Living was all very well, but Ed had gnawing at him an awareness that his own generation were in the vanguard of the fight against fascism. And Rex was languishing in the Strathmore Detention Centre. What was fair about his contemporaries sacrificing their lives and his brother being in prison while he enjoyed the country pleasures of farming bees? When Ed was called up to serve in the Home Guard, he was disgusted to find himself part of an elderly group who would interrupt a war exercise between 'enemies' to have lunch together.[17]

By the end of 1943 he could stand it no longer. He applied for the Air Force and in early 1944 was accepted for training at a camp on the eastern edge of the Kaikōura mountains in the north of the South Island.

CHAPTER 5

Escape into the Air Force

—=≫•◆•≪=—

I n the autumn of 1944, Ed began a six-month training course at the
Royal New Zealand Air Force camp in the South Island's Wairau
Valley. To the east the river wound over plains to the sea but inland
rose the rugged peaks of the Kaikōura mountains, clothed in dense
forest on their lower slopes, rising to tussock and the steep broken rock
of the ridges and peaks. In winter thick snow covered the tops. Ed
launched himself into his new life with zest, studying flying, playing
rugby – and climbing mountains, a pastime which interested very few
of his 260 fellow trainees. Given a choice between the warmth of a
dance hall or a bar on a Saturday night, not many could see the point
in heading off into a dangerous world of snow, ice, avalanches and
freezing winds.

The highest summit in the Kaikōura Range is Tapuae-o-Uenuku,
9465 ft, known affectionately as Tappy and visible from Wellington
in the north to Christchurch in the south. When James Cook sailed
down the South Island's east coast in 1770, he noted it in his log as 'a
prodigious high mountain'. And in November 1849, in the first written
account of an attempt to climb the peak, a Māori guide, Wiremu
Hoepa, slipped to his death on steep ice.[1] When Ed mentioned his
intention to climb Tappy, a couple of fellow trainees expressed vague
interest, but the next three-day weekend saw Ed off on his own,
trudging up a gravel road in the dark. It was winter, and he found an
isolated farmhouse where the farmer's wife fed him generously and
provided a bed.

66

Away early on the Saturday, Ed walked 25 kilometres to enter a sunless gorge winding into the bowels of the mountains, and by late evening he was lighting a fire in a mountain hut alive with mice and fleas. Sunday was summit day:

> By 4 a.m. I'd had only four hours sleep but prepared a quick breakfast and was away before five o'clock. It was dark and very cold as I groped my way across the river bed and up the side of the main ridge ... At 7000 feet heavy cloud came over the peak and it snowed quite heavily. I wondered if I should turn back. I was startled to hear what sounded like a thin human voice calling for help ... and then realized it was the eerie wail of the native parrot, the kea ... A strong cold wind had sprung up ... To the west above heavy clouds towered a range of snowcapped peaks. I didn't know what mountains they were. To the east was the blueness of the sea stretching all the way to Wellington ...
>
> The climbing became a lot harder. I had to make my way across the side of the Pinnacle, a tall rock tower ... and felt isolated and a little frightened ... I arrived at the last big bump as heavy cloud moved in and was half blinded by drifting snow ... I fumbled my way upwards until there was nowhere else to go and then I realized I must be on top.

Back at camp next day, 'I listened to the young airmen discussing their social conquests of the evening. But I didn't care! I'd climbed a decent mountain at last.'[2]

Ed, always the dutiful son, regularly wrote letters home. To Percy he wrote about rugby and the bees:

> Dear Dad, I suppose you'll be very busy from now on keeping all the hives fed. We get plenty of exercise and I rather enjoy it. A week ago we had a special football match, our squadron playing against our sister squadron. I played in the forwards and we managed to beat the other team by 11 points to 6. I obtained a score which rather tickled me. It was a very hard game and towards the end became rather rough. Tempers got a bit frayed amongst the forwards and one of the opposition was especially irate as I had accidentally bashed him in the

lineout and made his nose bleed and just about knocked a couple of teeth out. However all was well after the game and all animosity was forgotten. I do rather well in the lineouts due to my height and find small difficulty dominating them.[3]

In letters to Gertrude he was more open, and his affection is always apparent:

> Dear Mother ... Do you know what I miss most about home? Firstly our good old discussions... you know how I love to talk. And secondly my Sunday mornings in bed when you brought up my breakfast. How I used to revel in the luxury. I can still taste those delicious omelettes and feel the peace of our back garden floating through the window ...
>
> ... I think the varied experiences the five of us have had in the last five years will enable us to come together and form a mighty cohesive family team capable of overcoming any problem – this is Dad's old dream isn't it and I think it will come to pass. I intend seeing that you and dad get some return for all the love and effort you have put into us ...
>
> ... I suppose you'll be rather short of cash so I'm enclosing £5. Use it for yourself and keep the house going ...
>
> Love, Edmund.[4]

In September, the trainees sat their exams. With a motivation he had not known at school or university, Ed had applied himself to flying and navigation with such diligence that he came fourteenth in a class of 260. Where to next? At 25 he was a bit old to be a pilot, so was placed in a special group of 12 going to Bell Block in New Plymouth to train as a navigator.

In camp Ed shared a bunkroom with 19-year-old co-trainee, Julian Godwin. Julian remembered Ed as 'affable', someone who mixed easily with other men, though with women he became suddenly quiet. He had a distinctive 'drawly' voice.[5] Neither of them drank, smoked or went out with girls. They worked hard at their navigation, read books and listened to the radio which mainly aired popular music. Julian, of English parentage, described Ed as an 'anglophobe', an attitude which probably came partly from Percy's experience in Gallipoli under English leadership, partly from the determinedly egalitarian New Zealand ethic where Jack was as good as his master, if not better. Another Bell Block trainee was Ken Durrant who recalled how on most weekends Ed would set off for Mt Taranaki (then known as Mt Egmont), usually on his own. He also remembered Ed as a table-tennis player whose strategy was always to go aggressively for the winning smash.

The trainees worked hard on navigation during the week, but between midday Saturday and Sunday evening they were free, and Ed, who was always trying to persuade others to join his expeditions, was soon working on Julian, who in 2014 wrote:

> We'd been at Bell Block for a fortnight when Ed broached the idea of climbing Mount Taranaki. Although I'd done no serious climbing, or even tramping, I didn't take much persuading. By repute I knew Ed had spent his spare time at the Wairau camp climbing nearby peaks.
>
> The approach march began on bikes, hot pedaling on dusty roads, and then on foot. Ed set a cracking pace. We must have just passed the halfway mark when a cold wind came up with cloud obscuring everything. The track was never-ending and the wind got stronger and more icy by the minute. After two hours the hut was not in sight and visibility was down to just a few yards. The wind, fresh from its journey across the Tasman Sea, blew and flapped our wet clothes around our cold bodies as we discussed whether to turn back. Then we heard a clang, the sound of a loose sheet of corrugated iron. The wind was giving us a signal where to find the hut.
>
> Morning came with no sign of any let-up, the wind still strong from the west, so we admitted defeat and stumbled back down the track.[6]

About a month later, Ed managed to talk the transport section into supplying a driver and a canvas-top personnel truck for another assault. This time eight aspirants would be involved in a Sunday attempt to reach the summit. Ed's team of beginner mountaineers were wearing Air Force-issue boots with smooth leather soles of the sort that can send the wearer slithering to his death when a change in the weather turns wet snow to ice, but on this occasion all survived. Ed climbed the mountain in total seven times, enough to inspire Flying Officer Auld, a member of the New Zealand Alpine Club, to propose him for Associate Membership, the preliminary to the sought-after Full Membership.

When the exam results came through, Ed learnt that he had come second in his group of 12 trainee navigators, and that at the end of February he would be flying to Lauthala Bay in Fiji to navigate Catalina float planes. His pay would rise to £5 10s a week, of which he promised £3 to Gertrude.

A second encounter with the Hermitage–Mt Cook area

Before the move to Fiji, the trainees had their Christmas break from 18 to 31 December 1944. Feeling the need to test himself on more difficult peaks than Tappy or Taranaki, Ed set off for the Mt Cook region accompanied by two coerced companions who dropped out in Christchurch before they had even caught sight of a mountain.

The high peaks of the central Southern Alps that cluster around Aoraki-Mt Cook, 12,218ft, can be intimidating. On the scale of other ranges in the world they are not high, but their abiding feature is the fierce weather that sweeps in from the north-west driven by storm-force winds, dumping huge amounts of rain in the forests and snow on the mountains. The snow compacts into ice which flows down the higher slopes, seamed with crevasses, until steepening into the chaos of an icefall. The incessant, reverberant thunder of avalanches from these breaking walls of ice is a constant reminder of the mountains' dangers.

Ed's intention was to ascend the Hooker Glacier on the western flanks of Mt Cook and to examine its routes on that side, all of them steep, icy and exposed. He had some 'very ambitious plans' that now had to be realised on his own. Although he never said as much, one suspects that among those very ambitious plans might have been an attempt on Cook itself. His experience was of the benign peaks of the Sealy Range five years earlier; now, as he stepped out of the bus in view of the ice-clad walls of Mts Cook and Sefton, he sensed a challenge infinitely more daunting than his climb of Ollivier.

Ed's diary describes how he made his way to Hooker Hut en route to Mt Cook on the first day:

Packed my rucksack with food and clothes for a week. And what a load it made, at least 80lbs ... The view is stupendous with great peaks soaring up on all sides. The only noise to break the stillness was the rumble of avalanches from the hanging glaciers on Cook and Sefton, the crash of rocks tumbling down the precipices, or the swish of some rubble on the glacier sliding down into a subterranean depth.

I set off up the glacier. It looked very treacherous and I was too nervous to venture any distance out on it by myself. At 4.30 p.m. I was right up at the foot of Mt Cook ... Very tired back at hut but a sumptuous repast of sausages, chips and onions made me feel better ...[7]

By the morning he had decided to leave Mt Cook for another day. Looking around for an easier peak, he saw to the west on the Main Divide Mt Footstool, 9078ft, reached by a steep ridge flanked by icefalls, and with a tiny hut halfway up known as Sefton Bivvy. Ed was uncomfortably aware that though Footstool might be easier than Cook, it still had a threateningly big-mountain feel to it, and he was tired and lacking in energy. Having finally reached the bivvy which was half full of snow, he debated whether to go on. The slopes above were avalanching. The route looked impossible. Descent was the only option, and even then he had a short fall. 'Very lucky,' he wrote in his diary.

Chastened by his second tactical retreat, Ed realised that the only options open to an untrained solo climber lay to the east, on the gentler peaks of the Sealy Range which included his old friend Mt Ollivier. Next day he climbed to the Mueller Hut: 'Very hot day and heavy pack. Needed frequent rests ... toiled through steep soft snow ... It's a bit lonely by yourself.'

Late on the following day he was glissading down steep shingle slopes to arrive at The Hermitage Hotel on Christmas Eve. 'There's a big crowd here and I feel very neglected all by myself. This solitary trip is no good. I enjoyed the five days I've had but that's about all I can stand of my own company in one stretch.'[8] Christmas Eve is not the best night of the year to be overwhelmed by loneliness. Despite his 'very ambitious' hopes, there had been no advance on the trip in 1940 when he'd seen those two fit and tanned climbers just returned from Mt Cook. He had been overwhelmed by these mountains with their fearsome slopes of

To the right of the larger Mt Sefton is Mt Footstool, 9078ft, on which Ed made an abortive solo attempt in December 1944 while on leave from his Air Force training. The road leads to The Hermitage Hotel. COLIN MONTEATH/HEDGEHOG HOUSE

steep ice. He needed companions, skills, experience. He finished his diary entry for the 24th with the words, 'I'm coming here again though ...'

Meanwhile, he was returning to the disparate worlds of the Royal New Zealand Air Force in the Pacific, Radiant Living with Gertrude, and beekeeping with Percy.

He wrote to Gertrude:

> In Christchurch I spent two very pleasant days at the
> Theosophical Conference ... They wanted me to lecture to
> the conference but unfortunately I had to leave too soon ...
> I hope it won't be too long before I'm back with you all again
> and moving once more in the old spiritual atmosphere.
> I prepared a lecture using experiences I had on my holiday as
> illustrations. I've entitled it, Footsteps on the Path.

The footsteps he wrote about were in the steep snow on Footstool, and he gave his lecture the title 'Great was my indecision'. He finished with a short paragraph entitled 'Children of Eternity':

We are one with eternity and as such have no beginning and will know no ending. Humanity's great strength of life flows on slowly improving, slowly developing characteristics of beauty, godliness, learning to express outwardly the external truth of which they are spiritually a part. A great inevitable, unquenchable wall of flame that will in time devour all the dross of life and leave him spiritually purged and cleansed – the true child of Eternity.[9]

Serving in the Pacific

Like Percy going to Cairo in 1914, Ed was filled with excitement as he contemplated new adventures in exotic places. Halfway to Fiji in February 1945, the lumbering Sunderland passenger flying boat emerged from cloud into bright sun over an azure sea. Fiji itself was white-sand beaches, surf breaking on reefs, and inland forests. The war seemed distant, with both the Japanese and the Germans on their way back to where they came from.

The Air Force Catalina flying boats were central to the adventure. Designed initially in 1935 as patrol bombers for the American Air Force in the Pacific, they became one of the most widely used seaplanes of the Second World War. With their snub nose, boat-shaped hull, panoramic windscreens and slow flight, they looked too ungainly to be of use, but they were extraordinarily versatile. Their landing field was the whole of the Pacific. They could detect and destroy submarines, land beside and rescue aircrew shot down at sea, go on 15-hour reconnaissance flights, escort convoys. Painted black, they successfully attacked Japanese ships at night – though by 1945 the Japanese had been driven a long way north of Fiji, and Victory in Europe was only three months away.

For four months Ed worked as a navigator on flights out of the Catalina base at Lauthala Bay close to Suva on the main island of Fiji. The navigator was of crucial importance on long, slow flights, particularly when out of range of the radio beacons close to base. Between flights he had time to read, think and write long letters home:

> We've been doing a lot of night flying lately and I rather like it even though it entails a lot of hard work for me. On our last trip we crossed 600 miles of empty ocean to three small islands near New Caledonia and then returned making a

73

Ed's Catalina flying boat crew. On his left is Ron Ward, co-owner of the Jolly Roger.
HILLARY FAMILY COLLECTION

round trip of 1200 miles. We flew at 9000ft and it was pretty cool but very calm. Below us stretched in every direction tumbled layers of cumulus cloud sharply outlined in the bright moonlight. I spent most of my time bashing away at the stars with my sextant and getting fix after fix. We had to cross 600 miles of ocean and then hit a small peninsular only 1½ miles wide but I managed to hit right in the middle of it.

One of the islands is an active volcano and we zoomed over it at 9000ft. The crater was just like a great glowing cigarette end with every now and then sparks flying up as red hot boulders were thrown in the air. It seemed strange to me as we flew along in the cool, still air that on those little islands lying dark and quiet beneath us people were sleeping and dreaming. Here were we, unlimited by time or terrain, covering huge distances while these people build their whole lives out on these tiny specks of dust surrounded by nothing but hundreds of miles of ocean … High altitudes seem conducive to philosophical thought and I often turn thoughtful as we roar along a couple of miles above the sea.[10]

74

To Percy he wrote about his future with the family bee business:

> Well Dad, I've been putting quite a lot of thought into my
> future and as far as I can see if I stick to the bees I'll be as
> well off as in anything else. I've got a pretty fair idea about
> beekeeping and with you to keep me on the right path I won't
> go very far wrong. So if you want me to help you after the war
> it will suit me very well. The conditions I will leave to you.
>
> I've been reading two very interesting books lately dealing
> with the rise to success and prosperity of two families. Both of
> them stress some important points, namely that by having no
> bank debts and by having some monetary reserves they were
> able to weather the worst slumps and depressions. I think
> this has been your idea all along hasn't it Dad? You've built
> up some excellent assets in gear and equipment and there's
> nothing to stop us going on to great success. When we have
> about 3000 colonies we'll be in a pretty solid way.
>
> I'd be very interested if you have any good books on
> honey production and queen rearing. I have plenty of spare
> time and do a lot of reading ...[11]

To Gertrude, too, he wrote about his relationship with Percy:

> You know, Mother, what I'd like best from Dad as a birthday
> present? Well, it's just a note saying he'd like to have me back
> in the business and what I have to look forward to when I do
> return. I'm getting on in years – 26 in a few weeks – so I have
> to consider the future a bit ... I wrote to Rex. Poor boy, I think
> his incarceration is really beginning to weigh on him ...[12]

With June he was more expansive about his dreams for the future:

> Just lately I've been reading Admiral Byrd's book 'Alone'... I
> wouldn't mind a trip to the Antarctic though I'd much prefer
> one to the Himalayas. What do you reckon June? Would you
> come up into the Himalayas for a little trip? The idea appeals
> to me immensely and who knows? We may end up there yet.
>
> Here's something you could get for me June. Do you
> remember me mentioning I was keen on browsing through

a bit of geology. So, my sweet, if you have an interesting textbook on the subject and forward it to me immediately I would greatly appreciate it. I feel the need for some practical scientific subject to study.

I'd also welcome anything on NZ climbing, Nanga Parbat, K2 and Mawson ...

A couple of days ago a parcel of books arrived for me. Much to my surprise I found that they were Psychology and English textbooks. You remember I thought about taking these subjects. The Psychology looks reasonably interesting but the English is I think a bit beyond me at the moment. There's only one big snag and that is that I haven't enrolled in any University. I'm going to apply to Auckland and if they accept me I'll probably sit the Psychology exam. I'd like to scrape up some sort of degree even though it is a bit late...[13]

In July 1945 Ed moved to active service in the Solomon Islands. Active was a relative term: Germany had surrendered and the Pacific war was winding down. Far to the north, the Japanese were preparing a kamikaze defence of their motherland, but when on 6 August the Americans dropped an atom bomb on the city of Hiroshima and another on Nagasaki three days later, the war came to a swift end. Japan surrendered unconditionally on 15 August. For Ed there were still flights to be made, errands to be run, but there was no longer a war, just the long process of demobilisation.

He and his squadron were stationed at Halavo Bay on Florida Island, 30 kilometres north of the large island of Guadalcanal which had been so bitterly fought over when the Americans took it from the Japanese three years earlier. Apart from its steamy heat, Halavo was a tropical paradise. Against a backdrop of rain forest and black volcanic rock, tall coconut palms fringed the shore. Catalinas, enclosed by the arms of the bay, nestled against the palms or came waddling on lowered wheels out of the turquoise sea and on to the white sand. Seaward were reefs and scattered islands.

At Halavo Ed teamed up with Ron Ward, a kindred spirit looking for adventures. They went hunting, chasing pigeons with bows and arrows, poisonous snakes with sticks, sharks and stingrays with rifles, and on one memorable occasion a 2.5-metre crocodile with a rifle and a harpoon. But their most dangerous exploit involved the *Jolly Roger*, an abandoned motor boat with a flat bottom, 40 centimetres of freeboard and a very large, seized-up 170hp motor. The flight engineers got the motor going while Ed and Ron patched and painted the hull and drew a skull and crossbones on the bow. To their great satisfaction they found that its top speed of 30 knots was enough for it to overtake the Commanding Officer in his official runabout.

The *Jolly Roger*, however, had the distinction of bringing Ed the first of several near-death experiences in his life. He and Ron had agreed to ferry one of the aircrew six kilometres across the bay to the American Catholic church at Tulagi. It was a clear morning, but a fresh breeze made the sea quite rough. While filling the boat with petrol, Ed noticed that one of the tanks was a bit loose but didn't think a great deal of it.

After dropping off their passenger, Ed and Ron turned for home into a head sea that had their flat bottom slamming hard. Suddenly there was a loud crack as a petrol-tank support broke and a spurt of flame shot out of the engine compartment into the cockpit. The only option was to abandon ship, but as Ed got to his feet a wave threw him off balance, and he landed on his bare back on the burning engine cover. He rolled overboard to join Ron in the water as the *Jolly Roger* went careering off belching smoke and flame.

Both of them were burnt, but it was Ed's back causing most of the trouble as they set out to swim ashore through a choppy sea. Ed recalled:

> [I] kept going through a fog of pain. Every now and then I'd feel myself giving out and I'd flop over on my back. Ron was pretty well done in too but he'd give me a yell and I'd start again. Finally we reached the shore. The sun was so hot on our burnt backs that we had to walk along the road backwards. Finally we found two Americans who rushed us to hospital.[14]

The official telegram to New Zealand noted that 'Sergeant Hillary received first and second degree burns to the trunk and face and upper limbs. He was taken to a US Navy hospital where he was classified as dangerously ill but later reclassified to seriously ill.' If the burns had been third degree – full thickness loss of skin – rather than second-degree blisters which heal easily, he might have died.

ABOVE *An officer is pouring something that is not champagne over the bow of the* **Jolly Roger** *at its launching.* HILLARY FAMILY COLLECTION

OPPOSITE *Ed in the Solomons with the crocodile he and Ron Ward harpooned and shot.* HILLARY FAMILY COLLECTION

Remembering the explosion 63 years later, Ron Ward said, 'Ed was drifting in and out of consciousness and I had to urge him to stay awake. Mind you that water was good for us and would have cooled off our burns. It's a wonder too that the sharks didn't get us but I suppose they preferred their meat raw, not cooked …'

And what did he remember most about Ed? 'I remember his ruggedness and his determination to get the job done. He'd go to the bitter end to get something finished.'[15]

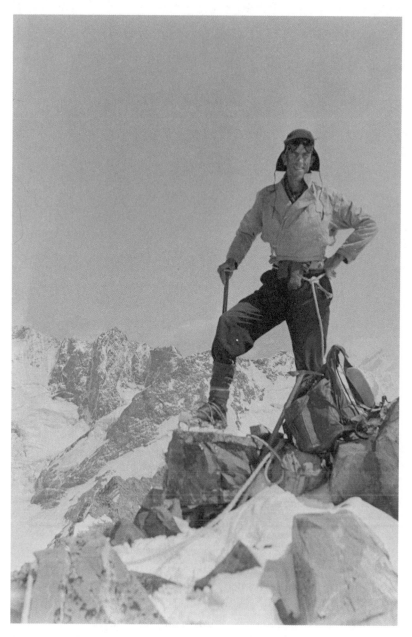

Ed on a summit in the Sealy Range, 1946. HILLARY MUSEUM COLLECTION

CHAPTER 6

Harry Ayres teaches Ed the craft of mountaineering

⟫◆⟪

E d was surprised on his return to Auckland in January 1946 that Percy was disclaiming any need of help. While his two sons were away, the one shooting crocodiles in the Solomons, the other serving time as a conscientious objector in a detention centre, Percy had employed paid help.

Ed needed no further encouragement. It was summer and the mountains of the Cook region beckoned, even though he was still on sick leave from the Air Force and his burnt back not yet fully healed. By now he belonged to the NZ Alpine Club and through its membership was in contact with other climbers. It was in the company of one of them, Alan Odell, a relative of Noel Odell of 1924 Everest fame, that he arrived at The Hermitage. It was a good season and the pair of them emerged from 17 days of unguided climbing with a useful bag of the easier peaks of the region: Malte Brun, Hamilton, Minarets, de la Beche, Sealy, Kitchener. Then it was back to the bees, Percy having agreed to accept back his prodigal son.

Early in 1946 Rex was finally released from the Strathmore Detention Centre. In May 1945 he had written, 'Yesterday saw me through three years of imprisonment – a long time but it has not been in vain – my conscience is clear and I am happy in my mind. I now have my second wind and could do another three if necessary ... I am giving up woodwork entirely and will put a lot more time into reading ...'[1]

Nevertheless he was relieved to be back in the relatively normal world of post-war Papakura and to be working with the bees alongside his older brother. Percy was by now aware that his sons, aged 25 and 26, were becoming more difficult to handle, whereas at age 61 he was tiring. He had kept Ed and Rex on a short leash through the good days of Radiant Living before the war, maximising the incoming honey flow through his sons' abilities whilst minimising the outgoing cash flows by paying them as little as possible. Now they were chafing at the bit. They wanted recognition, responsibility, the chance to become partners in the bee business. For undisclosed reasons, Percy wrote a reference:

> From P.A. Hillary, Managing Director, Clovergold Apiaries,
> 1 May 1946.
> This is to certify that Edmund Percival Hillary, a returned
> Airman, has been fully employed by me for eight years in
> beekeeping (in honey-production). He is an expert in all
> branches of the work and is one of the ablest and most
> capable of the younger beekeepers in New Zealand. He has
> acted as manager of the above concern for some time and gave
> every satisfaction.[2]

The reference seems not to have been used, and the two brothers settled into the family business. Ed was nominally still living with Percy and Gertrude at 730 Remuera Road, but in practice he preferred the View Road honey-house in Papakura. By 1947 Rex had married Winifred June Wilkie, daughter of a local headmaster. Rex was always more relaxed socially than Ed, and with his wavy hair and easy charm was attractive to women. Rex re-christened his wife Jenny to distinguish her from his sister June, and their home became an important retreat for Ed.

Throughout his life Rex was a good brother to Ed. In the early days he was a stand-in climbing partner when no one else was available. 'I enjoyed the trips in retrospect,' Rex said, 'but not at the time.' Later when Ed was taking time off to climb in the Himalayas, it was Rex who kept him supplied with cash from the bees. And later again, after 1970, Rex became Ed's chief school-builder in the Himalayas. As Rex resignedly said, 'Ed was very good at talking people into doing what he wanted them to do.'[3]

Ed with companion (probably Jack McBurney) and two unknown young women outside a corrugated iron hut. HILLARY MUSEUM COLLECTION

Throughout the late 1940s Ed and Rex increased their involvement in the business until they were running it as a partnership under the name of Hillary Brothers. The final purchase from Percy took place on 6 September 1953 when Ed, flush with cash from Everest lectures, agreed to pay £5518 spread over 12 years. There was dispute over this too. Did it include the big Papakura honey-house which by now had been replaced by a smaller building and the old one converted to apartments? In the end it was settled, but Percy had been difficult.

Meantime, the next climbing season came around and Ed still hadn't found the skilled, experienced partner he needed if he was to make progress on the big ice climbs clustered around Mts Cook and Tasman. He began 1947 at Malte Brun Hut with Alan Odell, but this time Chief Guide Harry Ayres was there with a client, Susie Sanders, and Harry was happy to have amateurs in his wake. A few days later they all moved up to Haast Hut, perched high among the great icefalls and crevassed névés that guard the central peaks. Harry Ayres was acknowledged as the best climber of his generation and now Ed, bringing up the rear, at last saw the maestro in action:

We had a chance to see Harry at his best when the last steep rise to the summit proved to be eighteen inches of powder snow over solid ice. Harry gave a fine exhibition of step-cutting up this face, brushing off the snow and hacking out bucket steps in the green ice underneath. Halfway up the face he was startled by an abrupt movement from Susie and it was an eye-opener to me to see the immense power and speed with which he slammed his pick into the hard ice for an emergency belay.[4]

A few days later, Ed had the breakthrough he needed. At short notice a client cancelled and Harry was available to guide Ed for a week, with an attempt on Mt Cook as the final goal. On 30 January, they set off from Haast Hut towards Cook under a starlit sky. In the dark Harry led through the crevasses of the Grand Plateau and the Linda Glacier with its litter of avalanche debris. Not long after dawn they reached the summit rocks. At the foot of the summit ice cap they put on crampons and climbed steadily up hard snow, with bouts of step-cutting on patches of ice. At 11 a.m. they were on the summit. To the north they looked on the ice-bound ridges of Teichelmann which they would climb five days later. Further north was Mt Tasman, New Zealand's second highest peak, which Ed would climb with Harry three years later. To the south, the mile-long summit ridge ran down to the Middle and Low peaks of Cook, and beyond them on the plains far below stretched the milky turquoise waters of Lake Pūkaki.

Ed was always unstinting in his praise of Harry Ayres:

> The technical climbing knowledge I gained in the New Zealand Alps came from Harry. We did some great climbs together and I was constantly amazed at his shrewd appraisal of difficult situations and his superb skill in overcoming them … Of moderate size but incredibly wiry and strong, he had the toughness and endurance to tackle any problem. His great ice axe cut innumerable safe steps in solid green ice and his arms seemed tireless. As a guide he was patient, encouraging and very secure … Up on the mountain he was incomparable.[5]

Ed and Harry Ayres on the summit of Aoraki–Mt Cook, 1947.
HILLARY MUSEUM COLLECTION

Harry had learned his craft largely from experience. He was born in 1912, almost exactly seven years before Ed. His father was a plasterer and lather in Christchurch; his mother died when he was only 12. He followed the path of many Kiwis born into straitened circumstances during the early twentieth century: he left school at 12, did a milk round and picked up low-paid jobs such as collecting spent hops from the local brewery. At age 16 he left home to look for work on the West Coast. He milked cows, cut scrub, laid railway lines in the Buller Gorge, went panning for gold in the Coast's brutally inaccessible gorges.

The break into guiding came through working on the farm of Mick Sullivan at Fox, where a hotel was being built. Tourists were taken on to the nearby glacier using steps cut into the ice by the guides – not death-defying climbing but the ideal training ground for Harry, who learned to cut perfectly shaped steps. In 1937 he went east across the Alps from the West Coast to take up guiding serious climbs on the high peaks around The Hermitage. This was the golden age of guiding when few amateurs would attempt high peaks such as Tasman or Cook on their own. Equipment was primitive. Boots had leather soles fitted with metal tricounis and clinkers which gave poor grip on rock and very little grip in small steps badly cut in ice. Crampons were available but required a modest level of experience and were not always used. The job of the guide was to know the route, judge the snow conditions and weather, and cut bucket steps in ice or frozen snow. And he had always to be ready with ice-axe and rope to hold a client who slipped on an icy surface and took off at high speed down an exposed stretch of mountainside.

For Ed, joining up with Harry was a quantum leap forwards in the development of his mountaineering skills. Country like the Kaikōuras was turning him into the tough all-rounder who could carry a big load over difficult mountain terrain, but it was Harry who led him into the big central peaks sheathed in dangerous ice. Where an icefall looked impenetrable, Harry could show him a way through. He passed on his knowledge of how to handle the multitudinous varieties and textures of snow and ice and how to use a rope for safety. From being just another Auckland amateur, Ed moved into the ranks of the best climbers of his day.

This is not to say that he, or any other New Zealand climber, had technical skills comparable with those of top Swiss, Austrian, German or Italian climbers who between the wars had been putting up routes on faces that had previously been thought impossible. Climbing in the Southern Alps was still at an exploratory stage of its development and its devotees were for the most part self-taught. The first ascent of Mt Cook in 1894 had been made by three patriotic young employees at The Hermitage who improvised a route up the north ridge when they heard that a British-American climber, Edward Fitzgerald, with his Swiss guide Matthias Zurbriggen, might beat them to it.

By the late 1930s and '40s Europeans were adopting smaller ice-axes as front-point crampons came into use, but in New Zealand, where step-cutting was still in favour, the long-handled variety of ice-axe was still used. Ed learned to apply his natural strength and stamina to cutting steps tirelessly in frozen snow or hard ice. He thrived on long, hard days in difficult conditions and bad weather. He was not aware of it at the time, but it was excellent training for the Himalayas.

His partnership with Harry Ayres was put to the test the following year when, in February 1948, they set out for the unclimbed South Ridge of Mt Cook with guide Mick Sullivan and client Ruth Adams.

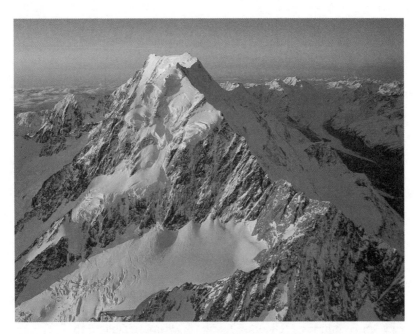

Aoraki-Mt Cook. The prominent rock ridge between sun and shadow is the South Ridge which was first climbed by Ayres, Hillary, Sullivan and Adams in 1948. It leads to Low Peak. The summit ridge continues to Middle and then High Peak.
COLIN MONTEATH/HEDGEHOG HOUSE

This was the outstanding challenge of the time. They began from a high bivouac at the foot of the ridge just north of Nazomi. The early morning light showed a fine, windless day as they ate breakfast and stuffed their sleeping bags into their rucksacks while looking up at the three rock steps guarding the ridge. Previous attempts had reached the top of the first step but no one had climbed further. The second step was steeper than the first, but they were fired up and strong, and by 9.15 had climbed it. The crux was the third step which was steep, smooth rock at the limits of their combined abilities; but Harry, with help from Ed's upstretched hand, was finally able to climb the last vertical section of rock and step on to the snow ridge leading up to the Low Peak. Back at The Hermitage, a watching crowd used mirrors to flash sun messages applauding their progress. Fourteen hours after leaving their Nazomi bivouac, the climbers were back at their base hut in the Hooker.

Three days later, the same South Ridge quartet started out on the week-long epic that became known as the La Perouse Accident. Before the days of the magical nylon rope, Beale's hemp rope was the preferred material for climbers, but it was awkward, unpredictable stuff that would invisibly rot from the inside. Older ropes would be cynically appraised as 'probably all right if you don't fall'. Ed's first letter after his 1947 climb of Cook had been to his sister June on her way by boat to England to study psychology: 'You'll be through Panama by now. I may as well get down to business straight away and say the only thing I really want is 120 feet of Beale's Alpine rope.'[6]

The accident happened when Harry, Ed, Mick Sullivan and Ruth Adams were close to the snow summit of La Perouse. Mick was protecting Ruth with a shoulder belay when she slipped on steep snow. Holding such a slip was routine for a guide, but this time the rope snapped and Ruth was gathering speed down a steepening slope. Just short of a fatal plunge over some cliffs, she was brought up short by a rock. Ed and Harry found her bloodied and unconscious and perhaps with spinal injuries. Helicopter rescues were unavailable in those times; instead they divided between them the work of calling in a rescue team: Ed to stay with Ruth; Mick to descend to the hut for bivouac equipment, warm clothes and food; Harry to run to The Hermitage to summon a rescue team of top climbers from Christchurch. Over the next week, they dragged, lowered and carried Ruth's stretcher down icefall, snow, rock, tussock, alpine scrub, thick forest and finally the bluffs of a river gorge to the West Coast. Ruth's father, who ran a cake-making business, air-dropped in 10 kilograms of his best fruit cake. She made a complete recovery. Ed had climbed another memorable mountain, participated in a vital rescue, and met some top climbers, among them Earle Riddiford who was to play such an important role in the next chapter of his life.

Harry's personal life had its ups and downs. His first marriage, to Cath Guise, a cook at Fox Hotel, was interrupted by war service in New Caledonia and the Solomons. Graham Langton comments, 'He was always attracted to women',[7] a weakness, or a strength, that he shared with Eric Shipton. Harry and Cath's divorce in 1948 was followed a year later by a lasting marriage to Jeanne Cammock with whom he had three children.

Harry Ayres's clients found him great company in a mountain

hut or on a climb, but down in civilisation he was at times uncommunicative and moody. His addiction to smoking was shared by many in a generation unaware of lung cancer. An idiosyncratic belief, surprising in our times when even the most sessile person drinks more than two litres of water a day, was his opposition to drinking water on a climb. Heavily sweetened tea or coffee was acceptable, but Harry said he had known only one or two people who could steadily drink water on a climb without being adversely affected. 'There are many people who founder, like horses, with drinking …' In later years he trained himself to do without water altogether until a climb was over.[8]

In the lead-up to the 1953 attempt on Everest, Ed pushed hard for Harry to be an expedition member, but guides were frowned on by the British Everest Committee and they already had two New Zealanders. How successful might Harry have been on Everest? Performance at high altitude is always an individual variable, but if he'd proved to be a good acclimatiser he would have been invaluable in the icefall, on the Lhotse Face and perhaps above the South Col. On one thing he would have had to compromise – he would have had to drink as much water as he could manage.

In 1956–58 Harry took a break from guiding to join Ed's New Zealand Antarctic party but as a dog-handler rather than with the South Pole tractor party. On his return he was appointed Chief Ranger of the newly formed Mount Cook National Park. Administration was not something he enjoyed, and in 1961 he resigned to run a motor camp at Hanmer. In 1981 he was awarded an OBE for Services to Mountaineering. But in 1987, at the age of 75, caught by a fit of moroseness and advancing years, he took his own life. Melancholia is a common thread in the make-up of mountaineers.

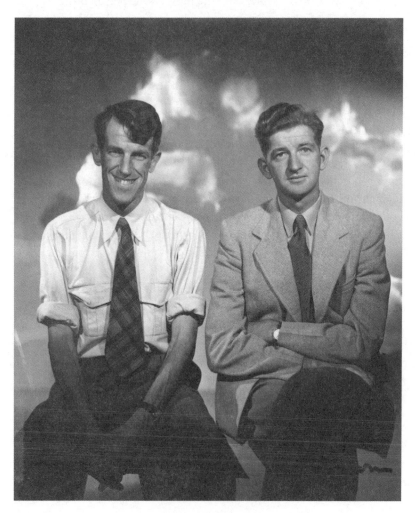

Ed with George Lowe, c.1952. HILLARY MUSEUM COLLECTION

CHAPTER 7

The New Zealand Garhwal expedition and the Shipton cable

If pressed to select someone for the title of Ed's best friend it would have to be George Lowe. Ed said, 'We just seemed to click and became friends almost immediately. George was tall and strong and very fit, and I admired his very effective mountaineering ability. But most of all I enjoyed his sense of humour – I don't think I ever laughed harder or longer than when I was with George in a mountain hut.'[1] George described their first meeting in the mountain bus that travels from The Hermitage up to the Tasman Glacier:

> One day I noticed a long-limbed, keen-faced young man sitting alone on the rear seat. Dressed in old tweed trousers with puttees around the ankles, a tartan shirt and a sweat rag circling his neck, all topped by a battered brown ski cap, he carried an ice-axe and a small rucksack, and his green eyes roved with a curious excitement over the scenery. I joined him at the back of the bus, and we talked easily about the mountains. He had been a wartime navigator, was four years my senior, and was now working for his father who kept a bee farm in Auckland.
>
> 'My father runs a fruit farm,' I told him, 'with beekeeping as a sideline. As a matter of fact we get our queen bees from a chap in Auckland – someone called Hillary.'

'That's us,' said the young man. 'My name's Ed Hillary.'

The bus jolted to a stop. We exchanged addresses and shook hands.

'Let's do a climb together, maybe next year,' he said.[2]

Like Ed, George came from the North Island, but from agricultural Hastings where his father owned an orchard. His future was directed away from manual work when at the age of nine he was knocked down the steps of the front veranda and fractured his left elbow, an awkward break which, despite seven attempts by the local GP to re-set it (on the kitchen table), left him with an arm which lacked its last 45 degrees of extension. George's father sought to strengthen the arm by having him milk the house cow each morning, but when he became eligible for war service nine years later he was declared unfit despite his elbow making him a crack shot. Instead he was manpowered into teacher training in Wellington.[3] On returning to Hastings he joined the Heretaunga Tramping Club as an outlet for his exuberant energy. He became club captain and through his breezy, well-written trip accounts was able to develop his writing and photographic skills. In 1945 he had his first encounter with mountains when he found a job as 'general hand' and later 'junior guide' for the busy months of January and February at The Hermitage. Guiding duties began with cleaning hotel windows, shelling peas on Christmas Eve, taking parties of tourists on to the Tasman Glacier, and carrying loads of blankets, kerosene and food to the mountain huts. But better things were to come when his employers realised that George had more to offer than as kitchen-hand and load-carrier. He was athletic, and unimpaired by his bent elbow. Easy climbs on Sebastopol and the Sealy Range led on to longer and more exacting climbs on the central ice peaks as a second guide, sometimes with Harry Ayres himself.

Ed and George met again in January 1950 when storm-bound for five days in Haast Hut which, at 7000ft, is the take-off point for many routes on Cook and the other central peaks. They played draughts using pieces carved from parsnips and carrots but they also talked about the Himalayas whose attractions had entered the alpine consciousness even in faraway New Zealand. For a start, Nepal had in 1949 opened its borders, making a host of big mountains available for the first time. Not one of the 26,000ft peaks had been climbed, though five months later on 3 June 1950 a strong French expedition created a sensation with their ascent of Annapurna. Maurice Herzog's account of the climb lost nothing in the telling and at around 15 million copies is still the all-time bestselling mountain book. Awaiting their first ascents, with fame of the mountaineering variety for their climbers, were Everest, K2, Kangchenjunga, Lhotse, Makalu, Cho Oyu – the list went on. It was something to dream about.

An invitation while climbing in the European Alps

The Hillary family was not in the habit of international travel, but in 1949 Gertrude and Percy splashed out on a boat ticket to England for the wedding of their daughter June to Norwich doctor Jimmy Carlile. They bought a car and travelled around England, but by 1950, when Gertrude had plans for the Continent, Percy had lost interest. Gertrude sent an SOS to Rex and Ed – if Rex would look after the bees, Ed could travel by boat to England and be their driver around Europe in May and June.

London made an indelible impression. Ed wrote:

> I made the usual pilgrimage to Westminster Abbey ... The royal tombs made history come alive for me and so did a hundred other relics of a mighty past. As a citizen of a new country with little history I felt I was being accepted back into the ancestral fold – it gave me an astonishingly warm feeling. In those days, like most of my fellow citizens, I was British first and a New Zealander second ...[4]

In Europe, he could hardly visit the Alps, the birthplace of mountaineering, without attempting some peaks, and he joined up with two fellow New Zealand climbers. The weather was fine. In Austria and Switzerland they luxuriated in comfortable huts and felt a swashbuckling superiority to the soft, guided clientele they met. They climbed a lot of peaks which they found 'pretty easy' while admitting these were routes described by the guide book as 'la plus facile'...[5]

But the most exciting event of the European trip was still to come. They had taken the train which climbs in a tunnel inside the bowels of the Eiger and Jungfrau to reach the highest railway station in Switzerland. Here at the Jungfraujoch post office, at 11,350ft, Ed

Ed at the Breslauer Hut in the Austrian Alps, 1950. A few days later he received the invitation to join the 1951 expedition to the Garhwal Himalaya.
HILLARY MUSEUM COLLECTION

received a letter from George Lowe. It outlined an expedition to the Himalayas being organised by Christchurch climber Earle Riddiford. George had been invited, but there was still a vacancy in the four-man party; George had suggested that Ed Hillary should be asked to join them. Percy encouraged him to accept. Rex would look after the bees. Ed had a ticket to the Himalayas.

Earle Riddiford
Earle was a member of an extended family which had played a distinguished role in the history of Wellington. Daniel Riddiford had arrived in the new colony in 1840 and for over a century family members were lawyers, politicians, and landholders in the fertile Wairarapa Valley. They were a large clan, however, and Earle's father was not wealthy when he died in a farm accident four months before Earle was born in 1921. His widow Helen was left with little money, and bringing up three children was a struggle, though Dan, a wealthy member of the extended family, helped from time to time and paid for Earle's private education

at Wanganui Collegiate between 1935 and 1938. As had happened to Ed Hillary a few years earlier, it was on a school trip to Mt Ruapehu that Earle Riddiford fell in love with mountains.[6] In 1937, when Helen re-married, they moved to Christchurch.

Earle worked in army intelligence in the Pacific during the war, but by 1945 he was back in Christchurch studying law and climbing mountains. It was mountaineering of a particular sort. Beyond the gold-bearing beaches and river beds of the West Coast, a complex network of icefalls and broken mountain ridges reaches up to the Main Divide. For a post-war generation of Christchurch mountaineers nothing could be more exciting than seeking out virgin peaks and ridges, and exploring these inaccessible gorges, névés and glaciers. They gave them names like The Garden of Eden, though a non-believer arriving during a nor'west storm would have understood why Adam and Eve were happy to take the apple and get out. Earle loved searching out these places and planning the expeditions.

It was an easy leap of the imagination from Westland to the Himalayas. Why not a New Zealand expedition? Kangchenjunga, perhaps? Even Everest? By 1950, Earle was planning a Himalayan expedition for 1951 with three engineering friends as founding members: Norm Hardie, Bill Beaven and Jim McFarlane. Who else could they invite? Harry Ayres was an early choice. Hardie proposed George Lowe after talking to him at a Federated Mountain Clubs meeting, and George suggested a strong, lean beekeeper from Auckland by the name of Ed Hillary. He hadn't actually climbed with Ed, but assured Riddiford that Ed 'is as good as you will get in ability and temperament'.[7]

Then Hardie remembered he'd met Ed twice in 1948, on the La Perouse rescue and later that winter when the bees were asleep and Ed was doing casual work on the Lake Pūkaki hydro-electric project. Norm Hardie was Ed's supervisor and described him as 'the easiest of blokes to get along with and possessed plenty of general ruggedness'.[8] A last addition was Ed Cotter, who had been asked by Earle to give a talk to the NZ Alpine Club in Christchurch and immediately afterwards was invited to join the expedition.

At its peak the party had eight members hoping to attempt Kangchenjunga, but then attrition set in. The engineers Hardie, Beaven and McFarlane were the first to leave, reluctantly giving preference to their professional careers. Harry Ayres lacked cash, and soon there were only four left – Riddiford, Lowe, Hillary and Cotter – and their objectives had shrunk to two much smaller peaks in Garhwal, an area of the Indian Himalayas just west of Nepal. They could hardly know it at the time, but these four had bought tickets in a lottery whose winner would become the most famous climber on Earth. Ed Cotter seemed to care least but the other three were fiercely ambitious. Hillary had dreamt since childhood of some famous achievement. George Lowe seemed to be the most modest of men but beneath his witty, easy-going exterior and studied understatement was a steely desire for recognition. Riddiford was perhaps the most ambitious of them all, though physically the least robust. He was the person who was driving the enterprise, gathering equipment, raising funds, obtaining permits, engaging Sherpas through the Himalayan Club in India, researching which peak in which area was most suited to their abilities and ambitions. Mountaineering was the way all four of them expressed their sense of being different, their sense of importance.

When he wrote about the Garhwal expedition, Ed noted Ed Cotter's whimsical humour, George's boisterous competence and Earle's cool intellect.[9] He acknowledged Earle's tenacity and other abilities too, but at a personal level he had more in common with George Lowe. In Garhwal Ed and George grew into a climbing team but their friendship was more than that. They were both good story-tellers, with George a natural comedian. They fed each other lines and laughed together. Both were competitive but somehow they never seemed to threaten each other. And in the end it was always George who deferred to Ed. Earle was quieter and more cerebral. He had the confidence arising from a large family of some distinction. Having a university degree, he was more at home with his Christchurch group of climbing engineers than he was with the pair that was Ed and George.

The Maximilian Ridge

Before leaving for Garhwal, Earle organised a dress rehearsal on the Maximilian Ridge of Elie de Beaumont. Although the summit of Elie is easily accessible by a standard route from the Tasman Glacier, the unclimbed Maximilian Ridge rose out of deep, inaccessible valleys to the north. George Lowe wrote in the journal of the Heretaunga Tramping Club, 'An invitation from Earle Riddiford (an illustrious

Ed Cotter, Ed Hillary (with bow and arrow) and Earle Riddiford under the bivvy rock at the foot of the Maximilian Ridge of Elie de Beaumont. LOWE COLLECTION

name in the alpine world as an explorer of virgin valleys and new routes on high hills) was accepted ... On a fine Christmas morning, we set off with cruel loads ...'[10]

It was a classic Riddiford plan, a topographical puzzle put together with pieces he had found in obscure accounts and by personally exploring Elie's gorges and icefalls from the west. He wrote of the first day:

> In the descent from the saddle ... the two ropes, Lowe-
> Hillary and Cotter-Riddiford, took varying routes adding
> a spice of competition. On this trip it was as well to get a
> running start in the morning if you wanted your share of the
> lead. When with George Lowe I would recommend hitching
> him to a ball and chain as well. It was at the camp on the
> floor of the Whymper that Ed Cotter first inflated his large
> collection of novelty balloons which completely unnerved the
> keas, the resident alpine parrots.[11]

Heavy rain set in for two days. They camped under a huge bivvy rock surrounded by a mass of celmisia daisies and thick grass. Ed made a bow and arrow and shot two kea which tasted like strong duck. On the ninth day they climbed the Maximilian Ridge rising in a series of six big steps with various smaller towers. Much of the climb was led by George. On the summit they parted, a separation that could be seen as symbolic of their time to come in Garhwal. Lowe and Hillary descended the Tasman to The Hermitage, while Riddiford and Cotter returned to their Westland camp.

Four Kiwis in Garhwal

On 3 May 1951 they flew across the Tasman to Sydney where they were to embark for Colombo on the *Orion*. Ed wrote in his diary: 'Very smooth pleasant trip with good food. Pleasant stewardess, Miss McCormack. On arrival Rose Bay accosted by half-a-dozen reporters. Gave story, had photos taken. All very important! Wandered around town, had grill for five shillings and then went to Kings Cross to meet stewardess – who did not arrive.'[12]

The NZ Expedition to Garhwal: Ed Hillary, Ed Cotter, George Lowe and Earle Riddiford (leader). HILLARY FAMILY COLLECTION

Ed discusses life with the daughter of the editor of the Melbourne Age *aboard the P&O ship* Orion. LOWE COLLECTION

Miss McCormack was probably more used to handling encounters with the opposite sex than were our climbers, of whom Ed Cotter said, 'We were all virgins.'[13] As the boat set sail, a group photo shows the party leaning on the ship's rail. Good companion Ed Cotter is smiling approvingly as step-cutter Ed Hillary tests the sharpness of his ice-axe; entertainer George has an engaging smile as he looks into the camera; planner Earle is looking in another direction as if he's a passer-by who got included in the photo by mistake.

From Colombo they travelled by train through Calcutta, Varanasi and Lucknow until finally settling into a forest bungalow at Ranikhet, where Ed shook a large scorpion out of one of his shirts. Here they met their four Sherpas whose sardar, Pasang Dawa, spoke some English and was familiar with the use of rope, ice-axe and crampons.[14]

For nine days they marched up-valley along the trail to their base at Badrinath, which was one of the most holy sites of Hindu pilgrimage in all India, mentioned in the Mahabharata in 500BC. In 1951 it appeared as a cluster of rusty corrugated-iron roofs surrounding the main temple dedicated to the god Vishnu. Steam rose into the air from the hot baths where pilgrims immersed themselves. The turbulent Alakananda flowed through the town on its way to the Ganges.

Rising magnificently as a backdrop to the town was their first objective, Nilkantha, only nine kilometres to the west, a spectacular pyramid framed by the dark walls of its gorge. For a fortnight they skirmished around its base searching for a feasible route, but like other parties before them they found none. The weather was indifferent, snowfalls heavy, and the altitude more enervating than they could have imagined. Ed's diary over the next two weeks records the Himalayan reality they were now facing: 'Country very steep … Nilkantha looks terrific and our hopes have sunk rather low … None of us going well … We are quite obviously not acclimatized to this height – have no energy or drive and at times breathe with difficulty … Killed a sheep.'[15] On 24 June they gave up and returned to Badrinath to lick their wounds and hope that Mukut Parbat would be easier.

Three days later they set off up a trail which would have taken them over the 18,400ft Mana Pass into Tibet had they persevered, but they turned right to gain the Chamrao Glacier leading to Mukut Parbat. Earle wrote, 'A fine array of ice peaks was to be seen gleaming in the sun at the head of the various branches of the Chamrao Glacier. One big rocky mass dominated everything else – Mukut Parbat. It was exciting to find that our objective was such a fine looking peak.'[16]

Over the next 10 days, with the two Eds and George doing most of the work, they found a route up relatively easy glacier and rock to a col from which an apparently climbable ridge of snow and ice led to the summit of their peak. The terrain might not have been difficult, but this was a Himalayan mountain with its ever-present difficulties of altitude and freezing winds. On one day the two Eds and George climbed a virgin peak of 20,330ft. 'Our first 20,000 footer!' exulted Ed in his diary. 'I was going better than the others and did a good deal of the trail-breaking.'[17]

On 10 July they moved into their Camp 3 at 21,000ft, and on 11 July they set off on their summit attempt, Ed Hillary and George on one rope; Earle, Ed Cotter and Pasang on the other. It was a bitterly cold day. On the crest of the ridge, where their route lay, a gale-force wind swept across from the south, penetrating the marrow of their bones. The inadequacies of their plain New Zealand boots became painfully apparent, particularly for George whose nailed soles conducted out whatever warmth he had in his feet. The others at least had Vibram rubber soles. During the four hours it took to reach the

Mukut Parbat from the south. The route to the summit is up the left-hand ridge.
LOWE COLLECTION

halfway point on their ridge, a subsidiary summit at 22,500ft, Ed Hillary and George stopped three times to remove their boots and massage circulation back into their frozen feet.

For the first half hour Hillary and Lowe were in the lead, but when the other three caught up Earle Riddiford politely asked if he could take the lead. George Lowe wrote:

> We followed slowly ... the wind shrieked and rocked us ...
> the rope between us billowing out over Tibet ... Earle and
> the others were in a little hollow cutting away slowly at some
> green ice ... we waited and gradually froze. Ahead was a steep
> rib of snow and ice that curled over in a cornice. The side we
> had to climb was sheathed in hard ice. Big Ed and I reckoned

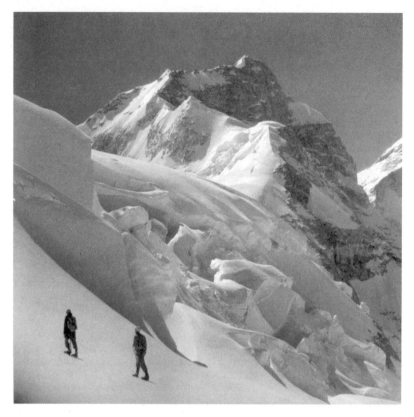

The north-west ridge of Mukut Parbat. The summit climb began from Camp 3 on the snow col on the other side of the broken ice. LOWE COLLECTION

it would take 3 or 4 hours to cut up this, and the chances of getting to the top were almost nil ...[18]

Ahead of them Riddiford was by no means confident either, but he knew that this was the climb on which the success of the expedition would be judged. It was still only midday and he was not ready to give up yet. Nor was Pasang, who surprised the other two by saying, 'Very little time to top, long way come, two hours to top.' Riddiford wrote:

Actually it took six slogging hours, battling with the wind all the time ... it was possible to avoid the worst of ... the green

ice by a delicate traverse up the crest of the ridge with one
cramponed foot in Tibet and the other in Garhwal. Ahead was
a series of bumps of mixed ice and rock, perhaps two hours,
but both Cotter and Pasang were keen, and we went on ...

We were beginning to get very tired ... We struck soft
snow. The wind, now much stronger, was direct in our faces
and made each step in the soft snow a stagger. We didn't know
whether we could make it but managed to push on slowly
up the final snow slope to the summit. It was a moment of
exhilaration. We closed up and shook hands. Below us the
great blue Tibetan glacier flowed away to the yellow plains of
Tibet ...[19]

Down at Camp 3, George and Big Ed were becoming concerned. It
was right on dark when they saw three climbers cramponing down the
last slopes at great speed.

Are you all OK? shouted George.
Yes!
Did you climb the bugger?
Yes!
Bloody good show!
What time did you get on top?
Quarter to six, said Earle.
Hell, you took a risk! said George.[20]

In his diary that night, Ed wrote glumly:

Mukut Parbat climbed today but alas George and I not in
the lucky party ... Pasang went very well and said of the
ridge, 'Very difficult.' Ed C. developed snow blindness due
to no snow goggles. I was very disappointed at missing the
summit especially as I was going OK when we turned back.
Great credit must be given however to Earle's persistence and
courage in continuing. The boys are all too tired to eat ...[21]

This was not the script Ed had written for himself. He was fitter and
stronger than any of them and by now his acclimatisation was really
starting to kick in. Surely if anyone was going to reach the summit of

103

Mukut Parbat it would be him. Given more time to reflect, Ed and George might have realised they were underestimating the Riddiford trio. Earle had a reputation for conserving his energy for the most important climb on a trip. If there was an important first ascent he was there, fired up and resolved. Ed Cotter was more laidback than the others. He observed ambition with amused detachment, but he was a natural athlete. His agility was such that he could walk considerable distances on his hands and had done so, to the alarm of both passengers and crew, on the rail of the boat travelling from Sydney to Colombo. When the expedition porters had been brought to a halt above Badrinath by a narrow log spanning a mountain torrent, Cotter had carried the first load across, then returned in the reverse direction on his hands to applause and laughter from the Tibetan porters who thereupon picked up their loads and carried on.[22] He was unlikely to let the team down on Mukut Parbat. Finally there was Pasang, who not only had the superior strength of all Sherpas at altitude but also was keen to achieve the climb.

Ed Hillary had learnt a lesson that the race is not just to the strong, but to those who have the courage and tenacity to see it through to the end. It was on Mukut Parbat he learnt 'It is not the mountain we conquer but ourselves.'

Down at Badrinath they looked at their thin bodies and weighed themselves:

	NZ	Garhwal	Weight loss	% loss
Riddiford	73kg	57kg	16kg	21%
Lowe	82kg	70kg	12kg	14%
Hillary	82kg	73kg	9kg	11%
Cotter	71kg	68kg	3kg	4%

'Big mountains eat flesh,' said Pasang.

Any two can join us

There was mail waiting for them at Badrinath, including an unsettling cutting from a London paper: later in the year Eric Shipton would be leading a four-man English reconnaissance looking for a route on Everest from Nepal. They talked longingly of what an excitement that would be, and in a moment of optimism Ed remembered the name of Scott Russell, a botanist who had lived and climbed in New Zealand and was now on the committee of the Alpine Club in London.

Unbeknown to the Garhwal group, the same idea had occurred to Roland Ellis of the NZ Alpine Club whose Otago chairman, Harry Stevenson, had known Scott Russell when he'd been climbing in the Southern Alps. The cable read:

> any possibility, one or more nz party, consisting riddiford cotter lowe hillary, at present successfully climbing garhwal himalayas, being included forthcoming everest expedition ... stop excellent type climbers who through being acclimatised should prove useful adjuncts[23]

The Garhwal group knew nothing of this second cable. They still had a month for some lesser climbs, and Earle's topographical curiosity led him back to Nilkantha where he identified a climbable route on a big ice ledge crossing the North Face. By mid-August, the expedition was over. Ed wrote in his diary, 'I just want to hurry home to the bees now,' but in the mail bag at the Indian border town of Ranikhet was a startling message.

Scott Russell had asked Shipton what reply he should send in response to the Stevenson cable.

'The correct answer was obvious,' Shipton wrote later:

> I had already turned down several applicants with very strong qualifications on the ground that I wanted to keep the party small; our slender resources of money and equipment were already stretched and I had no idea where these unknown climbers were or how to contact them. I was about to send a negative reply when, in a moment of nostalgic reflection, I recalled the cheerful countenance of Dan Bryant, and I changed my mind.[24]

Bryant was a New Zealander who had been on the 1935 Everest expedition. He had been good on ice and Shipton had liked him:

> The presence of Dan Bryant would have made dissension difficult to sustain, for any ostentation or humbug became

the target of his gentle mockery, which discouraged any of
us from taking himself or his grievances too seriously ...
Tough and thoroughly competent, he had a delicious brand
of humour and a huge fund of anecdotes, largely derived from
his acute observation of people ...[25]

And as the New Zealand cable pointed out, the Garhwal party would
be fit and acclimatised. Without reference to the rest of his party,
Shipton instructed Scott Russell to send a cable to Harry Stevenson
who in turn would contact the Garhwal group by way of a message to
the cable office at Ranikhet. The piece of paper on which it was printed
has been lost but the message was clear: ANY TWO CAN JOIN EVEREST
RECONNAISSANCE.

In his 1969 autobiography Shipton wrote:

> I soon began to regret this, for apart from the complications
> resulting from the last-minute inclusion of two new members
> of the party, still in some remote Himalayan valley and with
> no permits to enter Nepal, I found it far from easy to explain
> my totally irrational action to my companions. They could
> not altogether hide their dismay, though they were too polite
> to express it. Eventually the two New Zealanders caught us
> up when we were halfway across Nepal. Then for the first
> time, we learnt their names; they were Earle Riddiford and
> Edmund Hillary. My momentary caprice was to have far-
> reaching results.[26]

Back in Ranikhet the party of four was torn apart by this startling
invitation. Which two should go? Shipton was later to say that if he'd
known how traumatic the decision would be he would have invited all
four – and indeed Cotter suggested just that, reasoning that at worst
two of them would be told to go home. The other three, all of them less
casual, felt that *two* meant just that.

Ed Cotter was the first to drop out, a compelling reason being
that he didn't have the cash to continue. That left three who, in order
of physical fitness, were Hillary, Lowe and Riddiford. There was a
consensus that Hillary should be one of the pair to join Shipton. Cotter
wrote home shortly after the decision had been made: 'I wanted to see

Ed H. go, considering him the most suitable.'[27] Riddiford wrote in an explanatory letter nine years later: 'The first suggestion I made was that Ed Hillary should go as he had been outstandingly fit throughout the expedition.'[28]

Riddiford had a strong case too, though Lowe, with so much at stake, was reluctant to concede. George was physically stronger, and he and Ed had formed a good pair, but Riddiford had some arguments in his favour that were difficult to ignore. For a start he had organised the expedition. Without him none of them would have been in Ranikhet arguing about the invitation. He also had funds available from his uncle Dan Riddiford who had recently sent a donation to help the expedition stay solvent. More telling than anything, Earle had completed the first ascent of Mukut Parbat, while Hillary and Lowe had turned back.

Earle, the lawyer, had a strong case and argued it successfully. So it was that on 8 September, Ed Hillary, Earle Riddiford and Pasang Dawa set off to join Eric Shipton's reconnaissance of Mt Everest.

Two weeks later, Ed wrote privately to his beekeeping friend Bob Chandler who had donated £10 to expedition funds:

> I'll have quite a few interesting things to discuss with you
> on return including some of the personality clashes which
> occurred particularly between Earle and George. Earle proved
> rather difficult at times and I had to restrain strong impulses
> to give him a good kick. On the other hand George was
> something of a disappointment to me as under unpleasant
> conditions he proved rather lacking in drive and I, in some
> small measure, rather consider he cost me Mukut Parbat.
> Keep all this under your hat ...[29]

The Lowe–Riddiford feud played out for many years. George was unforgiving, even though a year later he received his own invitation to join the British prelude to Everest on Cho Oyu. Over the years, Earle's Christchurch friends stood by him, whilst George's friends – notably Ed – supported him. Earle, with his 'cool intellect', just wasn't Ed's sort of person.

CHAPTER 8

Everest Reconnaissance 1951

The decision made, Riddiford and Hillary threw themselves into preparations for their new expedition, buying food in Lucknow and cashing a money transfer of £200 thoughtfully sent by the NZ Alpine Club. Ed sent a telegram to Percy:

> Invited Shipton everest Expedition Could not refuse please forgive Erring son reply Rex November Writing Love Edmund[1]

The pair nearly missed the train leaving for the Nepali border town of Jogbani:

> We swept through the gates just as the guard appeared to blow his whistle. His firm cry of 'Too Late!' sounded the death-knell of our plans. But Riddiford was not the man to give in too lightly. His forceful persuasion (and judicious baksheesh) won the day. We leapt into a second-class carriage … a wild scattering of coins to our coolies, a sudden jerk that nearly threw us on the floor and another expedition had begun.[2]

Leaving the train after a two-day journey, they moved north to Dharan where they hired 17 porters to carry their loads into the rain-sodden hills flanking the great Arun River whose tributaries were in high flood.

The largest of them, 50 metres wide, was a torrent of brown, turbulent water. New Zealand climbers of Ed's generation prided themselves on their ability to cross flooded rivers using a long pole. With his ice-axe Ed cut a three-metre sapling. Then with a bow-wave breaking around Earle at the upstream end, Ed as anchor at the downstream end, and a cluster of laden porters in between, they surged across.

Further north they had to cross the broad Arun River, a massive body of fast-flowing brown water, in a dugout canoe with very little freeboard. As an encouragement for the boatmen to paddle hard, the oily surges on this stretch of river gave way to rapids that would be certain death if the boat failed to cross in time. The combined dangers of a mountainous terrain and widespread infectious diseases made the life expectancy of a Nepali hill dweller short at best, but for Arun boatmen life must have been exceptionally brief.

The dangers of the river behind them, Earle and Ed set off at a fast pace through steep, wet forest to reach Dingla, the village where they would join the British party. Ed wrote:

> As we climbed rapidly upwards, I couldn't help wondering what the four men we were meeting would be like. Of course we all knew about Shipton, his tough trips, his ability to go to great heights, and his policy of having cheap and mobile expeditions by living largely off the land. He was certainly the most famous living Himalayan mountaineer. But what did he look like? And what about his three companions? ...
>
> I looked at Riddiford. Thin and bony, with a scraggy beard and scruffy, dirty clothes, he didn't look a particularly prepossessing type. I knew from experience that I probably looked a lot rougher. But these Englishmen – for all I knew they might shave every day; they might be sticklers for the right thing. We'd have to smarten up a bit and watch our language.
>
> As we entered Dingla we were met by a Sherpa who informed us that the Burra Sahib was waiting to meet us ... We followed into a dark doorway and up some stairs ... and as we came into the room, four figures scrambled to meet us and my immediate impression was of large bodies in solid condition. My first feeling was one of relief. I have rarely seen

109

a more disreputable bunch, and my visions of changing for
dinner faded away forever ...[3]

A strongly built man with a short grizzled beard turned
towards me with a welcoming smile and I knew I was meeting
Eric Shipton for the first time ...[4]

He introduced his three companions: Bill Murray ... who had
led an all-Scottish expedition to the Himalayas; Dr. Michael
Ward, a well-built young chap with an easy impetuous
manner; and ... Tom Bourdillon ... an enormous chap ...
obviously as strong as a horse.[5]

How did the Kiwis look to the Shipton party? Mike Ward wrote:

Ed Hillary and Earle Riddiford charged up the hill carrying
immense Victorian-looking ice-axes. Both were gaunt figures
in patched clothes ... They were both wearing peaked cloth
hats with a flap down the neck. From the way they bounded
up the hill and the ease with which they wolfed down a
horrid meal of boiled rice and indeterminate green vegetables
they were both in training and used to the squalid aspects of
Himalayan travel.[6]

There was no doubt that by September 1951 Hillary and Riddiford
were able to hit the ground running, particularly when compared with
Ward, Bourdillon and Murray who had come from desk jobs. The New
Zealanders had been climbing for three months at heights of 15,000–
20,000ft. They looked, smelt and moved like mountain goats. Added to
this was Ed's occupational strength from carrying 40-kilogram combs
of honey around South Auckland for eight hours a day over 15 years of
harvests. It was an advantage that Ed would preserve through to
29 May 1953.

Shipton, Bourdillon and Ward
Of the six men sharing their meal of rice and local spinach that night,
four – Ward, Shipton, Hillary and Bourdillon – were, or would become,
major players in the history of Everest. Ed would not have heard of
Mike Ward, but in 1951 he was more important than anyone else. It

The British reconnaissance party 1951. Standing (L to R): Eric Shipton, Bill Murray, Tom Bourdillon and Earle Riddiford; Seated: Mike Ward and Ed Hillary.
ROYAL GEOGRAPHICAL SOCIETY

was thanks to his imagination and enterprise that the 1951 Everest Reconnaissance was taking place at all. He had been converted to mountaineering as a schoolboy at Marlborough by Edwin Kempson, a member of the Everest expeditions of 1935 and 1936. Cambridge University and its Mountaineering Club followed, and a medical degree in 1949. While completing National Service in 1950, Ward had the spare time to do some research on Everest at the Royal Geographical Society (RGS) in London. The traditional northern route used by British expeditions in the 1920s and 1930s had been closed by the Chinese following their occupation of Tibet in 1950 but at the same time Nepal had opened the unexplored southern approaches. Was there a route from this direction?

George Mallory in 1921 was the first to see the beginnings of a route in the chaotic and dangerous Khumbu Icefall. This led into the Western Cwm, a deep, high-walled trench whose upper reaches were hidden from view. At 26,000ft the South Col too was visible, but not the route from there to the summit. Nor was it known whether there was a climbable route from the floor of the Cwm up to the Col. 'I do not much fancy it would be possible,' was Mallory's gloomy opinion.

Wondering whether there might be some forgotten evidence, Ward searched the archives of the RGS for photos from the south. They were scattered and incomplete but they were there. Aerial photos taken in 1933, 1945 and 1947 showed a south-east ridge at a moderate angle rising from a broad South Col of wind-swept ice and rock up to the summit. The last thousand feet looked more promising than on the northern route. The big unknown was the terrain between the head of the Cwm and the Col. Was there an impossible headwall cutting off access or was it a slope of climbable snow and ice?

Ward was unaware that in November 1950 a small group led by eminent mountaineers H.W. (Bill) Tilman and Charles Houston had already entered Solukhumbu, the first foreigners to do so. They were distinguished climbers, but they the lacked time, fitness, acclimatisation and youth (Tilman was 52) to reach a point where they could see the head of the Cwm and the terrain from there to the South Col. Tilman's final summary for *The Alpine Journal* of 1951 was that 'although we cannot entirely dismiss the South Side, I think it is safe to say that there is no route comparable in ease and safety at any rate up to 28,000 feet to that by the North East'.[7] This was true but also irrelevant now that the Tibetan approach was no longer available. And the last piece in the topographical puzzle, the route to the South Col, had still not been found.

By June 1951, Mike Ward had persuaded the Himalayan Committee to support a small reconnaissance expedition from Nepal. Bill Murray and Tom Bourdillon had signed on as members, the latter from a new generation of English climbers who were taking on big routes in the Alps that had previously been the preserve of continental climbers. At the last minute Eric Shipton had appeared out of South China following the closure of his position as consul-general in Kunming. Here was the ideal leader for the expedition, and he accepted.

Shipton and Ward both had fathers who had worked in the outposts of empire. Ward's father had worked in the Malaysian civil service and been in Singapore when the Japanese invaded in February

1942. His mother had escaped in one of the last boats to leave the colony, but his father spent the war in a concentration camp. Eric Shipton's father had been a tea planter in Ceylon (now Sri Lanka) but died before Eric was three years old.

Is there an element of paternal deprivation in the make-up of mountaineers?

Shipton's mother, described as a woman of icy detachment, left the tea plantation to travel, taking her small son and daughter with her. Eric, shy and reputedly dyslexic, was sent to Pyt House, 'a school for failing or delinquent boys', having failed to gain acceptance into Harrow. He began to come into his own when, working in Kenya as a coffee planter, he met Bill Tilman. They climbed on Kilimanjaro, Mt Kenya and Ruwenzori, the Mountains of the Moon. Sometimes separately, sometimes together, they explored the Karakorum, entered the Sanctuary of Nanda Devi, made first ascents of Kamet and Nanda Devi, and went on the 1930s Everest expeditions. Above all, they wrote with wit and romance of wild and distant places, and their books have enthralled, amused and inspired countless mountaineers, whether armchair or practising.

When Ed met Eric Shipton in 1951, they seemed to develop an empathy. Certainly over the next two months Shipton chose Ed as his climbing companion. Did their shared lack of a university education make a difference? When required to pass Latin for the Cambridge University college entrance exam, Shipton took two years, and his interest in geology was discouraged when he was told the only job would be as a lecturer and then only with a first class degree. Biographer Peter Steele writes, 'This finished any aspirations he had for going to university, something that would dog him for the rest of his life and always give him a sense of inferiority in the presence of the university men who filled the ranks of the top British climbers at that time.'[8] Ed, too, was wary of anyone who assumed superiority because of his education.

This diffidence seldom showed, and Ed and Earle fitted in well with Shipton's group. Tom Bourdillon, a physicist, wrote to his wife Jennifer, 'I wish you could meet Ed. He is one of the best blokes I know. Earle is a good man – old NZ family, sheep farmer, soldier and now lawyer, 30 and he is a gentleman which Ed is not, but I would as soon climb or talk with Ed ... as anyone I know.'[9] Ed would hardly have understood the English concept of what makes a gentleman but he would have been gratified by his acceptance into this small group of climbers who simply liked him as a person.

Solukhumbu to the foot of Everest

From their meeting place in Dingla, the men walked for 10 days through dense forest infested with leeches, brown waving threads that would drop on to bare skin as it brushed past, then swell to the size of slugs as they gorged on blood. On 21 September the party at last entered the valley of the Dudh Kosi, the land of the Sherpas. This 'had become, for me at least, a kind of Mecca, an ultimate goal in Himalayan exploration,' Shipton wrote. 'Whenever we came upon a particularly attractive spot, Sherpas invariably said, "This is just like Sola Khumbu," and the comparison always led to a long, nostalgic discourse about their homeland.'[10] Even today, when 40,000 trekkers visit each year, this is a special place; in 1951 it was pure magic.

Shipton was loved by the Sherpas who worked for him, and their hospitality could not have been more generous. They supplied the group with eggs, chapattis, butter, honey, potatoes, corn, rice, mutton, pumpkin, peas, tea, and rice beer (chang) and spirits (rakshi). The party bought 10 pounds of honey, described by Ed as 'granulated and of good flavour'.

In Namche Bazar, a village of 60 houses at 11,290ft on the trade route to Tibet, they settled into a large house to sort loads before moving higher to Tengboche Monastery where the view opened out to display the great Khumbu peaks rising all around them, with Everest furthest away and displaying the top thousand feet of the all-important south-east ridge above and beyond the Lhotse-Nuptse wall. 'There are some really stupendous peaks which look quite unclimbable to me,' wrote Ed in his diary. 'They are the first peaks I have seen that make New Zealand climbs look easy … I could well imagine spending a year or so in this valley – it attracts me more than any place I have ever visited.'[11]

By 29 September the party was camped at 18,000ft in a lateral moraine and confronting the towering presence of Everest on whose flanks they hoped to find a route. Immediately in front of them rose the tumbling chaos of the Khumbu Icefall. Ed noted, 'Tom, Michael and Bill have not been going well due to altitude. Earle seems to be in good

Panorama of the Everest group as a backdrop to the Sherpa villages. The houses of Namche Bazar (photographed in 2010, not 1951) fill the steep little cirque in lower centre. Two tracks lead up and left to Khumjung and Khunde which are just visible in the flat valley running left from centre. Tengboche Monastery is on a spur on the other side of the main valley, which is the Dudh Kosi. Everest is the rearmost peak with all except its top 1500 feet concealed by the Lhotse-Nuptse Ridge. The prominent peak on the right is Ama Dablam with the Mingbo Valley in front.
LHAKPA SONAM SHERPA

OVERLEAF *The key 1951 view of Everest from Pumori showing a route linking the Khumbu Icefall and the Western Cwm to the South Col by way of the snow and ice slopes of the Lhotse Face. The actual route from Col to summit is just behind the skyline ridge.* ERIC SHIPTON

---

form, as is Eric, and I seem comparatively unaffected by height.' Three months in Garhwal was making acclimatisation easier and Shipton had the reputation of always being comfortable at altitude.

The party divided into three pairs, two to enter the icefall while Shipton and Ed climbed to a viewpoint on the slopes of Pumori. They made height quickly. It was an amazing day with an outcome better than they could have imagined. As they climbed, the obscuring ridges fell away and parted to reveal the extraordinary sight of a climbable route to the summit of Everest. The icefall was not looking any easier but, once surmounted, smooth slopes of easy snow led all the way up

the Western Cwm to the snow and ice face of Lhotse which, though steep, was nowhere blocked by walls of rock or ice. The route to the South Col was there and waiting for them, and they knew from photos that above it a south-east ridge of mixed rock and snow led at a moderate grade to the South Summit. The ridge beyond that was not visible. Down below they saw two distant figures, whom they recognised as Riddiford and Pasang, making excitingly fast progress to reach a point halfway up the icefall.

Four days later Shipton, Hillary, Riddiford and Pasang returned in an attempt to reach the Cwm. The sun beat down. 'We poured with sweat and before long our panting produced a tormenting thirst … Threading our way through a wild labyrinth of walls, chasms and towers, we could rarely see more than 200 feet ahead.'[12] By 4 p.m. they were close to the top when a snow slope they were climbing avalanched gently downwards. Pasang, who was in the lead, got a shaft in far enough to hold Riddiford, who was otherwise heading for a crevasse. The party decided to retreat from the icefall until snow conditions improved and the rest of the group became better acclimatised.

Returning on 28 October, all six climbers with three Sherpas re-entered the icefall. Their hopes of finding a more stable route on consolidated snow were shattered when they found that a large area of the most broken part of the icefall had collapsed, leaving an altered landscape of unstable blocks of ice scattered over huge crevasses. But they persisted, and after a fine lead on a blade of ice by Tom Bourdillon they could see into the gently rising Cwm. They were still cut off by a final crevasse stretching across the Cwm but, given time, a route could be made.

Returning in a subdued frame of mind, they discussed the route. The Sherpas declared it too dangerous for carrying loads day after day, and it was hard to disagree. The ice was changing constantly and from time to time there would be a major subsidence. On the left-hand side, avalanche fans offered an easier route but were being fed by cliffs of hanging ice above. It was like being in a zone of Force 9 earthquakes with tsunamis of ice. Eric said he would not ask porters to risk their lives in such a place. But when Ed pointed out that if a British expedition didn't accept the risk someone else would, they knew he was right. And maybe the icefall would be more stable pre-monsoon than now in the autumn.

That was the end of the 1951 reconnaissance: successful, though overhung by disquiet about the dangers of the icefall. Nevertheless, the group and particularly Ed were confident that the Himalayan Committee would lodge their claim for a British attempt for March– May, the spring season, of 1952.

It was not to be. Earlier in the year, the Swiss had requested that one of their climbers be invited on the Shipton reconnaissance but the English Himalayan Committee had turned them down. Instead the Swiss applied for, and received, permission to attempt Everest in both the spring and autumn of 1952.

Predictions that the icefall would be almost unacceptably dangerous and that expeditions would ignore the risk were proved right. There have been some 50 deaths in the icefall, culminating in the catastrophe of 16 porter deaths in April 2014 when an ice avalanche cut a swathe through a line of porters under the ice cliffs to the left of the icefall.

As it turned out, the British were lucky the Swiss got in ahead and made their experience available to those who succeeded them in 1953. The shambles that was the British Cho Oyu expedition of 1952 showed that the British were in no way prepared for a climb as demanding as the ascent of Everest, and had they tried that year the result would have been a humiliating failure. Possibly the French would have been first to the summit: an outcome that would have been as discomforting as when Norwegians were first to the South Pole.

CHAPTER 9

Everest from Tibet, 1921 and 1922

⟫⟩◆⟨⟪

T he ascent of Everest in 1953 raises the question why it took so long – 32 years since the first attempt in 1921. In 1852 the peak known to nearby Tibetans as Chomolungma was identified by Indian surveyors from a hundred miles away as the highest point on Earth. They gave it their own name, Mount Everest, after the British surveyor-general of India. It was on the border between Nepal and Tibet, but both countries forbade entry: it was not possible to learn more. Nevertheless, high mountains were being climbed, and in 1909 the Italian Duke of Abruzzi struggled breathlessly to reach 24,600ft in the Karakorum Range. Another 4,400ft higher would have seen him on top of Everest itself. Climbing into the thin air of its peak seemed, from a distance, to require just a track to its foot and some determination.

Set against this sanguine view were accounts of the sufferings of those who had actually climbed to such great heights – the breathlessness, the exhaustion, headaches, insomnia, the total debilitation. The stories from balloonists were not encouraging either. The few who had approached the altitude of Everest had been paralysed, rendered unconscious or died. Scientists had become fascinated by the mechanisms underlying the effects of altitude, and this culminated in the magisterial *La Pression Barométrique*, published by French physiologist Paul Bert in 1878. Having read about the symptoms of travellers crossing high passes in the Andes and balloonists ascending to great heights in France, he built a low-pressure chamber in which he could simulate altitudes up to 45,000ft, a level at which a human loses consciousness in seconds and will die not much later. His experiments proved conclusively that the problems associated with high altitude are not due to low air pressure as such but specifically to the low pressure (pO_2) of the single gas oxygen. He also proved that all symptoms and difficulties due to high altitude vanished when breathing pure 100 per cent oxygen in his low-pressure chamber set to the height of the summit of Everest.

The human body is optimised to function efficiently at sea level where the available pO_2 is 160mm.[1] On the summit of Everest, the atmospheric pressure is reduced by two-thirds giving a pO_2 of around 50–55mm, which will sustain consciousness in a very well-acclimatised subject but is incompatible with life for more than a short time. The record, held by a Sherpa, is 22 hours on the summit without oxygen. The situation is transformed, however, if the climber is breathing 100 per cent oxygen. At an ambient barometric pressure of 250mm on top of Everest, the available pO_2 to his or her lungs is 100 per cent of 250mm, more than at sea level. The climber is able to move easily, even when carrying a heavy oxygen apparatus.

So why was it that on the expeditions of the 1920s and 1930s, the climbers were not insisting on carrying large volumes of oxygen delivered through an efficient apparatus? For a start, they were hardly likely to have read *La Pression Barométrique* or any other physiological research. They were soldiers, surveyors, teachers and civil servants, trained through their public schools and Oxbridge in the classics and humanities. Science was a technical discipline carried out by people who were usually not part of their social scene. The Alpine Club had more than its share of literate romantics for whom science was an unknown mystery practised by serious people with the reputation of being poor company. In the 1920s and 1930s, and even as late as 1952, the occasional scientist on an expedition tended to be the butt of jokes. Scientists for their part might not be bothered to explain their evidence to unappreciative members of the Alpine Club. Paul Bert reserved his admiration for mountain guides, peasants who had learned their climbing as chamois hunters or crystal gatherers in the Alps and wore homemade metal crampons. He commented wryly that a guide

121

'furnished with a piece of bread and a few onions makes expeditions which require of the member of the *Alpine Club* who accompanies him the absorption of a pound of meat …'[2]

Besides, the Alpine Club had its code of ethics which, to begin with at least, forbade the use of such aids as crampons, though the ice-axe was always acceptable. An oxygen apparatus, with its heavy bottles of compressed gas, its pressure gauges, reduction valves and mask, was seen as abhorrent in a sport whose essence was its contact with nature at her most sublime.

Even to those who did not reject oxygen out of hand, use of oxygen was a great deal less simple than a scientific analysis in a French or English laboratory might suggest. Providing pure oxygen to a subject in a low-pressure chamber in a laboratory is easy; the same cannot be said about providing 12 hours of it to a climber above 26,000ft on Everest. It was difficult to demonstrate that oxygen apparatus helped on a high peak in the Himalayas because it had not been tried there. At an accessible altitude in the Alps of, say, 13,000ft, oxygen was close to useless – just a back-pack weighing 15 kilograms with a suffocating mask unpleasantly reminiscent of what one wore during a wartime gas attack. The ambient pO_2 in the Alps is not low enough for the advantages of the bottled variety to overcome the disadvantages of its weight and clumsiness. Move above 20,000ft, however, and the benefit of oxygen starts to be felt. Above 26,000ft, the oxygenless climber enters an environment so dangerous it is called the Death Zone.

What might have happened if oxygen had been offered to Dr Somervell and Colonel Norton on 4 June 1924 as they made their attempt on the summit of Everest? They had spent a sleepless, cold night in their high camp at 26,800ft. With difficulty they had found the energy to melt snow for a drink, but they lacked the appetite to eat anything solid. By a stroke of luck the weather was fine and windless. They climbed upwards with agonising slowness.

'Our pace was wretched,' Norton wrote. 'My ambition was to do twenty consecutive paces uphill without a pause to rest and pant on bent knee; yet I never remember achieving it – thirteen was nearer the mark.'[3] At 28,000ft Somervell could go no further. At lower altitudes he had been an oxygen sceptic but if he'd been offered a bottle here, at the end of his tether, he might have accepted. In less than a minute the desperation would have gone from his breathing and the torpor of extreme exhaustion would start to fade. He would see and think more clearly about his situation and surroundings. When he got up he could have moved without stopping. He would surely have become an oxygen convert.

To help Norton and Somervell even more, we would give them oxygen for their climb all the way from the North Col at 23,000ft to their top camp where, with new-found energy, they would spend hours melting snow for drinks and eat solid food before enjoying a good night's sleep breathing oxygen. When they set out next morning, on easy ground, they would be climbing at a rate of at least 600ft per hour. If the climbing had stayed easy – a big 'if' on the north side of Everest where there is the exceptionally difficult Second Step still ahead – and the weather had stayed fine, they would be on the summit within four hours. By evening they would be back to an ecstatic welcome on the North Col.

This is the template against which to compare the realities of the 1920s, 1930s and 1950s.

The story of Everest is also the story of oxygen.

The approach from Tibet, 1921

Until the beginning of the twentieth century, Tibet was closed to foreigners except for a few adventurers who darkened their faces with walnut juice, donned Tibetan dress, and crossed one of the Himalayan passes to the north of India – but this was not an option for a full-scale mountaineering expedition. Sir Francis Younghusband, in 1903–04, paved the way for British expeditions to Everest by establishing communications with Tibet – at the point of a Maxim machine-gun to begin with. In August 1904, a document was signed, agreeing on trade and the exclusion of foreign powers such as Russia and China. Another most useful exclusion was that of foreign mountaineering expeditions. The British now controlled approaches through both Tibet and India. For 30 years at least, Everest had become their mountain.

The First World War intervened, but after the armistice the Royal Geographical Society (RGS) and the Alpine Club formed a joint committee, the Everest Committee – later the Himalayan Committee – to launch expeditions: seven in all between 1921 and 1938. The expeditions in 1921, 1922 and 1924 came together as an extraordinary drama, a tragedy in three acts, with a cast of personalities who made

The 1921 British Everest party. Standing (L to R): Bullock, Morshead, Wheeler and Mallory; Seated: Heron, Wollaston, Howard-Bury and Raeburn.
WOLLASTON COLLECTION

the expedition members of the 1930s look pallid. The only person to take part in all three expeditions was George Leigh Mallory, the man who made Everest his own. He was supported by officers from the British Army in India, some of whom had been active in the Indian Himalayas for decades. They were all survivors of the Great War.

The 1921 expedition was an advance into terra incognita. Everest had been seen as a massive block of rock and ice on a distant horizon, but how to reach it and what it would look like from close up was unknown. A reconnaissance would be the first step, but there was always a chance, a slim hope, that there would be a linked route of ledges and broad snow slopes that would take them all the way to the top on their first encounter.

Lieutenant-Colonel Charles Howard-Bury was appointed leader of the 1921 expedition. At 39, he was a man of independent means thanks to his ownership of a large estate in Ireland. He trained for the army at Sandhurst, and was posted to India, which he used as a base for travelling into the Himalayas, Tibet and Russian Turkestan. After surviving a long war as an officer on the Western Front, the last eight months as a prisoner-of-war, he returned to Ireland but must have found country life too quiet: when the Everest expedition was announced in January 1921 he volunteered. The Everest Committee would have liked what they saw. He was strong, enterprising, battle-hardened, an able linguist, knowledgeable about Tibet and its neighbours, a hunter and a botanist. He was a good organiser and a good leader.

There was another 'leader', too: the influential Arthur Hinks, secretary of the RGS and of the Everest Committee. Born in 1873 and educated in Croydon, South London, he had an outstanding mathematical brain that took him to the Cambridge Observatory,

Arthur Hinks, the influential Secretary of the Royal Geographical Society.
ROYAL GEOGRAPHICAL SOCIETY

where he worked until 1913. He was also the RGS lecturer in cartography. He did not fit easily into Cambridge and when the position of full-time secretary to the RGS came up, he was pleased to be appointed there. Although not a mountaineer, he held firm opinions about who should go on Everest expeditions and how they should behave. His values were soon put to the test when J.P. Farrar of the Alpine Club recommended his two most favoured climbers, George Leigh Mallory and George Ingle Finch.

Mallory, the son of a vicar, had been educated at Winchester and Cambridge, where he took history without distinction. He enjoyed the intellectual stimulation of Cambridge, was on the fringe of the Bloomsbury group, took part in amateur theatricals, liked Picasso, Cézanne, van Gogh. Above all, he distinguished himself at climbing, a sport widely embraced in Cambridge and particularly in intellectual circles. Add to this his striking good looks and fine physique, photographed to advantage in Cambridge – and later bathing on the march in to Everest – and you recognise those star qualities that were to make him the prima donna of the Everest grand opera.

His younger sister recalled that as a child he 'had the knack of making things exciting and often rather dangerous. He climbed everything that it was at all possible to climb … He used to climb the downspouts of the house, and climb about on the roof with cat-like sure-footedness.'[4] On rock he moved with ease on the most difficult routes of the time, and attracted the admiration of Geoffrey Winthrop Young, doyen of the Alpine Club in the pre-war years. Mallory also wrote well, a valuable attribute in anyone who might achieve lasting fame. His diaries and letters to his wife Ruth are widely quoted in expedition literature and from time to time he expressed the hope that he might become a writer. Of climbing a peak he wrote: 'Have we vanquished an enemy? None but ourselves' – a sentiment adopted by various climbers since, including Ed Hillary.

Even more famous is his cryptic reply to a *New York Times* journalist in 1923. 'Why do you want climb Everest?' he was asked. 'Because it is there,' Mallory replied, expressing the compulsion mountaineers feel to climb a peak when they are confronted by it: because it is there.

On the downside Mallory was disorganised and forgetful, and was technically illiterate when it came to gear such as cameras and oxygen

George Finch in 1922, wearing his self-designed quilted jacket.
ROYAL GEOGRAPHICAL SOCIETY

apparatus, though a good minder could fill the gaps. Most importantly, however, he came to identify his destiny with that of Everest, and was willing to take ever greater risks to reach its summit.

The other Alpine Club climber recommended by Farrar was George Finch. By origin, temperament, upbringing and intellect, he was someone who asked questions of everything and sought his own answers. He was born in 1888 on an outback cattle station in Australia, and at the age of 14 was taken to Europe by his lively, theosophist mother who never returned to Australia. After rejecting a placement at an English public school, he was taught by a French tutor in Paris, then spent five years at university in Zurich studying physics and chemistry. Mountaineering in the Swiss Alps was at his back door.[5]

After training under a guide, George Finch and his brother Max began guideless climbing. This practice earned the strong disapproval of the Alpine Club of London whose members were for the most part gentlemen who left the sweaty business of hewing steps and grunting up steep rock to a guide, a trained peasant who provided the safety of a tight rope from above for his client coming up in leisurely fashion from below. Finch earned the undying enmity of some of this group by writing a dismissive article in *The Field* magazine about guided climbing. All you needed behind a guide, he said, was reasonable fitness, leisure and a secure income.

In 1912 Finch moved to London as a chemist and lecturer at the Imperial College of Science and Technology. He would be employed there for most of his working life, apart from during the First World War when he became an expert on explosives, and from 1921 to 1924 when he was involved with the Everest expeditions.

An invitation to join the 1921 expedition came partly because he and Mallory were recognised as the best Alpine climbers in England, and partly because his scientific and technical expertise was required for developing an oxygen apparatus and for improving primus stoves which were known to perform poorly at high altitude. This early interest in oxygen looks quixotically ahead of its time, given the antipathy to it that would soon develop. During the war, however, oxygen tanks and face masks had been developed for use by Royal Flying Corps pilots at higher altitudes over enemy territory. Finch visited Oxford to try out his stoves in the low-pressure chamber of a Dane, Professor Dreyer, who was the recognised expert in the use of oxygen when flying. Dreyer's experiments and measurements had shown that climbing at the oxygen pressure found on top of Everest was marginal to say the least. As a demonstration, Finch was placed in the chamber at a simulated altitude of 21,000ft, then given oxygen from a mask. The experience made Finch a life-long convert to the use of supplementary oxygen.

A mere two weeks before the expedition was to embark for India, Arthur Hinks and Alexander Wollaston, the expedition doctor, required its members to undergo a medical examination by two Harley Street specialists, one an orthopaedic surgeon, the other a paediatrician. To his astonishment, as well as that of his Alpine Club backer Farrar, Finch was declared unfit. The two reports, both brief, stated that Finch was sallow, in poor condition, anaemic, tired, losing weight, unfit and, if the test for sugar in his urine was correct, possibly diabetic. Dr Wollaston, whose interest in medical practice was fairly perfunctory, agreed that Finch could not possibly go on the expedition after two such damning reports.

When Finch went back to Oxford a few days later, he asked for an independent assessment. Professor Dreyer wrote that Captain Finch was slightly underweight but otherwise of excellent physique. He had an unusually large vital capacity, indicating a high degree of physical fitness. Tests in the low-pressure chamber proved that he possessed quite unusual resistance to high altitude. Of more than a thousand athletic young men Dreyer had examined, none had resisted high altitude so well.[6]

Dreyer and the Harley Street doctors seem not to have been examining the same man. Among explanations put forward for such discrepancies, the first, that Finch was recovering from treatment for recurrent malaria, is the least compelling, though this might have contributed to a 'sallow look'. The second, that the medical findings were rigged, is ungentlemanly, reflecting as it does on the integrity of the medical profession and the RGS. The third has a ring of truth and fits with the unconventional personality of George Finch.[7] It was a story of brief romance, pregnancy, marriage and divorce that must have been common during the war. Around the day of his medical examination for the 1921 expedition, Finch was unwinding an unsuitable marriage by providing evidence of adultery: he had reason to be tired and sallow. And Hinks, who never married, and the examining doctors must have felt that the end justified the means when they came to write their report. During the summer of 1921, Finch went on to complete a difficult climb on the south face of Mont Blanc. Farrar wrote acidly to Hinks, 'Our invalid Finch took part in the biggest climb in the Alps this season.'[8]

The other climber-scientist invited on the expedition, and this time accepted, was Arthur Kellas, a 53-year-old Scot with a DPhil from Heidelberg that secured him a lectureship in chemistry at the Middlesex Hospital Medical School. His enjoyment of hill-walking took him to the Sikkim Himalaya, where he organised six serious mountaineering expeditions between 1907 and 1914, with first ascents to a height of 23,180ft. Accompanied only by local porters, he recognised the special qualities of Sherpas, writing after his fourth expedition in 1912: 'Of the different types of coolie, the writer has found the Nepali Sherpas superior to all others. They are strong, good-natured if fairly treated, and since they are Buddhists there is no difficulty about special food for them – a point surely in their favour at high altitudes.'[9] He had become fond of his Sherpas and in the phrase 'if fairly treated' recognised their independent cast of mind. As a scientist he could hardly fail to become curious about the physiological problems that came with altitude, and by 1920 he was able to write a remarkably accurate prediction of the physiological situation of a man standing on top of Everest.

Having come from an expedition in Garhwal, Kellas should have been acclimatised and fit when he joined the 1921 Everest expedition, but he was unwell with persistent dysentery. He rode a pony, as did others, but became so weak with continuing diarrhoea that he was reduced to being carried on a litter. Nine days out from Darjeeling, he weakened further and died. Thus were lost to the expedition the two scientists – Finch and Kellas – who could have started an understanding of the physiological problems of high altitude.

By late June, with the recently arrived monsoon whitening the mountains in new snow, Howard-Bury and his reduced expedition had established a first base at Tingri, within 60 kilometres of Everest to its north. He spread his small band across the countryside, mapping and exploring the expanse of the wider Everest region stretching from the Nangpa La in the west to Kharta and the upper Arun Valley in the east. Centrally placed was Everest whose topography was completely unknown. The exciting task of examining its northern approaches was given to George Mallory and a companion from Winchester, Guy Bullock, who had been called in at short notice to replace Finch. The nominated climbing leader, Harold Raeburn, a tetchy 56-year-old Scot, had survived the medical examination in London but not the walk through Tibet. He retired sick at an early stage.

Discovering the North Col route on Everest
Tibetans advised Mallory that if he and his party wished to see Chomolungma, they should advance to the valley in which they would find the Rongbuk Monastery. On 25 June they had their first startling, close-up view. A bare valley flanked by mountains led to a vast mountain pyramid with the ribbon of the Rongbuk Glacier at its foot. The monastery, built only in the last 20 years, was a huddle of grubby, flat-roofed buildings with a large Buddhist stupa in their midst. There were said to be hundreds of lamas in the monastery or in caves and retreats in the surrounding hills. How could this grimly Spartan

Rongbuk Monastery with Everest and its North Face filling the head of the Rongbuk Valley. ROYAL GEOGRAPHICAL SOCIETY

community sustain itself? The answer was the deep spiritual charisma of its founder, the Dzatrul Rinpoche, who later would cross the Nangpa La to found a sister monastery at Tengboche in the Khumbu Valley.

In the often abysmal monsoon weather, Mallory and Bullock spent a month exploring the Main Rongbuk Glacier and its western tributary. They looked over the divide into Nepal to become the first climbers – perhaps even the first people – to see the Khumbu Icefall and, above it, the entrance to a deep trench which they called the Western Cwm. From the great cirque at the head of the Main Rongbuk they saw to their left a 23,000ft snow col which they called the North Col. The snow and ice face leading to it looked dangerous, but once on the col a relatively easy north ridge led to a north-east shoulder from which a well-angled ridge led to the summit. Here, in their first month of exploring, they had found a route which looked climbable.

An irritation for Mallory at this stage was a message from Tingri that the photographs he had been taking for the past month were all blank: he had probably been inserting the plates back to front. He vented his frustration by blaming the geologist who had instructed him and by writing to his wife Ruth a paragraph of positively Shakespearian invective at the expense of his unfortunate sardar – 'a whey-faced treacherous knave whose sly and cultivated villainy too often, before it was discovered, deprived our coolies of their food, and whose acquiescence in his own illimitable incompetence was only less disgusting than his infamous duplicity'.[10] One cannot say for sure that Mallory was being unreasonable, but there is a nagging suspicion that the military chaps were the ones who knew how to handle porters.

Three weeks later Mallory received another letter, this time from Oliver Wheeler, a Canadian surveyor attached to the expedition, who had been doggedly mapping from west to east, sitting out long patches of bad weather while he waited for brief clearances that would permit completion of his photo-survey. Entering the Main Rongbuk valley, he noted and then followed a stream coming in from the east through a narrow gap in the side wall. He was surprised to find that it emerged from a substantial body of ice, the East Rongbuk Glacier, which provided relatively easy access to the North Col. The missing piece of the route up Everest had been found and Wheeler had drawn a map of it. Mallory was annoyed with himself for missing the East Rongbuk and with Wheeler for finding it. Early in the expedition he had written to Ruth, 'Wheeler I have hardly spoken to, but you know my complex about Canadians. I shall have to swallow hard before I like him, I expect. God send me the saliva.'[11] Wheeler's map was just one more thing to be swallowed at an altitude where saliva was in short supply.

On 24 September, Mallory, Bullock and Wheeler, and three Sherpas, made Everest history by becoming the first men to set foot on the mountain. From the East Rongbuk they climbed to 23,000ft, and by 11 a.m. they were leaning into a torrent of wind and driven snow on the crest of the North Col with a gentle north-east ridge inviting them to go on. The wind was less welcoming and they were not equipped to climb higher. It was the end of the 1921 expedition. But what a success it had been, what a tough group they and their Sherpas had proved to be. Next year would surely see them to the top.

The 1922 expedition
The Everest Committee had permission from Tibet for an expedition

in 1922 but time was short. Howard-Bury might have thought his excellent leadership in 1921 had earned him the same role the following year, but instead they chose the colourful General Charles Bruce who, at the age of 56, would always, if things went wrong, have the excuse that he was too old. Educated at Harrow, Repton and then military college, he was the youngest of 14 children of the 1st Baron Aberdare whose fortune came from coal in Wales. In 1888 he joined the Indian Army with the 5th Gurkha Rifles and in 1915, as a Brigadier-General, he landed in Gallipoli where he was severely wounded.

In the Hillary archive is a memoir written by Percy Wyn-Harris (who was on Everest in 1933) that gives a flavour of the General:

> Here's a story about old General Bruce who led the 1922 expedition. In Calcutta I'd called to see him at his hotel. He was lying on his bed on a frightfully hot night looking like an overfed porpoise. He said 'Let me give you a piece of advice you'll find very useful. If ever you get into trouble with Sherpa porters there are two words that'll pull the porters up short. They are 'muji kas' and that means 'tighten your assholes.' Well, in 1933 at Camp 5 I found a big perched rock just waiting to be pushed off down the mountainside and I did. The porters were appalled and then I remembered that they believe that evil spirits live under rocks and I'd just let loose a whole cloud of them. Something special was called for from me. Then I remembered 'muji kas' and it did the trick. They tightened their assholes and they stopped being frightened![12]

In India Bruce joined some of the earliest Himalayan climbing expeditions, and in 1907 he made the first ascent of Trisul, 23,360ft, at that time the highest peak yet climbed. In his prime he was a man of great physical strength and a formidable wrestler. He was good-humoured, shrewd and a raconteur with a fund of bawdy stories. Through his personality and his fluency in Nepali he established a rapport with the porters and the herders of 300 yaks as they spent the month of April swaying across the windswept plains of Tibet. He sounds like the sort of Englishman on whom the British Empire was founded.

Mallory, of course, was again chosen by Hinks and his Everest Committee. He had arrived home in 1921 feeling tired, but the mountain had him in its grip. He had taken the lead in finding the route; he was Everest's spokesperson, its lead climber. Already, it seemed, the mountain was his destiny.

Then there was Finch, and this time even Hinks could find no reason to exclude him. Scientists were warning that deaths might occur above 25,000ft. Oxygen might help, but what would happen to a climber who ran out of oxygen close to the summit or whose apparatus malfunctioned? The expedition needed a technical person who understood the valves, tubes and gauges, and Finch was their man. Hinks was at his acidic best when writing to General Bruce prior to their departure:

> This afternoon we go to see a gas drill. They have contrived a most wonderful apparatus which will make you die of laughing. Pray, see that a picture of Finch in his patent climbing outfit with the gas apparatus is taken by the official photographer … I would gladly put a little money on Mallory to go to 25,000 feet without the assistance of four cylinders and a mask.[13]

Hinks's money would have been safe up to 25,000ft, a height not much more than that already reached by the Duke of Abruzzi, but on Everest there was still 4000ft of increasingly thin air before Mallory or Finch could reach the summit at 29,000ft. Even Finch must have been aware that his apparatus had its shortcomings. A standard rack of four oxygen cylinders – which they simply called 'gas' – on a carrying frame weighed a hefty 32 pounds (14.5kg). They contained in total 960 litres of oxygen which at a flow rate of 2 litres per minute gave eight hours of assisted climbing. Was this really enough, and could their Sherpas carry such a weight of oxygen high on the mountain?

By the end of April the expedition had its Base Camp in the Rongbuk Valley. Three weeks later Camp 4 was pitched on the North Col. Two parties would make summit attempts, the first led by Mallory without oxygen, the second by Finch with oxygen. Mallory was already fit and well acclimatised; Henry Morshead, who had been a surveyor in 1921, had also acclimatised well. Howard Somervell was new to the

Himalayas but had a strong background in the Alps. At age 25 he had joined the war effort as a surgeon, at first behind the lines, then in 1916 in a field hospital at the Somme. In the first 48 hours of the battle its surgical operating theatre was overwhelmed by 10,000 casualties, many of whom could only be left to die. Somervell emerged from the war as a pacifist, a Christian, and a surgeon who would devote his working life to medical work in South India. Of the fourth expedition member General Bruce wrote: 'Major E.F. Norton is an experienced and very reliable and thorough mountaineer. He is an officer in the Artillery, and well known in India for his skill and interest in pig-sticking.'

On 20 May, Mallory, Norton, Somervell and Morshead set off on the first serious attempt to climb Mt Everest. Stepping up on to the exposed crest of the col, they were immediately assailed by the great enemy, the west wind blowing at gale force. They had not yet understood how debilitating the wind was, penetrating windproofs that were adequate in the Alps but not at 23,000ft. During a stop, Norton's rucksack containing his spare warm clothes was flicked by the rope and disappeared down to the glacier 4000ft below. It was only after several hours of climbing that Morshead realised he ought to be wearing his outer windproof. They had not brought crampons so were slowed down by having to cut steps.

At a height of 25,000ft, higher than anyone had climbed before, they built two rock platforms for Camp 5 and retired for the night. Somervell described 'sleep in snatches of the most fitful and unresting variety'. Next morning they had gone only a hundred yards when Morshead announced that he was too weak to go on. They had no Sherpas carrying a higher camp; now there were just the three of them, taking the lead by turns, hoping they might climb the last 4000ft with enough daylight left for the return. When by 2.30 they had reached only 26,800ft, it was clear they had neither the time nor the strength to get even close to the summit before dark. Any future summit attempt would have to start from a camp at 27,000ft, not 25,000ft. 'We discussed whether we should go further ... we chose retreat with the minimum of regret ...'[14]

Down at Camp 5, a frostbitten, staggering Morshead was tied into their rope. They were crossing the head of a long, steep snow couloir when one climber slipped, dragging off the second, then a third until Mallory halted them with an ice-axe sunk into the snow. Morshead,

The first assault party, 1922: Morshead, Mallory, Somervell and Norton.
ROYAL GEOGRAPHICAL SOCIETY

Somervell thought, was not far from death. At the tents on the North Col there were no Sherpas, no climbers and no stove to melt snow. Slaking their thirst after 36 hours without fluid would have to await their descent to Camp 3 the following day. They could feel proud of the great height they had reached, but more than anything these two days had shown the magnitude of the difficulties high on this mountain.

Oxygen helps Finch on the second assault

The second assault on Everest would test Finch's belief in oxygen, though he'd be using an apparatus which had been assembled in England at short notice. On a first trial in Tibet, he had found the stiffness of the valves made the face masks suffocating, so had improvised a system using a rubber football bladder as a reservoir. Oxygen flowed from its cylinder into the bladder, whose outlet was a rubber tube held in the climber's mouth. The climber inhaled from a full bladder, then allowed it to refill with oxygen during exhalation by clamping the tube shut with his teeth. As a piece of technology it was crude, but it remained in use for the next 16 years.

Finch's party of three consisted of himself, Geoffrey Bruce (cousin of General Bruce) and the Gurkha Tejbir. Geoffrey Bruce had come as a transport officer, a role in which he excelled, but he had never done any climbing. The North Col was not the best place to start. Tejbir, a tough Nepali, was also a climbing novice and untrained in the use of oxygen.

Finch began using oxygen on the climb to the North Col and noted that it made climbing easier even below 23,000ft. On 25 May the three climbers with 12 porters left the North Col using oxygen and following the route made by Mallory. Arriving at Camp 5 they had time to move the tents 500ft higher. No problems so far, but Finch described a terrible night during which a storm came in from the west and 'rose to a veritable hurricane.'

> Terrific gusts tore at the tent …The wild flapping of the
> canvas made a noise like that of machine-gun fire … and we
> had to take it in turns to go outside and tighten guy-ropes
> … a great hole was cut in the windward panel of the tent
> by a stone, and the flaps of the tent were stripped of their
> fastenings.[15]

All next day and into the night they were tent-bound and increasingly cold until Finch had an idea:

> Like a heaven-spent inspiration came the idea of trying the
> effect of oxygen … almost at once I felt the painful, prickling,
> tingling sensation, due to the returning circulation of the
> blood, as the lost warmth slowly came back to my limbs. We
> connected up the apparatus so that all could breathe a small
> quantity throughout the night. There is no doubt that oxygen
> saved our lives; without it in our well-nigh exhausted and
> famished condition, we would have succumbed to the cold.[16]

The 27th was, in theory at least, their summit day. At 26,000ft Tejbir, carrying a load of oxygen cylinders, decided he'd reached his limit,

Oxygen apparatus used by Finch and Bruce in 1922 to reach a record altitude of 27,300ft. ROYAL GEOGRAPHICAL SOCIETY

and the wind was rising again. At a height of 27,300ft Bruce's oxygen developed a fault, and Finch knew they had no hope of getting near the summit. Leaving four oxygen cylinders on the rocks, they turned and descended into thickening mist. So easy was the ground that the 1800ft descent to Camp 5 took only half an hour. They woke Tejbir from a warm sleep and continued downwards. On the Col, hot tea and a tin of spaghetti gave them strength to descend to Camp 3 in less than an hour.

Finch could reflect that although oxygen had taken them higher than anyone had been before, they had not really been close to the summit. Their oxygen apparatus was crude, and the logistical problem of carrying a large number of oxygen cylinders high on the mountain was daunting. Climbing Everest had been harder than they'd thought it would be.

Down at Base Camp at the end of May, expedition members saw the first snowfall of the monsoon cover the mountain. They could with good reason abandon Everest, yet Mallory and Somervell had recovered from their ordeal of 10 days earlier. The line of camps was established and stocked with food, and four cylinders of oxygen awaited them at 27,300ft. It was worth one last try. When 6 June broke fine, Mallory and Somervell, with 14 porters, set off on a third attempt. They dug Camp 3 out of its new snow, which Somervell noted 'was of a thick consistency that we had not previously seen in the Himalayas'. Next day, with the weather still fine and mercifully free of wind, they set off on the climb to the North Col, 'ploughing through snow of a most unpleasant texture'.[17] They recognised the avalanche risk but judged it to be acceptable.

At 1.30 p.m. Somervell, who was breaking trail, described hearing 'a subdued report ominous in the softness of its violence', and a crack opened in the snow above him. Then the whole body of snow began sliding downwards, carrying 17 people with it. The avalanche slowed to a halt but not before nine porters had been carried over a 70ft ice cliff. One survived unscathed, another was dug out alive, but seven Sherpas were killed. It was a tragic end to an attempt on a brutal mountain of unpredictable difficulty.

Recollecting their experience when writing the book of the expedition in 1923, Bruce, Finch and Mallory all agreed that Everest was climbable, though they placed varying emphases on how oxygen should be used and when. One chance observation that would be largely forgotten over the next seven expeditions was that 'sleeping oxygen' restores appetite, gives sleep, and reverses the process of high-altitude deterioration. Even Finch failed to mention it when he summarised what was needed on Everest: 'The climbing equipment of the mountaineer in this zone should include, firstly, a supply of oxygen; secondly, warm and windproof clothing and footgear; thirdly plenty of food and drink.'[18] It sounded straightforward, but there were many problems involving technology, 'ethics' and leadership to be resolved before this simple recipe would be put into effect.

CHAPTER 10

Mallory and Irvine, 1924

⟹◈⟸

The Everest expedition of 1924 included Mallory but not Finch, who had easily been picked off by Hinks after he found that Finch was making money from lectures about the 1922 expedition. The lectures took place in Switzerland and were given in German, which made them no great threat to the commercial arm of the RGS, but permission had not been sought from Hinks. Finch gave his opinions freely on such matters as the selection of personnel and use of oxygen, but what made him especially intolerable, apart from being an Australian, was that he was usually right.

Bearing in mind Hinks's distaste for publicity, it was surprising that he included Captain J.B.L. Noel on the 1924 expedition. It was all about money. In 1921 King George V had donated £100 and the Viceroy of India all of 750 rupees, but Hinks was in need of £10,000. To his astonishment, Noel, who had been photographer in 1922, came up with the extraordinary offer of £8000 for the 1924 film rights. He was an unlikely pick for Hinks – he would have been at home in a late twentieth-century advertising agency – but £8000 was a very useful sum and would solve the expedition's funding problems at a stroke.

Noel's faith that he would profit from his investment reflected the confidence of the whole expedition. Sir Francis Younghusband, in his Introduction to *The Fight for Everest 1924*, wrote, 'The members of the expedition, marching across Tibet, took it as a certainty that they would reach the summit.' The better part of two years had been available for planning under the leadership of General Bruce, and in London it was

The 1924 party. Standing (L to R): Irvine, Mallory, Norton, Odell and MacDonald; Seated: Shebbeare, Bruce, Somervell and Beetham. JOHN NOEL

easy to look at a photograph of Everest on a fine day and be confident of success.

The first sign of misplaced confidence came in early April during their march through Tibet when the General succumbed to his recurring malaria and had to quit the expedition, leaving Norton as leader. Norton was a good replacement but Bruce was missed. He was liked and respected by the climbers, and above all had a rapport with the porters. Now Norton had to pick up the intricate details of a plan requiring that a thousand loads be carried up the East Rongbuk Glacier and built into a pyramid at whose apex would be a Union Jack on the summit of Mt Everest. On 14 April, Mallory wrote to his wife that Norton 'has appointed me second-in-command and also leader of the climbers altogether. I'm bound to say I feel some little satisfaction in the latter position.' Mallory drew up a plan in which Norton and Somervell, without oxygen, would be a first summit party, followed by himself and Irvine using 'gas', with which they were well supplied. He told his wife:

The gasless party has the better adventure and ... it is
naturally disappointing that I shall be with the other party.
Still, the conquest of the mountain is the great thing, and
the whole plan is mine and my part will be a sufficiently
interesting one and will give me, perhaps, the best chance of
all of getting to the top. It is almost unthinkable with this
plan that I shan't get to the top; I can't see myself coming
down defeated ... The telegram announcing our success, if we
succeed, will precede this letter, I suppose: but it will mention
no names. How you will hope I was one of the conquerors!
And I don't think you will be disappointed.[1]

On 30 April, the arrival of the expedition at a Base Camp was
celebrated with champagne and a five-course dinner. Summit day
was scheduled for 17 May, but snow fell in the afternoons, strong
winds blew, and the nights were thought to be unseasonably cold,
though no one really knew what was 'seasonable' in this bleak place.
Logistics were already disorganised when on 9 and 10 May the whole
expedition was shaken by a full blizzard. It was hard to distinguish
porters who were seriously ill with altitude sickness or hypothermia
from those who were simply demoralised. One led to the other,
anyway. Man Bahadur the cobbler, his feet frozen to the ankles,
would have ended up with bilateral amputations if he had not died.
Samsherpan became comatose and later died of a stroke. Tamding fell
and broke his leg below the knee.

On 12 May Norton ordered a retreat to Base Camp, followed by a
pilgrimage to Rongbuk Monastery for a blessing from the Head Lama
who now filled the role of chaplain to the expedition's bedraggled
front-line troops. Fine weather, of a sort, returned intermittently, but as
late as 27 May Mallory was writing: 'It has been a bad time altogether.
I look back on tremendous effort and exhaustion and dismal looking
out of a tent door into a world of snow and vanishing hopes ... The
physique of the whole party has gone down sadly. The only chance now
is to go for a simpler, quicker plan.'[2]

They agreed on three assaults mounted sequentially from a Camp
6 placed at 27,000ft. The first team was Mallory and Geoffrey Bruce;
the second Norton and Somervell; the third the two newcomers, Noel
Odell and Andy Irvine. They had oxygen at Camp 3, but with only 15

of 52 porters still fit, there did not seem to be the capacity to carry it to higher camps for use in the assaults.

On 1 June in fine weather Mallory and Bruce, considered the strongest climbers at this stage, climbed the familiar snow and broken rock of the route to Camp 5 at 25,300ft. The plan was to establish Camp 6 at 27,000ft the next day, but in continued fine weather that morning the watchers were surprised to see the party returning. Their three porters had refused to continue, they said, leaving them no choice but to come down. What had happened to Geoffrey Bruce's fluency in Nepali and his powers of persuasion? Mallory gave another explanation: 'I do not think it is possible without oxygen.'

Meanwhile Norton and Somervell, still in the window of fine weather, had climbed easily to Camp 5, and a day later, at 26,800ft, had pitched the single tent that was Camp 6. The fourth of June was their summit day, fine and nearly windless. The climbing was still easy and after 500ft they had passed the high point reached by Finch and Bruce two years earlier. Everything was going to plan, except that they were going ever more slowly as they hit a wall of exhaustion.

At midday Somervell was too exhausted to continue. Norton continued angling slowly upwards into what would become known as the Norton Couloir. Here the climbing problems multiplied: the angle was steeper, the footholds smaller and more sloping, the snow patches powdery and uncompacted. By 1 p.m., at a height of 28,100ft, he knew that he lacked the resources to climb out of this cul-de-sac. The easier route on Everest did not lie up the Great Couloir. Was he also up against a physiological ceiling? No one knew. The descent was a nightmare. Norton was becoming snow blind and seeing double. Somervell dropped his ice-axe which bounced 8000ft down the North Face. At 9.30 p.m. they staggered into Camp 4. It was an extraordinary achievement to have climbed so high, yet it asked more questions than it answered. If there was a climbable route, where was it? Would oxygen have helped? Was it, in fact, essential?

The third assault was to have been by Noel Odell and Sandy Irvine, but by 6 June when the third and last attempt set out it consisted of Mallory and Irvine, names that were to become indissolubly linked. Odell was a geologist, educated at Brighton and the Royal School of Mines, and a member of the Alpine Club. He first met Irvine during a Merton College expedition to the Arctic island of Spitzbergen. He

Mallory and Irvine set off from the North Col on their last climb. JOHN NOEL

was so impressed with the 21-year-old engineering undergraduate (and rower for Oxford) that he suggested to the Himalayan Committee that Irvine should be a member of the 1924 expedition. The Committee agreed. Irvine was a fine athlete, was of sound family background, could turn his hand to fixing technical problems with the oxygen apparatus, and was of attractive appearance and personality. Having travelled together by boat to India, Mallory wrote that Irvine was 'one to depend on for everything perhaps except conversation', which was not required on the last thousand feet of Everest anyway.[3] He might have added that Irvine had not actually done any mountaineering – but did it matter with Mallory in the lead?

Mallory had by now put together a strong plan. He and Irvine would be using oxygen all the way from Camp 3 at 21,000ft through to the summit four days later. Unlike the first and second assaults which had lacked the Sherpa numbers to carry oxygen, this time Camps 4, 5 and 6 would all be in place, and stocked with food, fuel and oxygen. Mallory had spoken dismissively of oxygen in the past but by June 1924 he was a convert, and he knew that Irvine could mend its pipes and valves.

Mallory had correctly identified the best route from below and its main problems. From Camp 6 at 27,000ft they would not cross into the Norton Couloir but rather would climb to the crest of the north ridge which they would follow to the First Step. This, he believed, could be bypassed on its right, taking them to the foot of the Second Step. This piece of rock looked altogether more difficult, an almost vertical, 100ft buttress with no obvious way of sidling around it – but it might be easier than it looked from a distance. Above the Second Step there was a small, benign-looking Third Step but no other apparent obstacles before the summit. The weather was fine and apart from intermittent cloud would remain so throughout their summit day.

The two men never returned to tell their story, but a part of what happened on 8 June has been pieced together from evidence accumulated over the years. As they settled into Camp 6, Mallory wrote two notes to be delivered by his returning Sherpas to those down at Camp 4. The first read:

> Dear Odell, We're awfully sorry to have left things in such a mess – our Unna cooker rolled down the slope at the last moment ... To here on 90 atmospheres for the two days – so we'll probably go on two cylinders – but it's a bloody load for climbing. Perfect weather for the job.
> Yours ever, G. Mallory

And to Captain Noel, the photographer watching from the North Col with his cine camera and telephoto lens, he gave some advice about when and where to catch their movements on film:

> Dear Noel, We'll probably start early tomorrow in order to have clear weather. It won't be too early to start looking out for us either crossing the rock band under the pyramid or going up skyline at 8.0 pm. [*sic*: he means a.m.]
> Yours ever, G. Mallory

Their oxygen sets carried two bottles each. At the set flow rate of 2.2 L/min (litres per minute), these would have lasted seven hours, which at a theoretical climbing rate of 300ft/hr would have got them to the summit, assuming they were not slowed by climbing difficulties of any sort.

One of their four discarded oxygen bottles was found at 27,800ft near the foot of the First Step, though with no indication whether the

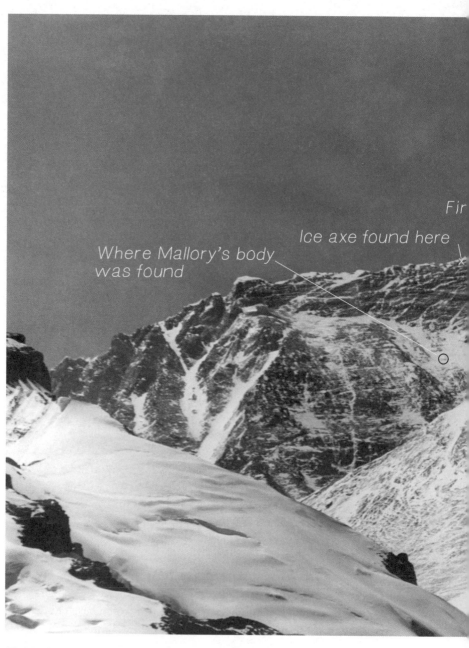

Fir

Ice axe found here

Where Mallory's body
was found

*The North Face of Everest in 1933 showing the First and Second Steps and where the
Mallory/Irvine ice axe was found. The circle marks the site where Mallory's body was
found in 1999 by the Mallory and Irvine Expedition at 26,760 feet. The expeditions
of 1924 and 1933 traversed into the Great Couloir at a height of 28,130 feet before*

he Great Couloir

Second Step

being brought to a halt by exhaustion and difficult rock. On his oxygenless solo ascent in 1980 Reinhold Messner also traversed into the couloir before continuing to the summit. ROYAL GEOGRAPHICAL SOCIETY

men were on their way up or down. In 1933, one of their ice-axes was found 200 metres from the foot of the First Step. It is hard to see why either climber would deliberately abandon an ice-axe and Wyn-Harris, who found it, believed the most likely explanation was that one of them had slipped and fallen here.

Dramatic proof that they had fallen came in 1999 when the Mallory and Irvine Research Expedition found Mallory's body on the mountainside some 300 metres lower than the axe. The first clue had come from a report in 1979 that a Chinese climber called Wang had told a companion four years earlier that, while at the 1975 Chinese Camp 6, he had stumbled on the antique body of 'English dead'. Adding to the mystery was that Wang was swept to his death in an avalanche the next day. In 1999, the Mallory and Irvine Research Expedition located the site of this Camp 6. They found themselves on a terrace which was 'a virtual graveyard of mangled, frozen bodies … a kind of collection zone for fallen climbers'.[4] Those first examined wore modern clothes and equipment. But lower down, where the edge of the terrace dropped away, they saw 'a patch of white that was whiter than the rock around it and whiter than the snow'.[5] It was another body, but completely different from the others. This one was wearing the clothes of 1924: woollen cloth, hob-nailed boots, fur-lined leather helmet. A manila rope around his waist was frayed, showing it had snapped during a fall. The legs, one of them broken, revealed bare bone, as did the face, but the back, its skin bleached white, was miraculously preserved as if made of marble. The arms were extended, fingers clawing into the slope as if to arrest a fall. There was a hole punched in the skull. Labels on the clothes read G. Mallory. The evidence showed that he had been on his way down the mountain and not using oxygen when he fell.

So it was known now that they had fallen rather than died of cold and lack of oxygen. No one could know who had slipped first, but the inexperienced Irvine would have been more likely to choose a wrong foothold than highly experienced Mallory. You can almost see, and hear, them. Two exhausted men stumbling down, roped together, their oxygen at an end. Irvine misjudges a downward-sloping ledge and, in an instant, his feet have shot from under him and he is gathering speed down slabs greased with snow. Mallory braces himself but his footholds on rock cannot withstand the jerk that drags him off. Now they are

Mallory (left) and Irvine. ROYAL GEOGRAPHICAL SOCIETY

---

both falling with sickening speed. The rope snags on a rock and snaps. Mallory comes to rest in the graveyard below; Irvine falls all the way down the North Face.

But had they reached the summit of Everest before their tragic end? The last and most enigmatic piece of evidence comes from Odell, and that was a sighting at 12.50 p.m. on the summit day of two dots he was sure were the figures of Mallory and Irvine.

Odell was the one-man support team who over three days, from 8–10 June, climbed twice, without oxygen and with apparent ease, the 4000ft between Camps 4 and 6.[6] He was on his own except at Camp 4, and wrote of his experiences almost mystically. At Camp 5 he described the sunset:

> The fact that I was quite alone certainly enhanced the impressiveness of the scene. To the westward was a savagely wild jumble of peaks … the brilliant opalescence of the far northern horizon of Central Tibet, above which the sharp-cut crests of distant peaks thrust their purple fangs … an ineffable transcendent experience that can never fade from memory.[7]

Of his last sighting of Mallory and Irvine, Odell wrote in his diary that night: 'At 12.50 saw M&I on ridge nearing base of final pyramid.[8] A few days later, he wrote a more detailed account for a press dispatch:

> There was a sudden clearing of the atmosphere above me and
> the entire summit ridge and final peak of Everest were unveiled.
> My eyes became fixed on one tiny black spot silhouetted on a
> small snow-crest beneath a rock-step in the ridge; the black spot
> moved. Another black spot became apparent and moved up the
> snow to join the other on the crest. The first then approached
> the great rock step and shortly emerged at the top; the second
> did likewise. Then the whole fascinating vision vanished,
> enveloped in a cloud once more. There was but one explanation.
> It was Mallory and his companion moving, as I could see even
> at that great distance, with considerable alacrity ...[9]

At this stage, Odell did not specify which rock step he was looking at, whether the easy First Step, the difficult Second Step, or the easy Third Step closer to the summit. In 1933, Smythe and Shipton, climbing towards Camp 6, deepened the uncertainty by suggesting that Odell had been looking at rocks, not men:

> Shipton suddenly stopped and pointed. 'There go Wyn and
> Waggers on the second step,' he exclaimed. Sure enough,
> there were two little dots on a steep snow-slope at the foot of
> the cliff. We stared hard at them and could have sworn they
> moved. Then simultaneously, we realized that they were rocks.
> And, strangely enough, there are two more rocks perched
> on a snow-slope immediately above the step; these again
> looked like men and appeared to move when stared at ... Is
> it possible that Odell was similarly tricked by his eyes? His
> view was between shifting mists and lasted only a minute or
> two. The effects of altitude, tiredness, and the strain of the
> climbing combine to impair the efficiency of vision ...[10]

Eventually Odell made a decision that indeed he had been looking at the Second Step, though the speed with which his two climbers had surmounted it suggested they were on the easier Third Step with the summit quite close. Did Mallory have the technical skill to climb the

The crucial pitch on the Second Step photographed in 1999. The low angle of view makes the rock look deceptively easier than it is. The five-metre ladder was fixed in place by the 1975 Chinese expedition and has been in use ever since. Conrad Anker's free climb of the step used the broad crack to the left of the ladder. DAVE HAHN, 1999
MALLORY AND IRVINE EXPEDITION

Second Step? In 1999 a top American climber, Conrad Anker, free-climbed it as if he were Mallory in 1924. The obvious line was an off-width crack, wide enough to take arms and legs. Anker was soon up and on to easier rock above. He rated it as Yosemite grade 5.8, which is defined as 'within the range of the average weekend climber'.[11] The average weekender in Yosemite climbs to a high standard using modern equipment; nevertheless, it seems likely that if the top pitch of the Second Step were in the thick air of North Wales, Mallory could have climbed it.

Whether he could have climbed it at 28,300ft on Everest, no one can say. They had oxygen but of a primitive sort. To reach the summit it would need to have been a day of miracles, but miracles do happen. Although it was the Chinese in 1960 who first documented the ascent of this route, in climbing legend this stretch of mountain will always belong to Mallory and Irvine.

CHAPTER 11

The 1930s, a decade of disillusion

O ne of the unintended consequences of the 1924 expedition
was that thanks to the entrepreneurial activities of Captain
Noel, all access through Tibet was forbidden for the next nine
years. He was undoubtedly right in seeing the dramatic potential of
filming the first triumphant ascent of Everest, but as the events of 1924
unfolded it was clear he was wrong in his belief that he could film it.
He had abundant footage of the expedition riding its ponies across
the plains of Tibet and setting up wintry camps on the East Rongbuk
Glacier but the mountain footage, which was to have been full of
action, merely showed panting climbers chipping steps slowly with
frequent rests. More and more the film's focus fell on the Tibetans and
their monasteries.

On the retreat from the mountain Noel had the idea that he could
add life to his showing of the film in a London theatre by having a
troupe of Tibetan lamas on stage. They could have trumpets made from
human thigh bones in one hand and drums made from human skulls in
the other. It was an opportunity, too, for the lamas to see how the other
half lived. In the event the Lhasa theocracy took exception to their lamas
being made objects of amusement; nor did they like the film of Tibetans
picking lice from a partner's scalp and eating them. Encouraged by the
political officer in Sikkim, Major Bailey, who disliked expeditions, the
Tibetan authorities cancelled forthwith all permissions for Everest. It
became known as 'the affair of the dancing lamas'.

Noel was unfazed and in 1927 published his own account of the expedition. His observations on oxygen were correct: 'Very powerful and able climbers might climb Everest without oxygen, but it would be safer ... to take oxygen in approved machinery which would be better than Expeditions previously have had.'[1] He even anticipated the commercial expeditions of the twenty-first century: 'Oxygen will render the climb possible to any fit human being; and probably some day in the future the journey to the top of Everest will become an adventurous excursion possible to the ordinary tourist.'[2]

It is tempting to speculate how the Everest story might have unfolded if Noel had been left behind in 1924 and Finch taken instead of Irvine. Without Noel, there would have been no dancing lamas and no withdrawal of permission. Finch was equal in ability to Mallory and would have been the natural choice to climb with him. With Mallory converted to oxygen, Finch would have been with him keeping the temperamental apparatus working as they attempted the Second Step. They might have been defeated in 1924 but they could have returned on another expedition with improved apparatus and a better understanding of how to use it. They would have relearnt that sleeping oxygen is essential. In 1926, or 1928, or 1930, using optimal flow rates of oxygen and fixed ropes, they would have climbed the crucial pitches, and finally someone would have reached the summit.

The four expeditions of the 1930s

By 1933, the Tibetan authorities had relented and gave permission for four expeditions. Those of 1933 and 1936, both led by Hugh Ruttledge, were large and expensive. Those of 1935 and 1938, the first led by Eric Shipton, the second by H.W. Tilman, were small. All four were failures. On the mountain they found too much wind, too much snow, too little oxygen, and rock that was more difficult than they had expected. In 1933 two assault teams reached roughly the same high point of 28,100ft as had Norton in 1924, and like him realised they had no chance of reaching the summit before dark, even if they found the strength to continue. The 1933 second team of Frank Smythe and Eric Shipton was thought to be the strongest but on the day of their summit attempt Shipton was struggling:

> It must have been about 7.30 when we started. It was a fine morning, though bitterly cold. I had a stomach ache and felt

as weak as a kitten … After about two hours I began to feel
sick and it appeared to me that I was approaching the end of
my tether … So I decided to stop and let Smythe go on alone
… after waiting a little longer I started back to Camp 6.[3]

Smythe entered the Great Couloir but found the way upwards blocked
'by a series of fearsome black overhangs … Time alone rendered the
summit inaccessible.' His solo retreat down the mountain was made
memorable by his conviction that he was being accompanied by a
person who was not Shipton, and by the sight of two curious-looking
objects in the sky, like kite balloons which seemed to pulsate and have
wings and a beak. The ethereal heights above 27,000ft were a place for
visions as well as terminal exhaustion.

Reflecting on how one might climb that last thousand feet, Smythe
conceded that he would use a large quantity of oxygen to overcome the
difficult section in the couloir:

> Prior to 1933 there were those to whom the thought of
> oxygen was abhorrent. I confess to a similar prejudice. There
> seemed something almost unfair in climbing what was then
> thought to be an easy mountain by such artificial means. I
> doubt whether there is a member of the present expedition
> who now thinks thus, for Everest has been proved to rely for
> its defence not only on bad weather and altitude, but on its
> difficulties too … its weapons are terrible … as exacting on the
> mind as on the body. Those who tread its last 1000 feet tread
> the physical limits of the world.[4]

It was an insight that came too late, for not a litre of the considerable
weight of oxygen the expedition had carried to the foot of the mountain
had been used, except in an unsuccessful attempt to treat frostbite. The
mountain was not entirely devoid of oxygen, however, and Raymond
Greene, expedition doctor and brother of novelist Graham, described
finding some old cylinders left behind by Finch at Camp 5 in 1922. One
was in perfect order. Greene sat down, opened its valve and breathed in
the oxygen that came hissing out: 'The result was remarkable: everything
around seemed to brighten; a lost sense of colour returned; for the
moment I felt stronger, and was able to resume the climb.'[5]

The 1935 party. Standing (L to R): Bryant, Wigram, Warren and Spender; Sitting: Tilman, Shipton and Kempson. DAN BRYANT

Drawing on his experience in 1933, Shipton argued that a small, cheap expedition had as good a chance of reaching the top as one that was large and expensive. Why not, he reasoned, reduce equipment and supplies to the bare minimum and live off the land as much as possible. Eggs were in relative abundance, mutton from the scrawny local sheep was tasty, the roasted barley meal called tsampa that formed the staple Tibetan diet was edible, to Shipton at least, when made into a paste with sugared tea.

Permission was granted, and in June 1935 Shipton's minimal expedition was exploring the Nyonno Range just east of Everest. Ironically, the monsoon arrived as late as 26 June. As they crossed unknown passes and climbed virgin 21,000ft peaks, they could look west to the snowless black rock of the route on Everest bathed in sun. As a year to climb the route from the north, 1935 was exceptional.

In July they moved to the East Rongbuk Glacier to make a token climb on Everest. At 21,000ft they found and buried the body of Maurice Wilson, a free spirit with an ambition to cure the ills of the human condition through fasting and faith. An ascent of Everest would provide the fame that would secure recognition and acceptance of his beliefs. His body was found half buried in snow just higher than Camp 3.

When the Shipton climbers occupied a camp on the North Col, the slopes were thickly covered in new snow, confirming that the monsoon is not the best time of year for climbing Everest. In confirmation, a vast area of new snow to a depth of two metres avalanched off the slopes of the North Col during the interval between their arrival and their departure four days later.

Ruttledge was back in 1936 leading the best-resourced of all the expeditions so far. The wireless equipment alone comprised 58 porter loads and there was newly developed oxygen apparatus of both the closed- and open-circuit varieties with variable oxygen flow rates up to a generous 6 L/min. They might have had the best equipment ever, but they were also plagued by the worst weather of any expedition to date and the highest point reached was a lowly 23,000ft on the North Col.

At the end of it all Shipton, a member of all four expeditions of the 1930s, could survey the great weight of equipment and supplies that littered the lower camps and reflect how much more easily his style of expedition could have achieved the same lack of results at a fraction of the cost. And medical officer Charles Warren noted that though the oxygen apparatus was tried once or twice, they would get no further with the oxygen problem until the climbers actually used it.

With the reputations of the Alpine Club and Royal Geographic Society suffering after repeated failures, the Mount Everest Committee appointed as leader H.W. Tilman who in 1936, with Noel Odell and Peter Lloyd, had made the first ascent of Nanda Devi, 25,646ft. Perhaps Tilman was a leader who would get his men to the top. When the expedition left Kalimpong, their four tons of baggage was carried on the backs of 55 mules, a tenth of the whole being oxygen equipment which again was under the care of Dr Charles Warren and chemist-engineer, Peter Lloyd, who broke new ground by using oxygen for three consecutive days while making a summit attempt. Tilman, without oxygen, accompanied him and conceded that Lloyd 'went better than he did'.

Despite this reluctant endorsement, Tilman still felt that the disadvantages of oxygen outweighed its advantages. His final statement was that 'the mountain could and should be climbed without oxygen ...'[6] And Shipton noted that purists agreed 'their task was to climb the mountain by their own unaided efforts, and that to use an artificial means of breathing in the rarefied atmosphere at high altitudes would be to overcome by unfair means Everest's principal weapon of defence'.[7]

Thus came to an end two decades of endeavour on the north side of Everest. The Mount Everest Committee could reflect that they were no closer to climbing Everest than they had been in 1924. The consensus seemed to be that a lightweight expedition, without oxygen, should be mounted each year, expecting to fail because of fresh snow, yet anticipating the *annus mirabilis* when they would find the conjunction of fine weather, no wind, and rocks dry and clean all the way to the summit.

In pursuit of this, the Everest Committee, on 14 June 1939, voted to apply for Everest expeditions in 1940, 1941 and 1942. But three months later Germany invaded Poland, and Britain found herself committed yet again to a terrible war which would consume all her resources of personnel and money for most of a decade.

Everest would have to wait.

Postscript: The Second Step

After the Second World War, the Chinese allowed only their own expeditions – strengthened by altitude-tolerant Tibetans – to attempt Everest from the north. On 24 May 1960 a summit team had reached the foot of the Second Step. Four times the lead climber fell off while making his attempt. A second climber in bare feet took his place. When this failed they formed a human pyramid, one climber standing on the shoulders of others to finally reach a line of holds at the top of the pitch. They summited in darkness, so had no photographs. The details aroused scepticism among Western climbers – the bare feet, the arrival on the summit in darkness – but eventually photos taken on the descent next day in daylight convinced sceptics that they had been taken from above the Second Step. No one could doubt the authenticity of the second Chinese ascent in 1975 by climbers who left a metal tripod on the summit. They eased the climbing of the Second Step by bolting in place a five-metre aluminium ladder which is still in use.[8]

CHAPTER 12

Lessons on Cho Oyu, 1952

———⟫·◆·⟪———

The British were in a subdued frame of mind as the news sank
in that the Swiss had ownership of Everest for the whole of
1952. True, they had permission for 1953 but if they failed it
was the French (merde!) who would take over. For the British, 1953
would be the last throw of the dice. As for oxygen, its ethical and moral
dilemmas ceased to exist. The Swiss were known to be developing their
own oxygen apparatus; the French would do the same for 1954. This
was war, and the enemy was using gas.

In the pre-monsoon season of 1952, the British had to console
themselves with a side-show on Cho Oyu, 26,906ft, where they could
combine an attempt on a mountain with preparations for 1953 if the
Swiss should fail. The Himalayan Committee had to look no further
than Eric Shipton for a leader, and when he chose his team he began
with those he knew from the 1951 reconnaissance: Ed Hillary, Tom
Bourdillon and Earle Riddiford. Missing from the list of first choices was
Mike Ward who declined Shipton's invitation because he was completing
his national military service and had an examination to work for as a
qualification in Surgery. These could probably have been deferred, and
in retrospect he might have seen that missing out on Cho Oyu was a
mistake. He could have helped with the oxygen trials and would have
carried over into 1953 the residual acclimatisation that is attained by
spending time at altitude. Although he was selected for Everest the
following year, he never acclimatised well enough to be a candidate for
the summit party – a position he coveted and indeed deserved.

Cho Oyu party, 1952. Standing (L to R): Colledge, Hillary, Shipton, Pugh, Riddiford and Lowe; Seated: Secord, Gregory, Evans and Bourdillon. RIDDIFORD COLLECTION

There were three newcomers on Cho Oyu who would play important roles on Everest. The first was Charles Evans, a surgeon who would become Deputy Leader in 1953 and would in 1955 lead a British expedition making the first ascent of the world's third-highest peak, Kangchenjunga. Then there was Alf Gregory, a photographer and travel agent from Blackpool who turned out to be a good acclimatiser, and George Lowe who came with a strong recommendation from his good mate Ed Hillary. Of the three remaining members, two – Campbell Secord and Ray Colledge – were climbers who did not go to Everest the following year. The third member, physiologist Griffith Pugh, came as an appointee of the Medical Research Council (MRC), where he worked in the Division of Human Physiology which studied the problems of personnel in extreme conditions such as cold or during physically demanding field operations. High-altitude climbing fitted comfortably under this umbrella.

Griff Pugh was born in Shrewsbury in 1909, the only son of a Welsh barrister in Calcutta who had a lucrative practice and a socially ambitious wife. They would return to England each summer, but when war was declared in 1914 they left Griffith, age four, and his sister Ruth, age three, in Wales, under the care of a nanny in a large country house rented for the duration of the war. For five years Griff lived in the unfettered outdoors of a country estate, with no school, no parent and no other company, apart from his biddable younger sister and Nanny Saunders who was a loving family servant.

At age nine he was packed off to boarding school. Of his formative teenage years at Harrow he said, 'The great thing about going to an English public school is that you know that nothing as bad as that can ever happen to you again … It took me forty years to recover from my public school.'[1] He went on to Oxford where, following in the footsteps of the Calcutta Pughs, he studied law. Long vacations were spent enjoying the pleasures open to the sons of well-off parents; in Switzerland he took cross-country skiing to a level where he was selected for the British Olympic team. A 'third' in law underlined that this was a subject without much interest for him, and he spent a further five years doing medicine. It was 1938 when he qualified; war was in the air, and when it broke out he quickly married a beautiful and wealthy young woman, Josephine Cassel. He had a varied wartime career, including training soldiers in mountain warfare in Lebanon, and studying their responses and needs, a job that suited his inquiring mind and ability to work in difficult conditions. On demobilisation he worked as a medical registrar at Hammersmith Hospital before moving to the MRC. Mike Ward had contacted him there to discuss the physiological problems of high altitude. He looked just right for field research in the Himalayas.

The expedition arrives

The Himalayan Committee, now uncomfortably aware that public expectation was building, decided to define objectives for the Cho Oyu expedition within the overarching goal of preparation for a British Everest expedition in 1953:

1. To develop a group of climbers who had proven ability to acclimatise and climb at altitudes above 24,000ft.

2. To attempt the first ascent of Cho Oyu.
3. To test clothing and other equipment.
4. To test the oxygen equipment that was in the process of being developed by Peter Lloyd and a group of technical experts in England.
5. To carry out a programme of physiological research that would lead to the informed use of oxygen at high altitude.

For all five objectives Cho Oyu seemed to be a good choice. It was on the border between Tibet and Nepal, but in 1951 Shipton and Ward had identified a route on a buttress on its south face that was comfortably in Nepal and close to the Sherpa villages of Khumbu. As the sixth-highest mountain in the world, it gave a good stretch of altitude for testing men and oxygen. On the glacier at its foot there would be a good site for a base camp where Pugh could set up his laboratory and send climbers as high as they could go while testing new oxygen apparatus.

There was less clarity about who would provide the leadership that would combine oxygen research with putting a route up a very big mountain. Though Shipton was the leader, he had often placed on record his opposition to oxygen, science and applying siege tactics to big mountains. Perhaps he thought it was Pugh's job to persuade climbers to collaborate in his research, but motivating a group of individualistic mountaineers was not one of Griff's skills.

The three New Zealanders in the party had their own objectives. Ed Hillary was determined to cement his place in the 1953 team by climbing Cho Oyu and as many of the nearby minor peaks as there was time for. George Lowe was the second on Ed's rope, not quite as strong but determined to prove his superiority over the third Kiwi, Earle Riddiford, who had kept him out of the Everest reconnaissance the previous year. Riddiford felt he had earned his place on Cho Oyu not only as a climber on Mukut Parbat and in the Khumbu Icefall but also through his work for the present expedition in London. His friend Norman Hardie, also in London, described preparations at the Royal Geographical Society:

> Earle was horrified to find that virtually nothing had been done. So he unofficially took on the duties of ordering and

161

shipping the considerable amounts of food and equipment for Cho Oyu that had to be forwarded to Nepal. Shipton was hard to pin down and reluctant to make decisions ... Oxygen supplies and physiological requirements were in hand, however, organized directly by Bourdillon and Pugh, and Peter Lloyd of the 1938 Everest expedition also did much work on the oxygen ... Each day Earle kept me informed on the frustrations he was encountering ... Though Shipton had been brilliant in the 1930s ... he did not enjoy the large expeditions ... Organizing such an event from a city office was distasteful to him. Earle did well in getting the party onto its ship.[2]

The expedition reached Namche on 16 April 1952, a day after the Swiss expedition had passed through on its way to Everest. By the end of the first week, Bourdillon and Riddiford had tried, unsuccessfully, to climb Khumbila, 19,000ft, unaware that this closest and most sacred of all the Khumbu peaks was the home of gods of such importance that local Sherpas thought no human should go near its summit. Shipton and Hillary, shotgun in hand, had chased thar up and among the grass-covered bluffs alongside the trail, and sardar Ang Tharkey had shot a couple of pheasants which made good eating. There is no way of knowing whether these activities made the gods restive, but certain it is that when they arrived in full view of their proposed route on the south face of Cho Oyu, the party knew immediately that the mountain was impossible for them from Nepal. Aesthetically the big buttress was superb, but it had no obvious camp sites and was relentlessly steep, particularly the bluffs at the bottom.

Thus, within a week their expedition was in disarray, their mountain without a route except perhaps from Tibet. From Namche a well-used trade route ran north to cross the Nepal border over the 19,000ft snow-covered Nangpa La Pass. The previous year Tom Bourdillon had seen a possible snow route just to the east of Nangpa La on the north side of Cho Oyu. There was a problem from the north, however: Communist China now controlled Tibet and had a military garrison at Tingri, the first occupied village after crossing the Nangpa La. A more isolated mountain might have been attempted without attracting the attention of the Chinese, but with Tibetans and Sherpas crossing the Nangpa La it would soon be known that British climbers

The North Face of Cho Oyu. The 1952 expedition turned back below the ice cliffs in the lower part of the face. Climbers on this expansive snow face might have been visible to Chinese soldiers in Tibet. ARTHUR COLLINS/HEDGEHOG HOUSE

were in Tibet and might well be using mountaineering as a cover for espionage.

The three Kiwis, believing that their tiny country made them less of a prize as captives than the British, were all in favour of carrying on with a full-scale attempt. Ed, who was by now feeling fit and acclimatised, felt sure he could outrun Chinese soldiers, if not their gunfire. Shipton, who had spent the war in diplomatic posts in Central Asia and China, was altogether more circumspect. An international incident leading to a Nepali cancellation of permission for Everest in 1953 would not go down well with the Himalayan Committee. As a grudging compromise, they finally settled on a quick lightweight attempt. In the week between 5 and 11 May, Bourdillon, Gregory, Hillary and Lowe placed two camps on the mountain and reached a height of 22,500ft before turning back on ice threatened from above by seracs. Had they had time and space to stand back and study the mountain closely, they would have found the route by which it is now climbed every year, but in 1952 there were too many uncertainties hanging over them.

The attempt on Cho Oyu having come to its embarrassing conclusion, the group split into smaller parties. Evans, Shipton and Gregory went exploring to the west. At Shipton's suggestion, Hillary and Lowe went east to attempt the first crossing of the Nup La to the Rongbuk Glacier in Tibet. A frustrated Riddiford went home, having developed a sore back and a high level of dissatisfaction with Shipton's leadership.

The oxygen trials and the physiology

Where was Griff Pugh? Although the attempt to make a first ascent of Cho Oyu had been a failure, the greater importance of the mountain had been as a testing venue for climbers and oxygen apparatus at heights of up to 26,000ft. Griff's research programme had made a slow start. The first weeks had been difficult as he discovered that he did not acclimatise well, and had been unable to avoid the fevers, sore throats and diarrhoeas that afflicted everyone to some extent. As with acclimatisation to altitude, the old hands such as Shipton had a degree of immunity to dysentery carried over from previous expeditions.

There was a realisation by now that, as a team leader, Griff the scientist had his limitations. He was full of physiological information and ideas but very much a loner. He flew separately to Nepal rather than travelling by ship with the others. On the march in he walked happily by himself, observing the local people and places around him but not getting to know his fellow expedition members. He had a tendency to be intolerant in the way he expressed his opinions. This would hardly have mattered if he had been a self-contained researcher, but his job was to use the people around him as his subjects. The oxygen story was compelling and would have been an easy sell in the mouth of the right person. Ed was hardly aware of the questions about the use of oxygen, let alone the answers, but a simple explanation that Everest was unreachable without oxygen, and that keeping the apparatus in working order would be a prerequisite for a summit team, would have had him first in the queue to learn its use.

A principal goal of the expedition was to have climbers test the open-circuit apparatus on extended climbs at the sort of altitudes that can be found only in the Himalayas. Ed's diary for 6 May notes, 'Cam and Tom to make an oxygen attempt', but does not say where or on what mountain. There is no record that the apparatus was ever used except during short bursts at the Menlung La laboratory camp. A bizarre event occurred during the last weeks of the expedition. A mail-runner arrived with an urgent message. It was a telegram advising that a cylinder of the sort that held the bulk of the expedition's trial oxygen had exploded, killing a factory worker. It instructed that all cylinders should be bled to a safer pressure. Exactly who was thought to be in charge of the oxygen, and who did what to the distrusted cylinders, remains a mystery but the outcome was that all except a few oxygen bottles were emptied completely. Ed makes no mention of this event in his diary, but by then he was on his way to the Nup La. It was a deeply frustrating outcome for Peter Lloyd, the engineer and climber who was an oxygen enthusiast through having used it on Everest in 1938 and was now in London applying his expertise to developing a better apparatus for 1953.

That left the physiology tests that were to be conducted in a controlled environment on a snow slope. Late in May, Griff Pugh had three subjects, Bourdillon, Secord and Colledge, camped on the gentle snow slopes of the Menlung La Pass. At 20,000ft this was a long way short of the heights above 23,000ft where the shortage of oxygen becomes so much more of a problem, but it was much better than London. There were the usual delays as they looked for porters to carry the research equipment to the laboratory camp, but by 22 May everything was ready for a week's intensive work.

Time was short. A measured track was stamped out for the exercise routines, and a laboratory tent set up with instruments for analysing air samples from the subjects' lungs. Supplementary oxygen was tested at flow rates of 4 and 10 L/min delivered from an open-circuit apparatus. The effects of using oxygen while sleeping were also measured. And as a final test, in lieu of the closed-circuit apparatus under development in London, the group did work tests on the measured slope while breathing from a 300-litre bag of pure oxygen. This reduced their apparent altitude to below sea level and seductively demonstrated the wondrous benefits that would – in theory – be delivered by a perfectly functioning closed-circuit apparatus.[3]

At the end of a week on the Menlung La, Pugh folded his tents and trekked back to Kathmandu. His findings would emerge as a report to the Medical Research Council during the next few months.

Ed and George cross the Nup La

Deaf to the call of science, or unaware of it, Hillary and Lowe were intent on making the first ascent to the Nup La Pass from Nepal, via an exceptionally difficult-looking icefall at the head of an arm of the Ngojumba Glacier. The previous year, Bourdillon, Murray, Riddiford and Ward had made an attempt while acclimatising on the Everest Reconnaissance but had had neither the time nor the acclimatisation to force a route up the crevassed and unstable masses of broken ice. Once in Tibet, however, the Rongbuk Glacier would be an easy mountain path running past Everest's North Face, the history of which both men knew well. The threat from the Chinese was almost non-existent. There were said to be soldiers at the Rongbuk Monastery to the north, but they would not be patrolling the desolate, unvisited moraines at the foot of the North Face.

They set out on their three-week excursion on 19 May accompanied by three of their climbing Sherpas and, for the first two days, half a dozen locals including a young Sherpa woman carrying 40 kilograms of potatoes. The route to the foot of the icefall went close to what is now the popular trekkers' destination of Gokyo, with the south face of Cho Oyu rearing up to the north. Their first sight of the route to the Nup La confirmed that it was not going to be easy: '... a great icefall tumbled thousands of feet in a chaos of shattered ice. The icefall was split by a great rock buttress, and the ice surged around it like the bow-wave of a destroyer.'[4]

There could be no holding back, however. Perhaps this was a test of their resolve and fitness for a Shipton-led Everest expedition next year. For the next eight days they were occupied with finding a route and carrying loads in a chaos of crevasses, collapsing seracs and deep snow. On 29 May they crossed the Nup La in fine weather. The head of the West Rongbuk Glacier swept smooth and unbroken for many miles and they made excellent time. They were moving into Everest history as they moved closer to the North Face, with its First and Second Steps, and the Norton Couloir.

Entering the East Rongbuk, they found a few collapsing rock walls marking the site of the old British Camp 1. Earlier they had expressed a distant interest in attempting unclimbed Changtse, 24,730ft, but it was hardly realistic and dark clouds were gathering to the south and west. It was time to return to the Nup La and down the icefall.

When Ed and George came down, they could feel pleased with themselves. The crossing of the Nup La had been a tour de force, partly sheer exuberance but also a barely disguised demonstration of their strength on snow and ice generally and icefalls in particular.

But this was irrelevant if Everest had already been climbed. Rather than head for Namche, they turned east across the 17,700ft Cho La Pass to the base of Everest where they found the still-warm ashes of a Swiss fire but no human beings. At the grazing village of Phalong Karpa they received the news that seven Swiss had reached the summit, 'which depressed us a little', but at Pangboche they met Eric Shipton who told them the Swiss had failed. Ed, deciding that he needed to go to Namche anyway, took off at speed, and in two hours was looking down in the evening light on the 'hotch potch' array of a few British tents and the neat lines of the Swiss encampment over which flew their flag.

Ed was invited to coffee and noted in his diary: 'I was very impressed by René Dittert, the Chef d'Attack, and Lambert, the toeless guide who reached highest on the mountain with the Chief Sherpa Tenzing Bhotia – about 28,100 ft.'[5] Dittert remembered Hillary: 'When I told him of the difficulties almost all of us experienced in freeing ourselves from our professional obligations for four months, he answered with a smile, that it was no problem for him because in New Zealand he had thousands of workers so conscientious that they required no special supervision and worked perfectly well in his absence … "I have lots of bees who do very well without me for a few months."'[6]

Ed wrote to his sister June:

> The Swiss were a very badly battered and dispirited group even though I think they did very well. It had become quite a national thing with the party and they rather feel they have let Switzerland down in not getting to the top …
>
> On this trip I've been lucky in being quite remarkably fit … I am hoping that next year I'll get a chance to go really high as to date I have found altitude effects relatively negligible. Here's hoping anyway.[7]

And to Jim Rose of the NZ Alpine Club in Auckland he wrote: 'The Swiss are convinced that no one will get to the top of Everest without efficient oxygen …'[8]

CHAPTER 13

The Swiss get close, 1952

W hile the British were on the expedition called Cho Oyu,
the Swiss were setting foot on the unknown terrain of
the Western Cwm, the Lhotse Face and the South Col.
There was a first expedition in the warmer pre-monsoon weather of
spring 1952, and another in the wintry cold of late autumn. Both were
bruising, hard-fought encounters by strong teams of climbers. Two
men stood out for their strength at altitude and the way they led and
inspired the others. They were Tenzing Norgay and the Swiss guide
Raymond Lambert who had gravitated towards each other, sharing a
tent and a climbing rope throughout both expeditions.

Tenzing was not a Sherpa but a Tibetan, known in his early
days in Darjeeling as Tenzing Bhotia – Tenzing the Tibetan. He
was born in Kharta, a mythically remote and lovely valley that lies
in the shadow of the Kangshung face of Everest. He was the son
of Mingma, a poor yak-herder, and Kinzom, a hardy woman who
outlived 12 of her 14 children, eight of them dead before the age of
five. When Tenzing was 12, his father entered the Tibetan equivalent
of bankruptcy following a disastrous outbreak of disease among his
yaks. To ease the family burden, Tenzing crossed the Nangpa La into
relatively prosperous Khumbu,[1] and became a servant to a well-off
family in Thame.[2] Socially his status could not have been lower. It was
not till many years after Everest that Tenzing was able to overcome
his shame at being forced to take any job he could find and admit
that he was born a poor Tibetan, not a Sherpa, even though in the

The Swiss spring expedition, 1952. Standing (L to R): Flory, Wyss-Dunant, Aubert, Hofstetter and Lambert; Seated: Chevalley, Roch, Asper, Lombard, Zimmerman and Dittert. THE SWISS FOUNDATION FOR ALPINE RESEARCH

eyes of the West, at least, Kharta had an air of myth and romance that Khumbu had partly lost.

He might have been poor, but Tenzing was also attractive and intelligent, with the result that the eldest daughter of his employer's family, Da Puti, fell in love with him. A penniless Tibetan migrant was not the sort of son-in-law any wealthy, clan-conscious Sherpa was looking for, but Da Puti was not inclined to be obedient. In 1932, when they were both 18, they ran away to Darjeeling, she to live in hardship but with the boy she loved, he to find what work he could, the best paid being as a high-altitude porter on the expeditions. There was not much work to begin with, but in 1935 Tenzing got his break. It came by way of Eric Shipton, who would later do the same for 31-year-old Ed Hillary. Shipton was looking for two more porters for that year's Everest expedition, and as he cast his eye over the assembled applicants he must have seen something in Tenzing that he liked. He chose him despite his lack of experience.

Tenzing was on Everest with the British in 1935, 1936, and in 1938 Tilman described him as 'young, keen, strong, and very likeable'.[3] Then came the war, which put an end to expeditions. He accepted a job in Chitral as orderly to a Gurkha major, and was joined there by Da Puti and their surviving child, daughter Pem Pem, their son Nima Dorje having died of dysentery. In 1944, Da Puti contracted some lingering disease, perhaps TB, and died at the age of 30, a tragic end to a loving relationship that had survived 12 years of hardship. Needing a wife and a mother for his family, Tenzing married Ang Lhamu. She was four years older, no beauty, but warm, intelligent, resourceful and an excellent stepmother. She was his companion in the years of his ambition to climb Everest and the first few years of fame after it.

After the war, climbing resumed in the Indian Garhwal Himalaya, one of them a Swiss expedition which included René Dittert and André Roch, both of them now members of the 1952 Swiss attempt on Everest. Tenzing had become their sardar in 1947 and was outstanding both as a manager of porters and, unusually for a Sherpa at the time, as a climber. So in 1952, Tenzing was invited to be both sardar and a member of the climbing team.

His climbing partner, Raymond Lambert, was at 37 a year younger than Tenzing. He had an exceptional record of difficult climbing in the Alps, including a famous winter ascent of the Aiguilles du Diable, during which he and his companions were holed up for three days in a crevasse and Lambert lost all his toes from frostbite. Along with the other climbers on Everest '52, he belonged to the Androsace, a club from Geneva limited to 40 elite climbers. Financially the expedition was generously supported by the Swiss Foundation for Alpine Research, whose scientific and geographic interests resembled those of the Royal Geographical Society in London.

The Lhotse Face

The Swiss established their Base Camp at 16,600ft on the Khumbu Glacier on 20 April. Ten days later, they made the difficult crossing of the deep, side-to-side crevasse at the top of the icefall, strung a rope bridge across it, and became the first humans to enter the ice-bound space of the Western Cwm. They called it the Valley of Silence, which was true enough during the cloud-filled afternoons under a blanket of new snow, but less apt when avalanches came thundering off the side

The Lhotse Face is mid-photo below the summit of Lhotse. The South Col is skyline left. On the right is the Geneva Spur. The Swiss route in spring 1952 climbed the steep ice slope to the Geneva Spur. The Swiss autumn route, which was also used by the British in 1953, wound up amongst the ledges, crevasses and ice walls of the Lhotse Glacier in mid-photo below the summit and face of Lhotse. THE SWISS FOUNDATION FOR ALPINE RESEARCH

walls, or when the deep roar of the jet-stream was heard as it blew its plume of snow off the summit 9000ft above them. The Cwm was a snow corridor rising 3000ft up which they plugged a trail winding from side to side to avoid crevasses. Snow fell most afternoons and maintaining the route was an endless labour. In Geneva the expedition had planned only four camps on the mountain, but everything was bigger and took longer than they had expected, and in the end they placed seven camps.

To a climber grown up in the Alps, the Lhotse Face looked reasonable, a 3500ft cirque of ice and snow that offered two routes. To the right below the summit of Lhotse was the steep but inactive Lhotse Glacier which came down in ledges that could be linked into a winding route with sites for camps. The more direct line to the South Col, which was marked by a sapphire-coloured patch of ice, was a couloir of steep, unbroken snow with a rock spur showing through its upper half. They called it l'Eperon des Genevois, the Geneva Spur. Set at an angle of 40 degrees, the couloir had no camp sites so would have to be climbed in a day. This was the route they chose.

On 15 May, their first big push on the couloir route, they realised how much more difficult the altitude was than they had anticipated, and how cold it was. 'The wind was sweeping its kingdom,' wrote expedition leader René Dittert. 'Its complaint rose from a murmur to a wail and to rending cries. It wore our nerves. Sometimes it raised a shrill note, as sharp as a blade of steel, vibrating like a knife thrown into a wooden target.'

> We gained about 300 feet an hour, scarcely more … The snow, which was now harder, obliged us to cut steps. Four, five, six blows with an axe were needed, while lower down two had been sufficient. We were in a bad way … Cutting steps exhausted me and stupefied me. I was empty-headed. I thought only of the moment when I would surrender my place to those who came behind … I leaned my forehead on the axe and waited for my heart to calm down … I watched the rope running up between my legs. It rose slowly, by jerks of eight or twelve inches, and I dreaded the moment when it would tighten again and I would have to start moving once more … Never in the Alps had we reached such a degree of exhaustion.[4]

They reached a height of 24,600ft, not much more than halfway to the Col, and here they suffered their first setback. The oxygen sets they had brought with them, based on apparatus used in mines, were almost useless.[5] They gave some relief at rest but were unworkable during climbing because of the resistance of the valves to the movement of oxygen during the violent breathing at high altitude. It would not be possible to climb the Lhotse Face to the South Col in a single day.

The definitive push from the Cwm to the summit began on 25 May after 10 days fixing ropes and carrying loads to their halfway depot in the Couloir. The schedule was ambitious: day 1 to the Col; day 2 to a high camp at 27,500ft; day 3 the summit. When Lambert, Aubert, Flory, Tenzing and six Sherpas set out, the weather was unusually fine, but after only an hour one of the Sherpas, Ajiba, dropped out with a high fever suggesting a relapse of malaria. There was no option but to send him down and share out his load. By midday they had reached the depot halfway up, and here they added food, fuel, oxygen and tents to their loads. At 4 p.m., with the Couloir now in shadow, two more Sherpas declared they were going back.

'How could we prevent them?' wrote Lambert. 'Had we the right to do so? ... Three Sherpas out of seven had gone. For those who continue, such an abandonment is always difficult to bear ... we moored what we could not carry; we should have to come back and get it.'

By 7 p.m., with no hope of reaching the Col that night, they scratched out ledges for two one-man tents, and the seven of them crammed inside: 'Pressed one against the other, we listened to the moaning of the wind. Suddenly the tent flap opened and the indefatigable Tenzing, he who always thinks of others, brought us something to drink. "Merci! Tenzing. Go and sleep".'[6]

Tenzing was first awake in the morning, melting snow for hot chocolate. The Sherpas went down to collect supplies from the depot below while the three Swiss and Tenzing resumed the climb. At 10 a.m. the Col was before them, and rising above it the first ever close-up view of the south-east ridge leading to the summit. Had they not been so pitifully weak they might have felt optimistic. Giving his load to the Swiss, Tenzing dropped down to help the three Sherpas lift loads from the depot below.

Lambert describes making camp:

> On the Col the wind was violent. There was not a trace of snow: nothing but stones welded together by the frost; a desert in miniature. One would have to be as hard as rock or ice to resist the gusts that had been passing across the Col for millennia and seemed in a rage to prevent us from putting up the two tents. On all fours, clinging to the earth like insects, we at last succeeded in bringing sense to the refractory

The South Summit (28,720ft) from the South Col (25,800ft). Lambert and Tenzing's camp was at 27,500ft and their high point was 28,200ft. THE SWISS FOUNDATION FOR ALPINE RESEARCH

cloth. It took us two hours, and then came the waiting. It is difficult to imagine what these hours of waiting mean for an expedition in the Himalaya.[7]

Somehow Tenzing found the energy to make three trips bringing up loads, but the other Sherpas were at the end of their strength. It was clear that they would be in no fit state to carry a high camp, and next day they retreated to the Cwm.

The three Swiss and Tenzing wondered how they should use their remaining strength. They were not strong enough to carry the full weight of a high camp. It was hard to contemplate two carries to the site of a camp on successive days, but what other option was there? Tenzing loaded himself with a tent. They added some food and oxygen, and decided to pitch the tent as high as they could before returning to the Col. The plan was not to stay high overnight, so they carried no sleeping bags and no stove for melting snow.

The weather was fine when they set out at 10 a.m. with the snow in good condition and the climbing easy. The tents below became smaller as they gained height. Late in the afternoon they were at 27,500ft with the weather staying fine. It was Tenzing who made the decision by saying, 'Sahib, we ought to stay here tonight!' They pitched their tent and moved in for a long night. Lambert wrote:

> We were overtaken by a consuming thirst which we could not appease. There was nothing to drink. An empty tin gave us an idea: a fragment of ice and the candle-flame produced a little luke-warm water. The gusts of wind made our heads whirl; it seemed to us that we took off with them into space, like those houses one thinks one sees moving when watching clouds in flight ... this was the boundary between waking and sleeping. I dared not sleep, must not sleep. Tenzing shook me and I awoke, and I shook him in my turn. Amicably we beat one another and pressed close together throughout the night. In the sky the stars were so brilliant that they filled me with fear.[8]

In the morning they were quickly on their way. They had spent the night fully clothed. They had no liquid and hardly any food. They had three canisters of oxygen and one of their pathetically inadequate delivery sets. They began to climb the 1500 feet separating them from the summit but it was painfully slow. Three steps, halt, suck oxygen. They were climbing at just over 100 feet per hour. Their oxygen would last for six hours. By 11 a.m., with their oxygen almost finished, they had less than 1000 feet of height above them, but it might as well have been 10,000 feet. Their bodies were empty of food, fluid, energy, oxygen, hope. Their stops on the descent were as frequent as on the ascent. They had reached their end.

The autumn expedition

A second spring attempt got no higher than the Col but autumn was still available. Only Lambert, Tenzing and expedition leader Chevalley returned for the harsher post-monsoon season. They were joined by four other Swiss climbers and they brought with them two new types of oxygen apparatus, both open-circuit. The better set, made by the German firm Draegar, was based on apparatus used by pilots and had flow rates that could be selected between 2 and 4 L/min. Climbers hoped to use oxygen during both climbing and sleeping above 23,000ft, and for this the expedition was carrying 30,000 litres. With a weight of supplies 50 per cent more than in spring, it was the best equipped expedition to attempt Everest, yet it never had the morale of the spring expedition.

Partly it was the weather passing from autumn into winter. On the march-in, as the huge train of porters was crossing the High Route between Ringmo and Ghat, two thinly clad lowland Nepalis died of exposure. Even before this, Chevalley was writing in his diary, 'We are becoming morose.'[9]

The placement of the route up the Khumbu Icefall and the Western Cwm went ahead through October, often in fine weather, though to the sound of wind roaring across the high ridges. The question was which route to take – the spring route direct up the couloir, or the longer winding route up the Lhotse Glacier? Perhaps made confident by their new oxygen, Lambert chose the couloir. On 31 October, two Swiss on oxygen were accompanying 10 Sherpas up the lower couloir when an avalanche of ice fell on them. Several Sherpas were struck and one of them, Mingma Dorje, was left hanging immobile at the end of his rope and bleeding from head wounds. His companions lowered him to Camp 5 but his condition was deteriorating. Chevalley noted widespread subcutaneous emphysema, showing that fractured ribs had punctured his lungs. He died shortly afterwards. The tragedy cast a long shadow; the Sherpas were their friends.

They retreated from the couloir and next day began a new route up the Lhotse Glacier. November was the beginning of winter with its penetrating cold, unceasing winds and shortening days. The sun was slow to reach into the Cwm and early to leave; not surprisingly, the morale of the Sherpas was low. When a runner arrived with mail, the climbers found that most of it had been stolen in India.

Chevalley noted, 'Gross is in a poor way with insomnia and anxiety; Buzio is too euphoric; Dyhrenfurth is ill; Spöhel is depressed; Reiss is enigmatical.'[10]

On 19 November, Lambert, Tenzing, Reiss and seven Sherpas set off for the South Col. They were using the new oxygen sets successfully and hoped to make a summit attempt. Fighting the wind, they pitched five tents on the Col. The cold, the wind and the altitude prevented sleep. Lambert described what happened next:

> Day broke, but the gale went on … Eventually we came out of our tents, prepared our sacks and at 11.30 set off in the direction of the south-east ridge to establish Camp 9. But the gale and the cold paralysed us gradually. We painfully crossed the Col and ascended the glacier facing the camp. Flattened by the wind against a wall of snow were the remains of an eagle …
>
> We were pierced by the cold despite all our equipment. Tenzing was ill in his turn, the Sherpas almost ceased to advance and we halted at about 26,600 feet. It was impossible to go on in such conditions and at such a height. We left the equipment where we were with the provisions and oxygen bottles and went down again to the Col where we abandoned the greater part of the 130kg we had brought up … This was flight …[11]

As they retreated off the mountain, the Swiss could look back on a year of exceptional achievement, but with deep regret that they had come close but not close enough. Given the Draegar oxygen sets in spring, they might have been successful. They knew, too, how the British would benefit from their experience. They had shown that the best route on the Lhotse Face was the glacier, not the couloir. There had to be a well-found camp on the South Col with good stoves for melting snow and enough oxygen to give climbers the energy to use them. Without effective oxygen sets, an expedition would fail. They had also learnt that despite their strength at altitude, Sherpas are not supermen; they too collapse, feel fear, lose confidence; the Swiss had needed twice as many of them. And finally they had seen from close up that the route to the South Summit had no insurmountable barriers. Only that last 300 feet to the summit remained unknown.

CHAPTER 14

Organising Everest, 1953

---◆---

The failure of the Swiss put the British in pole position for 1953, but there were many unknowns. There was the question of leadership for a start. Eric Shipton was the obvious choice. He was the only contemporary mountaineer well known to the general public. His books had made him a legend, and his public lectures filled the halls. So when he finally emerged from Nepal in late July to attend a meeting of the Himalayan Committee on the question of leadership, he was appointed despite his own suggestion that a younger person might be better.

It seemed the only sensible decision, but there was some unease, particularly as the details of the Cho Oyu and Swiss expeditions became known. The Swiss experience made it clear that a summit attempt had to be launched not from the Western Cwm but from the South Col or higher. A considerable weight of oxygen, tents, food and fuel would have to be carried to the Col, and this would require leadership skills of a high order. The problems of logistics and of using the skills of climbers and porters to best advantage made the ascent of Everest more like a military operation than a leisure activity.

All of this flew in the face of Shipton's own beliefs. He disliked big expeditions and was incapable of the planning they involved. Making climbing a race between competing nations was anathema to him. Until now he had believed that it would be better not to climb Everest at all than to use oxygen. The Cho Oyu group added their discontents, particularly Secord, Pugh and Riddiford, who attributed their lack of achievement to Shipton's inadequate leadership.

Ed was more circumspect in public, but in the privacy of his diary he too was critical. After meeting the Swiss in Namche he wrote:

> In my opinion Eric is now quite unsuitable as an Everest leader as instead of a powerful combining and shaping factor in the expedition he disturbs people's confidence, saps their enthusiasm and fills them with doubt entirely because he has now little or no confidence in his own judgments and is jealous of positive judgments of others.[1]

He made the same point to Jim Rose, his NZ Alpine Club colleague (and future father-in-law), though pointed out that his close relationship with Shipton would be advantageous when the British selected their team for 1953:

> Eric would like to see a party of four British and four New Zealand climbers going to Everest next year – at least that's what he told me. He knows there is a body of opinion in England opposed to the inclusion of any New Zealanders and certainly not more than two but Eric thinks he can handle them ...
>
> I don't think there's much doubt that Eric is far from the ideal big party leader – he realises this himself – but his influence is pretty terrific and even in Nepal and India he is treated by officials as someone of considerable importance.[2]

Ed never went public with these sorts of statements about Shipton. He was too fond of him, too much an admirer of his feats of climbing exploration, too aware of how much he owed to him. But his strongly developed competitive instincts were alight now that he saw a chance to be part of the expedition to make the first ascent of Everest – perhaps even in the summit team. He was, after all, stronger at altitude than anyone else in the Cho Oyu team. It was something to dream about.

There might have been reservations about Shipton, many of them unexpressed, but on 28 July he was offered the leadership and he accepted. Next day he wrote to Ed:

My Dear Ed,

There was a Him. Com. Meeting yesterday at which next year's trip was discussed in general terms. I was asked to lead it; I said I wasn't too keen ... Then I was sent out of the room while they discussed it. I was pressed to take it on (it's a great pity they didn't see me in the Himalayas this year as they wouldn't have been so keen) and I said I would, providing I wasn't necessarily expected to go high. Then we went on to discuss the party – I said I wanted you and George <u>and</u> Harry Ayres and this was agreed ... We are in the process of selecting a Secretary/Organiser, possibly John Hunt. Now could you three get together and draw up an exhaustive and detailed list of proposals about equipment <u>and food</u>. I'd like your ideas about boots, tents, sleeping bags, woollen clothing, etc and also about ice pitons, rope etc, and apparatus for crossing crevasses ...

I have suggested a party of 9 including myself ...

Yours, Eric.[3]

Whether this casual approach might have led to success if Shipton had remained as leader no one can say. Mention of oxygen is conspicuous by its absence. Ed claimed later that he, Charles Evans and Charles Wylie would have filled any organisational vacuum, but that was in old age when he had become more oracular.[4]

August 1952 went by with the doubts about Shipton only growing. When the Himalayan Committee began to think of alternative leaders, military personnel came to mind. They were experienced in logistics, and in the absence of any current war might be available immediately and free of charge. Two names were at the top of their list: Colonel John Hunt and Lieutenant-Colonel Charles Wylie.

Wylie was an officer with the Brigade of Gurkhas who had spent most of the Second World War in the testing environment of a Japanese prisoner-of-war camp. He spoke Nepali fluently and he was also a climber. As overall leader, Wylie was too understated to be a convincing candidate, but he gladly accepted the position of organising secretary in London and transport officer in Nepal, a position he carried out alongside sardar Tenzing Norgay. Unusually among expedition members, he did not write a book, so remained relatively unsung, but he played an indispensable role.

John Hunt had a far more impressive Himalayan record than he was generally given credit for. His military career had been in India and Europe, so he was largely unknown to the post-war generation of English climbers. He was born in 1910 in the Indian hill town of Simla. Four years later, he lost his father to the war in France. He was educated at Marlborough, where he excelled at French, German and rugby, and by his mid-teens was climbing regularly in the Alps. Coming from a family of soldiers, he applied for Sandhurst where he entered first of his year in 1928, and was again first when he passed out as a senior under-officer. In 1931, commissioned into the Kings Royal Rifle Corps, he moved to Calcutta where Bengalis were becoming restless under British rule, a movement which earned Hunt's sympathy.

When on leave from his regiment between 1931 and 1938, he went into the Himalayas where, with friends, he reached 24,500ft on the unclimbed Saltoro Kangri in the Karakorum, and attained the 23,350ft south-west summit of Nepal Peak just north of Kangchenjunga. He became a member of the Alpine Club and the Royal Geographical Society in 1935, and was accepted for the 1936 expedition to Everest only to be turned down by a doctor who heard a cardiac murmur – and reputedly told him he should take care when climbing stairs. Climbing to 24,500ft in the Karakorum would seem to be strong evidence that the murmur was of the common benign variety rather than an indication of heart disease, but the decision was not open to appeal.

Hunt returned to Britain in 1939, and was made chief instructor of the mountain warfare school in Braemar. In 1944 he commanded a battalion in the invasion of Italy, where he was awarded the DSO. His regiment subsequently took up a peace-keeping role in Greece, and this earned him a CBE.

Transferred after the war to Germany, he continued climbing in the Alps. Here one of his climbing partners was Basil Goodfellow, the secretary of the Himalayan Committee who in 1952 was wracked with uncertainty about the wisdom of committing next year's Everest expedition to the leadership of Eric Shipton. Goodfellow recognised in Hunt qualities the expedition needed: leadership skills in forming a team, organisational ability, a quick intelligence that could sum up what a situation required, fierce determination, extensive climbing experience – and Hunt's Himalayan experience exceeded that of any potential member apart from Shipton's.

Hunt expressed delight when sounded out privately in July 1952 about the possibility of a role such as deputy leader, but the situation was awkward. Shipton had already accepted the position of leader, with Charles Wylie as his deputy. How did one add a second deputy leader and, for that matter, one who had met neither the Himalayan Committee nor Shipton? A meeting set up at short notice between Hunt and Shipton illuminated the yawning gap between their visions for the 1953 expedition. Shipton's preferred style of organisation was relatively informal, relying on inspired improvisation to solve the climbing problems; the expedition was not a race, not a competition, not a situation in which national drum-beating played a part. Hunt, on the other hand, saw 1953 as the last chance for the British to make the first ascent of their mountain; and for this to happen, planning had to be intensively focused on every detail. The mood of the Himalayan Committee was that every possible step to achieve success must be taken. The prestige of England was at stake.

The axe fell at a meeting of the Himalayan Committee on 11 September, when Shipton was surprised to notice that 'Leadership of the Expedition' was an item on the agenda. It was an embarrassment for the committee too, but they had come to the decision that Hunt would be no less than co-leader. This was an awkward compromise. It might perhaps have worked with Shipton as the *éminence grise* beside Hunt the planner, but Shipton's response was to tender his resignation. It was a sad end for a man who aroused great affection in those who came to know him.

Looking back on the leadership controversy, Shipton admitted that he was 'not an efficient organizer of complicated projects':

> Even so, the chagrin I felt at my sudden dismissal was a cathartic experience which did nothing to increase my self-esteem. I had often deplored the exaggerated publicity accorded to Everest expeditions and the consequent distortion of values. Yet, when it came to the point, I was far from pleased to withdraw from this despised limelight; nor could I fool myself that it was only the manner of my rejection that I minded.[5]

Hunt chooses his team

There could be no mistaking the intensity of John Hunt's planning when he sat down at an Everest desk heaped with correspondence

John Hunt. The inscription reads: 'Ed Hillary. To remind you of our comradeship on Everest. John Hunt 7/1/54'. HILLARY MUSEUM COLLECTION

in the premises of the RGS in South Kensington. Top of his list was selection of the team. For a start there were the five who had proved themselves in 1952: Charles Evans, Tom Bourdillon, Ed Hillary, George Lowe and Alf Gregory. Tenzing Norgay would lead the Sherpas and also be a lead climber. Charles Wylie was Transport Officer and Organising Secretary. Mike Ward, instigator of the 1951 reconnaissance expedition, was appointed doctor, reserve climber and assistant physiologist. Three Himalayan newcomers were Wilf Noyce, George Band and Michael Westmacott. Griff Pugh was physiologist and adviser on food and fluid intake. James Morris was correspondent for *The Times*; Tom Stobart was movie cameraman.

Ed received his invitation in late October:

> Dear Hillary, I believe that Eric Shipton has written to tell you about the change in the leadership of the 1953 Everest expedition … it is most unfortunate that it should have happened in this way, and very bad luck on Eric Shipton. However, you will, I am sure, agree with me that there is only one way of looking at it – we must go ahead with the planning with a firm determination to get to the top. This is an interim letter to tell you that I am busy with the selection of the party and that I very much hope that you and Lowe will be ready to join the party …
>
> Yours sincerely, John Hunt

He replied on 2 November:

> Dear Hunt, Thanks for your letter. We were naturally very disappointed when we heard that Eric Shipton was no longer leading the party to Everest next year. Quite apart from personal feelings on the matter we owe Shipton a great deal of gratitude for his generous inclusion of New Zealanders in his two last expeditions.
>
> However, as you say, the main thing is to climb Everest and in this effort we can assure you of our wholehearted co-operation. We appreciate very much your invitation to be members of your party and will do our best to more than justify our inclusion.[6]

Evidence of Hunt's planning ability was not long in appearing, for the post brought a series of detailed plans which Ed 'reluctantly had to admit seemed to hit the nail on the head every time ...'[7]

A letter which invited him to be part of a three-man planning group secured Ed's loyalty and untiring hard work for the whole of the expedition.

> Dear Ed ... Planning. I hope that you, with Charles Evans, will accept the job of being part of a small planning group or if you prefer it, my counsellor in the making of plans. I shall, of course, call on advice from other members of the party as necessary; but I do not intend to make a habit of having full Party meetings to discuss plans, as this becomes too controversial and too unwieldy ...[8]

The 'proposed expedition appointments' included:

- Leader and planning: Hunt, assisted by Evans and Hillary.
- Transport: Wylie
- Oxygen: Bourdillon, assisted by Evans
- Medical and hygiene: Ward assisted by Evans
- Physiology: Pugh assisted by Ward
- Messing: Pugh assisted by Band[9]

Ed was flattered by the proposal:

> Dear Hunt, Your letter arrived yesterday and was, I must admit, something of a surprise even though a very pleasant one. I accept the responsibilities with much pleasure. I find that as the weeks pass and the time shortens before my departure for India that my enthusiasm for the task continually increases. It will be a great thrill to get to grips with the mountain.[10]

On 5 November, Hunt had released a 10-page *Basis for Planning* which proved to be a remarkably accurate blueprint for the expedition.[11] Its opening sentence read: 'The ultimate aim of the Expedition ... is the ascent of Everest during 1953 by a member or members of the party ...'

As Hunt himself said, this might be self-evident, but he was emphasising that there was only one goal that mattered. It was not making a film, or writing newspaper articles or books, or doing physiological research. It was getting to the top. He was aware that on Cho Oyu neither the expedition leader nor its members seemed to be clear about their aims. In 1933 and 1936, Finch had tartly commented that the goal seemed to have been to climb as high as possible on Everest without using oxygen. And in 1938 the object had been to prove that a small expedition could place its climbers almost as high on the mountain as a large expedition. What became apparent in 1953 was that its leader had an intense singleness of purpose, knowing that he and his expedition would be judged solely by whether a climber reached the summit of Everest.

A table shows how much the British had learned from the Swiss.

	Swiss Spring 1952	British Spring 1953
Climbers	9	12
High-altitude Sherpas	14	28
Oxygen	20,000 litres	193,000 litres
Weight of stores & equipment	4 ½ tons	7 ½ tons
Arrive in Namche	14 April	25 March
Man-days on & above South Col	18	33
Route up Lhotse face	Ice couloir with no camps	Lhotse glacier with two camps

The use of oxygen

Of all the uncertainties hanging over the expedition, the most critical was the development of the oxygen apparatus. It was given such urgency by the Himalayan Committee that a plan was requested from Hunt only six days into his role as leader. Britain was in the fortunate position that during a protracted, all-consuming war it had developed a technological infrastructure that could be used on Everest. Air crew had needed oxygen sets when flying at high altitude. What was needed now was an adaptation for mountaineers.

The choice between open- and closed-circuit delivery systems sparked off intense debate. Both consist of a bottle of oxygen connected to a reservoir bag which leads into a face mask. Beyond this basic similarity, there are major differences.

In the open-circuit apparatus, an inspired breath consists partly of bottled oxygen, partly of ambient air. The expired air, still containing a lot of unused oxygen, is blown off into the surroundings. Ninety per cent of a climber's precious bottled oxygen goes to waste, but enough is absorbed to reduce his apparent altitude to around 20,000ft.

The closed-circuit apparatus, which wastes nothing, is based on a compelling theory. The climber's mask is a perfect fit to his shaved face so that outside air is entirely excluded. He is breathing pure oxygen from his oxygen cylinder so is effectively climbing at sea level. Expired air from the lungs is passed through a canister of soda lime for removal of the carbon dioxide which is the waste product of energy metabolism. The purified oxygen is recycled. The climber is living entirely off gas supplied by the British Oxygen Co. Ltd.

In the few closed-circuit systems that had been trialled before 1953, there were serious problems which showed up erratically as feelings of heat, choking and suffocation. The open-circuit system was criticised for being inefficient and unwieldy, requiring a huge weight of oxygen cylinders to be carried up the mountain. But there were keen protagonists for both systems. Tom Bourdillon, physicist, climber on Cho Oyu in 1952, and selected for Everest in 1953, believed he could develop a successful closed-circuit system. Peter Lloyd, of the Himalayan Committee, believed equally strongly in the superiority of open-circuit systems. As a climber on Everest in 1938 he had found such a system of considerable benefit while climbing to over 27,000ft, whereas a trial of a closed-circuit system had caused such unpleasant feelings of suffocation that he rejected it as a future option. In late 1952 it was agreed that development of both systems would proceed – but time was running short.

Doomsayers predicted that when either form of apparatus broke down the climber would simply collapse, but the limited evidence available was against such pessimism. Finch and Lloyd had both switched off their oxygen at 27,000ft and found they could cope with problems and descend with no more difficulty than someone who had not used oxygen.[12]

The expedition assembles in Kathmandu

Of the members gathered at the British Embassy in Kathmandu on 5 March 1953, Ed already knew those who had been on Cho Oyu. Now there were important new acquaintances to be made. The first of these was John Hunt, of whom Ed wrote:

> Despite my pre-conceived prejudices I was immediately impressed. He greeted me with great warmth; told me he was expecting much from me and that he wanted me to share with Charles Evans the advisory tasks of his 'Executive Committee'; and how he personally intended to lead from the front ... he expressed a complete conviction that our party could get to the top ...[13]

Tenzing was there too:

> I was eager to meet Tenzing Norgay. His reputation had been most impressive even before his two great efforts with the Swiss expedition the previous year – and I certainly wasn't disappointed. Tenzing really looked the part – larger than most Sherpas he was very strong and active; his flashing smile was irresistible; and he was incredibly patient and obliging with all our questions and requests. His success in the past had given him great physical confidence – I think that even then he <u>expected</u> to be a member of the final assault party as he had been with both the Swiss expeditions although I am sure that neither John Hunt nor any of the rest of us took this for granted ... One message came through, however, in very positive fashion – Tenzing had substantially greater personal ambition than any Sherpa I had met.[14]

Two members who were peripheral to the climbing team, but sharp observers, were cameraman Tom Stobart and *Times* correspondent James Morris. Stobart was 39, and had a varied history filming in the Himalayas, the Antarctic, Africa and Australia. He described meeting Ed Hillary:

> My room-mate, who arrived in Kathmandu on the second day, was a skeleton, as tall as I was, with a New Zealand

The party and high-altitude Sherpa team at Advance Base on 31 May 1953. Standing (L to R): Stobart, Dawa Tenzing, Evans, Wylie, Hillary, Hunt, Tenzing, Lowe, Ward, Bourdillon, Band, Pugh, Gregory and Noyce; Seated: 21 high-altitude Sherpas – Topkie, Thondup, Chhangju, Annullu, Ang Tsering, Norbu, Balu Tensing, Mingma Tsering, Dawa Thondup, Ang Nima, Da Namgyal, Thakto Pemba, Pasang Dawa, Nawang Gombu, Gyaljen, Phu Dorje, Nanje Khancha, Ang Temba, Ang Dorje, Kirken and Ang Dawa. ROYAL GEOGRAPHICAL SOCIETY

accent, a hatchet-thin face, and seemed tied together with steel. I learned that this man was called Ed Hillary. I had just got a rubber torch in pieces and couldn't get it together again. This human machine took charge. 'Let's give it a go,' he said, using an expression we came to know so well in the following months. It may have meant that he would try to fix it, but it did not. Actually it meant he would fix it, a subtle but important difference so far as Ed and his fellow countryman George Lowe, were concerned.[15]

John Hunt working on logistics at the camp in the grounds of Tengboche Monastery, 12,688 feet. ROYAL GEOGRAPHICAL SOCIETY

Stobart had met John Hunt at the RGS four months earlier:

> John was sitting at a desk piled high with papers ... as I
> looked at this slightly grizzled soldier I felt there was no
> doubt that what a friend, who had served under him during
> the war, had told me was probably true. 'If nobody else can
> get to the top of Everest, John will think it necessary to go
> there himself.' Indeed truer words were never spoken or gave a
> better description of this formidably determined man.[16]

James Morris, 26, was the second-youngest expedition member after 24-year-old George Band. Having left school at age 17, he had served three years in the Middle East with the 9th Queen's Lancers. After two years at Oxford he became a journalist with *The Times*, later becoming a full-time author, writing 18 books as James Morris and, after 1972, more than 30 as Jan Morris. In 1953, *The Times*, which owned the copyright to the Everest expedition dispatches, recognised that they needed their own journalist with the expedition rather than relying on a leader writing articles in his spare time. 'Hunt,' wrote Morris in his book *Coronation Everest*, 'kindliest of commanders, digested the fact that I had never set foot on a mountain before and even summoned up a wan smile as, over lunch one day at the Garrick Club, he invited me to join his team as Special Correspondent of *The Times*.'[17] Morris added immeasurably to the legend of the expedition by having its success announced to the world for the first time in London on the morning of 2 June, the day of the Coronation of Queen Elizabeth II.

Aerial view of Everest showing route from Base Camp to summit.
ROYAL GEOGRAPHICAL SOCIETY

CHAPTER 15

'We were on top of Everest!'[1]

===>+<===

By the end of March the expedition had set up an acclimatisation camp in front of Tengboche Monastery in a meadow strewn with mauve primulas and surrounded by forests of rhododendron, birch and juniper. Small grey musk deer and brilliantly coloured monal pheasants enjoyed the protection of the Buddhist monks. Like all first-time visitors, John Hunt was overwhelmed by what 'must be one of the most beautiful places in the world'.[2] The great walls and ridges of the inner ring of Khumbu peaks towered around them, framing the view of the Lhotse–Nuptse wall to the north-east with Everest behind. The top 2000 feet of their route was easily visible, a broad south-east ridge rising to the South Summit and, beyond that, to the unknown ridge leading to the highest point on Earth's surface. Was it an impossibly corniced blade of ice interrupted by equally impossible rock steps? Until a climber stood on the South Summit, no one would know.

Two weeks were spent acclimatising on smaller peaks and being taught the use of the new oxygen sets by Tom Bourdillon. The assessments were enthusiastic. Even at heights of 18,000–20,000ft, the oxygen more than compensated for its weight. 'I like this open-circuit jobbie,' Ed wrote, and he applied himself to learning its habits.

April was the icefall month, somewhat difficult and more than somewhat dangerous, but there was no other way into the Western Cwm. Once the route was established, with its staircases of ice, its fixed ropes and aluminium ladder bridging the huge topmost crevasse,

Porters at the top of the Khumbu Icefall where it eases off into the Western Cwm.
ROYAL GEOGRAPHICAL SOCIETY

daily convoys of Sherpas carried supplies to Camp 3 in the Cwm. Each
group of laden Sherpas was roped to a climber to protect anyone who
slipped or had a snow bridge collapse under them. This happened to
Ed. Descending ahead of Tenzing, he jumped across a crevasse only to
have the block he landed on collapse. Had Tenzing not been able to
hold him with his belay, both would have plummeted into a crevasse
of unknown depth and the history of the expedition would have been
different. Audiences in years to come would say, 'You must have been
very grateful to Tenzing for holding you like that,' to which Ed would
reply, 'Well actually, I would have been very disappointed if he hadn't.'

May was when the more serious action took place. Advanced Base,
Camp 4, was established on a protected site in the upper Cwm at
21,200ft, an altitude that was tolerable for everyone once acclimatised.
From here there was a grandstand view of the next obstacle to be
climbed, the 3500ft Lhotse Face that formed the head-wall of the great
amphitheatre of the Cwm. When Bourdillon, Evans and Hunt set off
on 2 May using closed-circuit oxygen, they were hoping that this new
technology would work a miracle on the problems of altitude which

began in earnest from this height upwards. Who knows, given good snow conditions and oxygen sets working to perfection they might even reach the South Col ...

It didn't work out that way. Their route was up a mixture of deep snow or steep, hard ice; the oxygen sets were uncomfortably hot; and the maximum height they reached was still an alarming 3000ft short of the Col. The weather was following its established pattern of intense heat in the morning, switching to a fall of thick new snow in the afternoon. It wasn't going to be easy.

Down at Base Camp, the Hillary–Tenzing team was restlessly waiting their chance to share the lead. Ed had an idea. Bourdillon and Evans were up there trialling the closed-circuit sets. Why not mount a trial with the open-circuit system? With Hunt's permission, Hillary and Tenzing left Base Camp at 6.30 a.m. on 4 L/min. Five hours later they walked into Advance Base, 3300ft higher. Though tired, they still had the energy to return to Base Camp in a snowstorm that afternoon. Theirs wasn't a valid comparison with Bourdillon and Evans's trial of the closed-circuit system – they were using a well-made route at a lower altitude – but it helped their reputation as the strongest climbing pair in the expedition, and confirmed Ed's belief in the greater reliability of open-circuit oxygen.

Tom Bourdillon, developer and protagonist of the closed-circuit apparatus, was having his faith sorely tested as he trialled it in the Western Cwm. As well as the unpleasant heat of the closed system, he noted that after several hours of use 'some pronounced after-effects were observed. For possibly two hours after taking the set off at the end of a day the user suffered from most of the symptoms normal to him in hypoxia – that is extreme lassitude, drowsiness and various minor aberrations of speech and memory ... These effects were so marked that they became a standing joke.'[3] One could never quite know what toxins might have found their way into the tiny environment of the closed-circuit system. Or was inert nitrogen leaking in around a not quite gas-tight face-mask from the outside air and diluting the oxygen? Was the discomfort due only to the circulating heat and humidity? These were unanswered questions in 1953.[4]

The die is cast
On 7 May, Hunt called the climbers together for the key meeting at which he would announce the plan for the assault. It was held in the

big tent in the moraine-strewn squalor of Base Camp, and all of the 12 climbers were there except George Lowe and George Band who were at Camp 3. The broad outline was that between 7 and 15 May the route up the Lhotse Face to the South Col would have its steps plugged and cut, its ropes fixed and its camps established. This would culminate in a big carry of tents, food, fuel and oxygen by a team of 14 Sherpas to Camp 8 on the Col. When a window of fine weather arrived, a first assault would set out from the South Col using closed-circuit oxygen. A second assault, weather permitting, would follow next day.

The important questions for the climbers were who would do what. Some of the questions answered themselves. If there was to be an assault using closed-circuit oxygen, it would be led by Tom Bourdillon: no one else could cope with its problems. And accompanying him would be Charles Evans for the same reason. There would undoubtedly be an open-circuit attempt. Who was first choice for this? Hillary and Tenzing were the strongest pair.

From the South Col, Bourdillon and Evans would have 3000 feet of climbing between them and the summit. At the least they should reach the South Summit and, if the closed-circuit oxygen worked to perfection, they had a strong chance of reaching the top. The assault by Hillary and Tenzing, on the other hand, would take two days, with an intermediate Camp 9 at 28,000ft. For anyone laying bets, Hillary and Tenzing had the short odds.

That was four of the climbers accounted for, but what about the other eight? John Hunt had always seen himself as leading from the front. This meant he would position himself in the camp on the South Col, where he could direct and support five elite Sherpas who, if Bourdillon and Evans failed to reach the summit, would carry Camp 9 to around 28,000ft. He needed one other support climber on the South Col and, because Alf Gregory acclimatised well, Hunt gave the Camp 9 support position to him.

Two more climbers were required to accompany Sherpas on the carries between Advance Base and the South Col. Transport Officer Charles Wylie was an obvious choice. Wilf Noyce was selected alongside him, as he too handled the altitude well.

That left three climbers to establish the route up the Lhotse Face: Lowe, Band and Westmacott. The original plan had been for climbers to use oxygen while working on the Lhotse Face and also for

Ed Hillary at Base Camp. GEORGE LOWE

sleeping, but there simply wasn't enough of it, despite oxygen making up more than a third of the loads on the mountain. Lowe, Band and Westmacott would be cutting and plugging steps and fixing ropes all the way up the Lhotse Face without the enormous advantage of using oxygen. The twelfth man was Mike Ward, who was reserve climber as well as doctor.

Silence followed as each thought about his position. Charles Evans, as deputy leader, had been part of the planning so was not going to speak against it, but others might feel disappointed. George Lowe had started as Ed's climbing partner with an outside chance he would be part of an assault. Now he would be expending all his energies on the Lhotse Face without the opportunity to go higher. He later confided his disappointment to Wilf Noyce, who was praising his work on the Face.

'Ah, yes,' George said, 'but people judge you by how high you go, and it doesn't look now as if I'll make the South Col.'[5]

Then there was Mike Ward, who could have reasonably expected to have one of the stronger claims to a place in a summit team, yet here he was, a mere 'reserve'. 'Didn't like it either,' Ed wrote in his diary.[6] In the event of the first two assaults failing, Ward could expect to be a member of a third attempt but it was a disappointment.

James Morris of *The Times* was another observer at the meeting:

> Had anyone any questions or observations? Hunt asked, looking benignly around the tent with a soldierly air, as if he were about to order his company commanders to synchronise their watches.
>
> 'Yes,' said Michael Ward, with a vehemence that nearly knocked me off my packing-case. 'I certainly have. I think it's a great mistake that you're going so high yourself. It's a great mistake. You've done too much already. You shouldn't go with that support team. I feel this very strongly.'
>
> He spat this out with a flashing of eyes and a quivering of his saturnine head; and John thanked him gravely. The passionate doctor proved to be partly right. Hunt, who was forty-two, climbed extremely high ... to the absolute limit of his endurance; and of all the climbers he was the most exhausted, so that I used to wonder, after the event, looking at his tired drawn face and thin body, moving with an air of infinite weariness, whether he would ever be quite the same again. But there, it was the sacrifice of leadership.[7]

Slowing down on the Lhotse Face

On the Lhotse Face the team began to disintegrate before it had cut the first step. Band and Westmacott had not acclimatised well, as is common in first-time climbers, and both had suffered intermittently from dysentery during their time on the mountain. As well as this, Band had just developed a feverish cold.[8] When they made their slow way to the foot of the face, they discovered that the strength they needed was not there. On 10 May, Lowe, accompanied by the Sherpa Ang Nima, and unaccompanied by any oxygen, began his lonely assault on the route from the head of the Cwm to the site of the midway camp – Camp 7 at 24,000ft. The weather was no help. Every afternoon snow came down, filling in steps that had been laboriously plugged or cut in the morning. Oxygen would have made a huge difference but there was none to spare.

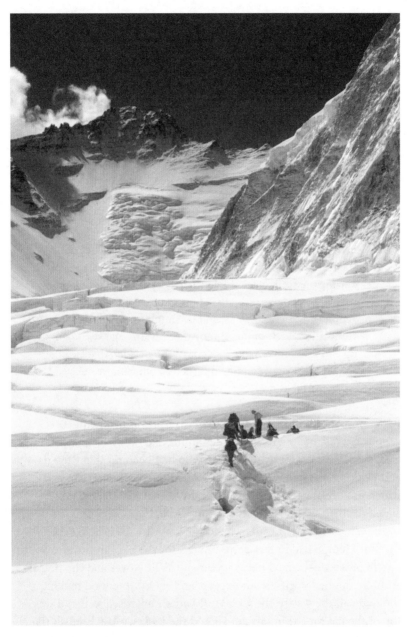

The Western Cwm leading up to the Lhotse Face and the peak of Lhotse, 27,941 feet.
ROYAL GEOGRAPHICAL SOCIETY

Down at Camp 4/Advance Base, 21,200ft, anxiety grew as the team now assembled there watched the snail-like progress of Lowe and Ang Nima. One day the wind was too strong for the two climbers even to go outside. Another day Lowe took such a dose of sleeping pills that he was semi-comatose all next day. Mike Ward went up to help but after five nights he had to retreat, defeated by the altitude: 'I tried as hard as I could to think of a reason for my poor condition, for I was going much worse than George all the time over 23,000 feet. I could think of none.'[9]

Ed later described how down at Advance Base he was getting edgy:

> By May 19th George Lowe, Mike Ward and Ila Tenzing were in Camp 7 at 24,000 feet but the Lhotse Face attack had almost fizzled out … The weather had not in fact been very satisfactory but there was also a clear lack of vitality in our thrust at this stage. I knew from experience that George needed someone to stimulate him into the considerable action he was capable of – and he simply wasn't getting this stimulation. I felt quite grumpy that I wasn't allowed to go up and give him a hand. Next day John decided that George should come down and he returned to our camp as relaxed and cheerful as ever.[10]

For a moment Hunt became less than his usual impeccably supportive self. Mike Ward recorded in his diary on 20 May: 'John EXCESSIVELY RUDE to George who had been up about ten days and working damned well. Quite ashamed to have him in the party which has been very friendly so far.'[11] In his autobiography, Ward added to this a cryptic quotation from Virgil: '*Flectere, si nequeo superos, Acheronta movebo* – If I cannot bend the gods, I will let hell loose.'[12]

But George had in fact done enough for the big carry to the South Col to proceed. The next day, 35-year-old Wilf Noyce and the Sherpa Annullu donned open-circuit oxygen, and set off intent on making the route all the way to the Col. Wilf had acclimatised well and was top of the list for a third assault should the first two fail. Like all the climbers, he marvelled at the difference oxygen made. He described the sensation of opening the valve on the oxygen set: 'When, after all the struggles, the switch was at last turned on, a taste or breath of metallic new life seemed to slip through the mouth to lungs, mocking every disadvantage and making life seem good once again.'[13]

It was 21 May, and in one of the turning-points of the expedition, they left the Lhotse Face below them and stood on the crest of the Geneva Spur, looking down on the South Col. Noyce recalled:

> ... the eye wandered hungry and fascinated over the plateau ... a space of boulders and bare ice perhaps four hundred yards square, absurdly solid and comfortable at first glance in contrast with the sweeping ridges around ... in among the glinting ice and dirty grey boulders there lay some yellow tatters – all that remained of the Swiss expeditions of last year ... We crunched down to the last of the wind-crust, myself still unwinding the rope. Then the flat. The yellow rags lay in dead little heaps, or fluttered forlornly from metal uprights that still stood. Round about was spread a chaos of food, kitbags, sleeping-bags, felt boots. Whenever people talk of the 'conquest' of Everest, I close my eyes and see that ghost-ridden scene.[14]

Reaching the South Col was a start, but there were no loads there yet, no Camp 8 as the springboard for the attempts on the summit. At Camp 7 there were now 14 Sherpas crammed into too small a space. Many of them were nervous about the huge physical effort required of them as they carried 30lb loads from 24,000ft to 26,000ft without oxygen. Recognising how critical was this last carry, Hunt agreed with Tenzing and Hillary that the two of them, on oxygen, should climb to Camp 7 where Tenzing would urge the Sherpas to expend all their energy on this crucial next stage. Hillary and Tenzing in front would make steps; Charles Wylie would encourage the stragglers in the rear. By the end he was carrying one of their loads. At last, with enormous relief, Hunt saw from Advance Base that 17 figures were crossing the top of the Geneva Spur.

Now he had a well-equipped Camp 8 from which the summit attempts could be launched.

Bourdillon and Evans
On the morning of 26 May, Bourdillon and Evans emerged from their

From the South Summit of Everest on 26 May, Bourdillon surveys the unclimbed final ridge. CHARLES EVANS

tent on the South Col. Evans swung his 50lb closed-circuit set on to his back, strapped the face mask in place and immediately knew that something was seriously wrong. Bourdillon identified a damaged valve that had to be replaced, a procedure that took over an hour. Once under way, however, the sets worked so well that the pair were climbing at the unprecedented rate of almost 1000 feet per hour. It did not last. At 28,000ft, when they changed soda lime canisters, something went wrong in Evans's set. Perhaps a valve had iced up during the change. This time the diagnosis eluded Bourdillon. Evans managed to keep going, but his breathing was painfully laboured.

At 1 p.m. they reached the South Summit, 28,700ft, higher than anyone had climbed before. Seated on the snow dome, they could look closely for the first time at the last 300 vertical feet of Everest. It was not the gentle snow ridge they'd hoped for. They were looking at a thin crest of snow and ice on rock, steep on the left, overhanging as a cornice on the right. Two-thirds of the way up, the snow was interrupted by a 40ft rock step which looked formidable indeed at such an altitude.

It was 1.20 p.m. They had two-and-a-half hours of oxygen left. Evans estimated that the step-cutting on the ridge and the attempt on the rock step would take three hours. Evans's oxygen set was malfunctioning. Descent from the summit would take more than three hours. If they went on they might reach the summit, but with no oxygen left the return would be dangerous in the extreme. Evans had no ambition to become another Mallory or Irvine, but Bourdillon was wracked by his awareness that this might be his, and the expedition's, last chance. He had worked for more than a year on the design of the oxygen sets for just this moment; there was only 300 feet of height to climb on a ridge that was difficult but not impossible. But Evans was sure they were making the right decision, and as they turned and began their descent a great weariness came over them. The last thousand feet to the Col began with a couloir of steep snow. They slithered from belay to belay. 'We yo-yoed down', they said.[15] Exhausted beyond belief, they staggered into camp on the South Col in the late afternoon.

Tenzing assisting Bourdillon and Evans after they have climbed, on closed-circuit oxygen, to the highest altitude ever reached, 28,700ft. ROYAL GEOGRAPHICAL SOCIETY

Hillary and Tenzing

On this same day, 26 May, Hillary and Tenzing arrived on the South
Col, accompanied by Alf Gregory and 11 Sherpas with more oxygen,
food and fuel. Also with them was George Lowe who, far from
exhausting himself on the Lhotse Face, had acclimatised and gained
strength. Mike Ward had commented that Ed and George were 'going
like greyhounds'[16] and now the two greyhounds were back together
again.

Five of the strongest Sherpas had been selected to carry the loads
for Camp 9, two of them with John Hunt on the 26th and three with
Alf Gregory two days later. When the time came, only two of the
five were willing or able to continue. None of the Sherpas apart from
Tenzing and Annullu had used oxygen up to the South Col, and
they were suffering from exhaustion, insomnia, apprehension and the
other ills of extreme altitude. When Hunt set out on the first carry to
Camp 9, he had only Da Namgyal and himself to carry three loads.
At 27,300ft Da Namgyal could go no further. Hunt was in no better

*The five men who helped Hillary and Tenzing to carry Camp 9 to 27,800ft: Hunt,
Da Namgyal, Gregory, Ang Nima and Lowe.* GEORGE LOWE

shape, but it was Da Namgyal who called the halt, and they dumped their loads of a tent, food, fuel and oxygen, including the bottles they had been using for their ascent. The descent to the Col without oxygen was a remarkable effort from Da Namgyal and a quite extraordinary performance from the 42-year-old leader.

The high winds that arose on the night of the 26th gave Ed one of the worst nights he had ever experienced, and prevented the second assault team starting on the 27th. But on the 28th the weather was fine though windy as Hillary and Tenzing, Gregory and Lowe, and George's Lhotse Face Sherpa Ang Nima prepared loads for the carry to Camp 9. At 27,300ft they added the Hunt–Da Namgyal loads to their own. Five hundred feet higher they'd had enough, and settled on a flattish spot beneath a rock bluff for their camp.

It took Hillary and Tenzing three hours, not using oxygen, to chip out enough ice and rock to convert their site into two ledges, an upper one for Hillary and the lower for Tenzing. While Tenzing melted snow and ice for the first of many brews of soup, lemon drink and coffee, Ed reviewed the oxygen situation. There was an immediate problem when they found that there was no adaptor for the 1400-litre cylinder of sleeping oxygen which would have given them 12 hours of sleep. And some of their four bottles of summit oxygen had been used on the day's carry. On the plus side, there were the two quarter-full bottles left behind by Hunt and Da Namgyal, and the two left by Bourdillon and Evans. These would cover their descent from Camp 9 down to the South Col.

They took their sleep in two lots of two hours, with hot drinks between times. There was ample fuel for their gas cooker whose sound and warmth helped them through the night. The wind came at them spasmodically in big gusts, but in the early hours of the morning it ceased. When Ed looked out through the sleeve of the tent at 4 a.m. the black sky was brilliant with stars and there was no wind. If conditions held, they would have the miracle of a fine, still day. At 6.30 a.m. they were on their way, the ridge in shadow but the mountain above glowing in the early morning sun. With their oxygen sets on 4 L/min., Tenzing took the lead, kicking steps in soft snow or climbing on the protruding strata of the rock. The steep face of soft snow below the South Summit felt dangerously unstable, but like Bourdillon and Evans they accepted the risk.

Hillary and Tenzing climbing on open-circuit oxygen above the South Col.
ALF GREGORY

At 9 a.m. the slope eased off to the comfortable snow mound of
the South Summit. Ahead of them they saw the bewitching, final
snow crest of the summit ridge of Everest. Ed was aware of a feeling
of astonishment that he should be here, so early in the morning, on a
fine windless day, with four-and-a-half hours of oxygen on his back,
and a companion as strong and committed as he was. No one had ever
been so well placed to stand on top of the world. The snow was steep
but looked no harder than on the best of the climbs he'd done in New
Zealand. If the snow was too soft, that might be a problem, and if it
was ice, that would be slow. And the rock step halfway up might be
impossibly difficult. But there was no question of stopping now. After
dropping off one empty oxygen bottle each and reducing the flow rate
to 3 L/min. on the remaining bottles, they moved together to where
the ridge steepened. A blow of the axe and Ed had the answer to his
question about the texture of the snow. It was crisp, indeed perfect. Two
easy scraping blows of the axe and he had a safe and comfortable step.

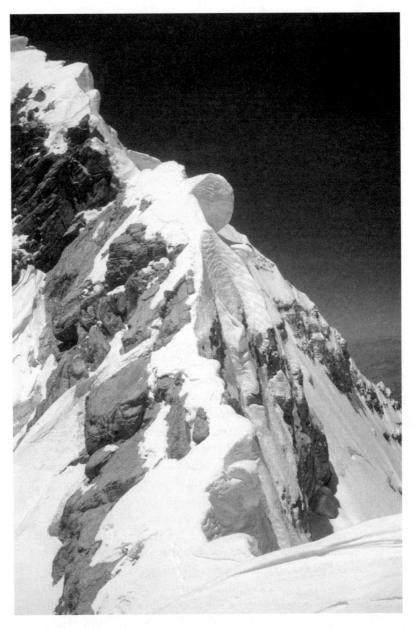

The summit ridge seen from the South Summit. The Hillary Step is three-quarters of the way up this photo. ED HILLARY

From here they moved singly, Ed always in front, cutting step after step, Tenzing protecting him with a solid shaft belay.

After an hour of steady progress they came to the foot of the rock step. Vertical it had looked from a distance, though maybe closer to 70 degrees in reality. Whatever the angle, there was no doubt that it might prove impossible. There was no way of sidling around it on the left, where it was all seriously difficult rock. Nor could they climb on to the equally steep ice-sheathed Kangshung Face on the right. In between the rock and the ice, however, was a more promising lead: a chimney of the right width where one's back and a cramponed foot could be getting a grip on the ice while the other foot and one's hands found holds on the rock. It was similar to ice chimneys they'd climbed in the icefall. Soon, with the flow rate turned up for this gruntingly hard pitch of climbing, Ed was into it, searching for holds, legs pressing up, oxygen set scraping on the ice. A lot of panting and he was up. Then up came Tenzing.

Nothing could stop them now. At 11.30 a.m. there was no more ridge to climb. As Ed would say thousands of times over the next 50 years, 'A few more whacks of the ice-axe, a few very weary steps, and we were on the summit of Everest.' In his 1955 autobiography he wrote:

> My first sensation was one of relief … but mixed with the relief was a vague sense of astonishment that I should have been the lucky one to attain the ambition of so many brave and determined climbers. It seemed difficult at first to grasp that we'd got there … I turned and looked at Tenzing. Even beneath his oxygen mask and the icicles hanging from his hair, I could see his infectious grin of sheer delight. I held out my hand, and in silence we shook in good Anglo-Saxon fashion. But this was not enough for Tenzing, and impulsively he threw his arm around my shoulders and we thumped each other on the back in mutual congratulations.[17]

Ed removed his oxygen without ill-effect, and took the famous photo of Tenzing with ice-axe aloft and the British, Nepali, Indian and United Nations flags flying in the breeze. In the summit snow Tenzing buried some food offerings for the gods who live there. Ed added a white cross given to John Hunt by a Benedictine monk. He went down

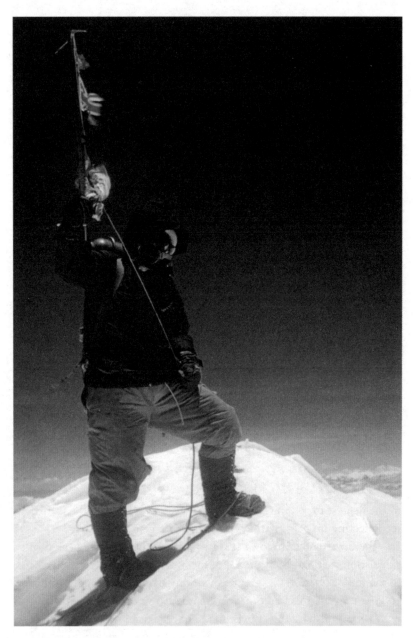

Tenzing on the summit of Everest. ED HILLARY

Hillary and Tenzing back at Advance Base after their first ascent. ALF GREGORY

to the nearest rock and collected nine stones as souvenirs, then, after reconnecting his oxygen, they began their descent.

There were no crises on the way down and none of the near-death exhaustion that had been the lot of most climbers who had been close to the top of Everest. Oxygen was working its magic through to the end. As they approached the Col, George Lowe came to meet them with a thermos flask of soup. Ed had not rehearsed what he would say, but as he felt an upwelling of affection for his friend and for this extraordinary mountain, the right words came: 'Well, George, we knocked the bastard off.'

Wilf Noyce and Pasang Phutar were there too, and they prepared hot drinks for unappeasable thirsts. The wind had got up again. It was a long cold night without oxygen, and next morning the five of them left the South Col without regret. Charles Wylie and some Sherpas were at Camp 7 but still the news had not reached Advance Base where John Hunt and the others were waiting in an agony of suspense. Failure would mean a desperate third attempt by a small weakened group, whereas success would mean, well, success! They could leave this hard mountain behind.

A few hundred feet above Advance Base, Hillary, Tenzing, Lowe and Noyce were met by a panting Tom Stobart carrying his camera. Tom knew that giving the news to Hunt could be a special moment in his film, the one his audience might remember when all else had been forgotten. He gave them his instructions: no indication of success until they were close enough together for Tom to catch the emotion of the moment. 'Please. Nobody give any signal until we are close enough for a picture. Not until I give the word.'[18]

As they came in sight of the camp, people began to come slowly to meet them. Mike Westmacott was in front, John Hunt a little behind him, eager at first but slowing as he looked at the expressionless faces of the returning party. They had failed, surely. Suddenly he looked and felt extremely tired. Quietly Tom was saying, 'Not yet! Wait a bit, get closer.' He recalled:

> Then I let go the rope, brought up the camera. 'Right, George, let it go.' As George gave the thumbs-up everyone stopped for a second, not taking it in, not daring to believe their eyes. Then they began to stumble forward. Flinging arms round the victors' necks, clapping them on the back, everyone talking at once.[19]

How the good news reached London

There was one expedition member whose work was unfinished, and that was James Morris. Everest had become world news, and journalists had converged on Nepal, making stories from what they could glean around hotel bars in Kathmandu. A couple of the braver sort had trekked into Khumbu and even reached Base Camp.

Morris had to get his news to London without interception. He had had a stroke of luck six weeks earlier when he found a radio transmitter in Namche controlled by an Indian called Mr Tiwari – who agreed to transmit the occasional message to the British Embassy. It would be in code, a code with two meanings: the first for the multitude who would intercept it, and the second for Ambassador Summerhayes who would forward the decoded version to *The Times*.

At 2.30 p.m. on 30 May in the Western Cwm, Morris had his scoop of the decade, and he wanted it to reach London as a headline in *The Times* for the coronation of Queen Elizabeth on 2 June. He strapped on the crampons he had worn for the first time less than a month earlier and set off in the direction of the icefall and Base Camp.

'I'll come with you,' said Mike Westmacott. Stumbling down the disintegrating chaos of ice, they reached Base Camp after dark. Morris wrote:

> Before I could sleep, though, I had a job to do. Leaning over in my sleeping-bag with infinite discomfort, for my legs were as stiff as ramrods and patches of sunburn on various parts of my body made movements very painful, I extracted my typewriter from a pile of clothing and propped it on my knees to write a message. This was that brief dispatch of victory I had dreamed about through the months. Oh Mr. Tiwari at Namche and Mr. Summerhayes at Katmandu! Oh you watchful radio men in Whitehall! Oh telephone operators, typists and sub-editors, readers, listeners, statesmen, generals, Presidents, Kings, Queens and Archbishops! I have a message for you!
>
> Now then, let me see. Pull out the crumpled paper code; turn up the flickering hurricane lamp, it's getting dark in here; paper in the typewriter, don't bother with a carbon; prop up your legs with an old kit-bag stuffed with sweaters and socks; choose your words with a dirty broken-nailed finger; and here goes!
>
> Snow conditions bad stop advanced base abandoned yesterday stop awaiting improvement
>
> Which being interpreted would mean:
>
> Summit of Everest reached on May 29 by Hillary and Tenzing.
>
> I checked it for accuracy. Everything was right. I checked it again. Everything was still right. I took it out of the typewriter and began to fold it up to place it in its envelope:

Times *correspondent James Morris.* ALF GREGORY

but as I did so, I thought the words over, and recalled the wonder and delight of the occasion, and remembered that dear old Sherpa who had greeted us with his lantern, an hour or two before, when we had fallen out of the icefall.

All well! I added to the bottom of my message.[20]

The message was carried by runner to Mr Tiwari at Namche on the morning of 1 June. Through the airwaves it went to the British Embassy, then by cable to London. And that is how the message reached the young Queen on the day of her coronation and gave immeasurable delight to the vast crowd gathered to see her.

Who got there first?

There are always revisionists. For Everest 1953, the first came in less than a month. When expedition members entered Kathmandu they were met by a huge crowd shouting, 'Tenzing! Zindabad!' as they held aloft banners on which were painted Tenzing standing on top of Everest while hauling up a supine Ed Hillary from below. Tenzing could sign his name but had never learnt to read or write, and when a chanting crowd surrounded him, and their leaders insisted he sign the document they held, he did so. It said that he, Tenzing, was the first to step on to the summit.

Only three years earlier, a Nepali uprising had overthrown the Rana family which had held the country in feudal subjection for a hundred years, and revolution was still in the air. Much of the impetus had come from the anti-British, anti-imperialist movement in India. Now here they were, the British, at it again, stealing from the indigenous people another of their treasures, the first ascent of their highest mountain. A Nepali had been there too, and surely he, rather than an effete Britisher, must have carved the trail to the summit. Or was he Nepali? He had no passport. He was called Tenzing Bhotia, Tenzing the Tibetan. He'd lived in Darjeeling for the past 12 years and now India was claiming him as one of theirs. Tenzing himself was out of his depth. He could not read a newspaper, or a letter, or even a street sign. He could speak four languages but his English was minimal. In this maelstrom of publicity and conflicting demands, he had no agent to guide him.

One wonders if Tenzing had been approached even before the expedition had set out. There had been the incident when the Sherpas mounted a protest that their accommodation in the Embassy garage was unsatisfactory when the British were in Embassy beds. Maybe, but most ordinary expeditions, including the climbers, would have been grateful for use of the Embassy garage and grounds. It sounded as though there had been some stirring in the background. In the accounts of the expedition as it unfolded, Tenzing comes across as not fully at ease. He showed disappointment when no Sherpa was included in the Bourdillon–Evans first assault. He'd been essential to the management of Sherpas and porters, but on the final climb he'd played second to Hillary's lead. Partly this was because Hillary was more used to cutting steps, but more important was the fact that they were almost wholly dependent on their oxygen equipment and Ed was the one who knew how to calculate flow rates and fix faults. It was the language problem again. Those who could describe how to use oxygen spoke only English. On the climb itself, communication was rudimentary: a few words of English from Tenzing, a very few words of Hindi from Ed.

When Ed agreed to a request from the Sherpas of Khumjung in 1961 that he build them a school where they would learn to read and write, he was correcting a crippling inequality in their lives.

As to who got there first – the question that would be put to Ed repeatedly for the rest of his life – it was answered by Tenzing in 1955. In his autobiography, ghost-written by American writer James Ramsey Ullman, Tenzing gave an unequivocal description of the last few feet:

> A little below the summit Hillary and I stopped. We looked up. Then we went on. The rope that joined us was thirty feet long, but I held most of it in loops in my hand, so that there was only about six feet between us. I was not thinking of 'first' and 'second.' I did not say to myself, 'There is a golden apple up there. I will push Hillary aside and run for it.' We went on slowly, steadily. And then we were there. Hillary stepped on top first. And I stepped up after him …
>
> Now the truth is told. And I am ready to be judged by it.[21]

The man who made it possible

The other revisionist proposition was that Griffith Pugh was the individual who made the 1953 expedition successful. This suggestion came from Mike Ward, who had already earned a special place in the history of Everest through his launch of the 1951 reconnaissance. Without him the British might well have missed out on their 1953 place. He has his own claim to be 'the man who made it possible'.

He was still important in mid-1952 when the 1953 expedition was taking shape. The 1951 team of Shipton, Ward, Bourdillon and Hillary, with Charles Evans added, were the core group for 1953. But then Shipton was eased out and replaced by an outsider, Colonel John Hunt, whose first task was to select the expedition personnel. Ward wrote of his meeting with Hunt: 'My first impression was of some disturbing quality that I sensed but could not define. Later I understood this to be the intense emotional background to his character …'[22]

Other expedition members initially expressed similar reservations about being led by a soldier who might simply bark orders from a command tent, but when they met him they found qualities of leadership, warmth and empathy that allowed the whole party to regard him with admiration and affection.

The whole party, that is, except Mike Ward who had been more displaced than most. He had wanted to be a full member of the climbing team and potentially someone who might get to the top. Hunt's decision to have a doctor who kept in good health by not pushing himself hard as a climber was a reasonable one, but not what Mike wanted. In the event, he was called into his role as reserve climber when the attack on the Lhotse Face was faltering, but he was not well enough acclimatised to be strong at 24,000ft. Later experience on Makalu in 1961 would show that this was around Mike's altitude ceiling. He happened to be one of those people who for individual physiological reasons do not acclimatise easily. But this was not clear in 1953, and at the important meeting on 7 May when Hunt announced that as leader he would go to the South Col in support, Ward gave his medical opinion that he was not strong enough. But Hunt carried his load and part of a Sherpa's to 27,300ft, and three days later the expedition achieved their goal. Two members reached the summit. The leader had got it right.

In 1951 Ward had begun reading about the physiological problems of Everest as well as its Nepali approaches. Through this he met Griff Pugh at the Division of Human Physiology of the Medical Research Council. When Pugh returned from Cho Oyu in June 1952, preparations for 1953, in particular the development of oxygen apparatus, were already well under way. When Hunt took over planning in October, he consulted widely, including with Pugh who had returned from the Himalayas with useful observations on oxygen, clothing, boots, fluid intake, food and hygiene. But there were also many others back in England who recognised that oxygen was the stuff that would make the climb possible.

In the book of the expedition Hunt wrote:

> Among the numerous items in our inventory, I would single out oxygen for special mention. Many of our material aids were of great importance; only this in my opinion, was vital to success. In this department perhaps more than in any other, those who worked to satisfy our requirements had the hardest task of all, for time was so short. But for oxygen, without the much-improved equipment which we were given, we should certainly not have got to the top.[23]

One might have hoped that everyone would live happily ever after, but Ward was troubled by the thought that the scientist Griff Pugh, and by association his companion Mike Ward, had received less than the recognition due to them. He pointed this out at the twentieth Everest anniversary in 1973, and noted in particular the physiological work on Cho Oyu that had led to success: 'Their results were of unprecedented value, [as] for the first time the problems posed by high altitude were defined in the field. This was the decisive advantage that we in 1953 were to have over all who had gone before us.'[24]

Ward's work did not go unrecognised, and in 1983 he was awarded a CBE. The next big anniversary was the fortieth in 1993, when the Queen attended a lecture presentation. Slides were shown as expedition members praised each other's achievements as being essential to the expedition's success. But then the unexpected happened. Mike Ward, who had a flair for drama, stood up and said he disagreed. There had been other expeditions on Everest with a good leader but they had failed. There had been other strong climbers but they too had failed. Success in 1953 was due to the work of one person, the unsung hero of Everest – Dr Griffith Pugh.[25]

There might have been a shrugging of shoulders – there goes old Mike again – but for one member of the audience, this strongly expressed opinion opened a door she had not known was there. This was Pugh's 46-year-old daughter, Harriet Tuckey. Griff had been a distant and awkward father, as she describes with disconcerting honesty in the biography she published 20 years later. She called it *Everest, The First Ascent: The Untold Story of Griffith Pugh, The Man Who Made it Possible*. It is a moving account of a daughter's discovery of her father. Mike Ward told her 'how Pugh had designed the all-important oxygen and fluid-intake regimes, the acclimatization programme, the diet, the high-altitude boots, the tents, the down clothing, the mountain stoves, the airbeds'.[26] Yet Hunt, in *The Ascent of Everest*, written within a mere month of arriving back from the expedition, had bestowed his acknowledgments much more widely. Tom Bourdillon wrote Appendix V on oxygen equipment. His last paragraph noted: 'A very large number of people and organisations contributed to the development and production apparatus for this expedition', and Appendix IX listed 19 suppliers and developers. The 10-page Appendix VII on physiology and medicine was written by Pugh and Ward, and Appendix VI on diet

Hunt and Pugh conducting oxygen concentration tests. ROYAL GEOGRAPHICAL SOCIETY

by Pugh and Band. H.W. Tilman commented unsympathetically in a review that he had found all the appendices very interesting except for the two 'irksome' articles by Pugh which were notable only for their 'questionable assumptions, platitudes and complacency'.[27] There they were, at it again, a mountaineer – admittedly a famously anti-science mountaineer – belittling scientists!

On his return from Cho Oyu, Pugh wrote a report for the Medical Research Council. Ward described it as 'this seminal report'. It was, he wrote, 'one of the most important in the history of scientific, high-altitude exploration. It formed the medical and scientific basis for the 1953 expedition and determined its "shape"... a scientific approach to the problems posed by the last 1000 feet, was fundamental to our success.'[28]

But here was another puzzle: it was never published. It 'had a very restricted circulation. All this scientific work was really separate from the mountaineers – and a good thing too!' wrote Ward.[29] Why restricted? Why not published? Publication is the currency in which scientists receive their recognition.

I began a search for this rare document. Requests went unacknowledged until at length I found that the original was in the Mandeville Special Collection of the University of California, San Diego, into which the papers of Griffith Pugh had been placed by Professor John West. A modest fee of $58 and I had my copy of the 1952 report.[30]

To say that it was an anticlimax is an understatement. I read it, turned it over, went back to the beginning – where was the content that made this 'seminal' report 'one of the most important in the history of scientific, high-altitude exploration'?

In the Discussion section of his report, Pugh talks only of the last thousand feet on Everest from a high camp at 27,600ft. 'Use oxygen at a flow rate of 4 L/min,' he advised. The big questions were not answered, or even asked:

- At what height should the climbers start using oxygen?
- Should they use sleeping oxygen, and if so from what height?
- Should flow rates other than 4 L/min. be made available?
- Should Sherpas use oxygen as well as Europeans?

The main reason for earlier failures on Everest was that pre-war climbers hadn't used oxygen at all. The most important decision for 1953 had already been made before Cho Oyu: that the expedition would use oxygen in whatever way might be necessary to place a climber on top of Everest. Discussion on when the oxygen would be used, by whom, how much, and whether open or closed circuit, would intensively occupy various engineers, scientists, technical designers and climbers back in England. Griff Pugh would be a significant contributor but was only one among others. During the expedition, logistics were all-important. One-and-a-quarter tons of oxygen had to be moved to nine camps. Of the weight carried to high Camps 8 and 9, 63 per cent was oxygen.

Can any single person be called 'the man who made it possible'? John Hunt used to emphasise that the climbing of Everest had been a team effort, and that the 'team' included the expeditions from the 1920s and '30s, as well as the Swiss in 1952. Was Hillary the man who made it possible? Probably not. Had the siren song of the closed-circuit apparatus been ignored and the whole effort gone into the open circuit,

219

Tom Bourdillon – and others – would have been strong contenders for a summit position. What about Tenzing? He led the Sherpas on the mountain, inspired the all-important carry of 13 loads to the South Col, and had the skill and stamina to reach the summit.

But if I were pressed into the invidious position of naming a single person as 'the man who made it possible', I cannot see how it could be anyone except John Hunt.

Everest after '53

The decade of the 1950s saw an expensive international race to climb the world's highest mountains, with first ascents of the 11 highest of the 14 peaks above the magic height of 26,000ft. The climb of Everest had broken through a psychological ceiling, but the invasion of the Himalayas would have happened anyway in the post-war world where people were looking for more acceptable forms of excitement. Oxygen, with its attendant high costs and many porters, was used in the first ascent of all five peaks above 27,000ft, but often not on those below. Equipment and techniques improved dramatically. Plastic, vapour-barrier boots, all-weather clothing and new bivouac equipment allowed climbers to survive nights out at high altitude that would have led to death or severe frostbite in the 1920s. Climbers advanced up steep rock or ice walls by fixing a line of ropes up which they jumared to where they had left off the day before.

A new breed of climber emerged, hardened and acclimatised to high altitude by experience accumulated year upon year in the Himalayas. They climbed the big faces and ridges of Everest and all the highest peaks. They made winter ascents for the first time, sometimes solo. They learned how to recognise and work at the boundary between acclimatisation and deterioration. They came from all parts of the world in pairs or small groups who shared resources and worked together from time to time. Where oxygen was used, it was usually only for the final push to the summit of a very high mountain. They had a fearsome mortality rate, but achieved feats of climbing that were regarded as impossible in the 1950s.

After 1990 came the development of commercial, guided expeditions which gave anyone the opportunity to reach the top of Everest. You have to be fit, masochistic, have an alpha-type personality, and be prepared to pay around $70,000, but serious climbing experience is not a prerequisite. The general scheme is that you settle into Base Camp where you acclimatise to 17,000ft before setting out on at least two training climbs up the icefall and Western Cwm, partly for acclimatisation, and partly to allow the guides to assess your strength, acclimatisation and skills to get to the summit without endangering either yourself or your minders. If you fail to convince, your expedition is over. But if you pass the assessment, you join several hundred others waiting at Base Camp for forecasters in the US, UK or elsewhere to announce the dates of a window of fine weather. Meanwhile teams of Sherpas have opened the route, fixed ropes up much of its length, and established camps equipped with tents, food, fuel and oxygen. They also have teams of porters clearing rubbish to out-of-the-way sites amongst the moraine debris lower down.

With the confirmation of the date of arrival of the good weather, there is a mass exodus up the mountain. From the Lhotse Face to the summit, open-circuit oxygen is used at flow rates varying between 2 and 4 L/min. The summit climb starts at midnight from the South Col. In a vintage year, over 600 people have climbed the mountain. In bad years, there are accidents such as the avalanche from the overhanging ice on the south-west face that killed 16 Sherpas in 2014, or the earthquake-triggered ice avalanche that killed 19 in 2015 and injured nearly 100.

There are many who deplore these commercial ventures, but it's not easy to frame acceptable rules. Guides have always been part of mountaineering. The Nepali government likes the income generated by expeditions. Sherpas want the work because they earn enough in three months to support themselves and their families for the rest of the year. Insisting on measurable skills in climbers is fraught with problems. A host of armchair mountaineers around the world enjoy the gladiatorial aspects of the sport. Let battle commence.

Ed and George in London where they adopt local dress. HILLARY MUSEUM COLLECTION

CHAPTER 16

'The most sensible action
I've ever taken'

⟫⟩◆⟨⟪

At dawn on 2 June 1953, the one million people lining the
streets of London to see the Coronation procession heard
that the British had climbed Everest. Back in a much quieter
Auckland, a young reporter, Pat Booth, was telling Percy and Gertrude
Hillary at 730 Remuera Road that it was their son and Tenzing Norgay
who had made the historic ascent.

Coming to the door, Gertrude expressed first astonishment, then
absolute delight. She called up the stairs, 'Perce, come quickly. Edmund
is at the top!'

Percy came down but showed less excitement. 'Edmund is a good
man under pressure,' he said. 'He always carries his weight.'

Would Edmund, Booth asked, find it hard to come back after all
that had happened?

Percy shook his head. 'He's a very hard worker with the bees. I'm
sure he'll be glad to get back to it.'[1]

The more effusive public announcement by Acting Prime Minister
Keith Holyoake neatly set New Zealand in its place in respect of the
Mother Country:

> I am able to announce that a newsflash has just come through
> advising us that the New Zealander, Hillary, has succeeded
> in conquering Mount Everest ... If this news is correct, and

I'm absolutely assured it is, then our New Zealander Hillary has climbed to the top of the world. He has put the British race and New Zealand on top of the world. And what a magnificent coronation present for the Queen. How proud we all are that this is from our loyal little New Zealand.[2]

One of the earliest personal letters of congratulation came from Eric Shipton, who may have been sidelined for the leadership but knew it was his intuitive acceptance of two New Zealand climbers in 1951 that had secured for Ed Hillary a place in 1953:

> My dear Ed, What a wonderful climax to the Everest story. The London newspapers started ringing me at about midnight on Monday and continued most of the night. I was absolutely thrilled when I found it was you who got there first, though I knew it would be you if anyone. You most certainly deserve it and I could not be more delighted. Now you will just have to come to England to tell us all about it and I shall expect an early visit from you. I spend most of my time just now in a day-dream picturing you and Tensing making your way along that last narrow ridge (droning 'Home on the Range' as you went) and then the colossal moment of getting there – it makes my heart thump just thinking about it. I had a wire … from Longstaff saying 'How right you were to back N.Z.' … We are all so delighted that Tensing was there with you, representing the Sherpas – no-one could have wished for a better combination … Again with my delighted and heart-felt congratulations on a really superb effort.
> Ever yours, Eric.[3]

Another consequence of Ed's achievement was a KBE, bestowed by the Queen on 6 June and accepted by the New Zealand prime minister on his behalf. The first Ed heard of it was a letter addressed to 'Sir Edmund Hillary, KBE' while on the trail halfway back to Kathmandu. 'My God!' he said. 'I'll have to get a new pair of overalls.'[4]

It was the sort of mock-heroic response that became a Hillary trademark, but he came to like his knighthood and he was impressed by the occasion on which it was bestowed:

Our most important invitation was to a Buckingham Palace garden party. Dressed in unfamiliar morning suit with long tails and top hat, the expedition members mixed with hundreds of dignitaries as though to the manner born – well, almost! At the conclusion of the garden party we were conducted deep inside the palace to quite a small but very pleasantly decorated room. There we waited rather nervously until an official entered and announced in stentorian tones, 'Her Majesty the Queen.' The Queen came in, followed by most of the royal family, and we were all greeted in a very relaxed fashion. The Queen was tiny and charming and behaved just as we expected a Queen to do in those days. Then for me came the most important moment. A small stool was placed in front of the Queen, I knelt on it, a short bejeweled sword was put in her hand, she touched me lightly on each shoulder and said, 'Arise, Sir Edmund.' ... It was quite a change from early days as a bee farmer in New Zealand.[5]

Louise Rose

Ed was now famous – and an eligible bachelor. In August he flew back to New Zealand, but made an unexplained three-day stopover in Sydney where the press caught rumour of a romance, though without tracking it to its source. On 8 August he and George Lowe received an ecstatic reception when they arrived back in Auckland. They also found that the news of a romance had crossed the Tasman: 'Sir Edmund, in a Press interview, said a cabled reference to his "girlfriend" had been in error. It was a misunderstanding. He had no "girlfriend" though he had three direct mail invitations from young women to "name the date".'[6] A week after this denial, however, came the announcement that Sir Edmund Hillary would be marrying Louise Mary Rose at the chapel of the Diocesan School for Girls on 3 September, only a fortnight away.

Louise Rose was the 22-year-old daughter of an Auckland lawyer, Jim Rose, also president of the New Zealand Alpine Club. More to the point, he was chairman of the Auckland section of the club in whose small firmament Ed had been a shining star even before the Everest reconnaissance of 1951. During the late 1940s Ed would visit Jim in his comfortable house at 278 Remuera Road, with its spacious view

Phyllis Rose née Joske and Jim Rose. HILLARY FAMILY COLLECTION

of harbour, hills and islands, and talk about his climbs and news from down south.

Jim Rose was one of the many great-grandchildren of Archibald Rose, a founding father of the fledgling city of Auckland. Archibald emigrated from Scotland in 1849 and started a drapery business, both importing and exporting, which eventually employed 500 people. He was active in public affairs as the first mayor of Auckland in 1851, and between 1860 and 1874 was intermittently a Member of Parliament. He married three times and had nine children. Jim Rose studied law and had a brief first marriage before, on a passage to Australia, he met and fell in love with Phyllis Joske whose large Jewish family lived in Melbourne. In their long and successful marriage they had two daughters, the second of whom was Louise Mary Rose, born on 3 September 1930. Her writing at the age of six gives glimpses of the style she will use 30 years later in her books:

> Hulloe Daddy, I hope you are very much better. Mummy has been very kind to me, she bought me a string for the violin and some stuff called Roslyn it is like a piece of kari gum you just

rub it on. The violin makes a lovely sound, nice and loud and squealy, it is a great success, I think I can play it quite well.

With love from Weasle

Good-bye

She ends with a pencil sketch of herself in a new frock.[7]

Louise had a gift for music. She started on the violin but at some time a tutor suggested her forthright approach might be more suited to the viola. By the time she entered Auckland University's School of Music, the viola was her preferred instrument and the one she played in local orchestras and taught to pupils. She also played the piano and sang in the university's madrigal group.

An acquaintance of those years, Graeme Gummer, son of the architect who built the Hillary house in 1955, remembered social occasions at the Roses' house:

> The Rose home was like a mansion really, with a lawn tennis court of fine English grasses. Phyl Rose was a good organizer. Louise's presence at these functions was always rewarding.

Louise Rose, age c.21. HILLARY FAMILY COLLECTION

She was neither shy nor forward but accepted each person for themselves. Her straightforward common sense and pleasant nature put everyone at their ease.[8]

If music was one thread in Louise's life, the outdoors was the other. In the Ruapehu Club hut book for 4 January 1940 appears the entry: 'Louise Rose 9 years old. Got within 75ft of top of highest peak, and then went down Gliding Gladys.' At university, Louise joined the tramping club as Ed had 12 years earlier. Weekends were often spent in the Waitakere Ranges. The Roses also had a bach on the lip of a line of cliffs between Piha and Anawhata, another favourite haunt.

On long weekends, the destination might be Mt Ruapehu. There was snow and rock climbing on the ring of peaks around the crater, a dip in the hot crater lake for the risk-takers, and skiing on the glaciers in winter. Transport to Ruapehu was variously by train, bus, car or truck. Graeme Gummer remembered travelling in the train by night, singing tramping songs and chatting. If the moon was full they looked out on 'a somber landscape of farms being broken in from the forest with burnt-out stumps, steep hillsides and bush. Many of the train stops were at timber-milling communities with drying kilns spouting steam, smoke and wood smells … Louise was always a natural leader. She got us going seemingly without any effort on her part.'[9]

In 1951 Ed Hillary and George Lowe make their appearance in Louise's diary, competing, from a distance, for her attention. In December 1951, the Garhwal climbers gave a talk on their expedition. Ed and Earle Riddiford, who had been christened 'The Tigers', had just arrived back from the Everest Reconnaissance on the *Wanganella*. Louise's account of the occasion gives a glimpse into the social customs of the early 1950s:

> Well, we went over to the Odells and I found to my relief that I was dressed properly. We all had an Uncle Jack which is a rather strong type of sherry made by Hetti Harre's uncle. Ed was taking a girl he met on the Wanganella. We went roaming to the Gummers with my feet in a box of bottles. We all got well stoked up and at about 8.30 went to the Road House. We had the most marvellous dinner and the six of us had a lot of fun. George and Ed talked Hindustani and

clapped their hands for waiters. They also said they would take me climbing and mentioned a traverse of Tasman. We got home at 2am. Going down our steps George slipped and I stopped him so now I can say I held George Lowe when he fell on a rock climb.

The boys gave us a terrifically interesting talk at Alpine Club section meeting held in our house with 55 people there. The two Ed's and George evidently got on very well together – Earle was the worker. The poor Odells have got George for an unknown period. He's a bit of a devilish fellow.[10]

In 1952 after the Cho Oyu expedition Ed, Louise and George travelled down to Ruapehu for skiing. Louise continued her diary:

All Sunday was spent doing orchestra but thinking about going skiing. Ed arrived at 11.30pm in his Austrian trousers and Everest down jacket with a devilish twinkle in his eye. Everyone muddled round in the dark packing the truck. We got to Taumarunui about 6.30 am in dense fog and got hot pies. From there until National Park the road was terribly twisty and bumpy but when the fog lifted there were wonderful views.

We got out of the truck and were just getting our belongings together when Pa came bouncing down the mountain looking marvellous and his eyes were twinkling. It was hot so I took off my woollen shirt much to the surprise of some garrulous schoolboys who were convinced I would have only a singlet or less underneath. People were asking us when Ed Hillary was coming, so we said he was just behind and we were the Sherpas. After we'd reached the upper hut George arrived in high spirits and Ed had all the boys out step-cutting which pleased them immensely.

Soon after that I went out on my skis and found that I was completely hopeless. Ed then took George and me in hand and led us down the ski tow run. I soon got left behind but learnt a lot in spite of that. When I got in, dinner was being prepared and I made fruit salad and jelly and then George found the AUC song book and we started singing right on through dinner until bedtime. George is very good at leading singing. I played the ukulele.

Next morning we made breakfast using the private Hillary coffee. George took Aileen and me step-cutting. Then he did a great big glissade and got out of control for a while and hurt his hands but the tourists were thrilled. I had just finished eating an orange at about 2 o'clock when I was told that Ed had dislocated his knee. Poor Ed, I think it hurt him a lot and he just got into his bag. He lent me his down jacket, they are the most marvellous things.

Next morning no one budged – everyone was waiting for someone else to get the breakfast.

Aileen and I started on Ed's leg which was very stiff and painful. We gave it baths in hot water and then snow-cold water. Poor fellow, he nearly hit the roof. He's very calm to have put up with what we did.

She finished on a wistful note thinking about her future: 'I only wish I knew what I wanted to do with my music. These good solid mountaineers are so much more fun and better friends than musicians …'[11]

Ed starts a campaign

By the beginning of 1953, there was a greater sense of purpose in the lives of Louise Rose and Ed Hillary, at least in the short term. Louise had won a scholarship to the Sydney Conservatorium of Music to continue her study of the viola, while Ed had his position as a leading climber on the Everest expedition. This gave him a new confidence and he was writing letters that he hoped would be persuasive. He called it his 'campaign'.

31 January

My Dear Louise,   I suppose you are well out on the Tasman with a calm sea and a bright moon. I wish I were there too! … You know Whizz, this early departure of yours is really most unsatisfactory. I'm just about the most backward wolf that ever lived but I'd really summoned up my courage and planned a strong attack on your depressingly formidable defenses and then you have to pack your bags and depart. My only chance now is on my passage through Sydney … I've

Louise was a gifted musician, winning a viola scholarship to the Sydney Conservatorium of Music. HILLARY FAMILY COLLECTION

finalised my booking. I'll cross to Sydney on Saturday Feb 28th and then leave on Monday night for Calcutta. I hope you will spare me some time, Whizz, as the thought that I won't be seeing you again for about five months doesn't appeal to me very much ...

Look after yourself, Whizz, drop me a line if you can find time. Love from, Ed.

18 February

My Dear Louise,   It's not long now before I step aboard the plane. I've been invited to stay with friends but that would be too restricting so I've booked in at the Wentworth Hotel which is meant to be frightfully posh and expensive. I've made no arrangements at all so am free until I leave on Monday.

What are you going to do Whizz? I can just see you shaking your head and saying, 'Well, I have ten minutes to spare on Saturday afternoon but I'm frightfully busy on Sunday, and I strum the old viola on Monday mornings, so what about a cup of tea on Monday afternoon?' What a depressing thought! I think it would be a jolly good idea if you came and had dinner with me at the Wentworth on Saturday night and we went to a show afterwards ...

The other night I did a bit of work on my new book 'Battle against Boredom.' Have I told you that I'm trying to write a book? Eric Shipton gave some encouragement ... Imagine it – me trying to be an author! For some people I know it would be the joke of the season ...

This is a frightful lot of bilge Whizz, but summed up it means that I'm hoping I'll see a lot of you, that I have no engagements and if you would like to do anything at all from symphony concerts to Luna Park I'll be very happy if you arrange it. I'm looking forward to hearing all your experiences and seeing you again ... love from, Ed.

22 February

My Dear Louise, I was very pleased to hear that you'll be down to meet me at Rose Bay on Saturday. I don't know whether I'll have the usual band of reporters ...

I was interested to hear of Fleur's efforts with you in the

cause of Christian Science ... I used to be pretty interested in a lot of so-called 'advanced' religions such as Theosophy and Anthroposophy ... I even used to give lectures at one organisation and I conducted a radio session over 1ZB every Sunday morning ... I still sometimes think about these things and harbour the hope that life has a real meaning and that all our trivial efforts and aspirations are not entirely wasted. It's a depressing thought that we are born, live and die all for nothing and I still prefer to think there's some reason behind it all ...

Love from, Ed.

PS. My one extravagance this year has been a new dinner suit – tailor made at 30 guineas – and it really looks extremely smart I must say ...[12]

A short paragraph in Ed's 1999 autobiography describes his weekend in Sydney with Louise on his way to Everest 1953:

I spent two days with Louise and they were possibly the two happiest days of my life. We sat on the grass in the Sydney domain and listened with great pleasure to outdoor musical concerts. We walked hand in hand across the Sydney Harbour Bridge and halfway across I kissed Louise for the first time ... by the end of those two days we had developed an understanding that we would see a good deal more of each other in future.[13]

There is greater intimacy in the letters that follow the Sydney visit, a belief that Louise will accept him. Getting to the top of Everest, has become part of his courtship of Louise Rose.

2 March

Well Whizz, I'd been really looking forward to my few days in Sydney but I never really thought I'd have so much fun. Everything went perfectly, right from the time I landed at Rose Bay. I really arrived all set to conduct some sort of campaign, not that I had much idea what a campaign of that nature demanded. But from the start everything seemed to flow along as we'd drift from one thing to the next. I really enjoyed myself enormously and you really are a darling Whizz. I'm going to be looking forward to my return the whole time I'm away so don't you go and forget all about me in the interim. I'd hate to have to come back and beat half a dozen musicians over the head with my ice axe … It's now about an hour out so I expect you're home in bed and fast asleep but the plane is just settling down to the usual routine. Everybody has removed their coats and ties and I've already had a glass of orange from the steward. Look after yourself – I really am terribly fond of you. Love from, Ed[14]

3 March
Hello Whizz Darling, Here I am parked in a luxurious room in the famous Raffles Hotel and all I can do is feel lonely and think of you … At least there's the consolation that once I get on the job the time should pass quickly and it won't be long before I'll be back in Sydney … I wonder what my chances are? … You know, Whizz, human nature is a funny thing. Here I am on a trip that I suppose any NZ climber would be most keen to go on and I spend all my time thinking of something quite different – in fact you! Mind you I'm determined to do well on this trip because my ambition has always been to get really high and also I know that if I can be really successful I might be able to do reasonably well with my book …
    All my love. Ed.[15]

4 March
Hello Darling, When I come back to Sydney I won't stay in a hotel as it is really a waste of money seeing I don't expect to stay inside much. I'll try and get a bed and breakfast place in the Cross and save my money for more important things.
    One of my pleasantest memories is sitting in your comfortable chair watching you practice. You really did look sweet Whizz, you have such graceful and attractive arms. I wished I'd arrived half an hour earlier and had the full session.
    Do write to me as often as you can, Whizz, as your letters will be the things I most look forward to on this trip. Look after yourself. All my love, Ed[16]

234

In a revealing letter of 8 March, Louise responds to Ed's declaration of his 'campaign'.

> Dear Ed, Heaven knows when you'll get this letter or where you'll be or how uncivilised you'll look. Anyhow I suppose you know all the new climbers by now and are really getting going and have your mind on the great task ahead without me getting in the way.
>
> You really don't need to worry about me you know and the long range campaign, as you actually won the campaign quite a long while ago …
>
> Tons of love from, Louise.[17]

Ed responded quickly:

> 21 March
> It was a terrific thrill yesterday to get two letters from you … John Hunt noticed my enthusiasm on receiving your letters and asked me if they were from someone I was keen on and I replied 'Too right!' … Love from Ed.[18]

> 19 April
> My darling Louise, The morning was still windy with light drifting snow but we set off in an endeavour to get to the top of the icefall. The ice above us was fantastic. Great crumbling seracs surrounded by piles of fallen ice. We were pretty scared most of the time but after a lot of false leads we finally reached the last line of ice-cliffs. There was no easy route but I managed to give my well known impersonation of Harry Ayres, cut up the lower section and then wedged myself into a narrow crack in the ice and wriggled and jammed my way up to the top. It was quite a moment as we are now at the entrance to the Cwm.
>
> Well Louise dear, it's getting jolly cold here so I think I'll crawl into my bag. It doesn't matter where I am, I always think of you before I go to sleep. You're sometimes mixed up in a confused jumble of seracs, crevasses and primuses but you're always there. I find it rather comforting … This Everest climbing is a strange sort of business – half the time you're

excited and half the time scared. Perhaps it's a little like being in love – but then I always have been a bit of a coward in a way. But I do seem to get over it with you.

All my love, Ed.[19]

Louise wrote again on 26 April:

My dear Ed, I got a letter from you two days ago, it was a beauty, with lots in it, so now I know a little more about what you are doing ... By the time you get this you should be starting on the main objective ... I've been staying with Aunt Enid who lives in a cottage in the bush 30 miles outside Melbourne and it was heavenly. She is a marvellous woman, very like Ma, and also terribly kind. It's so different from NZ with lovely gum smells and all the birds making a terrific noise. It was such a change being out in the open and out in the fresh air. We picked blackberries, gardened and I went each day across the paddocks to get the milk where there was a boisterous young bull calf that would dance all round me. One of the local ladies showed me a dead tiger snake and I had a bath with a Tarantula spider ...

Tons of love and lots of luck, Louise.[20]

A week after the climb Ed wrote a subdued letter from Tengboche which has a clear view of the last 2000 feet of Everest:

My dear Louise ... From where I'm writing this letter we can see Everest ... the position of our high camp, the long steep ridge running to the South Summit and all the details of the summit ridge ... it looks a long way up and at the moment I have no desire to go back again.

... The public interest has been colossal. We've had telegrams from The Queen, the Duke of Edinburgh, Winston Churchill.

I'm still far from back to my old vigour and strength. I'm exceedingly thin and rather lethargic. Actually I was going like a bomb the whole time I was high up and didn't think I was deteriorating. But on my return to Advanced Base I found myself a bit weak and the trip down the icefall was plain hell for all of us …

Well Whizz, goodness knows what will be happening now – there is talk of royal receptions and lecture tours. I don't expect it will take long for things to get back to normal and I'll be seeing you then. I'm certainly looking forward to that …[21]

A proposal of marriage in Sydney

Celebrations and lectures in England took up all of July, but in August Ed returned to New Zealand for a month before setting off on a six-month lecture tour of the UK, Europe and America. He had unfinished business in Sydney before crossing the Tasman to Auckland.

Ed is reticent about Louise in his autobiographies. In *High Adventure*, written two years after Everest, she receives no mention, not even in the Acknowledgments. In the 1975 autobiography, his first mention of Louise is when he spends three days with her in Sydney on his way home to Auckland.

> I made one stop … to see a young musician … I had been enamoured of Louise for some time, even though I was eleven years older. I asked her to marry me and go to England for the lecture tour I had agreed to undertake. Somewhat in a daze she consented and I was overjoyed – it certainly proved the most sensible action I have ever taken.[22]

In the 1999 autobiography, he describes briefly her acceptance of his proposal but reveals how worried he was about how this would fit in with his lecture tour and her music studies:

> We had sufficient time together to confirm to each other that we'd like to get married some time. But what about her music? And what about my forthcoming lecture trip around the world? We were a little too dazed to come to any sensible decisions on that.[23]

A day after her acceptance, he admits to Louise in a letter that he is nervous about telling her parents that she has agreed to marry him:

My dear, darling Louise,   You've no idea how much I
regretted leaving Sydney on Saturday morning. Really I do
feel frightfully lonely here in Auckland despite all the plaudits
of the locals. It was great to see your parents again. Tonight
I'm going to screw up my courage and tell them about you
and me! Whew! It's going to be tough. I'll let you know their
reaction but I'm terrified, I can tell you. Well darling, I must
stop now. I wish we could get away quietly somewhere for we
really haven't had much chance to be alone have we?
    All my love darling, Ed[24]

He needn't have worried. The interview was managed by Louise's
mother Phyl, a woman of great warmth and blunt good sense. She not
only approved of the marriage but launched into plans for the wedding:
'Why don't you get Louise across from Sydney, marry her, then both
of you go off on this world lecture tour together ... Would you like me
to ring her?'[25] Ed continues in the same paragraph with the puzzling
statement, 'So my future mother-in-law proposed over the phone on
my behalf,' though the evidence is clear that Ed had proposed and been
accepted in Sydney.[26]

Three weeks later, on 3 September, Louise's twenty-third birthday,
they were married in Diocesan school chapel. Alpine Club members
held ice-axes to form an arch for the bridal couple. The Best Man was
– who else? – George Lowe. A week after that, still accompanied by
George, they were flying off for their lecture tour of Britain, Europe
and the USA.

Louise writes long, unstructured letters to the Rose and Hillary
parents about this extraordinary new life she's been plunged into.
She loves being the wife of Sir Ed, the amazing mixture of people
she meets, the red carpets that are laid out, the adventures, the travel,
the good food, the variety. She's positive about the people she meets:
they're clever, brilliant, heavenly, and gorgeous. She's seldom critical,
showing only the occasional patch of irony. She's matter-of-fact about
herself, neither humble nor vain. Ed, for his part, loves and admires
his new wife whom he describes variously as radiant, bubbly, warm,
cheerful, friendly, charming, calm and full of common-sense.

Every day is hectic, every evening a social occasion, every meal a
banquet. Louise notes after meeting Queen Ingrid of Denmark, 'My

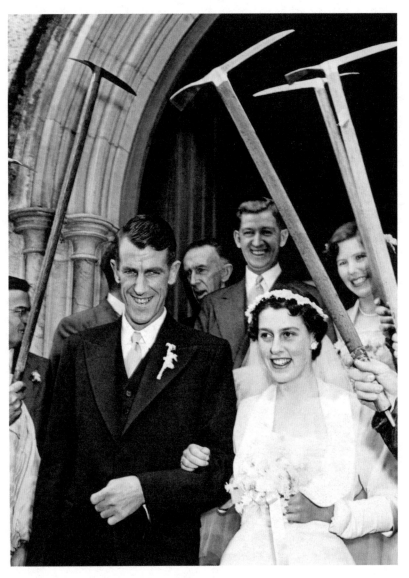

The Hillary-Rose wedding on 3 September 1953. In the background are Percy Hillary and George Lowe. HILLARY MUSEUM COLLECTION

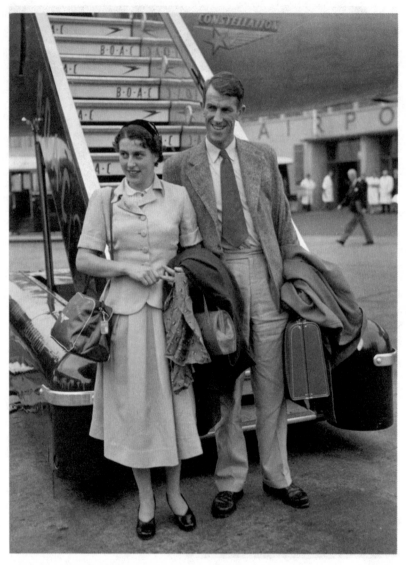

Louise and Ed set off on their combined honeymoon and lecture tour in 1953.
HILLARY FAMILY COLLECTION

fourth Crowned Head'; she was followed shortly afterwards by King Haaken of Norway:

> We were rather scared as he is such a terrific man but after a nerve-wracking 10 minutes wait we went into his amazingly untidy, cluttered-up, old study & sat down with him. He is very long & thin & grins & laughs heartily & enjoys life immensely. He was amazingly interested & we stayed 40 minutes. His false teeth click all the time & he is so energetic that we were wrecks at the end of it.'[27]

Louise warmed to Norway whose population, at 3 million, was not much bigger than New Zealand's. 'When we left about 20 of our new friends were at the airport … the country and the people are after our own hearts.'

They met the most important Crowned Head of all, Queen Elizabeth II, at the premiere of the Everest film at the Warner Theatre in London. Crowds lining the street outside 'cheered and yelled' when they saw Ed and Louise arrive. In the theatre they sat in the same row, only two seats away, from the royal couple. 'She is just so beautiful you feel that no one in the whole world could look so lovely.'

The party continued to the United States, enjoying their new affluence. Lecturing, they discovered, paid better than beekeeping. It was, said George Lowe, the 'only time in my life I had ever earned fairly big money'.[28] When John Hunt's *The Ascent of Everest* was released only three months after the end of the expedition, Ed's chapter was well reviewed, leading to a contract and advance for the book which would be his personal story. He called it *High Adventure*. When published in 1955, it would pay for the house he and Louise built on a piece of land gifted by Phyl and Jim alongside their residence at 278 Remuera Road.

CHAPTER 17

'A somewhat disastrous journey' into the Barun Valley

———❖———

W hen Ed and Louise returned to Auckland from their American lecture tour in early 1954 they were alone together for the first time. Ed writes:

> I quickly learned how lucky I was to have such a wife. Louise was warm and loving, yet very independent, with a great love of the outdoors and a multitude of good friends. She made it clear to me that she accepted me as a climber and was happy for me to go to the end of the world ... but for the first time in my life I had a strong reluctance to leave home.[1]

It was also the first time he'd been reluctant to go climbing, particularly in the Himalayas. But the previous year he had agreed to lead a New Zealand Alpine Club expedition to the Barun Valley east of Everest in April–May 1954. That meant he had only six weeks at home before his departure: 'six marvellous weeks', he described them, before an unwelcome separation.

The idea for such an expedition had been around since 1951, with an attempt on Everest as one of the less likely of its objectives, but by mid-1953 the focus had changed to Makalu, 27,826ft, fifth-highest peak in the world and still unclimbed. When it was found that an American Californian expedition had booked it for 1954, the New

Zealand objective became simply 'unclimbed peaks in the Barun', with the 25,200ft Makalu II – a subsidiary of the higher Makalu I – and Baruntse, 23,390ft, as attractive options.

Of the 10 expedition members chosen, two others apart from Ed had been on Everest '53. An obvious choice was George Lowe, who noted that the lean and restless Ed Hillary of 1954 was heavier and less fit following their lecture tour. The other Everester was Charles Evans, deputy leader in 1953 and now deputy leader to the Barun expedition. Ed had taken such a liking to Charles in 1953 that he had asked Jim Rose to find a job for him in Auckland so that they could go climbing together. Neurosurgery is not a field in which vacancies are easily found at short notice, and no more was heard of it. But the warmth of the friendship between Charles Evans and Ed is evident in a letter Evans wrote to Louise in the early part of the expedition:

> Dear Louise, Thank you very much for making me a hat – It is a very superior sort ... When we are both wearing our hats Ed & I are practically indistinguishable.
>
> The party has settled down together very well ... I like the boys a lot – I must admit it was rather daunting, the prospect of eight people all saying how good NZ is – but they've been very considerate ...
>
> Ed is gradually (he thinks) working off the effects of the American tour – I'm not so sure that he is. Every time he toils up a steep slope he says – 'There goes another old-fashioned' – or 'Let's get rid of the so-&-so luncheon'... I enjoyed the US tour a lot (in retrospect) & and it was nice to have a chance to get to know you ... Charles[2]

Of the remaining Barun members, six were New Zealanders: Bill Beaven, Geoff Harrow, Norman Hardie, Jim McFarlane, Colin Todd and Brian Wilkins. The medical officer, who would be hard-worked on the expedition, was Englishman Michael Ball, invited, along with Evans, as acknowledgement of and thanks for the English invitation to 'any two New Zealanders' to join Shipton's Everest reconnaissance in 1951.

During the latter part of April following the walk-in through lowland Nepal, the party split into three, with two groups surveying the unmapped Choyang and Iswa valleys, while Ed, with Jim McFarlane,

After the crevasse accident. McFarlane in front has been carried off the mountain by Pasang Dawa, the powerfully built Nepali to his right. Hillary is at the back on the left, Michael Ball, the overworked doctor, is near centre and Brian Wilkins is on the far right. WILKINS COLLECTION

Brian Wilkins and five Sherpas continued north to establish a base camp in the Barun Valley. Their next move was to carry a light camp to a higher altitude for a first look at the peaks they might attempt. On the morning of 27 April, Ed set out with McFarlane and Wilkins on what he would later describe as 'a somewhat disastrous journey'.[3] They climbed a 20,145ft peak up a broad ridge of broken rubble to a summit which gave a grandstand view of Makalu, on which they could see a good route. Ed noted that they had been 'going high very rapidly for a first acclimatisation trip', but the climbing had been easy and they had reached the top of their peak without too much trouble.

Ed had not been well, so decided to return to camp at 18,800ft where the Sherpas were enjoying a rest day. McFarlane and Wilkins continued higher to the divide between Nepal and Tibet from where they could see three of the world's five highest peaks: Everest and its

Kangshung Face, Lhotse and Makalu. The direct route back to camp was easy, a smooth névé dropping gently, the sort of terrain where gravity does the work as you swing easily downhill. Where the névé dipped down at a steeper angle, lines of crescentic crevasses appeared to right and left but with a smooth path down the centre. Wilkins was in front, McFarlane 10 metres behind with a few loops of rope in his hand. Without warning, Wilkins was suddenly through the soft snow of a bridged crevasse, and falling. McFarlane had time neither to get an ice-axe into the hard snow nor to brace himself strongly enough to hold the falling Wilkins. Slithering down the slope, he was able to slow Wilkins' descent with his ice-axe, but then that was out of his grip and he was falling free. Impact with the floor of the crevasse caused both climbers briefly to lose consciousness.

When Wilkins came to, he found himself in a sitting position in a mound of soft snow that had cushioned their fall. McFarlane was a metre away, groaning from pain. Though without any obvious fractures, he was unable to move. Wilkins, however, was able to climb along the floor of the crevasse to look for an escape route. Where they had landed, the crevasse was two metres wide and the blue ice of its walls unclimbable. Then he saw a point of light overhead to his right. The crevasse here narrowed enough for him to start climbing upwards, chimney fashion, his back against one wall and his cramponed feet on the other. It was a desperate climb, but by 4 p.m., two hours after the fall, he was out and moving as fast as he could to summon help from their camp a few hundred metres lower down.

When the pair had left Ed earlier in the day, they had agreed to reunite in time to shift camp down-valley before evening. By 3 p.m. Ed was irritated that they had not returned; by 5 p.m. annoyance had changed to apprehension.

Half an hour later, a distressed Wilkins, his face covered in blood from a cut over his right eye where his snow-goggles had been crushed into his face during the fall, returned alone. He related what had happened. McFarlane was conscious but immobilised 20 metres down in the icy depths of a crevasse.

With Wilkins too spent to return with the rescue party, Ed gathered his five Sherpas, ropes, a couple of sleeping bags and a torch, and set off. By the time they arrived at the site of the accident, it was almost dark. Communication between the Sherpas who had almost no English and Ed who had very little Nepali/Hindi was going to add unknown complexities to an already difficult rescue. In the last of the light, Ed crawled out on his belly to peer down the hole in the roof of the crevasse. He was relieved to hear a quick response from McFarlane when he shouted down into the crevasse, but it was clear that its overhanging roof might break off at any time.

Something had to be done quickly, either by hauling McFarlane to the surface or helping him into the two sleeping bags if the hauling operation failed. From experience, Ed knew that five Sherpas pulling together were strong enough to pull a climber out very quickly. He tied two ropes around his waist, one for himself, the other for McFarlane, crawled over to the hole and dropped over the edge. Immediately he knew that he had made a mistake. His weight should be in a foot loop, not a waist loop which was already riding up his chest, constricting his ribs and breathing. This might not have mattered if the lowering was completed quickly, but it went with agonising slowness. The Sherpas were unsure of what they were doing or how they should do it. After 15 metres they stopped lowering.

Ed was beside himself with pain, breathlessness and frustration. Finally he began to shout, *Upar! Upar!* – the easily remembered Hindi word for *Up!* Nothing happened. This was the stuff of recurring nightmares: spinning slowly around in the frozen dark, ribs cracking, while McFarlane, desperately in need of help, was unreachable below. Then McFarlane joined in, shouting with increasing urgency, *Upar! Upar!* Slowly the message got through and in uneven jerks the rope commenced its upward movement.

Worse was to come. The rope had now bitten deep into the soft lip of the crevasse and Ed was being dragged into a ceiling of soft snow rather than over the edge. He scraped, reached up and eventually, with a huge convulsive effort, got a hand on the rope above and hauled himself to the safety of the flat snow, where he lay recovering from the desperation of that final exertion.

What next? Ed shouted down the hole to ask McFarlane whether he could tie his waist loop on to a rope if they lowered it. 'Yes!' came the reply, and eventually he shouted back that he was tied on. With Ed directing operations from above, the rope came up quickly, but McFarlane too jammed against the snow roof and he was in no condition to make the effort that had just got Ed over the lip. There was no option but to lower McFarlane back to spend the night at the bottom of the crevasse. Ed lowered the two sleeping bags.

Have you got them, Jim?

Yes!

Well, get inside them.

In the darkness, Ed retreated to camp. This had been a day when his luck had run out. Breaking through the snow bridge into the crevasse had been the start of it, then the slow-motion agony of the rescue attempt assisted only by five frightened and uncomprehending Sherpas. Ed knew that he had made mistakes. The prescribed safety method of the times was to be lowered with one's feet in two Prusik slings, metre-long loops of rope attached to the main rope by a slip knot. The climber's weight is on his feet in the loops, not suspended through a constricting waist loop. When ascending, the slip knots allow the slings to be pushed up the rope, one at a time, until the climber has reached the top. That's the theory but the reality can be different at night, in the Himalayas, unacclimatised, with a cold wind blowing and no one to share the problems.

In the morning, in daylight, they returned accompanied by the recovered Wilkins, who was lowered through the hole he had escaped from the previous day. Down at the bottom of the crevasse he found McFarlane still alive, but he had not been inside the sleeping bags and his hands were bare. His feet were cold and hard up to the ankles, and his fingers had turned to ice. This time they cut away the overhanging lip of the crevasse so that when McFarlane was hauled to the surface they could drag him to safety.

For the next seven weeks a staunch and uncomplaining McFarlane would be carried in a cut-away tea chest on the back of an exceptionally strong Nepali porter until he reached the roadhead at Jogbani on the southern border of Nepal. After flying from Calcutta to Christchurch, he would undergo months of plastic surgery to his feet and fingers. He was able to resume a successful career as an engineer. He never climbed again.

Retreat from the attempt on Makalu II

The expedition still had the whole of May ahead of them, the best month of the climbing year. The irresistible challenge was on Makalu where a snow route led up to a col at 24,300ft. From here a good route

Makalu, 27,826 feet, fifth-highest peak in the world. The lower peak to the left is Makalu II, which was an objective for the New Zealand expedition until they were sidetracked into saving the life of Hillary. Between Makalu I and Makalu II is Makalu Col, which was the site of Camp 5 for the 1961 Hillary expedition to Makalu. NORMAN HARDIE

led to the unclimbed Makalu II, 25,190ft. To the south, accessible from the same col, rose the main peak of Makalu I, 27,826ft, but without either permission or oxygen this could hardly be considered a serious option.

By 14 May, six members of an increasingly fit and well-acclimatised party – Evans, Beaven, Hardie, Harrow, Lowe and Todd – had established Camps 1 to 4 and explored the route most of the way to the col. Ed was less well than the others, suffering especially from pain in his damaged ribs. Nevertheless he drove himself higher, confident that the old fire and strength of 1953 would return.

But on 15 May at Camp 3 his problems were getting worse rather than better: 'That night was an unpleasant one for me. I had considerable difficulty in breathing and every cough sent a sharp pain through my chest, but I was still stubborn in my belief that the condition would ease.'[4]

Next day he continued upwards to Camp 4 at 22,000ft with Hardie, Lowe and Wilkins, a decision that he later acknowledged was 'unbelievably stupid'. He was clearly very unwell, lacking in energy, stopping frequently to lean over his ice-axe. That night he felt feverish and was vomiting. He spent another full day at Camp 4 when common sense should have told him to go lower as quickly as possible while he could still move unassisted. By 17 May he was too weak to move.

> I commenced dressing but didn't seem able to get my boots on. George Lowe suddenly noticed my deplorable condition and realized they must quickly get me down to a lower camp. I managed to walk down the first long slope but then I came to an uphill grade and it was just too much for me. I fell on my face and everything went black.
>
> I had a period of terrible hallucinations and found myself clinging to the cliffs of Makalu with avalanches falling all around and people screaming for help … I came back to consciousness to find George tying me into a makeshift stretcher. Then followed a long period of semi-consciousness, of heat and extreme discomfort. It is the only time I can remember thinking that maybe it would be easier just to die …[5]

For three days the Sherpas carried a semi-conscious Hillary down the ice and then moraine to reach Camp 1, where the thicker air brought him quickly back to a normal state of consciousness. The expedition doctors, Charles Evans and Michael Ball, puzzled over the diagnosis. It might have been some sort of bacterial pneumonia but the chest signs heard through a stethoscope were not striking, and Ed's quick recovery at a lower altitude was faster than would be expected with a bacterial infection. An outlier was a flare-up of malaria that he might have caught in the Solomons in 1945, but there is no record of Ed having malaria then or later.

News of Ed's illness travelled down to the American Makalu expedition on the south side of the mountain, and they sent up some oxygen. When the news reached *The Times* of London, the paper

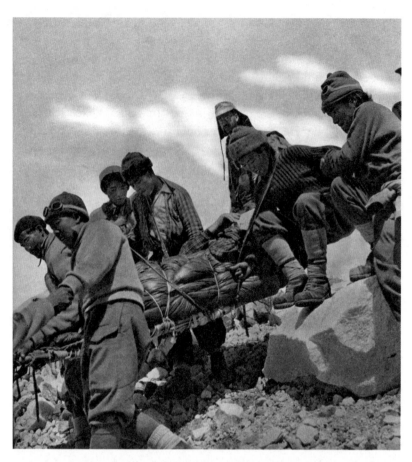

Sherpas carry a semi-conscious Hillary down to Makalu Base Camp.
HILLARY FAMILY COLLECTION

was alarmed to find it had no obituary for the world's most famous
mountaineer and sent an urgent request to Sir John Hunt.

With the danger past, the still fit members of the expedition went
exploring and made some first ascents, including of the handsome
Baruntse, 23,390ft. For Ed and frostbitten Jim McFarlane sitting in his
cutaway tea chest on a porter's back, it was the long walk south to the
flatlands at the Nepal–India border.

In retrospect it is clear that Ed was suffering from one or both of
the two malignant forms of high-altitude sickness, pulmonary edema

and cerebral edema.[6] Evans and Ball could not have diagnosed these conditions in 1954. At that time they were unknown to medical science except in the Andes, where a few astute physicians had described them in miners living at high altitude. In pulmonary edema, fluid leaks from blood vessels into lungs, causing breathlessness and cyanosis as less and less oxygen is absorbed from the lungs. In cerebral edema, fluid leaks into the brain, leading to coma. Suffering either of these is a vicious spiral which will often result in death unless the person is given oxygen or taken to a lower altitude where rapid recovery is a diagnostic feature.

Ed could hardly have suspected it then, but this was the first episode of a form of high-altitude sickness that would recur throughout his life, and at a lowering altitude ceiling. He always believed that some lasting damage had been done in 1954. He had been unwell before the crevasse incident and in a letter to Jim Rose described lack of appetite, sore throat and fever. Brian Wilkins described a persistent, undiagnosed malaise: 'Something was wrong with [Ed] prior to the crevasse accident, though the signs I observed during several weeks in close contact with him were too convoluted to be interpreted clearly ... in the weeks before the crevasse accident I had seen him battling, almost daily, against a persistent problem.'[7]

These are interesting observations. Ed believed that it was the injury to his ribs and lungs during the crevasse rescue that caused permanent damage. The pain from cracked ribs would have made his illness in 1954 worse by limiting the deep breathing which is an important defence against mountain sickness. But another possibility is that he was developing an increasing hypersensitivity to the hypoxia which is the cause of altitude sickness. It seems bizarre that someone who had been so strong at altitude only a year earlier should now have developed such a sensitivity – but even now our understanding of the processes underlying high-altitude illness has large gaps.

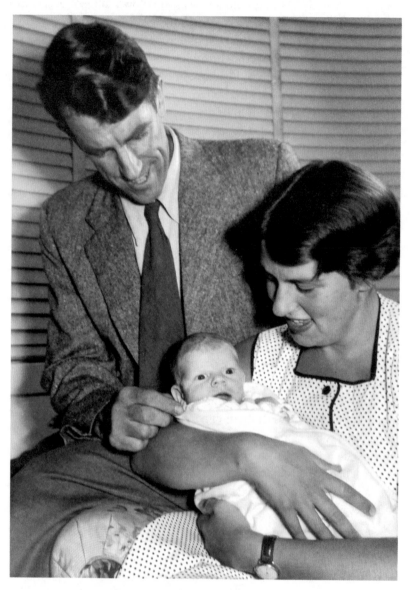

Ed and Louise with Peter, born December 1954. HILLARY FAMILY COLLECTION

CHAPTER 18

Employment opportunity in the Antarctic

───◆───

B y mid-1954 Ed was back in Auckland, where he would stay
for most of the next 18 months. He resumed his work in the
honey-gathering partnership with Rex, though with the bees
deep in their winter hibernation there was not much to be done. The
Sunbeam Talbot motor car, gifted to Ed and Louise while they were
in England, arrived and was christened *Jaldi*, the Hindi word for
quick. They moved into a cottage at 8 Patey Street, Remuera, while
they built a house at 278a Remuera Road. Their son Peter was born on
26 December.

The land at Remuera Road, valued at £1700 and with sweeping
views over the Waitematā Harbour and the Hauraki Gulf beyond,
was a gift from Jim and Phyl Rose after it was subdivided from their
own property. Gummer & Ford, a well-known firm of architects, was
commissioned to design the house. It rose two storeys on a steep site,
with a half-acre of grass, orchard and mature trees dropping away
below. A long, narrow terrace formed the footprint, giving each room
full sun and a view to the north. A kitchen, large living room and Ed's
office occupied the ground floor, all decorated with Tibetan carpets
and a host of memorabilia and photographs. It was the hub of a busy
life, and when Ed was away – as he was often, and for long periods –
Louise had her parents next door for company and child-minding.

Ed's first autobiography, *High Adventure*, financed the £6802 house

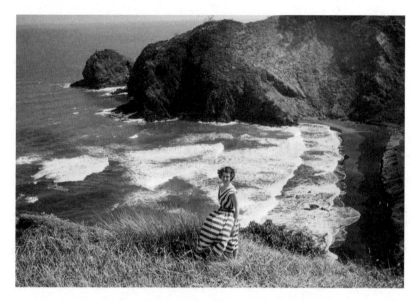

Louise near the site of the family's Anawhata bach above the west coast cliffs.
HILLARY FAMILY COLLECTION

build, but he had already ventured into the literary world with his account of the summit day in John Hunt's *The Ascent of Everest*. Some reviewers felt *The Ascent of Everest* was a bit dry, but it contains a wealth of well-told information and was an instant success with the reading public. Considering the stress of completing the book within a month, Hunt's achievement is remarkable. At the launch of the French edition in Paris on 21 November 1953, Louise noted in a letter to her parents that 'Poor John is not at all well & has an abscess on his neck.'[1] Ed was learning some French. When asked by a radio journalist to say what it was like getting to the top of Everest, he replied without hesitation, '*C'était très bon.*'

Meanwhile, Ed had begun on *High Adventure*. In July Hodder & Stoughton had offered him an advance of £5000 for his personal account of Everest – an amount which, even after the Himalayan Committee had taken its 40 per cent, compared favourably with the £400 per annum earned from the bees. A year later, George Lowe helped supplement this when he introduced Ed to literary agent

George Greenfield, whose sharp eye quickly spotted that the Hodder contract failed to include serialisation rights – which Greenfield was able to sell to *John Bull*, a high-circulation English literary magazine, for £7500. Greenfield remained a good friend and trusted agent for all Ed's later books.

Ed liked the challenge of writing and recognised it as part of his new persona. Louise wrote from London in December 1953: 'Ed worked at the typewriter until midnight … He really is a wonderful writer … very enthusiastic just now and can think of nothing else.'[2] Even on the Barun expedition, writing occupied his spare time. Brian Wilkins, with whom he was sharing a tent, wrote in his diary: 'We are in a tent 5000 ft higher than the summit of Mount Cook. Ed is banging away on his typewriter, thinking hard, and periodically reading the result to me for comment …'[3]

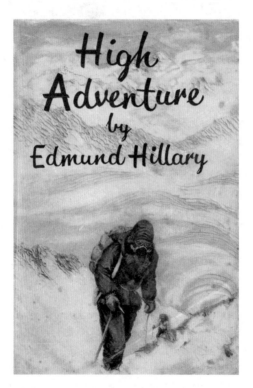

The cover of High Adventure, *published in 1955.*

Ed signing copies of High Adventure. HILLARY FAMILY COLLECTION

High Adventure begins with a dedication to the four people to whom he owed so much:

> TO **HARRY AYRES for** his superb mastery of snow and ice
> TO **ERIC SHIPTON for** his inspiration and unquenchable spirit
> TO **JOHN HUNT for** his courage and singleness of purpose and
> TO MY OLD FRIEND **GEORGE LOWE for** so many years of cheerful comradeship

The focus of the book is Everest, with only seven pages describing his life before the Shipton reconnaissance of 1951. The story of the big climb is sharpened into the form it will take for the rest of Ed's life, though with room for different emphases. Reviewers liked it. The prose was direct, engaging, straightforward, good-humoured, spare, dramatic, nonchalant; its author was self-effacing, humble, a good story-teller.

It was not all praise. For some it was too plain. Elizabeth Cox in *The Spectator* wrote: 'Sir Edmund Hillary is not interested in Tenzing's feelings, or in any feelings, not even his own.'[4] Some complained that the inner Hillary did not reveal himself, but Ed, like most of his countrymen, would have been shy of attempting to reveal the inner Hillary, even if he knew what it was.

Tenzing's autobiography, *Man of Everest*, was published at the same time as *High Adventure*. There was a cultural labyrinth to be traversed as the narrative crossed from non-English-speaker Tenzing, by way of Nepali-speaking friend Rabi Mitra, to American writer James Ramsey Ullman, but there is no mistaking that parts of Ed's account in *The Ascent of Everest* rankled with Tenzing. Ed's description of the climbing of the Hillary Step is an example:

> After an hour's steady going we reached the foot of … a rock step some forty feet high … I could see no way of turning it on the steep rock bluff on the west, but … on its east side … running up the full forty feet of the step was a crack between the cornice and the rock. Leaving Tenzing to belay me as best he could, I jammed myself into the crack, then kicking backwards with my crampons I sank their spikes deep into the frozen snow behind me and levered myself off the ground … As Tenzing paid out the rope I inched my way upwards until I could finally reach over the top of the rock and drag myself out of the crack on to a wide ledge. For a few moments I lay regaining my breath and for the first time really felt the fierce determination that nothing could stop us reaching the top.
>
> I took a firm stance on the ledge and signaled Tenzing to come on up. As I heaved hard on the rope Tenzing wriggled his way up the crack and finally collapsed exhausted at the top like a giant fish when it has just been hauled from the sea after a terrible struggle.[5]

Tenzing commented:

> I must be honest and say that I do not feel his account is wholly accurate … He gives the impression that it was only he who really climbed it on his own, and that he then practically

pulled me, so that I finally collapsed exhausted at the top like a giant fish...

Since then I have heard plenty about that 'fish,' and I admit I do not like it. For it is the plain truth that no one pulled or hauled me up the gap. I climbed it myself, just as Hillary had done ... I must make one thing very clear. Hillary is my friend. He is a fine climber and a fine man, and I am proud to have gone with him to the top of Everest. But I do feel that in his story of our final climb he is not quite fair to me: that all the way through he indicates that when things went well it was his doing, and when things went badly it was mine. For this is simply not true ...'[6]

The fish disappeared from subsequent accounts. It had been a misplaced attempt to add a colourful simile to the story, not an assertion that Hillary was in better physical shape than Tenzing – which was certainly untrue. There were differences between the New Zealand beekeeper and the Asian sardar, but there were also similarities. Both came from humble backgrounds; both were competitive, and nurtured an intense ambition to prove themselves by climbing Everest; both were thin-skinned and sensitive to slights whether from within an expedition or from the larger world into which they had been propelled by their fame.

In August, a couple of months after publication of their books, Tenzing used his friend Rabi Mitra to write to Ed:

> My dear Hillary, You don't perhaps know how very anxious I am to meet and talk to you. Believe me, I still have the same warmth of feeling and love for you as I had in those lone and trying days we were together on Everest. I admit certain unpleasant things have happened after our return from Everest and these have cast a shadow over our achievement – which, no doubt, is extremely regrettable.
>
> Everest has been a great teacher to me. I now realise the truth of the saying that – We ourselves become great by appreciating greatness in others. I am much more humble now and I fervently pray that the glow of love may shine forth again and dispel the darkness that seemed to have gathered in the corner of our hearts. As a token of my deep love and

258

friendship, I am sending you a casket of two pounds of best quality Darjeeling tea and a copy of my book, which I am sure you and your wife will appreciate.

If, however, you find mention of certain things (relating you) in my book which you don't quite seem to agree to, – 'Leave that aside' will be my request to you. I see and think with my own eyes and brain and so you with your own. Our viewpoints, naturally therefore, may not exactly be the same in all cases. We may differ and disagree on certain points and issues, but for that reason we should not allow ourselves to be separated from our mutual love and esteem for each other. We are and should remain friends forever and in eternity. Let nothing again stand in between us.

Here are my arms extended in love to offer you my EVEREST embrace and to your charming devoted wife my warmest good wishes.

Looking forward in much eagerness to hear from you soon.

Ever yours, Tenzing[7]

Ed replied:

My dear Tenzing, I was delighted to receive your letter. I too have felt that it is time that small things should be forgotten and that the main things to remember are those great moments we had together on the mountain. These minor shadows are soon dispelled and the world, after all, is still applauding the primary fact that two men, each helping the other, managed at last to reach the summit. Please be sure that I have nothing but the warmest affection for my old Everest comrade.

I have read your book and enjoyed it. It only increased my admiration for a man who could start life with few material advantages and through his own courage and strength become a national – and world – hero. I did not expect your story in all minor details to coincide with mine – each man must observe for himself. But I have only scorn for the newspapers and people who revel in pointing out minor differences. I hope you will view my own book with tolerance.

At the moment I am fully occupied with the organising of a New Zealand Expedition to the Antarctic. The problems are rather different from the Himalaya but the snow and ice are the same. I may be returning from England to New Zealand next April through Calcutta and if so I will make every effort to pay a visit to you in Darjeeling. It would be a great thrill to meet my old comrade again and also to greet once more all my friends amongst the Sherpas.

It is very generous of you to send me such a fine gift of tea and your book. I also will be sending you a copy of my book which has been recently published. I am enclosing in this letter a photograph of my little family. Please give my kindest regards to your wife and two charming daughters.

Yours affectionately, Ed[8]

Vivian Fuchs and the Trans-Antarctic Expedition

George Lowe met Fuchs casually at the Royal Geographic Society (RGS) in London after Everest, but the more significant meeting was in November 1953,[9] when Fuchs invited him to a meeting, gave him a copy of *Plans for a Trans-Antarctic Journey, by V.E. Fuchs, M.A., Ph.D.*, and invited him to be the expedition photographer. Fuchs had added a request that might have been the most important item on the agenda: 'If you will also write to Ed Hillary and sound him out, I'd be glad. I want to know if I can get a New Zealand party interested.'[10]

A few days later, Ed met Fuchs in the expedition office in London. 'I really knew nothing about him,' wrote Ed, 'in fact I'd only heard his name the first time from George – but I was immediately impressed by his forceful personality and his air of determination and confidence … he was powerfully built and obviously kept himself in fine physical trim.'[11]

Fuchs explained that the overall concept was a crossing of the Antarctic continent from the Weddell Sea to the Ross Sea, an attempt to replicate the expedition planned by Shackleton in 1914–15 but terminated when his ship *Endurance* was crushed in the Weddell Sea pack ice. The total distance of the crossing was 2300 miles, two-thirds of it across the 6000–12,000ft high Polar Plateau, in the middle of which is the South Pole.

Fuchs would be using motorised transport in the form of Sno-Cats. These would travel well on the plateau but might have difficulty ascending crevassed glaciers from the Weddell Sea to the plateau, and

Vivian 'Bunny' Fuchs. ROYAL GEOGRAPHICAL SOCIETY

on the other side descending from the plateau by way of a glacier to the Ross Ice Shelf. This is where Ed and a New Zealand expedition came in. Fuchs wanted New Zealand to build a base (later called Scott Base) in McMurdo Sound adjoining the Ross Ice Shelf. From here dog teams and small aircraft would explore the mountains and find the glacier best suited for the descent of the Sno-Cats. At their furthest point, about halfway between McMurdo and the Pole, the New Zealand party would use ski-equipped planes to stock a depot with fuel and other supplies for the Fuchs party en route to Scott Base. The advantage in having Sir Edmund Hillary join the Trans-Antarctic Expedition (TAE) was that his fame and presence might encourage New Zealand to make a large contribution to expedition funding. Fuchs was largely unknown, but Hillary was arguably the most famous adventurer on the planet.

Fuchs was born in 1908, the son of a German father, Ernst Fuchs, and an English mother, Violet Watson.[12] His English grandfather on his mother's side, Charles Watson, had emigrated to Australia as a young man, and eventually became wealthy as a partner in a wholesale importing business. Following a second marriage at age 43 and the birth of Violet, Charles returned to England, gentrified by his affluence. Violet's marriageability was diminished through being partially crippled by a childhood accident, but at age 32, while travelling in Europe with her mother, she met and fell in love with a young German in the hotel trade. His name was Ernst Fuchs, he was 24 years old, and he and Violet resolved to marry despite opposition from both families. Ernst had no obvious way of earning a living in England but Violet's well-off cousins came to the rescue with enough money for the couple to establish a country home on seven acres of land in Kent.

The future looked settled, but in August 1914 their two countries were at war. Ernst was now an enemy alien, and so, through her marriage, was Violet. Their money and property were confiscated, and Ernst was interned, at first for a few months, then, following the sinking of the *Lusitania* with the drowning of 1500 civilians, for the duration of the war.

In the event, there was a happy ending. When wealthy grandfather Watson died, half his considerable estate went to Violet, and in 1927 the government released all property that had been confiscated in the war. The family bought a country house on 33 acres in Surrey. Vivian enjoyed the better sort of education via prep school, public school, and Cambridge where he studied natural sciences. The nickname 'Bunny' was acquired at school after Fuchs had learnt to walk on his hands, holding himself in balance by his legs hanging below his head like a rabbit's ears. A tutor at Cambridge was Scottish geologist James Wordie, who had been with Shackleton's famous 1914–17 Imperial Trans-Antarctic Expedition. Wordie was leading almost annual expeditions into the Arctic, and it was on one of these, in 1929, that 21-year-old Fuchs fell in love with the remoteness and beauty of the polar region. In his diary he wrote, 'I keep on feeling how impossible it is to realise my luck in being here to revel in and marvel at all these things'[13] – an epiphany of the sort so often described by climbers on a particular first encounter with a mountain. Over the next three decades, Wordie would become an inspiration and mentor.

During the 1930s, Fuchs gained his PhD from Cambridge and went on geological expeditions to Africa. He was also there during the early years of the Second World War. He began his long association with the Antarctic when he was appointed Field Commander to the seven shore stations of the Falkland Islands Dependencies Survey (FIDS) in 1947. The Dependency claimed by Britain included South Georgia, the Falkland Islands, and the Antarctic Peninsula, the finger of mountains and ice which is an extension of the South American Andes and contains the Weddell Sea to the east. Because most of this area was also claimed by Argentina and Chile, an important function of FIDS was 'effective occupation' of shore stations. Here on the Antarctic Peninsula Fuchs learned about pack ice, about Antarctic travel using dogs, and acquired the toughness and stoicism that can make the harsh southern environment so fascinating for a select few.

It was here too in 1949 that he first dreamt of taking up where Shackleton had left off by making a crossing of Antarctica. James Wordie warned him that the times in 1949 were not propitious for a venture of such magnitude but after the excitement of Everest in 1953, Fuchs began cautiously sounding out potential supporters.

The committees in London and New Zealand

Like the expeditions of Scott and Shackleton, Fuchs's TAE was privately conceived and was structured as a limited liability company. Its budget would depend on what could be raised from governments, companies and the public. At a meeting of the Polar Advisory Committee in September 1953, reasons for supporting the TAE were listed:[14]

1. Prestige of nations involved
2. Romantic appeal
3. Justify territorial claims to Coats Land [eastern shore of the Weddell Sea] and the Ross Dependency
4. Knowledge of meteorological conditions at the South Pole
5. Knowledge regarding air routes potential
6. Knowledge of the Antarctic ice sheet and biology
7. Training for service personnel.

Fuchs liked to frame his expedition as a scientific endeavour but he was aware of the other advantages.

The TAE made slow progress through 1954 but began suddenly to take shape in 1955 with the formation of a UK Committee of Management under the chairmanship of Marshall of the Royal Air

Force, Sir John Slessor. As members he had five other Knights of the Realm, a general, a senior partner in a London law firm, a banker, the Bishop of Norwich, and finally a New Zealand representative, Charles Bowden. Funding was a problem but in February 1955 Sir Winston Churchill made a start by announcing a government grant of £100,000. More would follow, including the very expensive funding of all fuels by British Petroleum.

To begin with the New Zealand government showed little interest in funding the TAE or the scientific activities of the International Geophysical Year (IGY), but pressure began to build when they were reminded that they were responsible for the administration of the Ross Sea Dependency. No one owns any part of Antarctica, but claims had been lodged for various 'sectors', triangles with the South Pole at their vertex. The Ross Sea Dependency sector, which includes the Ross Ice Shelf, McMurdo Sound and Ross Island, had been claimed by the British in 1923 but placed under the Governor-General of New Zealand, the British Dominion closest to the Ross Sea. It was on the shingle beaches of Ross Island that Scott and Shackleton had built huts during the three expeditions of 1902, 1908 and 1911, and it was here that the Americans had already begun building the largest of their seven IGY bases on the continent. The advantages of Ross Island were its access to open sea for cargo ships in summer, and a runway on sea ice for cargo planes from Christchurch during spring and most of the summer. For Pole-bound parties it had access to the Ross Ice Shelf all year round.

In May 1955 the New Zealand government began its commitment by making a grant of £50,000 to the TAE. In Wellington a Ross Sea Committee (RSC) was established to manage New Zealand's expanding Antarctic activities and liaise with Sir John Slessor's TAE committee in London. An early task was to appoint a leader of what was being described as the New Zealand Antarctic Expedition. On 9 June 1955, while Hillary was on a lecture tour in South Africa, he received the invitation:

> committee offer you leadership ross sea expedition with
> assurance will appoint deputy leader of administrative ability
> and on understanding that while serving primary function of
> laying depots and bringing home crossing party you must pay

due regard to scientific aspects of expedition also leader must be
subject to direction fuchs and committee please reply = helm.[15]

The invitation was expected and Ed cabled his acceptance immediately.
The boundaries of a line such as 'LEADER MUST BE SUBJECT TO
DIRECTION FUCHS AND COMMITTEE' would need to be tested, but for
now all parties were in the honeymoon phase of their relationship.
The secretary of the RSC was Arthur Helm, a knowledgeable
enthusiast from the New Zealand Antarctic Society which had been
unsuccessfully promoting the cause of Antarctic research for many
years. The chairman, Charles Bowden, was a political appointee, an MP
and Cabinet minister. Now approaching 70, he felt honoured to fill this
uncontentious position which might lead in a couple of years to a well-
earned knighthood. Sadly for him, it never worked this way. 'Who will
rid me of this turbulent mountaineer?' was a thought that could have
crossed his mind from to time.

The leader's mission in the Antarctic

Although the first task was to build Scott Base to house the TAE
support team, this was a big investment for an uncomplicated task
of limited duration. They would have dog teams, planes, explorers,
surveyors, scientists – surely they could also explore and map the
untouched mountain country in the adjacent Victoria Mountains and
study its geology? It was soon agreed that five New Zealand scientists
linked to the IGY would be added to Scott Base. On top of this, a new
objective was developing in the fertile imagination of Edmund Hillary.

A month after his appointment as leader, Ed was at an IGY
conference and writing to Arthur Helm, who shared Ed's excitement
about the possibilities awaiting them in Antarctica:

> Dear Arthur, I went to the IGY Conference in Paris ...
> The main surprise was the enormous extent of the planned
> activities ... the biggest surprise to us was the announcement
> that the United States was putting a big base in McMurdo
> Sound ... The Americans were very hearty and made
> numerous offers of assistance ... Admiral Dufek will take
> 1000 tons of gear to McMurdo for us ...
> I had some useful discussion with Fuchs ... subject to

the limits of finance that although the objective for NZ must be the establishment of a dump on the Polar Plateau … the expedition should have sufficient supplies and equipment that they could travel out as far as the South Pole …

Fuchs seemed reasonably happy with these proposals …

The greatest weakness of our plan is the lack of tracked vehicles … as it might be possible to get vehicles onto the Polar Plateau …

Regards, Ed Hillary[16]

No one could say that Ed had not laid his cards on the table with both Fuchs and with the RSC from the beginning. If he was to build New Zealand's Scott Base, and establish depots for Fuchs from the Polar Plateau down to the Ross Ice Shelf, he wanted the option, if time was available, to go to the Pole. He wanted tracked vehicles as well as dog teams for making the route to the Plateau and its depot. Later it would be said that he nursed his ambition to go to the Pole in secret, but the truth was that no one had listened to what he was saying or taken him seriously.

The committees in London and Wellington could have asked themselves what a restless, competitive Ed Hillary might aim for in Antarctica where he had no scientific interests. The thought could have crossed their minds that he might like to add a visit to the Pole to his curriculum vitae. But they could also see that his expedition would lack the necessary resources for such an endeavour. He was not an Amundsen with a lifetime's expertise in dog-handling and cross-country skiing in high latitudes. He was not a Scott with the determination to man-haul even unto death. He was not a Fuchs with Sno-Cats that could bestride the continent. He was a mountaineer, and the South Pole had lodged itself in his brain as the next mountain he wanted to climb.

The IGY populates Antarctica
The Antarctic is for the most part empty, particularly in winter, but during the IGY of July 1957 to December 1958 and the support years of 1954–59, the continent was, relatively speaking, teeming with people occupying more than 40 bases from 12 countries. This was a remarkable collaboration of scientists studying such subjects as aurora and

airglow, cosmic rays, ionospheric physics, solar activity, geomagnetism, glaciology, meteorology, rocketry and seismology. The importance of the composition of the atmosphere on the earth-level environment was being recognised, as was the importance of the polar ice cap which contains 70 per cent of Earth's fresh water. Significant areas of ice cap had their base below sea level – and it was apparent that the continent had more inlets and adjacent islands than anyone had appreciated.

Rocketry had a link to the IGY, and the Soviet Union and the USA showed off their ability to launch Earth-orbiting satellites for the first time, the Soviets with Sputnik 1 in October 1957, and Sputnik 2 carrying the short-lived dog Laika a month later. In January 1958, the USA's Explorer 1 was launched into orbit. For all countries taking part in the IGY, it was a chance to display their interest in the geopolitics of the most remote of the Earth's continents. For its part, the USA was spending $250 million over five years, most of it on logistics and support provided by the US Navy but $5 million for the science.

Although the TAE was following in the footsteps of Shackleton and Scott, its safety margins were immeasurably wider. Radio networks kept field parties in daily contact with bases whose ski-equipped planes could mount a rescue mission or fly scientific parties into remote locations: with its vast expanses of snow and ice, the whole continent was an airfield. Flying could certainly be hazardous, particularly in whiteout conditions, and crevasse country needed to be treated with circumspection, but compared with the dangerous isolation in which Scott, Shackleton and Amundsen had operated, the Antarctic had become a relatively safe place.

CHAPTER 19

Scott Base

⟫⬦⟪

Although Ed had met Fuchs several times, he could not claim to have even begun to know him until they shared a small ship's cabin as they sailed south on the *Theron* from Montevideo to the Weddell Sea in December 1955. Ed, who had been invited along as an observer, would have preferred a cabin with one of the other three Kiwis on board – his old friend George Lowe, or his deputy leader Bob Miller, or chief pilot John Claydon – but Fuchs decreed otherwise. It was a first lesson: Bunny Fuchs didn't discuss preferences, he made decisions.

George Lowe observed with fascination the differences between Bunny Fuchs and Ed Hillary. He noted, as did others, that Fuchs was not in the habit of sharing a problem or seeking advice from anyone. As he put it, 'We did not sit around as a party discussing the pros and cons of a move. Pros and cons were announced by Bunny, who worked them out in camera.'[1] He described how reading at meals throughout the winter became an accepted custom:

> I think it was Bunny himself who started it, and eventually it
> was agreed to maintain a 'quiet' table for those who wanted
> to pore over books, and a 'noisy' table for those preferring
> to chatter. There was a suggestion of method in Bunny's
> encouragement of the reading habit, for there was no doubt
> that he disapproved of any discussion touching on the
> expedition's plans or progress. Indeed, the one spark that could

268

Aboard Theron *approaching Antarctica.* HILLARY MUSEUM COLLECTION

be guaranteed to jerk Bunny away from his book was the start
of a conversation, even a desultory chat, on some expedition
topic such as vehicles and equipment.

One day a group of three or four were listening with
interest while Geoff Pratt held forth on the subject of the
gloves we wore. 'These things are no bloody good,' said
Geoffrey. 'I wouldn't mind betting I could design a far more
efficient glove for conditions like ours.'

Bunny glanced up sharply from his book, took off his
glasses, laid them on the open pages and spoke. 'When you
know a good deal more about Antarctic conditions,' he said
quietly, 'you'll know more about gloves. Those gloves have
been designed after years of experience – and I think you'll
find they do the job they're intended for.'

Bunny replaced his glasses, picked up the book and went
on reading. After his intervention the glove topic, like many
another, was dropped.[2]

Ed would have been of the party who liked to yarn rather than read, and on *Theron* he was soon finding Fuchs a chilly companion. Ed's opinions were not of interest to Fuchs who had spent years of travel with dogs along the ice-bound shores of the Antarctic Peninsula. As Fuchs tartly pointed out, Hillary 'at that time had never even seen sea ice'.[3]

There might not have been a lot of talk in the top cabin, but Ed was to learn a great deal during his more than two months aboard *Theron*. There was an almost terminal setback at the outset when the ship was beset in the pack ice of the Weddell Sea between 24 December and 20 January. Not many ships had entered the south Weddell Sea, but the consensus, such as it was, had been to keep east until open water to the south gave passage to Cape Norwegia on the Antarctic continent. From here the prevailing easterly winds would briefly open a providential lead of hundreds of miles of open water skirting the ice cliffs of the continent.

Fuchs had studied the oceanography of the Weddell Sea and, according to rumour, believed that the elusive central route used by Weddell in 1823 was the key to a fast passage to the ice shelf where he would build his base. In his accounts Fuchs avoids giving reasons for his decision to enter the ice at a point less easterly than other vessels that year.[4] He made an enigmatic journal entry on 23 December: 'purposely entered the ice as far west as 30°W to allow diversion to the east'.[5] Whatever the reason, the reality was that soon they were being slowed by thick sea ice. To compound their frustration, radio contact with the Royal Society's IGY vessel *Tottan* showed she was making fast progress out east. There was additional annoyance for Ed. When expedition meetings were held when *Theron* was immobilised in the pack ice, Ed was not invited to them. 'I don't think Bunny had any concept of how irritating I found this – after all I was the leader of the other half of his expedition.'[6]

The expedition was led out of its entrapment by John Claydon in the Auster float plane. After a risky take-off down a dog-leg shaped pool in the pack ice, he was able to find a lead to the north and then east and so into open water. Without this vital reconnaissance, which on 20 January was already almost too late, the expedition would have failed before it had even reached a site for its Shackleton Base. Once north into these leads, they were soon travelling in open water but they had lost a crucial month.

Eight members of the British Trans-Antarctic Expedition wintering party wave goodbye to Theron. HILLARY MUSEUM COLLECTION

On 30 January they found a landing site in Vahsel Bay on a mile-wide bench of thin sea ice adjoining an ice slope leading up to the ice shelf that would be a secure site for their hut. Their troubles were not over yet. Two days after unloading had begun, a storm from the north forced *Theron* to stand out to sea while big waves flooded supplies stacked on the ice edge. When the wind dropped and the ship moored alongside again, the men worked around the clock emptying the holds and towing its contents to the foot of the inland ice slope. There was still hauling to be done from sea ice to hut site, but on 7 February the north wind again forced *Theron* to head for the open sea, this time without a chance to return.

As those aboard, including Ed, drew away from the eight small figures waving forlornly from the ice, the enormity of the tasks confronting the wintering party were apparent. The consequences of losing that month in the pack ice were now starkly clear. That was when the whole party would have sledged supplies to the hut site, built the hut, stored a supply of seal meat for the dogs for winter, and set up the instruments for the scientific programme. Now all this had to be done by only eight people in colder and less stable weather. An overhanging worry was a storm that would break up the sea ice and threaten the loss of supplies not yet moved to high ground. The storm came on 20 March and blew for seven days. By the end of it, 300 drums of fuel, a tractor, most of 25 tons of coal, a boat, most of the dog food and many engineering stores had been lost to the floor of the Weddell Sea.

The winter the eight men endured was grim even by Antarctica's demanding standards. Their story is told in *Eight Men in a Crate*, based on the diary of medical officer Rainer Goldsmith. Antarctic enthusiasts liked to see the Trans-Antarctic Expedition (TAE) as the last expedition of the Heroic Era, and right from the beginning these eight men earned their place in this august company.

The Ross Sea Party builds Scott Base

As *Theron* sailed back to Montevideo in February 1956 Ed could be thankful for Fuchs's invitation to join him in this brief encounter with the harsh Antarctic. In his diary he noted that the number of Ferguson tractors for Scott Base should be increased from two to four, and fitted with Norwegian full tracks. His experience had shown that although the TAE tractors worked well dragging loads across flat ice, their small halftracks were useless on steeper slopes. By contrast, the full tracks of Weasels or Sno-Cats coped with ease. On a trip to London later in 1956, he and Bob Miller visited the Ferguson factory in Norway which made full track vehicles for use in the Arctic, and ordered them for Scott Base. Planning continued in New Zealand throughout the rest of the year. Ed and Louise's first daughter, Sarah, was born on 29 June.

In December 1956 the New Zealand party sailed south into the Ross Sea in a wooden ship that had begun life in 1944 as an American netlayer before being bought by the British for the Falkland Islands Survey. After a decade she was on the discard list, but a refit in Southampton and a renaming to *Endeavour* was enough for the New Zealand Navy to buy her for transporting people and freight to the yet unbuilt Scott Base. On the voyage from the UK to New Zealand she had leaked badly in the Bay of Biscay, causing damage to expedition supplies. Now she survived a fearful storm south of New Zealand, but on 3 February Ed noted in his diary, 'Land ahead, Erebus and Terror …

272

It was wonderful in the warm sun and fresh air speeding along through the blue seas and all the time the two great peaks getting closer and closer ...'[7]

The land was Ross Island, on the south coast of which the Americans had built McMurdo Base adjoining the Ross Ice Shelf. Based on his study of Scott's records of 50 years earlier, Fuchs, in London, had suggested that the best route for his expedition as it dropped off the Polar Plateau would be the Ferrar Glacier, which came down to the west coast of McMurdo near Butter Point. Fuchs also believed this would be the best site for Scott Base, a recommendation supported by geophysicists because it would be free of magnetic interferences from Mt Erebus.

But when Ed in the *Endeavour* arrived in McMurdo Sound in January 1957, he found Butter Point more difficult to access than he had anticipated. The Americans, in their role of good neighbour, had sent their powerful icebreaker to open a channel through the sea ice, and that first night *Endeavour* tied up alongside the *Glacier*. This was the flagship of Rear Admiral George Dufek, commander-in-chief of America's huge Operation Deepfreeze which had already built its main base on Ross Island close to Scott's old hut. Dufek had at his command around the Antarctic seven shore stations, three icebreakers, three cargo ships, a fleet of Globemaster and Neptune planes, 1000 men and a budget of $250 million. In a long and distinguished naval career, Dufek had served in the Second World War and the Korean War, and had been with Admiral Byrd in the Antarctic. He came to like Ed, and during 1957–58 used his massive resources to help whenever he could. As journalist Douglas McKenzie wrote, he came to regard the whole TAE 'with baffled affection'.[8]

Ed gladly accepted an invitation to dine aboard the *Glacier*, where Dufek expressed his doubts about their plans. On a reconnaissance by helicopter next morning, Ed saw what Dufek meant. Butter Point was hard to reach, and once the sea ice had gone out was cut off from everywhere. A couple of days later, Ed was back in a helicopter looking at a site on Ross Island recommended by Dufek. This was Pram Point at the southernmost tip of the island where it has permanent access to the ice shelf.

It seemed such an obvious place to build. There was room for the whole of their planned base. An airstrip for their Beaver and Auster

New Zealand's Scott Base on the southernmost tip of Ross Island in McMurdo Sound. HILLARY MUSEUM COLLECTION

aircraft was only half a mile away. The main ice airstrip handling flights from Christchurch was within four miles. The next day an American bulldozer lumbered over and levelled the few irregularities in the site. Five days later, the first of six huts had been built using prefabricated panels ordered from Australia to a design developed in their Antarctic bases.

Ed wrote to the Ross Sea Committee (RSC), notifying them of the change of base site, and in return received from Bowden a letter written in a large flowing hand:

> Dear Ed, We followed the progress of Endeavour with keen interest and suffered with you all the pangs of seasickness in the buffeting you received ... Now today your signal has come advising that you have decided to establish the base at Pram Point on Ross Island. Needless to say I am surprised at this change of plan. I would have thought there would be obvious advantages in being on the mainland, where you would not be dependent on, or affected by, the condition of bay ice, as well as being so many miles nearer to Ferrar Glacier. However

you are on the spot and know all the factors, and will have weighed one thing up against another; and I have no doubt that you had weighty reasons for making that momentous decision … Meantime I send kindest regards and very best wishes … to each and all of your expedition and summer party and the Ship's Company.

God keep you all,

Yours Sincerely, Charles Bowden[9]

There is here the first twinge of discomfort as the chair of the RSC notes that his leader in the field does not necessarily follow the plan drawn up in London.

Finding the route to the Plateau

There was one more task before the autumn cold of March closed in, and that was to establish the vehicle route to (and from) the Polar Plateau, and fly fuel and other supplies to what became known as Plateau Depot, 280 miles from Scott Base.[10] Reconnaissance of the Ferrar Glacier had shown that it was impassable for TAE Sno-Cats, but geologist Bernie Gunn had been taken on a long American flight to examine other glaciers coming down from the Plateau. He was intrigued to find that a feature marked on the map as Skelton Inlet was in fact 'a great wide glacier … there were odd crevasses but it obviously gave relatively easy access to the Polar Plateau which none of the others did'.[11] Ed had confirmed these findings on a more recent flight and now dog teams were flown in to find a route up the glacier at ground level. The scale was vast. A hundred miles of glacier and 8000 feet of height separated them from their destination. The Plateau when reached was a terrain of gently undulating ice and snow the size of Europe, and in most places the ice was more than a mile in depth.

The ascent of the Skelton by two dog teams, one driven by Richard Brooke and Murray Ellis, the other by Harry Ayres and Murray Douglas, began on 26 January. At first they wore crampons on hard ice but as the teams advanced into the upper névé the surface changed to soft snow. On 9 February they had passed through the gap they called The Portal to reach the Plateau. Above them was John Claydon, circling overhead before coming in to land with the first supplies for a depot to be used by the crossing party in 1958. By flying around the clock,

Claydon and Bill Cranfield completed their initial stocking of the depot within three days. Between the Plateau and the Pole there would be two more depots, D480 and D700, the latter 700 miles from Scott Base and 550 miles short of the Pole. Ed and his party had now completed much of what had been requested of them, and with a year to spare.

Throughout this time, Ed was writing frequently to Louise.

> 8 February
> My dearest Louise, Well, it's pretty cold outside although the sun is shining and a bitter wind is blowing down off Mt Erebus. It is now 9.30pm and everyone is stopping work and having their evening cup of tea. I can hear the busy hum of voices in the mess room behind me and the strains of music from our magnificent radio-gramophone. We have such a doughty band of chaps that the field work will at least come up to the standard of the base. I sometimes find it hard to grasp that not only have we built such a fine group of buildings but that already we have found an admirable route to the plateau up the Skelton …
>
> Well, sweetheart, I am viewing the months ahead with very mixed feelings. I have a big responsibility here and much of it is intensely interesting and exciting and, I think, worthwhile. However I'm afraid I really do miss you terribly – sometimes I almost ache to see you again. It's funny how our feelings have grown and developed since we were married. I have come to depend on you so much that you are never far out of my thoughts. And Sarah too after the trip to the South Island has a special little niche in my thoughts – she really was such a dear. Peter of course, the little devil, will always have a place that none of the rest of our children will dislodge … I really am a most unsatisfactory and neglectful husband, I fear, but at least I am as fond of my wife as any husband ever was …[12]

> 21 February 1957
> I had a talk on the phone to Bunny a couple of mornings ago. He appears to have some major problems ahead and I just don't know how he'll get on. He wants us to put depots out much further if we can. If I could get some tractors up onto the plateau it would make an enormous difference and

I'm planning to give it a go. As you know I'm rather partial
to tractor transport and it will be fun to try to get something
to the South Pole. I can then retire and write a series of
bestsellers on my adventurous life ... your Edmundo[13]

Winter at Scott Base

With the departure of the last transport for the summer, Ed's scientists,
surveyors, dog drivers, engineers and tractor drivers were left on their
own with a long, dark winter ahead of them. His deputy leader was
Bob Miller, a surveyor who filled many roles. With Dr George Marsh,
an Englishman with Antarctic and dog-handling expertise, he explored
on foot the route up the Skelton Glacier and south to Depot 700 –
the depot 700 miles from Scott Base – ahead of the tractors. Miller
had excellent people skills and helped keep harmony at Scott Base
through the winter. Ed wrote to Louise, 'Everyone has been working
well, particularly Bob Miller who has been working like a Trojan. I
sometimes feel I'm the butterfly of the outfit. I flit around from job to
job and then duck off for a flight in the plane or on a visit to Admiral
Dufek ... I've come to depend on George Marsh a lot too.'[14] Marsh
and another Englishman, Richard Brooke, had been recruited for their
expertise with dogs and to balance the two Kiwis – George Lowe and
pilot Gordon Haslop – in the Fuchs team.

Winter at Scott Base and the personalities of its inhabitants are
described in an unpublished memoir, *Land of the Long Day*, written by
geologist Bernie Gunn. He described Marsh as 'polished, urbane, and
one of the most likable and entertaining men on the expedition'. His
ambition was to better the average of 20.8 miles per day achieved by
Amundsen's party on their way to the South Pole in December 1911,
and he and Bob Miller achieved this when they covered 1800 miles at
an average of 22.4 miles per day.

The scientists were led by Trevor Hatherton, born a Yorkshireman
but by 1957 a fully integrated Kiwi. Regrettably, the scientists hardly
appear in the non-scientific accounts. They had their space, their
instruments and their links to the rest of the IGY, and there was not
much else Ed could offer.

Ed's task was to plan for the group selected to support the Fuchs
crossing party. There were 12 people at Scott Base, with three dog
teams, three Ferguson tractors, a Weasel, and two small planes, the

The New Zealand Antarctic wintering party, 1957. Standing (L to R): Balham, Miller, Gawn, Ayres, Hillary, Marsh, Cranfield, Brooke, Claydon and Mulgrew; Seated: Gerard, Bates, Macdonald, Tarr, Gunn, Orr, Hatherton, Carlyon, Warren, Bucknell, Ellis, Sandford and Douglas. HILLARY MUSEUM COLLECTION

larger Beaver being preferred when stocking depots. Much of this was surplus to the requirements of Fuchs's journey from the Pole to Scott Base. With no one keen to spend an uncertain number of days or weeks waiting for Fuchs to arrive at a depot, Ed split his 12 men into four groups, of which only one, driving tractors, would link with Fuchs.

A northern party of Brooke, Gunn, Warren and Douglas, with dogs, would spend four months exploring and mapping the area north of the Skelton. Ayres and Carlyon, also with dogs, would survey the Darwin Mountains south of the Skelton. The tractor party would be preceded by the Miller and Marsh dog team who would be surveying the route to D700 to steer the motorised parties away from crevassed areas. They would then explore and map the Queen Maud Mountains. Coming behind them would be Hillary, Bates, Ellis and Mulgrew who would attempt to drive tractors to D700. Not written into the plan but generally understood (if not always approved) was the intention to continue to the Pole if machines, fuel, conditions and time permitted.

This was a far more extensive plan of exploration, surveying and geology than had originally been envisaged. Gunn described the reaction within the wintering party when the plan was pinned to the Scott Base noticeboard – and the response from Charles Bowden of the RSC:

> It was a historic document. I wonder if it survives? ... its proper place is in the Scott Polar Institute. The reply from the Ross Sea Committee was a monument to bureaucratic caution and indecision. In brief, it completely rejected the plan and directed that our entire field staff should concentrate on establishing depots. 'However,' it concluded in a tone of pomposity that could almost be heard, 'a limited amount of exploration may be carried out in True Antarctic Tradition, within a distance not exceeding fifteen miles of the Depots.' There was of course no land within fifteen miles of the depots! We roared with laughter, we booed, we jeered! 'In True Antarctic Tradition' was to become a catchword for doing nothing! Within minutes Sir Ed had banged out a reply which said in effect, 'The deployment of field personnel is best left in the hands of the field executive who are in a position to appreciate the problems and the capabilities of the people concerned.' Thus did Edmund Hillary lay himself, his career, his future, squarely on the line. We used to refer to him with a touch of sarcasm as 'Our Leader', considering in our juvenile arrogance that we needed little leading, but a real leader is there to make difficult decisions and stand by them, and by doing so he won our respect and support.
>
> The greatest weight fell on our air support group, Claydon and Cranfield, with their single Beaver having to range far and wide delivering supplies to four New Zealand groups as well as fuel for the Sno-Cats of the British party. It was an ambitious plan ...[15]

Reinventing Ferguson tractors

The tractors were still far from perfect, and throughout the winter Ed pressed his two engineers, Jim Bates and Murray Ellis, to improve them.

Although both were described as 'engineers', Jim Bates and Murray Ellis had very different backgrounds. Jim Bates had trained as a mechanic but he had an eccentric flair for invention. Gunn wrote:

Jim Bates working on diesel motors at Scott Base. HILLARY MUSEUM COLLECTION

Jim Bates was the nearest approach to a mad inventor I have ever met. Craggy of face with wild black hair and unshaven chin, Bates on the trail of a new invention was something to step aside from in a hurry as electric arcs crackled and gas-jets flared. Although I doubt he had a single formal qualification, he was probably the most intelligent man on the expedition with an insight into mechanical, physical, political and social problems that few others shared. I was often sounding out the views of that unlikely seer James Bates.[16]

Murray Ellis had taken an engineering degree and worked in the family business of Arthur Ellis and Co. which manufactured mattresses, sleeping bags up to Everest specifications, and down jackets. It was his father Roland, a good friend of Ed's, who, as a committee member of the NZ Alpine Club, had launched the telegram that led to the invitation to Everest in 1951. Murray was large and strong with a nice sense of humour and a twinkle in his eye. Like Jim Bates he had a remarkable ability to fix a tractor, Weasel or other piece of machinery that had broken down. This was difficult enough in winter in the garage they had fabricated from metal fence supports and packing cases, but to do the same thing, sometimes with bare fingers, at a camp on the Polar Plateau seems miraculous. Without them, the three tractors would never have left the environs of Scott Base, let alone reached the Pole.

The caboose, a caravan on sledge skis, was designed by Ed to provide something warmer than a tent. Although originally fitted out with five bunks, it was quickly apparent that it could take only two in reasonable comfort. One was Ed; the other, Chief Petty Officer Peter Mulgrew who had been co-opted from the Royal New Zealand Navy to manage radio communications. Wherever the party went, Mulgrew kept them in contact with Scott Base and a waiting world press. Ed had selected him from a number of Navy applicants, partly because of his skills, but also because he didn't salute or address Ed as 'sir'. He was small, combative, competitive, had a lively wit and a full repertoire of Gilbert and Sullivan songs. He and Ed developed an easy, bantering relationship. Ed wrote in his diary, 'Peter is doing a first class job with the radio … he's my most loyal supporter and will go on with me as long as I wish.'[17]

Murray Ellis working on the tracks of a Ferguson tractor at Scott Base.
HILLARY MUSEUM COLLECTION

CHAPTER 20

'Hellbent for the Pole'

—⊰◦⊱—

It was not a race, but as the two expeditions came closer to the Pole, the press enjoyed itself and boosted newspaper sales by portraying it as such. Fuchs's goal was to succeed where Shackleton had failed, to cross the continent by way of the South Pole and thereby bring prestige to his country and consolidation of its claim to the Falklands Dependencies sector of the Antarctic. It would also bring renown to the expedition leader, though he would have disclaimed any interest in this. Additionally, the UK party would carry out a scientific programme including measurements of the ice thickness along the line of their traverse which might show that in parts the underlying rock was below sea level. Antarctica might be an archipelago of islands rather than a single continent.

Ed's letters and diary give no indication that he felt he was in a race, but there is no doubt that he wanted to reach the Pole. Where do you go after you've been first up Everest? In a trip to the Pole he could see a challenge. Whether you admired or deplored this attitude depended on where you came from. The New Zealand response was usually 'Good on you, Ed.' The English, however, regarded the Pole as theirs.

Fuchs and Hillary resembled each other in their ambition, strength and determination, but there were also some large differences. Ed's basic tasks were setting up Scott Base, supporting his scientists and explorers, and establishing fuel depots for the British party. Beyond that he was driven by two goals: the first was to reach the Pole; the second to be back at Scott Base in time to catch transport back to Louise, Peter and Sarah in New Zealand. He did not want to endure another Antarctic winter.

There were external constraints. He had signed an agreement that he was subject to the direction of the Ross Sea Committee (RSC), the London Committee of Management under Sir John Slessor, and the Trans-Antarctic Expedition (TAE) leader Vivian Fuchs – a division of management which would have its repercussions in the field. Ed before Everest would have happily accepted this junior status, but by 1957 he had become a world celebrity. It was this fame and New Zealand's financial and logistical support that Fuchs sought when he encouraged Ed to be his support leader on the Ross Sea side of the continent. Fuchs wanted Ed's energy and charisma but failed to recognise that these were indissolubly linked to Ed's competitiveness and need for recognition. Fuchs was not famous, or not yet, but he had behind him the formidable resources and self-assurance of what had until recently been the world's greatest empire.

Then there was the question of styles of leadership. Ed could be authoritarian at times but he could also be very flexible. He would listen to other people and adopt their ideas if they were better than his own, though not always with an acknowledgement. Fuchs was more certain that he was right. With his three years of field experience as leader of the British presence on the Antarctic Peninsula, he could see no reason why he should consult with anyone. This would be acceptable if he was always right, but he was not. Fuchs had extensive experience with dogs in the Antarctic but none with vehicles such as the Sno-Cats he would lead through heavily crevassed country to the Pole. Stephen Haddelsey, in his account of the TAE, quotes criticism of Fuchs by glaciologist Hal Lister who had driven snow vehicles in Greenland. Lister quoted TAE deputy leader David Stratton: 'You are not here to think, Bunny and I do that for you; you are here to do as you're told.'[1] One needs to qualify such diary entries with the reservation that irritations and animosities easily incubate in the isolated conditions of polar exploration. Scott v Shackleton was a famous example on the expeditions of 1902 and 1908, and the same tensions were in play for Ed at Scott Base, where many were critical of his ambition to take tractors to the Pole.

On the plus side for Fuchs were his unshakeable self-confidence, and his physical strength, stamina, courage and determination. George Lowe described how during the voyage of the *Theron* a young Norwegian called Alf, the crew's champion arm-wrestler, put out a challenge which was accepted by the 48-year-old Fuchs:

> They sat down together, gripped hands and set about it, the crew watching all agog, though feeling that Bunny did not have much hope of success ... They pressed and strained, and as the seconds ticked by the audience fell silent. The veins on Bunny's handsome head were beginning to swell, his face reddened, his eyes shut tightly as he fought. Almost a minute passed, and then the Norwegian began to falter. Before long there were murmurs of applause – for Vivian Fuchs had beaten the champion.
>
> The game was trivial enough ... Far more interesting was Bunny's demeanour during the next few hours. He was oddly elated, jubilant, less severe than usual, and his eyes seemed to glint with the expression of a man who is compulsively determined, almost dedicated, to demonstrate an absolute, unshaking and unshakeable confidence in himself ...
>
> Bunny, the oldest among us, would throw himself with silent passion into every form of silent activity, every game and exercise, until he could beat every one of us into the ground ... Even at the most strenuous games the powerful, greying leader of our expedition could match himself against three or four people, one after the other, and when he could vanquish all of them several times running, would cast about him for a new opponent ... he was incredibly strong, single-minded, full of endurance and determination...[2]

A question of timing

A determining factor for Ed's ambitions would be whether Fuchs could reach the Pole around Christmas Day as planned. By this date the New Zealand group would only just have finished their task of stocking fuel depots, leaving them no time to reach the Pole. For Ed the best outcome would be for Fuchs to reach the Pole a few days ahead of the New Zealand group. Fuchs would have his priority and Ed his Pole. The more difficult scenario would have Fuchs a long way behind schedule, with Ed, embarrassingly, reaching the Pole weeks ahead of the official party.

From the start the Fuchs party had a delay of a month built into its plans. The New Zealand group was setting off from Scott Base on 14 October, whereas the main British party planned to leave Shackleton on 14 November. The reason for the delay was that Fuchs had decided to precede his main departure with a preliminary reconnaissance of the 350 miles of ice shelf and crevassed glaciers separating Shackleton from the Polar Plateau. This would be carried out in a Sno-Cat and three Weasels driven by Fuchs and three others. They would end their reconnaissance on the Polar Plateau at the hut known as South Ice which had been flown in the previous summer. From there they would fly back to Shackleton for the departure of the main crossing party heading for the Pole and Scott Base.

On the Ross Sea side, the equivalent of South Ice was Plateau Depot, 280 miles from Scott Base, but a longer distance, 970 miles, from the Pole. Between D280 and the Pole, the Kiwis were scheduled to stock two additional depots, D480 and D700, with the latter at roughly the same distance from the Pole as was South Ice.

The early timetable, made when optimism reigned, had Fuchs being first to the Pole, but there were large areas of uncertainty. His route to South Ice had not been traversed on the ground. Ed's group had taken dogs up the Skelton but not tractors – which might be hopelessly unsuitable for polar travel anyway.

When the New Zealand party set off on 14 October, they were in three tractors and a Weasel, dragging sledges heavily laden with drums of fuel. Their progress was so slow that by the time they camped they had covered only six miles and, ignominiously, were still in sight of Scott Base. The sceptics might after all be right that tractors couldn't even cross the Ross Ice Shelf let alone climb to the Plateau and the Pole. There was no option but to lighten the loads by dropping off drums of fuel.

After a week, with 180 miles behind them, Ed allowed himself the indulgence of some purple prose:

> I was pointing my tractor towards the distant mouth of the
> Skelton Glacier and as I bumped along I looked out on a

The Weasel and Ferguson tractors ascending the Skelton Glacier.
HILLARY MUSEUM COLLECTION

strangely beautiful scene. To the south of us the sun was a
molten ball of fire on the horizon and its low rays brought
into sharp relief the jagged sastrugi and transformed the hills
and hollows into a mottled patchwork of flame and shadow.
The white sky glowed with a delicate purple while the great
peaks standing all around us were dressed in crimson robes.
We were swimming along in a sea of glorious colour and for a
while I forgot even the cold and the discomfort.[3]

When they drove into Skelton Depot at the foot of the glacier, they
were met by Bob Miller and George Marsh and 18 excited dogs who
had been flown in to save sledging across the ice shelf. Skelton had
become a mini airport, with a dump of aviation fuel to be used when
the two planes, the little Auster and the larger Beaver, were relaying
freight into the next three depots, Plateau (D280), D480 and D700. It
was the use of the planes, and the skills of their pilots, John Claydon
and Bill Cranfield, which provided the flexibility to transport people,
dogs and freight between Scott Base and the depots at will.

286

The ascent of the 100 miles of Skelton Glacier took 10 days. Wind as well as drift and ice poured down between the mountains on either side, but the dog teams had already found a route the previous autumn, and Miller and Marsh and their dogs were back in the lead again, marking the best route for the tractors. Ed described their arrival at the Plateau camp on the last day of October:

> I was in the Weasel at the back of the train and I saw Jim suddenly change direction a few degrees … I looked ahead, and there on the horizon several miles away was a tiny black triangle – a tent. It was the Plateau Depot.
>
> My first feeling was one of enormous relief. With the bad visibility we had been experiencing I didn't know how accurate my navigation would be … To see our four battered vehicles and the laden sledges at the Plateau Depot seemed to be the fulfilment of an impossible dream. I don't think that ever before, even on the summit of Everest, had I felt a greater sense of achievement.[4]

The Beaver, flown by Claydon and Cranfield, was the principal load carrier for establishing Trans-Antarctic Expedition depots. HILLARY MUSEUM COLLECTION

He might have added a word of praise for Bates and Ellis who had adapted and maintained the three tractors that were the beasts of burden on which he might ride to the Pole.

They spent 12 days at Plateau Depot, waiting restlessly for planes to fly in during breaks in the weather with the drums of fuel for the Fuchs party. Harry Ayres and Roy Carlyon set off with two dog teams to explore and survey mountain country at the head of the Darwin Glacier. One of the teams was almost lost down a deep crevasse when a dog broke through the crust and was followed by the rest of its team and the sledge. Fortunately, the sledge got jammed 10 feet down, leaving the dogs hanging free in their traces in the space below. Harry climbed down, and he and Roy extricated them. One dog slipped out of its harness and fell to its death, the only casualty on the whole TAE.

From Plateau Depot three of the Hillary party flew temporarily back to Scott Base: Murray Ellis because an old rugby injury to his back had flared up; Peter Mulgrew with painful ribs after falling off the roof of the caboose and on to its towbar; and Ed to do leadership tasks, phone Louise and write letters.

> My dearest darlingest Lulu, My telephone call with you tonight has been quite a tonic for me. You really gave me the works and it's done me a lot of good and made me feel closer to you than I have for a long time. I really need a good roust up from you now and then when I get too morbid … Actually the job of leader is a pretty lonely one I find … I'm afraid this plan to use tractors has rather become a besetting sin with me and I probably drove everyone to distraction with it all winter as I was determined to carry it through despite a good deal of lack of confidence here at base …
>
> It's blowing a howling blizzard here tonight and up on the plateau but perhaps this will clear away the unsettled weather. I don't doubt in the least that we'll establish D480 and D700 but I would still like to push through to the Pole. I've come to the conclusion I'm ambitious or competitive or something but anyway I'd dearly love to get to the Pole, but fear that time is against me. Thanks for your pick-me-up darling. It makes me realise how much I need you …[5]

As a husband and father Ed was not always aware of the strains on a beleaguered solo mother raising two anarchic infants:

> By the way darling I was a bit aghast at the way you were yelling at Peter when we were on the phone the other night. I'm sure you don't realise how it sounded ... I think you'd be far better off to give him a damn good swipe rather than shout at him like that – probably do him and you far less harm ... it's easy to criticize from down here I suppose ...[6]

The weather prevented flying for a week, but in a clearance on 10 November Ed flew south from Scott Base to Plateau Depot, D280. Two days later they set off on the 200-mile journey to D480, which they reached a fortnight later. Ed could be dismissive of the dangers of travelling on the Plateau – 'the dangers of this sort of trip to my mind don't compare with a Himalayan expedition,'[7] he wrote to Louise – but the ever-present risk of a tractor breaking through a snow bridge into an apparently bottomless crevasse could be wearing.

A confusion of messages

When chairman of the RSC, Charles Bowden, was more clearly informed of Ed's polar ambitions, he expressed alarm at the risk involved, and pointed out that it would require approval of both Fuchs and the London committee. Ed replied briskly that risk could be assessed only by those in the field. 'We do not wish to deny you the functions of leadership ...' was the reply,[8] and there the matter rested. Did Bowden ever sound out Sir John Slessor in London? There is no mention of it in the record.

On 21 November Ed's diary records the receipt of two significant messages. The first was from Fuchs describing a delay in the departure of his main expedition.

> ... start delayed 10 days ... Leaving Shackleton 24th [November] ... Could be up to fortnight late arriving Scott Base ... possibility remains we do not arrive till 9th March ... If conditions difficult we can accept intended D700 at 600 miles ... Time so gained may be useful to you for your work in the mountains. As it seems unlikely we can meet at

D700 would appreciate guide from Plateau Depot if possible. Delighted you have vehicles on plateau and going so well. Congratulations from all. Bunny

Ed was alarmed to hear that the main party had not even started and that the crossing might not be completed until 9 March – a month later than an earlier estimate of 8 February. Predicting arrival times was an inexact science, but by 9 March – which could end up being later still – they might miss the last transport back to New Zealand. There was also the puzzling 'If conditions difficult we can accept intended D700 at 600 miles.' Compared with Fuchs, the New Zealand group was positively racing along. How could it fail to reach D700? Or was this code for the message, 'Keep away from the Pole …'?

The second message was from the RSC as a phone call from Arthur Helm to Scott Base. It was relayed to Ed via John Claydon and showed a startling change in attitude towards a Pole trip:

> Helm rang saying following committee meeting Monday it appears greatly increased interest in expedition and stocks particularly high. Committee interested in your prospects reaching Pole and whether you have considered this. If you are prepared to go for Pole, Committee will give you every encouragement and full support following formal approval from London. If you intend to proceed Helm requests you seek Committee approval for the venture following which they will get OK from London. Could you wire Helm re this on same day as you send 'Times' dispatch from D480. Good work. Claydon[9]

There was need for some approvals here, but there was no doubt that the overall tone was one of encouragement. Ed replied:

> On establishment of D700 the tractors carrying sufficient fuel to reach Pole will continue south to meet Fuchs. Unless Fuchs requires the assistance of the vehicles which is unlikely, we will continue on after meeting him and leave our vehicles at the Pole where they can be of some use. Admiral has agreed to evacuate us by air to Scott Base. I will join Fuchs at the Plateau Depot and guide him down the Skelton and across the Ross Ice Shelf. Hillary[10]

The tractor train on the Polar Plateau. HILLARY MUSEUM COLLECTION

It was not difficult to find good reasons for continuing to the Pole rather than waiting for Fuchs to reach D700 which, as events turned out, would be in eight weeks' time. By going to the Pole rather than waiting, Ed would be prospecting the route for the Fuchs party and speed their onward progress. For his own party it would be easier to drive the 550 miles from D700 to the Pole than to drive the tractors the 700 miles back to Scott Base. He would ask John Claydon to fly extra drums of fuel into D700 for the Pole trip, and he would approach the Americans to fly the party from the Pole back to Scott Base. To this the ever-obliging Admiral replied, 'Yes, of course, with pleasure. Best regards. Dufek.'

The tractor team reached D480 on 25 November, followed three days later by the Miller–Marsh dog team who pointed out that Ed's navigation was a bit approximate, the tents being six miles away from the position he had given them. There was competition between Ed with his tractors and the dog-drivers who saw the Pole trip as a 'stunt' compared with the exploration and mapping they planned. If they wanted someone to go to the Pole, why not a dog team – though to supply it with food for dogs and drivers might not be easy.

The group spent 11 days at D480 waiting for the weather-dictated arrival of the Beaver with its drums of fuel. Ed wrote to Louise:

> I'm heading for the Pole ... Although Bunny is so very much delayed he definitely could make it up if he only makes the effort but his mental processes are a bit beyond me ...
>
> I think you're right when you say I'm ambitious – I'm damned keen to get to the Pole anyway and honestly can't see the slightest difficulty in doing so apart from continuous bad weather for flying or major breakdowns in several vehicles. I still think that apart from anything else it will be damn good for NZ prestige for us to get to the Pole and I intend to have a go anyway. I still have a feeling that Bunny and London may not be too favourable but I doubt if I'll take too much notice of that ... Well, sweetheart, all my love and thank goodness December is here and time is passing...[11]

On 6 December, a fortnight after he had sent his gung-ho message to the RSC about going to the Pole, Ed received a dampening message from Bowden:

> Overriding consideration is that nothing should be done that involves any risk ... Depot 700 must not be left unmanned ... In view of many uncertainties ... the Ross Sea Committee cannot agree with your proposals ... We must await ... Fuchs' arrival at South Ice after which his future movements might be more clearly indicated. Bowden.[12]

Ed 'stamped around outside ... in something of a turmoil',[13] but there was nothing to be done apart from setting off for D700, a journey that took 10 days.

Miller and Marsh were ahead of them searching out the best route, but only 10 miles short of D700 the tractors had their worst encounter yet with a crevasse. Hillary and Mulgrew were ahead, probing their way through a more than usually maze-like area of crevasses, when they saw the rear of Jim Bates's tractor sink backwards through a snow bridge. For a moment it looked as though the whole tractor and its driver would disappear, but the vehicle came to rest more than half-buried with its front end pointing skywards. Ed rushed over and called

Nearly gone! Encounter with a crevasse on the Polar Plateau.
HILLARY MUSEUM COLLECTION

out, 'How are you, Jim? Are you all right?' to which Jim replied after a pause, 'Yes, but I don't like the view!'[14]

There was a strong chance that the immobilised tractor would not be recoverable – and this would put paid to their trip to the Pole more effectively than the wavering directives from the RSC. Even Ed would have accepted that two tractors had too small a safety margin to attempt a 550-mile trip to the South Pole. They dug deeply to create a ramp in front of the disappearing tractor. Then with tow-ropes in place they gave full throttle to the other two tractors, and breathed again as they dragged the threatened vehicle out of the crevasse and on to the flat snow above.

On 15 December they reached the site of D700, the last depot before the Pole, and the Beaver began flying in its loads. Two days later, Ed received a telegram from Bowden:

> Please accept heartiest congratulations from Committee and myself on reaching D700 in such good time ... In considering your future programme, you should know that the Committee

recently agreed that if Fuchs or London Committee requested you should carry on toward Pole the Committee would raise no objection provided this could be done within existing resources ... you should now make every endeavour to discuss your next steps as fully as you can with Dr Fuchs personally ... You should then be able to make a joint recommendation to Committee and to London.[15]

Bowden was probably aware that this suggestion had built into it the delays imposed by Fuchs's dislike of communicating with the outside world, including with *The Times* which, in theory at least, had bought exclusive rights to the expedition. The enterprising correspondent for the *Daily Mail*, Noel Barber, who had hitch-hiked a flight to the American polar station, was often able to glean 'information of a later nature than any that appeared in *The Times* for which the doctor [Fuchs] was writing laconic dispatches when the mood took him'.[16] Although Fuchs argued that he was too busy to write articles or give radiotelephone interviews, the failure to provide such basic information as to where he was located was undoubtedly a source of deep frustration, not least to Ed.

On 17 December Ed received a message from Fuchs that he expected to arrive at the South Pole between Christmas and New Year.[17] Ed wrote to Louise:

> My dearest ... I'm quite resigned to whatever happens with respect to the Pole trip. Now that we're completing our supporting task we'll just have a stab at going on further south making an attempt to dodge all crevasse areas and getting a clear run. If the going is very good we may possibly go to the Pole but probably we'll do a couple of hundred miles recce and then return to D700 and either fly out or return with Fuchs if he's as early as he says he's going to be. I'll just be counting the days now to get back to Auckland ...

To Fuchs he wrote:

> Pleased to hear you anticipating arriving Pole by New Year. You should arrive Scott Base in February ... Have had difficulty in following your progress and would appreciate

confirmation that you have reached South Ice ... On completion of D700 intend heading south-west with three Fergusons to try and clear crevasse areas and get clear running towards Pole. I don't know how far we will get but will keep you advised ... Ed Hillary[18]

On 20 December the five-man tractor party left D700, travelling south and carrying 20 drums of fuel which, with luck, should be just enough to travel all the way to the Pole. If there was too much deep snow they would turn back to D700.

With Fuchs from Shackleton to South Ice

When Fuchs and Hillary set off on their journeys in October 1957, Fuchs on the 8th and Hillary on the 14th, both knew from aerial reconnaissance that there were no impassable obstacles on the routes they had chosen. Hillary also had information from an on-the-ground survey in early 1957 by Brooke, Ellis, Ayres and Douglas who had driven their two dog teams the full 100-mile length of the glacier and knew exactly where the best route lay along the line broadly defined from the air. When they began the main journey eight months later, they again had dog teams out front marking the best route.

Fuchs had hoped to make his own preliminary reconnaissance in early 1957 but there had not been time. When the four of them set out on 8 October – Fuchs, mechanics David Pratt and Roy Homard, and seismologist Geoffrey Pratt – they were driving a Sno-Cat and three Weasels. The start was inauspicious when one of these broke down and had to limp back on Day 2 and another was abandoned after a breakdown. Fuchs's original estimate for the 350-mile journey to South Ice had been 14 to 21 days, but problems on three extensive crevasse areas meant the journey took 37 frustrating days. The result was that the departure of the main expedition, in three Sno-Cats, two Weasels and a Muskeg, was delayed until 24 November.

Worse was to come. With their knowledge of the route, the second trip from Shackleton to South Ice was expected to be much quicker – eight days was Fuchs's estimate – but at 28 days it was not much quicker than the first. The problem was that several weeks of warmer weather had softened the snow bridges. While the single Sno-Cat on the first trip never had a break-through, three major recoveries

295

were needed on the second.[19] The dramatic photographs of these long red vehicles with their pontoons angled down into empty space and embedded in crevasse walls are well known. To the inexpert eye the vehicles look impossible to retrieve, but all were miraculously brought back to the surface.

As a result the expedition lost a month which could not easily be recovered. Fuchs might have regretted that he had not combined all his resources into a single journey from Shackleton. The firmer bridges of the colder months of October and November would have given his four Sno-Cats less trouble. He would have had 10 people throughout to do the scientific and mechanical work of the expedition. And he would have had his dog teams for roving ahead to find the best route through the crevassed areas.

Although radio links could be sporadic, the expedition members were able to tune into the BBC and the NZBC, both of which gave reports from the Antarctic. Stephenson, the Australian geologist with TAE, noted that although there was usually a brief informative report from the New Zealand group, news from the British party was infrequent because Fuchs 'distanced himself from publicity'. Stephenson expressed the exasperation of all of them when he wrote: 'we found ourselves increasingly irritated by the persistent Hillary reports. We welcomed his progress but not the endless publicity.'[20]

Included in the news on 18 December was the information that Hillary was intending to drive to the Pole. It is not clear where this statement came from, as Ed was still at D700 and still being coy at an official level, but the rumours had been around for a long time. Fuchs sounds unsurprised in what could be read as a disingenuous comment in his diary of 19 December:

> I cannot imagine that Ed would have set this ball rolling without letting me know what he wanted to do … While there is no objection to his going on to the Pole, there is also no value for he can do no work on the way.[21]

The finishing straight is 550 miles long

The TAE had been generating little public interest until December 1957 when the world's press realised a story was unfolding in the Antarctic with a newsworthy end-game being played out. Reporters

New Zealand leader in the Antarctic. HILLARY MUSEUM COLLECTION

from around the globe converged on McMurdo and the Pole Station. They were calling it a race. On the Weddell Sea side was the Fuchs team with four 170hp Sno-Cats, three Weasels, a Muskeg and two dog teams. With 550 miles separating them from the Pole, they would leave South Ice on 25 December after listening to the Queen's Christmas Day message to her subjects. On the Ross Sea side was the Hillary team driving three 26hp Ferguson tractors. They would leave D700 on 20 December, five days ahead of the Sno-Cats, and they too had 550 miles of sastrugi and soft snow between them and the Pole. It was a distortion of what the TAE was about, but pitching it as a race made an irresistible story. The Fuchs party may have had more powerful vehicles but they were committed to their halts for seismic shots every 30 miles. The dogs no longer had an obvious role but there was no way out for them except by trotting alongside the vehicles. They were happiest travelling not much more than 20 miles a day, so they too were a limiting factor. There were the usual demands of vehicle maintenance in the sub-zero polar environment, and finally there were the sastrugi, the wind-formed ice ridges that hinder progress across the Plateau.

Not all of Ed's team were enthusiastic about a dash for the Pole that could end dangerously at the bottom of a crevasse, or ignominiously with a call for help from an American plane if the tractors broke down or ran out of fuel. Ellis and Bates were both fed up with patching up worn-out old tractors. Murray Ellis wanted to join a dog team. 'Tractors don't sit up and wag their tails when you feed them,'[22] he said. Derek Wright, the photographer who had been co-opted as a driver, knew he was going to get good photos no matter how it turned out. Peter Mulgrew was all keenness: 'Let's go to the Pole, Ed.'[23] As for Ed, the Pole was a mountain that had to be climbed.

John Claydon flew in a last load of fuel to D700 on 20 December. Then, at 8.30 p.m., Ed signalled the start of the push to the south. 'Didn't sleep very well as my mind kept churning over,' he noted in his diary, and the churning might not have been helped by a message from Bowden: 'Meanwhile you should not proceed beyond Depot 700.'[24]

On 21 December, the day Fuchs rolled into South Ice, Ed sent him a message:

> Have completed stocking of depots ... Left D700 yesterday
> with three Fergusons and 20 drums of fuel with intention of
> proving the route another 200 miles and then if going proved
> easy doing a trip to the pole. Did 27 miles yesterday ... Will
> scrub southward jaunt if vehicles and fuel can be used in any
> way to expedite your safe crossing either by further depot
> or anything else you suggest. In the interim until I get your
> reply will continue out to 100 miles from D700 and will cairn
> crevasse areas ... Best wishes ... Ed Hillary.[25]

One can only speculate which messages were getting through and when, but three days later, on 24 December, a message was received from Fuchs which made no mention of Ed's intention of 'doing a trip to the pole':

> We arrived South Ice 21 December after severe crevasse
> trouble and three major recoveries of Sno-cats ... Consider
> this worst stage of journey and expect rapid travel from
> here on. Thanks for your information and proposed crevasse
> reconnaissance ... We expect leave South Ice 25th ... Happy
> Christmas to you all. Bunny[26]

Ed replied:

> Glad to hear of your arrival South Ice ... We are 390 miles
> from Pole. Have cairned two areas of crevasses since D700
> but last fifty miles has been clear going. Waiting one day here
> then will push on. Will attempt contact you as arranged and
> advise you of progress. Best of luck, happy Christmas and an
> early New Year at the Pole. Ed Hillary[27]

Ed felt pleased with the way events were shaping up, and he wrote
in his diary, 'Slept like a log. Lovely morning and found excellent
travelling surface. Long low folds and extensive vistas in every
direction. It really looks like a plateau.'[28]

By 26 December, with no word from Fuchs, Ed could no longer
contain his exuberance and sent out an arresting press release: 'Am
hellbent for the Pole, God willing and crevasses permitting.'[29]

But that evening in the caboose, Peter Mulgrew's radio delivered
the sort of message that might have been expected at any time over
the previous week. It was headed, 'Urgent personal Fuchs to Hillary'
and began with a discussion of how there was a risk they would run
out of fuel:

> ... this risk was accepted when we thought you would have
> difficulty stocking D700. In interests of whole expedition I
> do not feel we should continue to accept this risk and am in
> difficult position of feeling I must accept your offer to clear
> present crevasse area then establish additional fuel depot at
> appropriate position from D700 thus abandoning your idea
> of reaching Pole. Know this will be great disappointment
> to you and your companions, but the additional depot will
> enormously strengthen the position of the crossing party ...
> Bunny Fuchs[30]

The reality was that Fuchs had ample fuel to reach D700, where more
was stockpiled.[31] He had written in his diary a week earlier that 'there
is no objection to his [Hillary] going on to the Pole',[32] but since then
someone seems to have pointed out the undesirability of the Ferguson
tractors arriving before he did. It was bad enough that the Americans

'The Old Firm' who nursed and drove three tractors to the Pole (L to R): Hillary, Ellis, Bates, Mulgrew and Wright. HILLARY MUSEUM COLLECTION

had built a centrally heated base on top of the Pole, complete with regular plane flights and a canteen serving Coke and hamburgers, without the support party preceding him in their makeshift vehicles.

Ed was now unstoppable:

> Personal to Fuchs, 27 December. Your message has arrived too late as we are now 240 miles from the Pole with only ten drums left. Have neither the food nor fuel to sit here and await your arrival … Your previous messages gave no indication of your concern about your fuel so I presumed you were satisfied with the depot stocking as arranged. I am sure we can fly more fuel in to D700 and the other depots and in an emergency you could no doubt get a few drums from the Pole Station. We have seen no crevasses from 60 miles on the Pole side of D700 and you should make fast time over this section. Expect to arrive Pole in six days … Hillary.[33]

At this stage the vehicles at significant risk of running out of fuel were the three Ferguson tractors labouring towards the Pole. A couple of days of deep, soft snow and the expedition would end up man-hauling or calling on the Americans for an air drop. This was, as journalist Douglas McKenzie pointed out, 'a situation which the United States Navy in Antarctica, with its close knowledge of the New Zealanders' dog-team, twenty-six horse-power tractors, and single-engine air transport, accepted with affectionate resignation'.[34]

When the tractors wearily bucked and slithered into the Pole station on 4 January 1958, they had half a drum of fuel left of the 22 they had set out with 15 days earlier. It was a close-run thing.

Although there may have been a touch of polar remorse after arrival, Ed never really regretted what he'd done, even if he had exceeded the instructions framed for him back in 1956. He'd laid the depots but Fuchs's fleet of vehicles was a month late. Was Ed, as leader of what he saw as the New Zealand Antarctic Expedition, really expected to sit around at D700 waiting for the uncommunicative Dr Fuchs to arrive at an unknown date? Why shouldn't he go to the Pole? And as Fuchs had always been quick to point out, not always convincingly, his own main interest was the scientific programme, not the physical achievement of traversing the continent. For Ed, accepting the challenge was all: 'I would have despised myself if I hadn't continued – it was as simple as that – I just had to go on.'[35]

That was how Ed saw the matter, but the British press, not surprisingly, saw the dash to the Pole in a much less favourable light. Jon Stephenson expressed in restrained language the view of his fellow expedition members when he wrote: 'At the time most of us on the crossing party felt it was underhand.'[36]

The New Zealand press, also not surprisingly, liked to see resourceful, under-funded Kiwis achieving above expectations. The 75-year-old English-born New Zealand prime minister, Walter Nash, had even asked his Foreign Office for advice when Ed was still between D700 and the Pole. Their reply read:

> The most important considerations in the present situation are that:
> (a) Hillary has carried out his primary obligations with notable success

(b) If he were to wait for Fuchs at Depot 700 he might have to wait many weeks doing nothing

(c) A further reconnaissance would obviously assist Fuchs if and when he reaches the area

(d) Hillary is confident – and no one in New Zealand can question his judgment – that he can reach the South Pole with his present resources …

It appears, therefore, that there are no good grounds for instructing Hillary to return to Depot 700 there to await Fuchs' arrival – nor would such an instruction be easily explained to the New Zealand public.[37]

Ed wins the race but loses the game

If Ed had adopted a low profile after arriving at the Pole – perhaps some shoulder-shrugging modesty and a claim that he was doing it to help Bunny – there would have been some grumbling but not too much. Regrettably, he did not. On 3 January Ed made a bad move. If this had been a game of chess, it could have been said that Ed was playing a risky game against an older and more experienced opponent – and that what he did next was to lose his queen and put himself in check. The message he sent was this:

> Dear Bunny, I am very concerned about the serious delay in your plans. It is about 1,250 miles from the Pole to Scott Base, much of the travelling from D700 north being somewhat slow and laborious with rough, hard sastrugi. Leaving the Pole late in January you will head into increasing bad weather and winter temperatures plus vehicles that are showing signs of strain. Both of my mechanics regard such a late journey as an unjustifiable risk and are not prepared to wait and travel with your party. I agree with this view and think you should seriously consider splitting your journey over two years. You still probably have a major journey in front of you to reach the Pole. Why not winter your vehicles at the Pole, fly out to Scott Base with American aircraft, return to civilisation for the winter and then fly back in to the Pole Station next November and complete your journey. This plan would enable you to do a far more satisfactory job of your seismic work and I feel fairly confident that Admiral Dufek would assist …[38]

*International cooperation: Admiral George Dufek and Ed Hillary at the South Pole,
February 1958, awaiting arrival of the Fuchs party.* HILLARY MUSEUM COLLECTION

There were many reasons why Ed should not be handing out this sort
of advice. For a start, he'd have known better than anyone that Fuchs
could pick up speed once he'd joined the route established to Scott
Base. The tracks would lead them around or through the crevassed
areas, and Ed knew in detail which slopes to descend through the
snakes and ladders of the Skelton Glacier. The Sno-Cats with their
four broad pontoon feet could handle soft snow better than the
tractors and could bridge crevasses more easily. The dog teams, which
had been a limiting factor, were to be flown out to Scott Base by the
Americans. Seismic shots would become less frequent. Removal of
these limitations meant that on a trouble-free day the vehicles could
cover 60 miles.

More important than this increase in speed was the personality
of Bunny Fuchs. He was not a person who gave up, yet here was his
deputy – someone who had just upstaged him with his dash to the

Pole – advising just that. British bulldogs do not give up. There could be only one response to Ed's suggestion, and two days later, while still more than 300 miles from the Pole, Fuchs delivered it:

> Appreciate your concern but there can be no question of abandoning journey at this stage … I understand your mechanics' reluctance to undertake further travel, and in view of your opinion that late season travel is an unjustifiable risk I do not feel able to ask you to join us at D700 in spite of your valuable local knowledge. We will therefore have to wend our way using the traverse you leave at the Pole … Bunny Fuchs[39]

If you're in a hole, stop digging, but Ed now compounded his error by sending a long cable to Sir John Slessor, finishing with the advice:

> To my mind enough prestige will have been gained by the arrival of Fuchs and ourselves at the South Pole to enable a modification of the plan to allow the task to be carried out in a reasonable and safe manner over a two year period whereas a forced march late in the season could well cause most unfavourable publicity. Your instructions are the only things that can enable Fuchs to save face and adopt a modified plan so I would earnestly request that the Management Committee should give this matter its earliest consideration. Hillary[40]

Up to now, the exchange of messages between Hillary and Fuchs had, in theory at least, been private, but confidentiality was always fragile. The final, unfortunate act in the saga took place in the Wellington post office through which was passing Ed's private recommendation to the London committee. The clerk handling cables from the Antarctic had noted as a general rule of thumb that a long cable was a press release while the shorter communications were for the committees. The cable to Slessor and Bowden was long – so was delivered into the incredulous but grateful hands of a waiting press. Slessor and Bowden read the contents of their private cables as banner headlines in the London and Wellington dailies. As Arthur Helm said to Ed in the course of an explanation and apology, 'From there on the whole thing blew up.'[41] The message went viral.

Why was it that Ed Hillary made such a bungle? There could be no excuses, but at least there might be an explanation. Ed had lost his respect for Fuchs. He disliked Fuchs's assumption of superiority despite the imperfections of some of his decisions. He disliked his reluctance to communicate and his lack of empathy with other people. He was seriously worried that Fuchs was travelling so slowly that the whole expedition would miss the boat which was due to depart for New Zealand in March. Fuchs was averaging 20 miles a day on the Plateau from South Ice to the Pole, and at that rate he wouldn't reach Scott Base until the end of March, the date when Scott had died of starvation and cold. This wasn't going to happen to the TAE, but if the last transport departed before they arrived at Scott Base, Ed faced the unappealing prospect of spending the winter and spring of 1958 in the close company of Bunny Fuchs.

Who did Ed turn to for advice on his dash to the Pole? If Louise had been available for consultation, she would have recognised the folly of advising Fuchs to give up. But instead of Louise he had Peter Mulgrew as his companion in the caboose, the 12-by-4-foot caravan on skis which housed the radio and their bunks. The other three had their own tents, heated by a primus stove, and they cooked their meals separately. The isolation of living and travelling in the colder corners of the Antarctic can bring people close to each other but can also feed paranoia. One can imagine Hillary and Mulgrew entering a *folie à deux* as they read and wrote their radio messages and expressed their exasperations as to what Fuchs was doing or not doing. Combine this with hubris and it was a dangerous brew.

There was an unaccustomedly rueful note in the letters Ed wrote to Louise:

> 8 January 1958
> Well, darling, I'm rather glad we did get to the Pole even if it does appear to have provoked a bit of a storm. It was most unfortunate that they released to the Press my private note about Bunny pulling out at the Pole – it certainly stirred up a lot of comment ... I think Bunny's pride has been so hurt that he'll be keen to cross whatever happens. I've received a swag of telegrams just like the old Everest days ... and an

enthusiastic cable from Hodders wanting to sign me up for my personal book on the same terms as High Adventure which was pretty useful financially …

In the last week I had a lot of worry as to whether our fuel was going to hold out and also the small nagging voice wondering if I was going to find the place. Well, as usual, everything turned out perfectly and we arrived without difficulty on our last drum of fuel. My navigation has been most encouraging. However it has all been a time of high tension and I'd driven everyone pretty hard and we hadn't had much sleep so we were very pleased to arrive. I can quite honestly say I haven't got the dash for this sort of thing anymore. I certainly still can push things pretty fiercely but it takes more out of me and I don't get the same satisfaction out of it. Also … I have to make myself do things involving much risk …

15 January
My dearest Louise, In a way it's a slightly trying time at the moment … As you no doubt realise, I'm fed up to the gills with Bunny … I've been hearing all the gossip … Bunny is being most secretive about his activities and progress and we find it extremely difficult to prise even the smallest amount of information out of him … When I examine the position objectively I must admit I feel quite confident that Bunny will get to McMurdo OK … The newspaper controversy was a bit sickening … my main interest now is to get away from it all…'[42]

Fuchs and his Sno-Cats, flags flying bravely, arrived in triumph at the Pole on 19 January 1958. Ed flew in from Scott Base to display as warm a welcome as he could muster before returning to the base. By 7 February, averaging 37 miles per day, the same speed as the tractors, the Sno-Cats had reached D700, where they were joined by Ed, flown in to be Fuchs's guide down the Skelton. They reached Scott Base on 2 March. Within an hour of arrival, Bunny Fuchs had become Sir Vivian. He announced in a self-deprecating way that he had taken 99 days rather than the 100 days he had predicted – a claim to accuracy that avoided discussion on how far astray his early projections had

Civic welcome of Antarctic heroes: Fuchs and Hillary in Wellington, March 1958.
HILLARY MUSEUM COLLECTION

been. Nevertheless, the limelight shone on Bunny Fuchs, leaving Hillary in the background, a position he had not been used to after Everest.

Ed never admitted in his autobiographies that he had made mistakes in his dealings with Fuchs, but their incompatibility was made clear. Travelling with Dufek he wrote, 'I boarded a plane with George Dufek and flew back to Scott Base. Why was it, I wondered that I always felt slightly uncomfortable with Bunny and yet completely relaxed with Admiral George Dufek?'[43] Over the years one never heard Ed talk much about his dash to the Pole. It became part of his mythology, taking farm tractors across the ice, but there were some sore spots there that were best left alone.

Louise and Ed with their children, 1959. Sarah is holding tiny baby Belinda.

CHAPTER 21

Beekeeper in search of a
better-paying occupation

———◆———

S ince Everest and through the Antarctic, Ed had been kept busy,
but by 1958 he was looking at a future with not much to support
a wife and two small children. A year or two back there had been
talk of joining Bunny Fuchs on a lecture tour, but this now had little
appeal for either party. Ed was named co-author of the expedition
book, *The Crossing of Antarctica*, but as the Author's Acknowledgements
not too obliquely indicate, the main author was V.E.F. Ed's account of
the establishment of four depots and the trip to the Pole was tucked
into a chapter entitled 'Spring and Summer Journeys from Scott Base'.

Rear-Admiral Cecil R.L. Parry wrote on 7 October 1958 that the
Finance Committee of the TAE had met to discuss honorariums for
the book and 'it was decided to give you £250 for your contribution'.[1] It
was a small reward for the startling publicity generated by Ed's dash to
the Pole and his subsequent self-harming free advice to Fuchs. Fuchs
himself wrote with clarity and precision, and the book sold 130,000
copies in hardcover alone.[2] But anyone interested in the clash of
personalities, or personalities at all, would have been disappointed.

Ever since Everest, Ed had been reassured that money would never
again be a problem. Don't worry, he was frequently told, 'you'll get lots
of directorships and good government jobs. They're sure to make you an
ambassador or something! … Mostly I was approached by people who
sold cigarettes or hair cream and thought my title would look good in

one of their advertisements even if I didn't use their products. I was in considerable demand for luncheon talks and as a guest of honour at country balls ...'[3] With a population of just over two million, many of them in the farming sector, New Zealand in the 1950s and '60s offered lean pickings for its few celebrities. Business consisted largely of import licences which gave the owner a steady stream of income from a monopoly whose maintenance required little work. There were few company boards looking for enterprising directors, and Ed saw himself as left-wing anyway. The Great Depression of the 1930s was the background to his formative teenage years. His pacifist, anti-imperial father was a powerful influence: 'I admired his moral courage – he would battle fiercely against society or the powers-that-be on a matter of principle.'[4] And even in the more prosperous decades of the 1990s and 2000s, Ed was never interested in acquiring wealth beyond the ordinary comforts of a New Zealand middle-class family.

What about a diplomatic post? Ed had probably disqualified himself from a job requiring diplomacy. Officialdom, whether in Wellington or London, was unforgiving. As Douglas McKenzie wrote in 1963: '... the effect of official disapprobation was pervasive ... Edmund Hillary had embarrassed the Ross Sea Committee ... and he had embarrassed the government – than whom there is no body in New Zealand more easily chilled by United Kingdom disapproval.'[5]

Ed shared his restlessness with George Lowe, who had decided to live in England rather than return to New Zealand – but doing what?

> '11/8/58. Dear George, Your life seems to have dropped back into the old routine without much indication of substantial progress ... What has happened to all those movie cameraman possibilities? The lecturing life produces a comfortable income but it doesn't seem to have a helluva lot of future ... Mind you I can't talk as I'm still somewhat at a loose end. All the rosy ideas that were floating about on my return from McMurdo about worthwhile Public jobs have effectively disappeared making it obvious that nothing will be handed out on a platter. So for the next year or two I'll be combining the writing of my personal book with part-time bee-keeping ...'[6]

George was in the middle of writing his own personal account, but books could not be published within three years of 1 March 1958 without permission from the London committee of the TAE. Lowe was granted permission, but Ed had to wait until 1961. George's preferred title for his book, published in 1959, was the elegant *No Latitude for Error*, but his English publishers favoured *Because It Is There*. But *No Latitude for Error* was too good a title to waste, and Ed gladly used it himself. In his Foreword he wrote:

> This is an account of my personal participation in Antarctic exploration from my first meeting with Sir Vivian Fuchs in 1953 until the conclusion of the Trans-Antarctic Expedition in 1958 – by which time my party had completed the first tractor trip to the South Pole and Fuchs the first crossing of the Antarctic Continent.
>
> It does not seek to follow the pattern of an 'Official Account' which, by custom, eschews all personal problems and conflicts and details only the inexorable progress of the expedition, step by step and according to plan, until the grand but inevitable conclusion is reached. Instead I have sought to recreate the whole adventure as I lived it at the time – my pleasures or disappointments, successes or failures.
>
> Much of my story covers the activities of the first New Zealand Antarctic Expedition, which though an integral part of the Commonwealth Trans-Antarctic Expedition yet had very much an entity of its own – and an irrepressible enthusiasm which resulted in widespread exploration and scientific activity. Success in an expedition is only achieved through a combined effort, and for this I must thank the members of my New Zealand party; for my mistakes I have only myself to blame.

Ed's request to publish earlier than 1961 was considered by the London committee, which made its acceptance dependent on payment of 10 per cent of royalties to the TAE and manuscript approval by Fuchs – which was not forthcoming. Fuchs 'found the tone of the book distasteful'.[7]

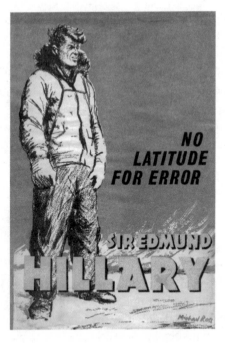

Cover of No Latitude for Error, *published in 1961.*

A handful of reviews in Ed's files show some New Zealand reactions to the book after it was published in 1961. The *Auckland Star* reviewer wrote:

> It is unfortunate that the controversy that has arisen over the author's relations with the Ross Sea Committee over his dash to the Pole has put the viewing of this book out of focus. Basically it is a story of thrilling adventure, of hazardous deeds, of privations and the dogged overcoming of difficulties. And it is the best book written on Antarctic exploration. Sir Edmund's powers of authorship have increased and through the story one sees the steady development of his qualities of leadership ...[8]

The *Wairarapa Times* gave a variant of the title: *No Room for Latitude.*[9]

E.R.S., in *Zealandia,* asked:

What was the point of making a trip to the South Pole by tractor and dog-team when it could so easily be reached by air?

For Sir Edmund it was just another adventure with no more purpose than playing a Rugby match. The game was the thing: the geophysical objects and the detailed examination of the southern land mass were secondary ... The planners fell into two categories, the scientists and the publicists ... The publicists wanted a story of endurance with Fuchs as its hero – whereas Hillary felt that whoever won the race to the South Pole was the hero ... The humorous angle, that planes were flying to and from the Pole almost every day, seems to have escaped both Hillary and the publicists. It was a fine feat of endurance but about as much an exploring trip as walking cross-country from Hamilton to Te Kuiti.

What sort of man is Edmund Hillary? To judge by his own account, an old-fashioned blood-boots-and-sweat explorer, whose tragedy it is to be born a hundred years too late. Machines do much more efficiently what was done laboriously by the pioneers of yesteryear. So Hillary and his like are reduced to climbing mountain peaks and making expeditions which serve, in the main, no very great purpose.

Hillary is also quite obviously a leader of men, the kind of person who can get things done by rule of thumb when more complicated methods only add to the confusion.

The controversy? The truth is that Hillary was on time while Fuchs was late. The people who wrote the script had Fuchs as hero but if they wanted to keep the story straight, they wouldn't have put Hillary in a minor part – he was too big to fit it.

Admiral Dufek could have been forgiven if he had greeted Hillary and Fuchs at the Pole with the war-time slogan: 'Was your journey really necessary?' It says something for his urbanity and kindness that he did not, but treated them instead with the kindness and helpfulness of a big brother helping the children with their games.[10]

When Ed was not writing his book or encouraging Rex to look after the bees, he was landscaping the steep slope on which he had built the family's new house, described by a visiting French journalist as *très bijou*. The property below the house was an old orchard, and in the winter of 1958 Ed dug paths, planted grass and created narrow garden beds where flowers, mint and parsley could be grown. As he worked on his book in his study he could watch winter squalls of rain change quickly to theatrically brilliant light on a distant sea varying from grey, through green, to bright azure.

In July Ed had tried to assuage the old restlessness with an attempt on an unclimbed ridge on Scott's Knob in the Kaikōuras, an area for which he retained a perverse affection from his Air Force days. Accompanying him were the ever-loyal Rex, Antarctic accomplice Peter Mulgrew, and Louise who was three months pregnant with Belinda. Leaving the road late one afternoon, and carrying heavy loads, they set off up a gorge where there was ice on every pool and on the fringes of the river. Ed and Peter shot two pigs which they roasted over a camp fire. Four days later, leaving Louise behind in the tent, they made their attempt on Scott's Knob up an icy unstable ridge, watched by nearby wild thar and chamois. But the ridge was too long and the winter daylight too short, so they abandoned the climb and returned to the waiting Louise who might have been reflecting that this would have been an inhospitable place to have a miscarriage. In his diary next day Ed wrote, 'Have decided that Kaikouras too tough for Louise and she will go to Christchurch.'[11] We do not have Louise's account of this or similar trips.

On 30 December 1958 Ed, still restless, wrote to John Hunt:

> Dear John, I've been putting some thoughts into my future activities. Although I have a number of expedition possibilities, I don't particularly want to follow this type of existence for ever, even if I could … I investigated the prospects of getting some sort of NZ Diplomatic job such as NZ High Commissioner in India but although the Government hastens to laud my mythical virtues in public, there has been singularly little response … The problem is not a financial one – I am getting a reasonable living out of being an Apiarist cum Author – but it is mainly the need to

get sufficient mental satisfaction and stimulation out of the
work I'm doing … I don't know if I told you that I'd put in an
application to the Chinese People's Republic for the North
side of Everest in 1960 … Ed

There is no reply to this letter in the files, but as a boost to morale,
if not to the bank account, a telegram came on 18 March 1959 from
Larry Kirwan of the Royal Geographic Society:

happy to inform you that her majesty the queen has
approved award to you of rgs founders medal 1958 for
your contribution to antarctic and himalayan exploration
stop all hope you are coming england to lecture june
and could receive gold medal then stop congratulations =
kirwan[12]

The seed of a Himalayan Expedition is planted

Ed always had at the back of his mind a shortlist of expeditions he
would launch if he could find the funds. Two of them were centred on
Everest. The first was an attempt to complete the pre-war British route
from the north through Tibet, now the Tibetan province of China. The
second was an ascent of Everest without oxygen. Best of all, combine
the two.

A third reason for such an expedition had been added the previous
year in the Antarctic when Ed by chance stumbled on Griff Pugh,
physiologist to the Cho Oyu and Everest expeditions. Griff was
carrying out the sort of physiology he did best: studying, in difficult
conditions, adaptation to cold while living in a tent pitched close
to Scott Base. Ed's diary notes: 'Had a long talk to Griff about a
Physiological Expedition in Feb 1960.'[13]

Inevitably, they talked of Everest. Was it possible without oxygen?
The British expeditions between the wars, and Lambert and Tenzing in
1952, had reached 28,000ft unaided, but in both cases there had been
reasons other than altitude why they could not go further. Surely, with
a support team using oxygen to establish camps, two unladen climbers
could use this prepared route to reach the summit without oxygen sets?

Then they asked, how could acclimatisation be improved? During
the couple of months or so when expedition climbers are at or above

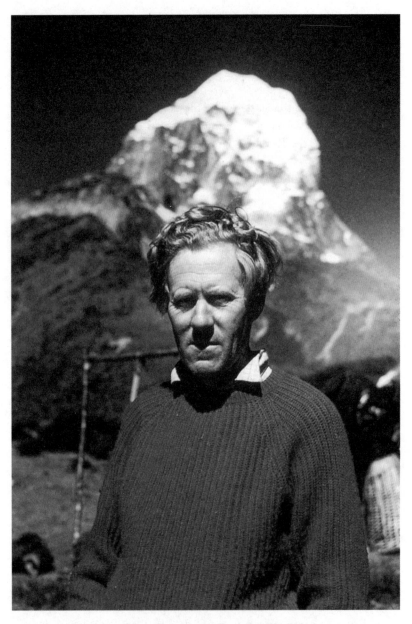

Dr Griffith Pugh, research physiologist and scientific leader of the Silver Hut expedition at Mingbo in the Himalayas with Taweche behind.

HILLARY MUSEUM COLLECTION

20,000ft, they steadily improve their acclimatisation. Why not live at 20,000ft for six months, through a Himalayan winter, and then make an oxygenless attempt on Everest?

Griff, the physiologist, envisaged them living in a high-altitude laboratory hut where he and other scientists could study the processes of acclimatisation in comfort. The problem, as always, was who would pay for it. Ed was too aware of the magnitude of the task to spend much time on it, though Griff wrote five months later that 'I and some of my colleagues will be formulating a draft proposal which we will send to you.'[14]

Over the next 10 months there were a couple of desultory exchanges. Ed was not at all enthusiastic about Everest by way of the South Col route. Failure – a strong probability – could only tarnish the glory of the ascent of 1953, and he knew that he was past his prime as a high-altitude climber. But the gleam of a challenge caught his imagination: 'I'd quite like to have a crack at Makalu.'[15] There was some unfinished business there.

In April 1959 Griff delivered his draft plan for an attempt to get two climbers to the summit of Everest via the 1953 route without using oxygen. He had been impressed by the standard of comfort of the huts at Scott Base and the way Antarctic depots could be established months in advance of their use. The huts he envisaged would be warm and comfortable, and equipped with modern laboratory facilities. Two of them would be built, one at Everest Base Camp, the other in the Western Cwm at 20,000ft.

During the winter expedition members would become increasingly well acclimatised, and in spring, the plan explained:

> a safe route should be established as far as the South Col, and
> a series of dumps laid, as in polar practice. For this purpose
> sledges should be provided, which would be man hauled as far
> as the Lhotse face, and drawn up from there by a wire cable
> and mechanical winch. In order to avoid the strain of repeated
> visits to 26,000 feet, oxygen equipment should be used during
> this phase. Before the assault phase, 2 further camps should
> be laid at 27,000 feet and 28,000 feet by parties using oxygen
> equipment.[16]

Two ascents of the mountain would be made, the first using oxygen, the second without.

Ed's reply was non-committal:

> Dear Griff, Thanks for your letter of 6th April and the enclosed draft plan for a combined Scientific and Mountaineering Expedition to Mt Everest. As you probably know my request to the Chinese for permission for a go at the north was rebuffed (as was only to be expected after the recent troubles in Tibet). Your draft plan is in many respects similar to my own …[17]

He might have added that this was not an expedition for the faint-hearted: it involved climbing the dangerously unstable Khumbu Icefall throughout winter, man-hauling camps up the Cwm to the Lhotse Face, establishing a winch and cable lift to the South Col, and finally putting in two camps above the Col.

When Ed wrote again in more detail, he dropped the idea of a winter hut in the Cwm, and added a second group of climbers who would arrive in March without wintering over and whose performance could be compared with that of the winter group. Ed was conscious of the limited public appeal of physiology, and in an earlier version had the winter party observing yetis and 'chasing them on skis'.[18] Conversely, no doubt, the yetis would be observing the climbers and chasing them on foot.

To Griff's suggestion that Ed should apply for Everest permission 'forthwith', Ed replied:

> I find it difficult to raise too much enthusiasm for the attack by the old route until something more tangible is available on the financial side … I'm damn certain we'd get someone to the top without oxygen but we'd need a lot of cash … Don't bother about me if you'd like to rake John Hunt in to run it – he'd probably be a lot more suitable and has the advantage of living in the UK … not that I don't think that you and I would work in rather well together.
>
> Best of luck Griff. Regards, Ed.[19]

The American connection
One day in the middle of 1959, when these ideas for another

Himalayan expedition were brewing, Ed's meagre earnings from beekeeping were supplemented by the useful sum of US$1000. *Argosy*, a men's adventure magazine, had chosen Ed as the recipient of its annual Explorer of the Year award. This involved a trip to New York to address the award banquet. As he and Louise boarded the plane, Ed could not have guessed that the trip would provide more money than $1000, or that it would lead to a large and complex expedition and a paid career for the rest of his life.

This change in fortune came about through John Dienhart, a lateral-thinking marketing director working for World Book Encyclopedia, the world's bestselling encyclopedia made up of 21 volumes of concise, carefully crafted entries. When he heard Ed's acceptance speech in New York, he was impressed not only by the famous explorer's physical presence but also by his ability as a speaker, the enthusiasm and energy with which he could engage an audience, his sense of humour, his infectious laugh. Here was a personality who could connect with a generation of children and parents buying World Book Encyclopedia, and inspire its sales force to greater heights.

He invited Ed to World Book's headquarters in Chicago to take part in an educational film for television. One evening after an unusually good dinner, Ed talked expansively about his dreams for the future, including his expedition that would combine yeti-hunting, physiology and an oxygenless attempt on Everest or perhaps Makalu.

In 1953 it had been natural for Ed to appear as an engagingly self-deprecating, even naïve mountaineer from a small country. Six years of fame might have gone to his head, but by now Ed recognised that people loved him for his simple modesty – which by now had become just a little less simple and a little more knowing. Ed had developed a bond with Americans during his time in Antarctica. They were generous, of course, but there was something about their easy-going nature that he responded to, just as they responded to his easy and unassuming sociability.

Ed had not been long back in New Zealand when he received a phone call from John Dienhart. He replied:

> Dear John, Your telephone call was something of a surprise
> and has made me do some quick thinking. I have a number
> of plans under way already and these may well not be of the

type and magnitude to appeal to World Book Encyclopedia. My big ambition, as you know, is to take a Physiological Expedition to the Tibetan side of Everest and attempt to get a party to the top without oxygen, but this is not possible due to the political situation.

Perhaps I might give you an idea of my plans for the next 18 months or so. I hope you will keep them confidential.

October–December 1959: A short trip in New Zealand to attempt the unclimbed north ridge of Mt. Hopeless followed by a fortnight hunting deer, chamois and thar in isolated mountain areas of New Zealand.

July–September 1960: In London and the USA lecturing and launching my new book on the Antarctic and hoping to raise $40,000 for my 'Around Everest' expedition. I hope you will keep it very much to yourself as any publicity could result in me having to dodge a Chinese army reception committee.

March–July 1961: This expedition will be the first complete circuit of Mt. Everest. Although this expedition will not descend below 18,000ft, over half of the route will be in Tibet so secrecy will have to be observed until the conclusion of the expedition. The party will need to be mobile and fast.

As you can see, these plans do not include a search for the Abominable Snowman. In my view the best time of year for such a search would be during the winter. By moving around on skis it should be possible to keep a very close watch on some of the suspected haunts of the Yeti. However any sponsor of such an expedition would need to realise that the chances are definitely against finding the creature – although of course this might just be the lucky party.

In general, John, everything is pretty well definite up to until September 1960 but I have only just started the ball rolling for 'Around Everest'. The main problem in organising an expedition is that you need finances before you go, whereas the money producing items such as films and articles aren't available until the end of the expedition.

If any useful purpose will be served by my coming to Chicago I will arrange a suitable date.

Kindest regards, Ed Hillary[20]

This somewhat disingenuous letter was a bait for the more expensive yeti/physiology expedition. An attempt on the unclimbed north ridge of Mt Hopeless, 7472ft, sounds like a comic sequel to *The Ascent of Rum Doodle*. A circumnavigation of Everest, most of it in Tibet, would almost certainly lead to capture, a major international incident and a long stay in a Chinese gaol. An unknown New Zealand beekeeper could cross the Nup La undetected for a few days in 1952, but his famous reincarnation could hardly escape notice in 1961 as he crossed the headwaters of the Rongbuk and Kharta valleys to re-enter Nepal alongside Makalu.

Dienhart responded with a request for a plan of the yeti expedition. Ed summarised the objectives as:

> A thorough search for the Abominable Snowman or Yeti, plus an extended programme of physiological research into the acclimatisation of the human body to high altitudes …

> 1. Evidence either proving or disproving the existence of the Yeti.
> 2. A party of climbers to winter for the first time at 20,000ft as a physiological experiment …
> 3. As the culmination of a long period of acclimatisation, get a party of men to the summit of Mt Makalu 27,790ft without using oxygen …[21]

He continued with an elaboration of these themes in terms vague enough to arouse the admiration of the World Book marketing team. 'It is obvious that this creature is very elusive and that the slightest sound or smell of humans is enough to send it to ground.' Ed noted that an advantage of searching in autumn would be that yeti would be working their way down-valley ahead of the advancing winter snows.

Promoting the physiology of acclimatisation was more difficult than the prospect of finding a yeti, but there was always the tenuous link to space travel: 'Man is reaching out to the stars and research into the technique of how to live in air of low oxygen content could well prove useful on some other planet in the not too distant future … I think an overall cost of $120,000 would produce a good expedition.'[22]

The result was an invitation to Chicago to meet the board of World

Book. In a letter to Louise, Ed sounds vaguely stunned as he describes the occasion and takes in the size of the task ahead:

> My dearest Lulu, Well everything has gone almost too easily and here I am with $125,000 to spend ... I flew to Chicago in perfect weather. Tuesday was the big day. At 9.30am I attended the meeting of the Directors and explained everything to them. They proved to be an extraordinarily pleasant crowd ... Anyway they agreed to support the whole expedition to the tune of $125,000 and gave me practically a free hand.
>
> They were particularly interested in the aftermath of the Expedition and wanted me to lecture on their behalf for 6 or 8 months around High Schools and Clubs etc. – at a salary to be agreed. They offered to transport you and the family over as well. I said I thought it would be possible ... We agreed that I would receive 20% of all the proceeds from books, magazine articles films etc. They are advancing me against this a salary at the rate of $10,000 a year. So we won't be poor ...[23]

Let planning commence

Suddenly it was all happening, and with less than a year before departure. Griff Pugh quickly arranged nine months' paid leave and began to plan the scientific programme and its personnel. An easy choice was Mike Ward, Griff's medical associate on Everest in 1953. Mike's everyday work was a far cry from physiology – he was a surgeon practising in East London – but Griff knew that he could rely on his unqualified support. Griff then sent out an appeal on the grapevine for interested respiratory physiologists, and found three more members.

An early response came from John West, a talented Australian physiologist working with the prestigious Respiratory Group at Hammersmith Hospital in London. He had heard about the expedition at a meeting of the English Physiological Society, applied to Griff and was accepted.

Jim Milledge, a respiratory physician who had graduated from Birmingham, had read about the expedition in the *Telegraph*. Like John West, he kept fit and was familiar with mountains through skiing. A third application from within UK came from Sukhamay Lahiri, a graduate from Calcutta now doing research at Oxford. From outside the UK came Tom Nevison from the US Air Force. Then there was me, Mike Gill from Ed's home city of Auckland. In 1959 I was at medical school at Dunedin, but saw myself as working towards an unrecognised PhD in mountaineering, with medicine as a back-up in the event that I should need to earn a living. I came to the expedition through a brief item on the back page of the *Auckland Star* of 23 December 1959: 'Sir Edmund Hillary is looking for two young New Zealand climbers to accompany him on his forthcoming Himalayan Expedition – and he is willing to receive applications from anyone interested.'

I dropped the newspaper, took up pen and paper, and spent two hours drafting as persuasive a letter as I could. The age limits were 25 to 35. I was 22, too young, so after some consideration decided to give myself an extra year. Climbing qualifications: I could muster a good record of climbs new and old. 'I have an ape-like build peculiarly suited to climbing,' I added. And then my trump card: the expedition was concerned not only with mountaineering but with physiology, and I had a Bachelor of Medical Science research degree in physiology. I sealed the letter, walked the mile and a half to Sir Edmund's home, and dropped it in his mail box. The following afternoon I was called to the phone. A voice barked out of the earpiece at me: 'Is that Michael Gill? Ed Hillary speaking. I got your letter today. What about coming up and having a yarn.'

'Yes,' I said. 'Yes. Certainly. When?'

'Well, why not come up now if you can spare the time.'

Within an hour I was knocking nervously on the door. I was warmly welcomed by an attractive Lady Hillary who looked at me with some curiosity as she invited me in. 'We've been just dying to know what this ape-like person looked like,' she explained.

It was not a very formal interview. The climbing record was fine and Ed had made an inquiry about my degree. 'I was talking to a doctor friend and he said this B. Med Science degree is a pretty good one. I'll let you know later whether there's a place for you on the expedition.'

Three months later in Dunedin an urgent telegram arrived: 'Appreciate you call me at your earliest convenience. Hillary'.

The call came through:

'That you, Mike? Thanks for your letter. Are you still interested in this expedition?'

'Yes I am.'

'Well. I guess you may as well come along. And look, I don't know how tied up you are down there, but if you can get the time off I'd like you to go over to London for three months before the trip starts and work with Griff to get yourself *au fait* with the physiology side of things. How does that sound to you?'

'That – that sounds incredible.'

'Well, I'll let you know a few more details later. Louise and I are going to Chicago and you could travel with us. How about dropping Griff Pugh a line in the meantime – here's the address ...'

I put the phone down, stunned. A flatmate standing nearby had picked up the conversation. He looked enviously at me.

'You lucky bastard.'

Chicago and London

Close to midnight on 29 May, anniversary of a more famous occasion, I found myself walking across the wet tarmac towards the first plane I had set foot in, an Electra gleaming against the black backdrop of the night. Four stops later, we landed in Chicago where Ed had publicity events to attend to. There was a luncheon for the whole staff of World Book on the top floor of the Merchandise Mart where Ed was to tell them about the expedition the company was funding. As the time came for Ed to address the assembled multitude I thought to myself what an ordeal it must be, but then I saw a professional in action: a few sentences that linked him to World Book, which made him one of them; a story that made them laugh; a lucid account of the expedition, with the occasional back reference to the Himalayas or the Antarctic. It was masterly and the audience loved him.

A television interview followed in the open space on the roof of the Mart. The main spokesperson for the yeti part of the expedition was Marlin Perkins, the 50-year-old director of the Lincoln Park Zoo in Chicago and well known for his zoo programme, *Wild Kingdom*, on TV. He was slim, quietly spoken, distinguished-looking, with a fine head of silver hair. Standing beside him was a 2.5-metre high artist's impression of a yeti, a barrel-chested primate that could have crushed any of us with one hand.

'Tell me, Marlin,' said the interviewer, 'what makes you think there is such a thing as a yeti?'

Expedition member Marlin Perkins explains to Chicago TV how he hopes to capture a yeti for his zoo. HILLARY MUSEUM COLLECTION

'Well, Dave, everyone who goes to the Himalayas hears about them and after a while you begin to think that, well, where there's smoke there's fire. But I think the best evidence is these photos of yeti tracks I've got here. Eric Shipton took these in 1951 right in the place where we're going hunting. All I know is that something must have made these tracks.'

'And you hope to catch him, do you?'

'Yes we do. We've got powerful spotting telescopes, we've got cameras set off by trip-wires and we've got tape-recorders for picking up the noise he makes.'

'But how are you actually going to catch him, Marlin?'

'Well, I'll show you, Dave. You see this gun I've got here? This is a Capchur gun which shoots a needle loaded with tranquilliser. All you have to do is estimate the size of the yeti, adjust the dose and let the critter have it. Like this.' And, raising the gun, with great deliberation he plunked a dart into a padded area on the animal's belly.

'Of course, if I make the dose too big, I might kill him.'

'And I guess if you make it too small he might kill you.'

'Yes, Dave, I guess that's so.'

'Just one more question, Marlin. What are you going to do with the yeti once you've got him?'

'Dave, I couldn't think of a better place than the Lincoln Park Zoo in Chicago.'

After a week in Chicago, we moved on through New York to London where we were met by Griff Pugh, a tall, stooped figure with splendid thick orange hair. He had a hesitant charm, a mildly deprecating smile and a quietly British way of greeting that set him apart from his more effusive American counterparts in Chicago.

'Hello Ed. Nice to see you. Where's your luggage. I've got a car outside.'

It was a new, silver-grey, two-seater Austin Healey. 'Nice little car,' said Griff as he climbed into the driver's seat. We tied our luggage on the back as best we could. Ed took the front seat while Louise and I perched on top of luggage in the space behind. As the car drew out and picked up speed, we felt the force of the wind striking us at shoulder level.

'I hope he doesn't go too fast,' Louise shouted to me. We could just hear Griff talking to Ed.

'I'll take her down the M1 and show you what she can do …'

'That was a hundred and ten miles an hour,' explained Griff when we had slowed down. It was the first of a series of car journeys that turned out to be the most exciting and dangerous moments of the expedition.

For the next few days Griff and his wife Josephine kindly put me up in their grand house at Hatching Green. There were large oil paintings of ancestors on the walls. The Pughs appeared in *Debrett's Peerage*, and Josephine was an heiress to part of a large fortune created by her great-uncle Sir Ernest Cassel. These were levels of sophistication and wealth that hardly existed in New Zealand.

Each day Griff drove me into his laboratory at the MRC building beside Hampstead Heath. The morning drive at 10 a.m. was after the main commuter influx, but at 6 p.m. the homeward-bound traffic was bumper-to-bumper in its single lane. Griff, pulling out into the empty oncoming lane, would accelerate past a line of slow-moving commuters until a corner, or an approaching car, made it necessary to re-enter the slow lane, thumb on horn as a request for a space to be made. These were moments of high emotion: exhilaration for Griff, terror for his passenger, impotent rage for the line of less adventurous commuters. Griff was an accident waiting to happen – and it did shortly after his return from the Himalayas. The Austin Healey was a write-off, Griff laid up with a broken hip.

At the laboratory I met Mike Ward, Jim Milledge and John West as they came in for their baseline studies, riding the bicycle ergometer at five work rates ranging from easy to maximal. I learned to handle the bags and tubes, to measure O_2 and CO_2 levels in expired air samples, and calculate the results. As the day of departure came closer, I was increasingly involved in sorting and packing equipment:

> Dear Ed, The chaos at Hampstead this week is indescribable: the lab is littered from end to end with apparatus of all sorts, half-packed cases, wrapping, new parcels arriving all the time; Griff shuffles round amongst it all with a hunted look, cursing everyone for their inefficiency. The phone rings continuously in the background, usually with some irate person complaining bitterly about suddenly receiving an order that they can't possibly hope to deliver on time. Meanwhile Pam, the lab-girl, and I, struggle on with packing … I spent a profitable three days at Cambridge learning how to do psychometric tests … Mike[24]

By the last week of August the loose ends had been tidied up. The last of the sea-level tests had been completed, and we had spent a weekend assembling the pre-fabricated Silver Hut designed in England by the Timber Development Association in association with Griff. The future looked rosy. Deliver a yeti to the Lincoln Park Zoo in Chicago. Live in the comfort of this fine hut through a Himalayan winter at 19,000ft. Then a quick, oxygenless ascent of Makalu. What could go wrong?

CHAPTER 22

The Silver Hut expedition

$\Longrightarrow\!\!\!\!\diamond\!\!\!\!\Longleftarrow$

Kathmandu in 1960 had only recently been opened to the rest of the world. In 1951 a bloodless revolution had overthrown 180 years of feudal rule, first by Hindu King Prithvi Narayan Shah and his descendants, and then for a hundred years by the Rana family whose vast Italianate palaces overshadowed the humble dwellings of poor commoners. For someone from a makeshift new country like New Zealand, its labyrinthine bazaars and old temples with their Buddhist and Hindu gods were achingly romantic and picturesque. There were hardly any vehicles except a few trucks and the occasional royal Rolls Royce carried over tracks from India on long poles. The early September of our arrival was the end of the monsoon when emerald-green rice fields filled the valley from wall to wall.

Our base in Kathmandu was the Hotel Royal, a reconditioned Rana Palace run by a larger-than-life White Russian by the name of Boris Lisanevich – rhymes with son-of-a-bitch, he used to say. He was a man of wide-ranging abilities and experience: he'd been chased out of Russia by the revolution of 1917, had danced with Diaghilev's Ballets Russes in Paris and London, established a nightclub in Calcutta, was friend to King Tribhuvan in the lead-up to the anti-Rana revolution of 1950. He lived with his Danish wife Inger and a leopard cub in a penthouse on top of the Hotel Royal from which he practised his entrepreneurial skills. His occasional imprisonments and bankruptcies were celebrated with a Russian banquet, which kicked off with three glasses of vodka, each of a different colour.

Already in residence at the Hotel Royal was our journalist, Desmond Doig. He was born in 1921 to Anglo-Irish parents in the city of Allahabad on the banks of the Ganges. His schooling at Kurseong, south of Darjeeling, had just ended when war broke out. After joining the Gurkhas, amongst whom he learned fluent Nepali, he fought in North Africa and Italy. Post-war England held no attractions for someone of his background who was also gay, but jobs were not easily come by in post-Independence India. Salvation came in the form of an offer to join the *Calcutta Statesman* as one of its few remaining English staff. He came to the expedition when World Book commissioned a search for a journalist. Desmond describes how he came to be the lucky one:

> One day I was called, surprisingly, into the office of the Editor of the Statesman. 'Ah Doig,' he said. 'How would you like to spend a year in Nepal looking for the Abominable Snowman? Somewhere near Everest. With Sir Edmund Hillary and assorted mountaineers and scientists.' He presumed that I could climb a bit, withstand the cold, and generally carry The Paper's flag through snow and ice. The important thing was that I could speak Nepali and had experience of Yetis ...
>
> 'Of course, Doig, there's no guarantee that you will go. I have merely been asked, as have editors the world over, to put forward a name for the job of the expedition's scribe. If they like the sound of you you'll be interviewed in London by Hillary.'
>
> I found myself on the short list amongst whom were names famous in the British newspaper world, ink-stained giants of the breed. The interview opened with the comment from Hillary that I was 'damned fat' but my knowledge of Nepalese people, their language and their Yetis, did the trick. 'You'll have to lose some weight,' said Hillary. 'I advise some exercise, cut down on the wine.'
>
> Also present was John Dienhart of World Books who later confided to me, 'You know something, I've started wondering whether I should have encouraged this venture or not. I actually worked the whole thing. It's the greatest publicity stunt a Public Relations man has ever pulled off. What do you think about that?[1]

Ed Hillary and Desmond Doig examine Khumjung Monastery's yeti scalp.
HILLARY MUSEUM COLLECTION

There was an element of boasting in this – a PR man has to promote himself as well as his company and its product – and also an element of truth, for the yeti hunt could reasonably be described as a stunt. The scientific side of the expedition was serious enough, however, and fitted with the educational mission of World Book Encyclopedia. As for the attempt on Makalu, it could be read as a scientific experiment, a stunt, or a high-risk sporting activity indulged in by a small, deviant sub-section of the community. For the expedition to be seen as successful it would need to satisfy the expectations of World Book, the scientists and the mountaineering community – which in the event it did. John Dienhart was pure American, with a crew cut, a treasure trove of current slang, and a round boyish face that crinkled easily into laughter. On the grounds that 'everyone should spend a year of their lives in the Himalayas', he joined the yeti group, but when the romance of sleeping in a tent with no bathroom had worn off he abbreviated the year to a week and retreated to Bangkok. Nevertheless he, with Ed and Griff Pugh, was one of the triumvirate who launched the expedition.

By the end of the first week in September, members of the

expedition had gathered in Kathmandu. Loads were sorted, 160 for the yeti-hunters and 310 for the scientific group. Griff established his independence early in the expedition by arriving late.

> Dear Griff ... I was a little aghast to find that you hadn't sent off to me the lists of equipment ... Thinking about the possibility of your late arrival in Kathmandu I have some further thoughts ... As the Director of Physiology and Medical Services it's not a bad idea to be in at the start of things when decisions are being made – in Kathmandu. Temperamentally I think you'll find it rather difficult if the other boys have made up all the loads, initiated the medical programme, and generally got things going ... What do you want to do? Regards, Ed[2]

On the day of departure Ed wrote another note:

> Dear Griff, Your late arrival is slightly complicating arrangements ... I have received a letter from a chap called Lahiri thanking me for including him in the expedition. I do not remember having done so – do you know anything about it? Regards, Ed[3]

Ed was quickly informed that Dr Lahiri was one of Griff's scientific team but there were early signs of flawed communications.

Clues to the yeti

Ed had chosen the Rolwaling Valley as a destination partly because it was reputed to be a yeti stronghold. It was in this region that Eric Shipton, Mike Ward and the Sherpa Sen Tenzing had photographed by far the best-defined yeti footprint on record. The valley's remote Sherpa community centred on the village of Beding, a cluster of 20 stone houses huddled under the immense cliffs of unclimbed Gauri Shankar. Desmond Doig entered the village announcing that he would pay for a yeti, dead or alive, or parts thereof. Within a week he had his first yeti relic, a man-sized skin of thick black fur with an ivory band across the shoulders and brown fur on its face. To the zoologists it was clearly the skin of the rare Tibetan blue bear, and indeed the owner had acquired it in Tibet where blue bears had always been strong yeti

Journalist Desmond Doig. HILLARY MUSEUM COLLECTION

candidates. Two more identical skins, all identified by Sherpas as being those of a yeti, would be bought during the next two months, along with a goat skin, a dried human hand, two small red pandas, a fox – and a yeti scalp.

Having spent three weeks gradually acclimatising, Ed and his troops deployed themselves at their ultimate locations around the rim of the Ripimu Glacier at 18,000ft with telescopes, trip-wire cameras and capchur guns. We had with us somewhere, we were told, an instrument that produced the sound of a yeti mating call. There was debate as to who would use it. Would it be answered by an angry, territorial male or by a sexually aroused female? Neither could be contemplated with equanimity. There was also the problem of how we would handle a live yeti emerging from a drug-induced coma, for we had no facilities for containing a large, disgruntled ape who would not have been placated by the promise that s/he was about to spend the rest of her days in the Lincoln Park Zoo in Chicago.

Sightings of yetis, as distinct from footprints, had been recorded only by Sherpas and Tibetans and even then at second hand. One of our Sherpas, Siku, had had a narrow escape from a yeti. He had been left on his own one stormy night in a mountaineering camp at 17,000ft when he heard a yeti coming towards the tent. There were sounds all around, the wind gusting fiercely around the rocks, the wild flapping of the tent, but above it all came clearly the whistling sound that yetis are known for, and it was getting louder. In a one-on-one encounter the yeti has the advantage of size and strength but when running downhill they are hampered by their long hair (and the females by their breasts) which gets in their eyes. Spurred on by terror, Siku took to his heels straight down the steep grass and rocks of the mountainside to appear in the nearest village an hour later, wild-eyed, exhausted and bleeding from his falls in the dark. The yeti itself regrettably left no tracks but there could be no doubting that to Siku it was terrifyingly real.

Yeti tracks, on the other hand, had been reported by mountaineers for many years. Some were fox tracks, some were bear tracks, others so altered by melting that they were unidentifiable, but Sherpas always swore they belonged to a yeti. We found them ourselves in 1960 on a névé at the head of the Rolwaling: tracks in the snow that were badly blurred by melting, but at a stretch they might have belonged to a large primate. At least one set was made by a fox, for where it walked in permanent shade the big single prints separated into two much smaller prints with the toes and pads of a fox. At least twice on the expedition we saw foxes purposefully crossing snowfields and a pass.

At the end of October the yeti party left the Rolwaling by crossing the 19,000ft Tashi Laptsa Pass to enter the Khumbu region. A destination here was Khumjung, in whose monastery was one of the best-known relics, a scalp said to be 200 years old. It was a domed affair covered in coarse, henna-stained hair except along its ridged crest where the hair had been worn away by being used as a hat during festivals. As the scalp of a primate it was unconvincing but the possibility existed. 'Could we,' asked Ed, 'borrow the scalp for examination by our scientist friends in Paris, London and Chicago?'

The agreement with the village elders included three conditions:

- A payment of 8000 rupees (about $80)
- A village elder must accompany the scalp on its travels
- The expedition will build a school in Khumjung.[4]

It was an intriguing set of requests, particularly the last, which is the first mention in Ed's diary of building a school. Thus did the all-powerful yeti weave a potent new thread into the course of Ed's life: the provision of education for Sherpas.

The scalp was duly taken to Europe and the USA to be examined by experts who declared that it had been fabricated from the skin of a serow, a goat-antelope. Khunjo Chumbi, the village elder who accompanied the scalp during these examinations, was in no way discomfited:

> In Nepal we have neither giraffes nor kangaroos so we know nothing about them. In France, or London, or Chicago, there are no Yetis so I sympathise with your ignorance. When I return to Solu Khumbu I will find a yeti for you. When you have gone to such trouble to prove the existence of the yeti, it is up to us Sherpas to help you. We cannot have you doubted by your own people.[5]

How were Ed's beliefs standing up to all this? The yeti had been essential to sustaining the interest of World Book Encyclopedia, and its funds, and the creature *might* exist. For a while at least he became a supporter. In France he was reported as saying in an interview: 'You will come with me on the greatest adventure of my life, the chasse à l'abominable homme des neiges dans l'Himalaya. Yes, the Yeti exists and I am going to prove it to you.'[6] Later he was to become equally emphatic that the yeti did not exist:

> Sir Edmund Hillary says the abominable snowman of the Himalayas is only a myth in the superstitious imagination of a simple mountain people, according to a report from Kathmandu. 'Nothing called yeti exists in flesh and bone,' he says, 'only in stories. Any further expedition in search of it would be sheer waste of money.'[7]

But what about that footprint photographed by Eric Shipton and Mike Ward in 1951? There were two photographs, one from a distance showing Ward looking at a line of tracks typically blurred by melting. The second was altogether different, a close-up on a thin, fractured plate of snow of a track so sharply defined that it seemed that if the observers looked up they would see the animal itself walking off.

Jim Perrin in his biography of Shipton and Tilman follows the yeti thread through the writings of these two best-known of Himalayan explorers and writers.[8] Both have a well-developed sense of humour, a disbelief in science and a dislike of pomposity. Shipton and Tilman, says Perrin, had 'a running yeti gag' that they kept up for years, trying to outdo each other with word play and practical jokes. In 1951 Shipton realised he had the chance to upstage Tilman by finding and photographing the best ever footprint. In 1984 Perrin interviewed Hillary about that photograph. Ed said:

> What you've got to understand is that Eric was a joker. He was forever pulling practical jokes, fooling around in his quiet way. This footprint, see, he's gone around it with his knuckles, shaped the toe, pressed in the middle. There's no animal could walk with a foot like that! He made it up, and of course he was with Sen Tenzing who was as big a joker as Eric was. They pulled the trick, and Mike Ward just had to keep quiet and go along with it. We all knew, apart from Bill Murray maybe, but none of us would say, and Eric let it run and run. He just loved to wind people up that way.[9]

Perrin continued:

> Ten years after the Travellers' Club interview I had Mike Ward on the end of a rope on the upper cliff of Glyder Fawr. Michael was an immensely talented rock climber in his day … As I was leading it, the heavens opened and the rock was soon streaming with water. Leaning over from the good belay ledge on top as Michael followed the pitch, I spotted him tussling with a particularly recalcitrant section of vertical crack coated with green slime, and yelled down: 'So Michael, about that photograph of the Yeti footprint …?' As I did so, I paid out

six inches of slack on a rope which hitherto I'd kept snug and tight. His eyebrows disappeared under the rim of his helmet. 'Take in, you bastard,' he gasped, face ruckling into a smile. It told me everything.[10]

A last word comes from David Snellgrove, Tibetan scholar, writing in his *Buddhist Himalaya*:

> In popular belief the yeti is an entirely mythological creature, identifiable with the rakshasa of Indian mythology. He belongs to the entourage of the 'Country-God' of Khumbu (Khumbu-yul-lha) who sends him forth as an emanation, when he intends harm to anyone. Thus to see a yeti is a very bad omen, only to be countered by directing effort forthwith towards accumulating merit. The yeti-caps are used once a year in the temple dances, when a monk masquerading as the yeti accompanies the 'country-god' on his reeling rounds. Mountaineers have on several occasions mentioned the existence of unexplained foot-prints, which their Sherpa assistants regularly identify as those of a yeti. Whatever these foot-prints may be, the only connection with the yeti exists as an extension of the popular imagination.[11]

Mingbo Camp and the building of the Silver Hut

The more serious arm of the expedition carrying in the Silver Hut had been led by Norman Hardie, who was on his third Himalayan expedition. He was accompanied by New Zealand builder and mountaineer Wally Romanes, English physiologist and physician Jim Milledge, and American photographer and climber Barry Bishop. They were escorting 310 Nepali porters carrying the silver segments of the laboratory hut, its physiological equipment and the wherewithal to survive a Himalayan winter at 19,000ft. In 1960 Nepali porters were among the poorest people in this poor country, and among these 310 was a tail end who were too old, too young, too poorly clothed, or too sick with disease to cope easily with the climb up to the high altitudes of the Khumbu region. After 12 days, the route took them over a 14,000ft pass where there was snow on the ground and a bitterly cold wind. None of the porters died, but for Norm it was an anxious crossing as he helped those who were losing strength at the rear of his straggling band.

Having passed through Namche Bazaar and Tengboche Monastery, Norm had set up a base at the tiny village of Changmatang, near the entrance to the Mingbo Valley at whose head the Silver Hut would be assembled. Surrounded by rhododendrons, Changmatang was a sunny place and its modest height of 13,000ft made it a comfortable altitude for everyone. An easy trail led up-valley to the open grass of the little summer grazing village of Mingbo, nestled into a hollow at 15,300ft. During the benign months of the monsoon from June to September a few families with grazing rights settled here to fatten their yaks and calves on the grass and wild flowers which briefly grow in abundance. But by autumn they were returned to their houses in the larger villages, leaving only a few stone-walled shelters which Wally Romanes converted into a snug kitchen and dining space. Mingbo soon had its small village of tents as it became an advance base en route to a 19,000ft location for the Silver Hut.

Norm had already had a look at the snowy upper reaches of the Mingbo with its gentle névé backed by a headwall of steep ice flutings leading to the Mingbo Pass at 19,500ft. Ed, drawing on memories of a traverse with Eric Shipton in 1951, had chosen the crest of the pass as the site for the Silver Hut. Norm was unhappy with this. Powerful winds funnelled over the pass, and the 500ft slope of steep ice leading up to it was a substantial barrier to porters carrying the hut and its contents. Nor would it be a place of easy retreat if something went wrong during the winter – an illness, or a descent under duress.

Arrived from the yeti hunt, Ed and I joined Norm and Wally for a night camped on the col in gale-force winds which quickly convinced us that a safer and more peaceful winter was likely on the broad reaches of the névé below. But there was an element of uncertainty about any site. Would the slopes rising above the hut bring down avalanches of winter snow that would carry the hut over the nearby cliff? Would the powerful katabatic winds from Tibet that unroofed Sherpa houses in January and February wrench a hut free from its moorings? The answers were not known but a decision was made to level a site on the downhill lip of a shallow snow gully which would, we hoped, offer some protection. In the event, the weather treated us remarkably well. There were nights when the hut lurched alarmingly in the winds, but there was not a great deal of snow and no avalanches. For much of the winter we were bathed in sun.

The head of the Mingbo Valley from Ama Dablam. Silver Hut and its accompanying tent are visible as two dots just below the isolated crevasse protruding into the smooth névé in the middle of the photo. HILLARY MUSEUM COLLECTION

With the site for the Silver Hut agreed on, the team launched into its building. Within a couple of days the base frame had been built, a floor laid, the curved pieces of the cylindrical outer wall fitted together, and the whole structure anchored to snow-filled kitbags buried two metres deep in the névé. It was a brilliant piece of English design and it served us well throughout the months we lived there. Aesthetically it was pleasing with its silver skin glinting against the fluted ice of the steep slopes behind. The Himalayan Scientific and Mountaineering Expedition was the original name, but in history it became the Silver Hut expedition.

Leadership

Meanwhile Griff Pugh had been in residence at Changmatang for a fortnight before venturing up the Mingbo. When he heard the hut had been built not at 19,500ft on the col but on the névé 500 feet lower, he expressed his displeasure, and the fault lines between him and Ed began to show. Ed was by nature impatient to make decisions, and when it came to a choice between col and névé for the Silver Hut, he and Norm had no

338

doubts as to which was the safer site. Griff himself, when he walked up-valley to see for himself, agreed, but he had not been consulted.

Although he was the scientific leader he was not always around to do the leading. On Everest in 1953 as research physiologist he was often at Base Camp where James Morris and Tom Stobart got to know him. Morris wrote:

> I always enjoyed his company. He was full of peculiar knowledge, and passed it on at surprising moments in a hesitating, slow-spoken, pipe-puffing manner; as if some gentle country parson, settling down for a quiet scriptural chat with his parishioners, were suddenly to present some theories about Kafka, the dipping hem-line, or space travel.[12]

Cameraman Stobart also enjoyed his company. He described him as:

> ... a large red-haired man who combined the two traditional qualities of the professor – clear-sighted intelligence and absent-mindedness. Of all the members he was, I think, the one I preferred to be with because he had that sort of

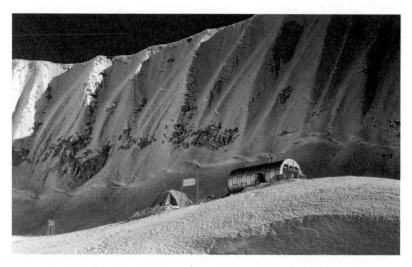

Silver Hut with Mingbo Col, on the route to Makalu, behind.
HILLARY MUSEUM COLLECTION

speculative curiosity, wonder and originality of thought possessed by all the scientific elite. He never became dull and we never ran out of topics for conversation.[13]

Despite his detachment from everyday life, Griff was unhappy at the way he had been presented in the Everest book and film, partly because he felt his contribution had been insufficiently acknowledged. For the Silver Hut expedition he became more assertive. On 2 August while still in London he had written:

> My Dear Ed, I am not at all happy about the turn of events since your last visit ... It turns out that in referring to me as Senior Physiologist you do not give my position adequate recognition before the public with the result that we have articles in the press which are distressing to me personally ... I am continually having to assert myself to keep Jim [Milledge], and even Mike Gill, from making independent plans which do not fit in with my arrangements ...
>
> So please send me your assurance (1) that you will see that my position and work for the expedition are properly recognized, and (2) that I am referred to not as Senior Physiologist which, so far as the press is concerned, merely means the oldest physiologist, but as Director of Medicine and Physiology for the expedition, or some equivalent title. I have come to feel that this is so important to the success of the physiological programme that I cannot allow any MRC equipment to be shipped until I get your answer.
>
> As you know, dear Ed, I have always had the highest personal regard for you, and I feel sure you will understand my point of view. Yours ever, Griff[14]

Ed replied by telegram:

> Have just received your letter of 2nd August and can appreciate your concern over your status stop However as we both know that the physiological programme depends on your direction and experience I suggest you have more confidence in yourself and me to work this matter out satisfactorily in the field. Regards Ed Hillary[15]

Grievances can swell disproportionately on expeditions, and by 9 November Ed was muttering in his diary that Griff 'has been sculling about down below doing nothing useful and getting on everyone's goat'.[16] Griff for his part was writing, 'I shall have to have another straight talk with him soon and, if the result is not satisfactory, return home ...'[17]

Ed described in his diary the straight talk that came three mornings later:

> A rather trying day for me. Griff visited me and from a notebook reeled off a long and detailed list of my weaknesses and inadequacies ... I think I can be excused a few harsh words at the end – but they were very few – and we decided to part in some disharmony. However the discussion continued in Desmond and Marlin's tent and they attempted to calm the troubled waters ... By afternoon things were much more harmonious and Griff had obviously improved by letting off steam. Perhaps things will be OK after all, though old Griff is decidedly eccentric. Both John Hunt and Eric had their flare ups with Griff – and so have I – I hope it's the last one.[18]

Griff might have felt relieved that he had let off steam, but it was not a way to endear himself to Ed. But for the time being at least, peace had been restored to the Mingbo Valley.

Science at 19,000 feet

The scientific phase of the expedition based in the Silver Hut lasted four-and-a-half months from mid-November 1960 through to the end of March 1961. It was a special time remembered with great affection by those who lived through it. The setting could hardly have been more spectacular, with the cirque of steep ice and rock of the Mingbo La at our backs and the vertiginous walls of Ama Dablam rising high above us in the other direction. The altitude was in the grey zone between acclimatisation and deterioration, but most of the time we achieved an equilibrium and kept at our work consistently. Each evening after a day in the laboratory, with the sun setting behind the mountains to the west, we would ski down the slopes of the névé to where it broke up into an icefall. Our isolation from the rest of the world was almost

The wintering party (L to R): Bishop, Lahiri, Pugh, Siku, Ward, Dawa Tensing, Milledge, Mingma Norbu, West and Gill. HILLARY MUSEUM COLLECTION

complete, and we never missed it. The party fitted together seamlessly. We were a happy group.

The tunnel-shaped hut was six metres long by three wide with windows at either end. A central kerosene stove separated a living space with eight bunks and a dining table from a laboratory with benches for equipment and a yellow bicycle ergometer for tests at varying workloads. The window filling the laboratory end offered a fine panorama.

The detailed physiological measurements we were making at 19,000ft were unique. At this altitude the oxygen content of air is half that at sea level, and at first our work capacity was also half our sea level ability, though it increased to around two-thirds as we steadily acclimatised. Assessment of lung and heart function required measurements of oxygen and carbon dioxide in lungs and blood. Blood leaving the lung at sea level is close to 100 per cent saturated with oxygen, but in the Silver Hut it was down to 70 per cent. An important finding was that during exercise the saturation dropped a lot further, sometimes below 50 per cent, despite a huge increase in the rate of breathing. This helped explain why climbing upwards at high altitude is such an extraordinarily exhausting business, even though one may feel relatively comfortable at rest.

For the most part we felt well at the Silver Hut, but we all lost weight, an indication of the high-altitude deterioration that could accelerate if one's defences were weakened. It happened to me in early February when I was well acclimatised. Up till then I had lost only three pounds in weight, but one day Mike Ward and I put in a long hard day climbing a steep fluted peak behind the hut. The approach was in deep snow and the fluting required hours of step-cutting. When we arrived back at the hut after dark I was completely done in. Over the next nine days I became lethargic, lost appetite, slept poorly and lost eight pounds in weight. On the tenth day I walked 6000 feet down to Changmatang. I ate a huge meal, slept for 12 hours, and by the morning was back to normal. It was a good case history of high-altitude deterioration and its cure.

It was not my first altitude illness on the expedition. Shortly after arriving at 13,000ft in the Rowaling during the yeti hunt, I found

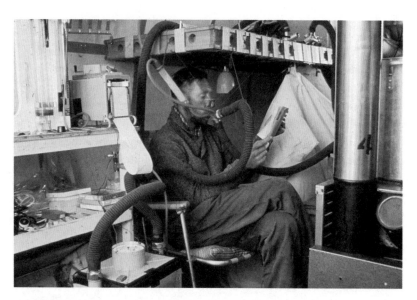

John West measuring his lung diffusing capacity at Silver Hut.
HILLARY MUSEUM COLLECTION

Silver Hut in a winter storm. HILLARY MUSEUM COLLECTION

myself increasingly breathless when walking uphill. Next morning
I awoke stuporose and cyanosed with my lungs full of fluid. Tom
Nevison made the logical diagnosis of pneumonia and started me
on antibiotics and oxygen. Within 12 hours my colour and general
wellbeing had improved to a remarkable extent. Tom was not to know
that just then an article by Dr Charles Houston was appearing in the
New England Journal of Medicine describing an illness exactly like mine,
with the additional evidence of a chest x-ray which showed extensive
pulmonary edema. This was HAPE, High Altitude Pulmonary Edema,
which is rapidly cured by administering oxygen. Without doubt I had
HAPE in the Rolwaling, and with a degree of severity that might have
killed me had the miraculously curative oxygen not been available.

Shortly before he moved up from Mingbo to the Silver Hut in
February, Griff was presented with the sort of natural experiment
that intrigued him. It involved adaptation to cold, one of his major
research interests. The subject was Man Bahadur, a Nepali from down-
valley wearing thin cotton clothes, a red turban and no footwear. He

presented himself at Griff's Mingbo laboratory and was occasionally found eating a piece of laboratory glassware. He slept comfortably outside with no bedding in sub-zero temperatures. Here was someone who truly had a special adaptation to cold. How did he do it? Griff had the necessary equipment: one set of temperature sensors attached to skin and another inserted into Man Bahadur's rectum to measure core body temperature. Measurements showed that he maintained his body temperature not by the unadapted person's response, which was to shiver throughout the night, but by turning up his basal metabolic rate – a sort of central heating.

One evening as the Sherpas filled in the hours between dinner and sleep in their usual way, which was drinking and telling stories, they talked about Man Bahadur. What were all those wires for? And the one protruding from his rectum? Pugh Sahib was known to be unusual, but this was more than the usual mystery. Finally Annullu, he who had been first on the South Col in 1953 with Wilf Noyce, decided he should take a look. It didn't look right. Encouraged perhaps by a relieved Man Bahadur, Annullu dismantled the experiment by removing all the wires – an action that won him banishment to the Silver Hut which was too cold even for Man Bahadur. Griff published his findings in the *Journal of Applied Physiology* in 1963: 'Tolerance to Extreme Cold in a Nepalese Pilgrim'.

First ascent of Ama Dablam

Before leaving with the yeti scalp in November, Ed, always keen that his expeditions should be looking at unclimbed peaks, had suggested that the wintering party should establish a high camp for a preliminary look at unclimbed Ama Dablam. It had not occurred to him that they might be strong enough to climb what looked like an impossibly difficult mountain. So when he heard in mid-March that a party consisting of Mike Ward as leader, accompanied by Barry Bishop, Mike Gill and Wally Romanes, had made the first ascent on 13 March, he was surprised as well as pleased – though with the note in his diary that there might be a problem with the Government of Nepal about permission to climb, or rather lack of it.

My memory of Ama Dablam is of a benign extension of our days in the Silver Hut. We had so many advantages. We were fit and as well acclimatised as we ever would be up to the 22,500ft summit. The

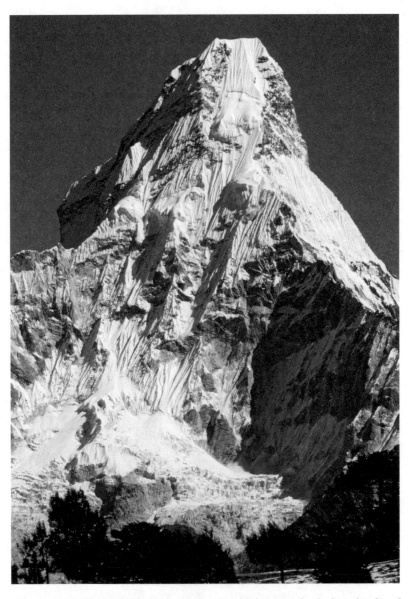

Ama Dablam. The route follows the south-east ridge between the shadowed rock and the sunlit snow. The snow cave camp was on the lower ice bulge. The route to the summit climbs to the right of the upper ice bulge to reach the snow spur slanting up the final snow face. Peter Hillary's party in 1979 was climbing the face direct when they were struck by an ice avalanche. HILLARY MUSEUM COLLECTION

ridge we were attempting was familiar in that we'd seen it in profile every time we stepped outside the hut. The route was south facing, capturing the late winter sun and sheltered from the prevailing north-westerly wind. There were three-and-a-half weeks between Wally's first reconnaissance and our arrival on the summit, but the climbing had been fitted into short bursts when we could be spared from the physiology programme. The most difficult part of the climb, the vertical rock of the first step, was led brilliantly by Mike Ward and Barry Bishop on 24 and 25 February. Our two Sherpas agreed with alacrity when we offered to do the load-carrying ourselves to the two higher camps. On 11 March the four of us carried loads to the lowest of the two ice bulges on the face and dug ourselves a snow cave. The next day Mike Ward and Wally climbed up to the ice cliffs skirting the upper ice bulge, the 'Dablam', which might have stopped us. Again luck was on our side. Shining cliffs of green ice rose above us, but between the ice cliff and the rock face plunging vertically for thousands of feet was a narrow rock ledge leading to the top of the 'Dablam.' After that, a long line of steps chipped up the central 55-degree fluting carried us to the summit. Looking across at the immense Lhotse–Nuptse wall with Everest looming high over it, we felt suitably humbled. But it had been a good climb.

CHAPTER 23

Makalu unravels

———⇒•◇•⇐———

In late 1960 a political crisis in Nepal was heading towards its climax, and on 15 December, as Ed, Desmond Doig and the yeti scalp were being welcomed in Chicago, King Mahendra abruptly closed his parliament and took control. Peter Mulgrew, Ed's Antarctic companion, had been with the yeti-hunters managing radio communications and was in Kathmandu when Parliament was dismissed. He sent Ed an analysis of what had happened:

> Dear Ed, Arrived a couple of days ago to find a revolution in full swing. Everyone seems to be in jail, and the way things are going I may well be Prime Minister when you return ... Peter[1]

The after-shocks of the crisis were not being felt in the Mingbo Valley – or not until the ascent of Ama Dablam became known. And when Ed wrote to Louise during his travels with the yeti scalp, he was more interested in how he was being received in London than in what was happening in Kathmandu:

> My Dearest Louise, I always have mixed feelings about my visits to England. There's so much I enjoy and so many people I like and yet it's the place where I'm greeted with the most suspicion by the pukka sahibs. Even Larry Kirwan agrees that this is true – although I think I've been successful in calming the fears of the scientists here that I might be trying to use

them for my own ends. Still it's not nice to feel that official circles view one a little askance – and rightly or wrongly that's the impression I always get in London. Despite our good reception here by the press and radio I'm really quite happy to be leaving and will be happy to get the damn old Yeti scalp back to its home and then get on with the routine work of the expedition.[2]

After helicoptering in to Khumjung on 5 January to return the scalp, and visiting Griff Pugh in Mingbo, Ed flew back to New Zealand for a holiday with the family. He returned to the Himalayas in late February. The next three months would be focused on an attempt on Makalu as part of the physiological programme, but for the first 17 days he'd be joined by Louise and a group of other expedition wives who called themselves 'The Women's Expedition'. It was Louise's first visit to the Himalayas.

As she and Ed passed through Calcutta, they visited The Indian Aluminium Company which, encouraged by the inimitable Desmond, had donated a prefabricated aluminium school for Khumjung.

Their arrival in Nepal coincided with the State Visit of Queen Elizabeth to Kathmandu. At the last minute, Sir Edward [*sic*] Hillary and Mrs E. Hillary were invited to a banquet in her honour on 27 February. Louise described the occasion to her family:

> I went to my room to attend to my hair as shortly before we had been commanded to appear at the State Banquet given by King Mahendra. This had come as a great surprise. Ed had only his dark suit while everybody else had their most glorious garments complete with decorations. I used Gita's makeup and June's pearls which fell off with a ghastly plastic clatter as I was saying Hello to the Earl of Home. We met many wonderfully important looking people. There were only 100 guests. We all had to shake hands and curtsy. I sat next to the Head of the Nepalese Royal Household, a darling little man. The King gave a speech in Nepali and the Queen gave hers in English and a very lovely one too. She had the most marvellous emerald and diamond tiara and jewellery.[3]

'The Women's Expedition', March 1961 (L to R): Lila Bishop, Ed Hillary, Louise Hillary, Irene Ortenburger, Leigh Ortenburger, Peter Mulgrew, June Mulgrew, Gita Bannerjee and Fred Moodie (Ed's GP). HILLARY MUSEUM COLLECTION

The King's speech to Queen Elizabeth touched on the awkward question of democracy:

> Your Majesty's land, justly called the land of the Mother of Parliaments, is also, I believe, aware of the difficulties that beset a country recently dedicated to the development of this system.
>
> Although on account of many and diverse errors and shortcomings, my desire to work out a strong and unalloyed form of parliamentary democracy for the betterment of my Kingdom could not be a success at this moment, I am still firm in my earlier belief that your experiences in the development and working of your institutions can be and are of great value to us. At the same time it is but natural for any good and successful system to take time to strike roots.
>
> Despite the courage and well-known devotion of our people to art and matters cultural, there is a lack of modern

amenities in our ancient land and this fact must have told on Your Majesty's comforts. Even then, I trust that our honoured guests must have felt today how happy and pleased my people are to welcome Your Majesty ...[4]

King Mahendra need not have been too apologetic about his failure to implement within 10 years a system which Queen Elizabeth's forebears had been working on for many centuries, but he and his ministers were sensitive to traces of criticism. This was an element in the storm that burst on Ed when the world media ran headlines that his expedition – and scientists of all people – had made the first ascent of Ama Dablam. It was not a high mountain but it was a spectacular and much-photographed presence looming over Tengboche Monastery.

The summit had been reached on 13 March while Ed was arriving in Khumbu with the Women's Expedition. On hearing news of the ascent two days later, they sent a message of congratulation to the climbers. But Ed's pleasure turned to dismay when, eight days later, a plane arrived at Mingbo with an alarming and uncompromising message from the Nepali Foreign Secretary:

> To Sir Edmund Hillary, Party Commander.
> In view of unauthorized ascent of AMADABLAM permit for Makalu has been cancelled.
> You are advised to abandon your plan on Makalu and return as soon as possible.
> Yours faithfully, Y M Khanal, Foreign Secretary[5]

This was out of left field. Permission was a recent innovation for the big peaks, the Everests and Makalus. No one in the Silver Hut had thought for a moment there was need for permission to climb one of the smaller mountains. We hurriedly looked at our permit. We could work in the Mingbo and 'climb adjacent peaks'. Ama Dablam was very adjacent, but it seemed fine legal discriminations were irrelevant.

Ed needed to return post-haste to plead his case in Kathmandu. Helicopters were not available in 1961 but fortuitously Ed had arranged for his Sherpas to build a rough airstrip at 15,500ft above Mingbo during the winter. It had been requested by the Red Cross who were flying in food for Tibetan refugees and had been scraped out in a short side-valley, the entrance to which was at right angles to the 400-metre strip. When Captain Schrieber made his first crab-wise landing, a rock demolished the rear landing wheel. 'Ach!' he said. 'Mingbo is not for beginners.'

The Antarctic had hardened Ed to risky flights in small planes, and an hour after leaving Mingbo he was with Desmond Doig in Kathmandu. Guy Powles, New Zealand High Commissioner in Delhi, wrote: 'Rumour here says Nepal is more upset about the publicity given to the climb than about the lack of a permit. In this connection Doig's despatch in today's Statesman is not exactly helpful. There may be some more "knee-bending" required.'[6]

More reasons came to light for this excessive punishment for the ascent of a 22,700ft peak – cancellation of a large and expensive international expedition. One was that Ed had attended the State Banquet in a lounge suit rather than dinner suit with decorations. But a more compelling explanation was that King Mahendra had been offended by English criticism of his action in closing down Parliament. Our expedition had become a scapegoat as Nepal sought a way of showing its displeasure.

In the end it was Desmond Doig who rescued the expedition. He had known Dr Tulsi Giri, the new prime minister, from way back, and when all hope seemed lost, Dr Giri agreed to hear Ed and Desmond at two early-morning breakfasts. Moving from unyielding to non-committal, he suggested that if Sir Edmund made an unqualified apology and promised never to make such an error again he might be forgiven.[7]

A few days later Ed received a letter:

> My dear Sir Hillary, In view of the unqualified apology submitted in your letter dated March 23, 1961 and in consideration of the undertaking given therein that no such incident would occur in future, His Majesty's Government of Nepal have been pleased to give a sympathetic consideration on the subject and, as a special case and without creating any precedent whatsoever, to permit the party to continue and complete the scientific study in the Makalu range, including an attempt on the peak, up to the end of May. His Majesty's Government of Nepal have decided to impose a fine of rupees

800/- on the party for having climbed Ama Dablam, a virgin
peak, without the sanction of the Government, in addition to
royalty amount of 3200/--N.C. for Ama Dablam.
Yours sincerely, Y M Khanal. Foreign Secretary.[8]

Three hundred loads to Makalu Base Camp

Ed flew in to Mingbo on 5 April having lost two weeks of
acclimatisation and fitness in Kathmandu. He already knew that the
route to Makalu would be difficult for an expedition carrying 300 loads
to the foot of the climb. It involved cutting a route and fixing ropes
over three snow and ice passes at around 20,000ft. Some of the porters
would be unused to carrying loads in mountain terrain and at such an
altitude. When he'd spoken to Griff Pugh at Mingbo on 5 January, Ed
had floated the idea of reducing the amount of scientific equipment
and cutting back the loads of oxygen to a minimum for medical
purposes. Griff rightly protested about reducing either. Oxygen would
be essential in the event of illness on Makalu, and continuing the
science programme at very high altitudes was a primary goal.

The tactics of the expedition had become less clear with time. An
early plan had been to have two groups of climbers, one using oxygen,
the other not. The oxygen team would do all the work, cutting steps,
fixing ropes, plugging a path in soft snow, preparing food and liquids,
making scientific observations and collecting specimens. The oxygenless
group would be the experimental animals, and carry nothing while they
climbed a route prepared for them. If an oxygenless climber reached
such a state of exhaustion he could go no further, he would be given an
oxygen set and helped down.

It was a plan that had been lost along the way for the 10-man
climbing team who began crossing to Makalu at the beginning of
April. The five scientist/climbers who had spent the winter in the
Silver Hut and should have developed a super-charged level of
acclimatisation were Mike Ward, John West, Jim Milledge, Wally
Romanes and myself. Ed, Peter Mulgrew and Tom Nevison had taken
part in the yeti hunt, returned home for the winter, and were now back
for the Makalu phase of the expedition. Finally we had two newly
arrived climbers: Leigh Ortenburger from the US and John Harrison
from New Zealand. Ed was overall leader, with Mike Ward as his
deputy. Griff was scientific leader but decided in the end not to go to

353

Makalu Base Camp with Lhotse and Everest behind. HILLARY MUSEUM COLLECTION

Makalu: 'On mature reflection I think my place is here [in the Mingbo] rather than in the Barun. The copying and coordination of results and the packing and listing of equipment in a calm and orderly way will keep me fully occupied …'[9]

The plan that evolved was simply to select assault teams of two or three climbers and have them sequentially attempt to reach the summit without using oxygen. There would be three scientific camps: one at Base Camp at 17,500ft; the next at Camp 3 at 21,000ft; and the last on Makalu Col, Camp 5 at 24,400ft. The bicycle ergometer would be assembled at each of these and the usual specimens collected at differing work rates. At Camps 6 and 7 and on the summit, only alveolar air samples would be collected.

None of us knew how hard it would be.

Ed is eight years older than he was in 1953
Determined to make up for lost time, Ed threw himself into a hectic itinerary of movements back and forth between the Mingbo and Makalu base in the Barun.

354

His letters to Louise show an uneasiness with his physical condition: 'I've been a little affected by altitude since my return ... This dropping in by plane is rather a shock to the system ... I've been dashing furiously around but I'm definitely finding it far harder work than I used to and am being forced to realise that with age plus my sojourn in Kathmandu, fitness can't just be picked up in a few days ...'[10]

He was also missing her, as he did in the Antarctic, and often wished he was back home rather than facing a difficult encounter with the fifth-highest mountain in the world. On 25 April he wrote from Base Camp:

> The mail arrived in yesterday with four letters from you. I almost hate it at times – it makes me so nostalgic ... I'm really rather glad that you are missing the Sherpas and the mountains – it does show how much you enjoyed it all. And I certainly did too. Wouldn't it be fun if we could do another walk in with Mingma and no big expedition to worry about. I don't think it would be impossible to arrange this and I'd love to do it with you. I really am terribly fond of all my Sherpas & intend to see them all again. We could even bring some of the children too when they're old enough ...
>
> All is going well here. Actually I sometimes think I'm not a bad organizer ... I'm not going too badly myself but not quite my old self I'm afraid. However I've a very strong team who can carry the ball very well once we get to grips with our climbing.[11]

There is not the total commitment of 1953 – more an eagerness to get the climbing business over and done with. Perhaps there was some complacency too, and a too-easy disregard for his near-death encounter with this same route in 1954 when he had lapsed into coma at 23,000ft with cerebral and pulmonary edema.

The team had been misled also by the ease with which the French expedition of 1955 had placed nine French climbers and a Sherpa on the summit. There were major differences between that expedition and this one. For a start the French climbers were stronger both as a group and individually. Even more importantly, the French used oxygen day and night from Camp 4 at 23,000ft, whilst the Sherpas used it from

Camp 5 on Makalu Col, 24,300 feet. The route for the summit attempt traverses left then ascends alongside the inconspicuous central glacier to Camp 6. Camp 6½ is on the other side of the glacier. Camp 7 is on the snow slope at 27,000 feet, and the highest point reached by Mulgrew and Nevison is on the pointed snow tongue entering a gully on the final rock face. HILLARY MUSEUM COLLECTION

Camp 5 at 24,300ft on Makalu Col. In his account of the climb French expedition leader Jean Franco wrote, 'Oxygen was the *sine qua non* of the expedition.'[12] A strong expedition with an abundance of oxygen had made Makalu look easy.

May is summit month for big peaks, and by 1 May Camp 3 was well established on a roomy névé at 21,000ft. From here a steeper section on snow and ice led to Camp 4 on a small flat area at 23,000ft. The climbing was not difficult but by now the altitude was making itself felt more seriously. This was the same height as Camp 6 on the Lhotse Face of Everest, where Band, Ward and Westmacott had reached their ceilings. It was the camp above which the French had used oxygen for sleeping and climbing all the way to the summit. And it was the camp at which Ed had collapsed in 1954.

On 2 May Ed was cutting steps and fixing ropes with Wally Romanes on the route to Camp 4, and hoping that he was about to reach the state of acclimatisation and strength he had known in 1952 and 1953. He wrote in his diary that night at Camp 3, 21,000ft, that he was 'tired'. On 3 May: 'A wild night and I didn't feel too good – not at all well acclimatized.' The next night was 'fearsome with gusts of wind as strong as I have experienced. I had a very poor night with headaches and backaches and all the signs of anoxia.'[13]

The next day Mike Ward and I climbed to Makalu Col, 24,400ft, another landmark on the route to the summit, but two days later Ed was feeling so unwell that he went down to Camp 2 at 19,000ft, accompanied by Mike Ward. His diary describes 7 May:

> Had a reasonable night but woke feeling miserable with a temperature. During the day Jim Milledge and John West staggered down with Aila who had bad pneumonia [pulmonary edema] and was on oxygen …
>
> I felt pretty seedy all afternoon and in the evening I had a frightful pain on the side of my head and face. When a Sherpa came to give me my evening meal I couldn't get him to understand that I didn't want it. I was sort of helpless, divorced from my limbs and although perfectly rational, when I tried to say something it just came out as gibberish – most unpleasant. The pain was pretty grim. I managed to shout for Mike Ward who finally came. He and Jim put me on oxygen. I went off to sleep later and when I awoke was human again – but rather fumbling in speech, shaking in hand and poor of balance – also seeing double. They said I had to go down to 15,000ft. I think the whole thing has been a result of my foolish efforts to catch up on everything after the Ama Dablam business. Well, we did catch up on everything but it all caught up on me as well …[14]

That afternoon, accompanied by Jim Milledge who for the next fortnight would become his personal physician, Ed walked down to the more benign altitude of Base Camp. He recovered rapidly but there was no question of returning to higher camps. The safe advice was to leave Makalu and take a low-altitude route back to Khumjung accompanied by Jim. It was a sad end to Ed's involvement with a mountain that had become his personal nemesis and it marked the end of his days as a serious climber.

Mike Ward becomes leader

On Makalu we now had a climbing/scientific group of eight people:

Mike Ward, leader, age 36, London surgeon who had been on Everest in 1953 and reached Camp 7, 24,000ft, which was around his altitude ceiling. He had led the Ama Dablam climb.

The others, in alphabetic order, were:

Mike Gill, age 23, medical student and physiologist, had wintered over and was on Ama Dablam. There was anecdotal evidence that 23 was too young for extreme altitude, and I became so much in agreement that I never again went above 22,000ft.

John Harrison, age 29, New Zealand artist and designer. In 1955 had climbed to 23,000ft on Masherbrum. He was regarded as the best hope for the third assault.

Peter Mulgrew, age 33, chief petty officer in the New Zealand Navy and Ed's radio operator on the 'dash to the Pole'. Had less mountaineering experience than the others but made up for it with more determination.

Tom Nevison, age 32, physician with the US Air Force. Had climbed to 24,000ft on Broad Peak in the Karakorum where he had acclimatised well.

Leigh Ortenburger, age 32, American statistician specialising in the propagation of radio waves. Climbed widely in the Andes and Tetons.

Wally Romanes, age 31, New Zealand builder who spent the winter in the Silver Hut and was on Ama Dablam. Christened Wally for Work by John West because of his untiring work throughout the expedition.

John West, age 32, Australian physiologist working in London. A clever scientist who applied his brain to the problems that arose on the mountain. Though without much climbing experience, he acclimatised well and easily coped with the climb to Makalu Col.

You could say we were strong on science and Sherpas but lacking in elite climbers. Nevertheless, on 12 May six of us were in a well-established camp on Makalu Col at 24,400ft in the finest weather we had experienced in a month. We did not know that days like this were rare. 'Makalu Col is the kingdom of the wind,' wrote Jean Franco. 'The few times we stayed there had convinced us that there must be only a very few days in the year when it is possible to stand up on the Col ... Usually a perpetual gale rages in this funnel ...'[15]

West and Ward assembling the bicycle ergometer on Makalu Col.
HILLARY MUSEUM COLLECTION

The first priority was the physiological programme. The bicycle ergometer was assembled and ridden to exhaustion while samples were collected and measurements made. We never knew what the Sherpas said to each other as they watched this strange ritual of climbing onto a stationary bicycle so high on a mountain.

We were now starting to test the theory that the Silver Hut group would be much better acclimatised than the new arrivals. There was no doubt that the long-stayers were happily acclimatised to 19,000ft, and even the climb to the top of Ama Dablam at 22,500ft had not been a problem. But 24,300ft on the Col was altogether different, and the wintering group was having to concede that there was no consistent difference between those who had had the most time at altitude and those who had the least. For all of us sleep was patchy, unrefreshing, and interrupted by periodic (Cheyne-Stokes) breathing – better described as periodic non-breathing. Our appetites were poor. Climbing uphill was accompanied by breathlessness far beyond anything we had experienced before, and it became immeasurably worse as we went higher. It was clear that climbing Makalu without oxygen was not going to be easy.

The first assault: Gill, Romanes and Ortenburger

From Camp 5 on the Col we had a good view of the last 3,500ft, a snow and ice face enclosed between two rock ridges converging on the summit. The centre of the face was a steepish icefall but so slow moving as to carry no risk from falling ice or collapsing seracs. On either side of the central ice were steep snow gullies which did not look too difficult. The last 400ft to the summit was on rock which we knew, from the French account, was not unduly difficult either.

The morning of 13 May was still miraculously fine when the three of us in the first assault team set off. The day began with a wrong move. The French route made a level traverse on an easy snow ledge to the far snow gully running up to the left of the central ice. But when we emerged from our tents to follow the load-carrying Sherpas, they were already far up the right-hand gully. Pemba Tensing, who had been with the French, said he knew the route, and the porters had followed him. They were beyond shouting distance and to get them back would lose us a day. We decided to follow and find a route across the central ice the next day after spending a night at Camp 6 – which was established that afternoon at 25,800ft, the height of Everest's South Col.

During the night the wind came up, but because it was at our backs we set off across the central ice, Wally and I sharing the lead, cutting steps across a mixture of steep ice and hard snow, or plugging steps in deep, soft snow. It was desperate work, and by the time we had crossed the icefall and reached the left-hand snow gully in the early afternoon we were done for. The wind had risen to gale force, and as we turned into it we were engulfed in driven snow. We decided to make a depot, calling it Camp 6½, and go back to Camp 6. Just short of it, I misplaced a step on an ice bulge, slipped and dragged Wally off. Down we tumbled to find ourselves embedded in a drift of soft snow 50 feet down and with lungs screaming as our bodies fought to replace the oxygen we had expended trying to save our fall. Back at a sombre Camp 6 we passed another endless night.

Next morning the gale was still blowing full force. Even going downhill I was breathless, and on the level traverse to the Col I was taking frequent rests. The wind drove into our faces with such force it was hard to keep a footing. Loose snow had been stripped away, leaving polished ice so hard that our crampons jittered across its surface. Though the powder had gone there was still, in parts, a thin

Wind on Makalu. HILLARY MUSEUM COLLECTION

layer of compact snow, and slabs of this, caught by the wind, were being whipped into the air and sent spinning towards Tibet like huge autumn leaves. There was a cry behind us and, turning, we saw Nima Dorje being blown across the ice on his back. The rope tightened, he clawed his way to his knees, to his feet, then continued on unsteadily in the slow motion that is the normal pace at high altitudes. Two of our small Meade tents on the Col, empty at the time, had blown away into Tibet in big gusts.

The big Blanchard tent was surprisingly warm. All the climbers were there now, Peter Mulgrew and Tom Nevison forming the second assault party, and John Harrison and Mike Ward forming the third. Leigh, who had not been on the leading rope and was less exhausted than Wally or I, decided to stay at Camp 5 and join the third assault. As we sprawled among the litter of sleeping bags and down jackets we told them of our two days on the upper slopes of the mountain. The altitude was much tougher than we'd expected. To reach the top, the summit pair had to be spared the punishing task of breaking trail except on the final push to the top. When compared with oxygenless

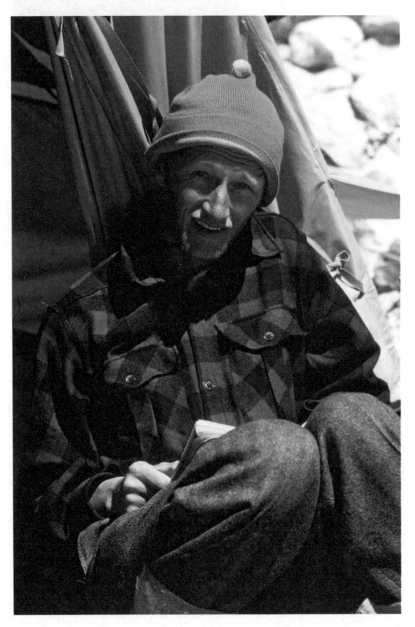

Peter Mulgrew before the Makalu climb. HILLARY MUSEUM COLLECTION

climbs on the north side of Everest ours had not been too bad an effort, but it was below expectations.

The second assault: Mulgrew and Nevison
Over the next two days Wally, Leigh and I retreated to Camp 3 at the wondrously comfortable altitude of 21,000ft, leaving behind us five climbers supported by a dozen Sherpas on the wind-blasted Col. The wind on 16 May had dropped as Mulgrew, Nevison and six Sherpas set off for Camp 6 on the second assault. That was the easy day. There was a well-plugged line of steps, a climb of 1400ft and tents already in place.

The following day was not so good. The wind had returned in force. One could say they were only 2000 feet short of the summit but at 26,000ft they were entering the death zone. All went to plan as the six loaded Sherpas and two climbers crossed the icefall, but at Camp 6½ one of the Sherpas slipped and began sliding down the steep slope. Belay techniques were not well taught to Sherpas in those early years. All of them were joined on a single rope, and as the falling Sherpa gathered speed the other five were plucked off one by one. Death seemed certain until suddenly they were arrested by the lip of a bergschrund 500 feet lower down. Ang Temba's ankle was so badly twisted he could not continue, but they were all still alive. Accompanied by Mingma Tsering, Ang Temba limped back to Camp 6 while the others re-grouped, adding two more loads to their own.

The Sherpas were now apprehensive but with persuasion from Annullu they climbed to where they could pitch Camp 7 at 27,000ft. Mulgrew, Nevison and Annullu would attempt the summit next day.

By morning the wind was again strong from the north-west. Nevison's diary describes their climb up the snow face to the foot of the rock: 'Pete was again feeling nauseated and vomited a little but after a while seemed better and we started off. He was moving slowly from the start and seemed to gradually slow down after that until it was clear he couldn't go on. We were at 27,450 feet.'[16] Mulgrew described the sudden onset of severe chest pain consistent with the later diagnosis of pulmonary embolism causing failure of a part of one lung. It marked the end of the struggle upwards and the beginning of an even more desperate five-day struggle down to Camp 5 on the Col.

Usually descent is the easy bit, with gravity doing the work. But the snow was soft and Mulgrew found himself repeatedly collapsing and unable to continue without a long rest. By the end of the day they had got no further than their camp at 27,000ft. Annullu's morale, so strong up till now, was in sharp decline. He could sense that death was not far off.

Nevison's diary continues next morning:

> Pete was again nauseated and vomited, or coughed up, some brownish material, presumably blood. A few rope lengths down he complained of an excruciating pain in his abdomen … we coaxed and cajoled him, a few steps at a time, with belays from above and below. Sometimes Pete stumbled, sometimes he slid down. After an eternity we reached Camp 6½ where Pete could go no further.[17]

They had neither tent nor stove, and had no strength to cross the icefall. They would not survive without a tent, so Annullu set off for Camp 6 where to his intense relief he found Ortenburger, Harrison and two strong Sherpas, Pemba Tenzing and Pemba Norbu. Ortenburger and Harrison had arrived at Camp 6 on their way up for the third assault but it was clear from the non-return of the second team that something had gone wrong. Now they loaded the two Pembas with a tent, stove and a bottle of oxygen and sent them off. 'They saved our lives,' said Nevison. 'In our debilitated state we could not have survived a night in the open. We also knew that we couldn't move next day unless Pete had oxygen.'[18] Nevison was in the early stages of pulmonary edema as shown by his frothy, pink sputum. Mulgrew was beginning the first of two appalling nights at Camp 6½.

Harrison and Ortenburger realised that one of them had to cross the icefall from Camp 6 to 6½ to rescue Mulgrew while the other went down to the Col to organise a rescue team of Sherpas. To decide who did which, they tossed a pill in lieu of a coin: Ortenburger 'won' the trip with two Sherpas carrying their single bottle of oxygen to Mulgrew; Harrison went down. But at Camp 5 on the Col there was more bad news. When Harrison entered the big tent to discuss the situation with Mike Ward, he found him disoriented and obviously ill with cerebral edema. 'Who are you?' he asked.

Ortenburger's first glimpse of Camp 6½ was no less dismaying:

> We reached 6½ quite easily – I was feeling much better than
> the day before. My first impression on seeing 6½ was one of
> horror. The tent was pitched badly and full of snow, the worst
> sight of misery I have ever seen, yet the occupants were more
> or less of good cheer. Peter was not doing too much talking
> but Tom was lucid and we spent an hour discussing what to
> do. It was decided that he should take the oxygen and go down
> with the two Sherpas while I stayed at 6½ with Peter and
> await the arrival of help. Sleeping bags were 50% water-soaked
> and we had no air mattresses. It was a miserable night.[19]

Nothing happens quickly at high altitude. Mulgrew next morning
was spaced out, but Ortenburger, in full possession of all his faculties,
could feel the clock counting down. Getting Mulgrew across the ice to
Camp 6 was going to be exceptionally difficult, but his life expectancy
was only a day or two if he remained at 6½. Then at 1 p.m. they heard
voices, and suddenly three lively Sherpas were there with oxygen. They
were Pemba Tharkey and Siku from Phortse, and Tenzing Norbu from
Pangboche. All three were 'low-altitude porters', which meant less pay,
no down clothing and no climbing higher than 20,000ft. The joke went
around that giving them an extra pair of socks had turned them into
high-altitude Sherpas. They were unbelievably alert and strong. None
of them spoke any English.

Mulgrew had one crampon missing, but with four people and an
oxygen set to help him, he was nursed across the ice traverse. It was
8 p.m. and dark when they reached Camp 6 where, inexplicably, there
were no air mattresses and no stove. It was another desperate night.

The route to Camp 5 next day would have taken three hours for
a climber in reasonable shape in fine weather, but they were in poor
shape, without food or drink, and the wind was as bad as it had ever
been and driving into their faces. To make matters worse, the three
Sherpas suddenly decamped downhill, leaving the two climbers on
their own. Ortenburger's diary describes what followed:

> Peter was going very slowly belayed by me and the Sherpas
> got further and further ahead until they'd left us behind. Peter

would take 3–15 steps at a time before he'd lose his balance and collapse. We had no idea whether the Sherpas would return so our only hope for Peter's life lay in this slow unaided progress. A night out, I believed, would finish him and might well finish me. So after allowing a rest after each collapse, I'd talk him into continuing the struggle.

In the late afternoon we reached the low angle icefield across which very strong gusty winds blow making it difficult to maintain one's balance. I saw two Sherpas standing around on the other side of the icefield. I signaled for them to come and after some time one of them started across. I thought he had the oxygen but when he arrived all he had was a pair of down pants. Summoning most of my remaining strength I drove this fellow, Nima Gungi, back across the icefield to the other Sherpa who had the oxygen and then drove them both back to Peter. There was only half an hour of oxygen in the bottle, the first bit of ice was uphill, and these two incompetent Sherpas were almost no help at all.

Then I noticed five Sherpas approaching at a good speed, among them Urkien, and in no time they had Peter across the icefield. He was able to walk with assistance during this portion, but his strength gave out on the other side and it grew dark just about then. The weather was very bad by then, strong and gusty wind driving snow and ice particles – it was worse than when the first assault team turned back. We realized that Peter had to be carried so a Sherpa went down to Camp 5 to get a headband and once we had this and on a Sherpa's back we made rapid progress since the terrain was easier.

The difficulty now was in finding Camp 5 – we had no flashlight. After travelling for half an hour, all of us peering into the darkness, Urkien said he was going to look for camp, and after 15 minutes he found it. In the dark we would have passed it had not Urkien found it. In addition to this feat and his personally carrying Peter part of the way, probably the greatest thing that Urkien did was to realise that if Peter was to get off the mountain it was his responsibility and not that of the terminally-exhausted climbers.

We reached Camp 5 at 8pm. Harrison and West were

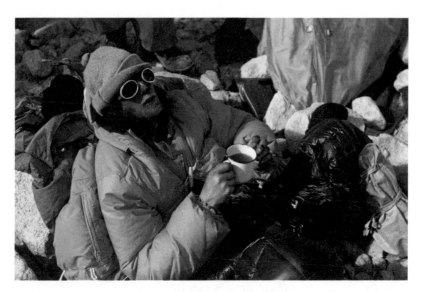

Peter Mulgrew alive after the Makalu climb but seriously ill with a pulmonary infarction and frostbite. HILLARY MUSEUM COLLECTION

most helpful and kind. Peter was completely out of it by then and had to be put into his sleeping bag. Some assistance was given to me and I certainly appreciated the warm and dry sleeping bag which was given to me. Warm drinks were brought and eagerly drunk.[20]

West had come up from Camp 3 the previous day using oxygen – 'Never let anyone tell you that oxygen doesn't help,' had been his comment – and had brought fresh energy to the retreat from the mountain. Mulgrew was an appalling sight. In the past week he had changed past recognition. The flesh had shrunk beneath his skin, leaving him gaunt and cadaverous; his colour was an ashen grey and his eyes had sunk back into their sockets; black patches of frostbite were showing on his face and hands, and his feet, were a pale lilac colour and cold as ice from the ankles down. Whenever he moved, an agonising pain shot through his chest. It was a miracle that he was still alive.

But the worst was over now. From Base Camp we had a radio link with Desmond at Silver Hut where he managed to contact Kathmandu via an intermediary 'ham' operator in Bangkok – who knew a Jesuit priest in Kathmandu, who found a helicopter to pick up Peter Mulgrew from a grazing pasture at 15,000ft in the Barun Valley. On 29 May, 11 days after his collapse at 27,400ft, Mulgrew was lifted into the bladed Perspex bubble that dropped out of the sky to carry him back to Shanta Bhawan Hospital in Kathmandu.

What went wrong?

For a start there was the sheer size and complexity of what were in reality three expeditions linked to each other over a period of nine months. The yeti expedition was a lightweight affair from a climbing point of view but was important for the sponsors. The scientific expedition was anything but lightweight, while Makalu with its combination of science and oxygenless climbing was a major attempt on the world's fifth-highest peak. At the end there was an element of expedition fatigue added to physiological fatigue.

We could claim that we'd had some bad luck – pulmonary infarcts are rare – but that was only part of the story. None of us had understood what we were up against. I have no memory of us ever sitting around discussing the problems we would face on Makalu or how the experience of the climbs on Everest in the 1920s and '30s was relevant to what we were attempting. We knew the successful stories of Everest in 1953 and Makalu in 1954, but all those climbers had used oxygen for both climbing and sleeping above 23,000–24,000ft. We had a reasonable supply of oxygen – 50 cylinders compared with 160 on Everest – but we never discussed how or when we might use them. Griff had emphasised to Ed the importance of taking plenty of oxygen to Makalu, but I can find no record of how much was actually carried to our Base Camp. We never practised its use below Makalu Col. We had not appreciated, except in a distant and theoretical way, how desperate life can be at extreme altitude, and how thin the safety margins are in case of illness when oxygen is not at hand for a quick retreat.

But against these negatives, there were some strong positives. World Book had justification for their funding in the publicity given to the yeti and the drama of the climb on Makalu. Peter Mulgrew's life had been saved by the resolution of Tom Nevison, Leigh Ortenburger and a handful of Sherpas – Urkien, Pemba Tharkey, Siku and Pemba

Tenzing – carrying a tent, a stove, a few bottles of oxygen and in the end Peter Mulgrew himself.

The scientific programme had been an unqualified success. The Silver Hut expedition became one of the classic studies in high-altitude physiology. West, Ward and Milledge wrote a textbook, *High Altitude Medicine and Physiology*, now in its fifth edition. And John West, who became an authority on altitude physiology, in 1998 published a fascinating account combining a history of the subject with science.[21] He dedicated it *To Sir Edmund Hillary who, with Griffith Pugh, introduced me to high-altitude physiology through the Silver Hut expedition in 1960.*

CHAPTER 24

Three new careers

——⟫◆⟪——

It was a subdued Ed Hillary who walked down-valley from Makalu Base Camp with Jim Milledge and five Sherpas. He seemed to be reassuring himself when he wrote in his diary, 'I'm not too worried about the climb – my work is mainly done.'[1] When he'd retired unwell to Base Camp, Peter Mulgrew had come down too, offering to leave Makalu so as to be with Ed as he took his low-altitude route back to Khumbu, but Ed refused the offer. 'I'm very fond of Peter but think he should go as high as possible on this climb for his own sake in the Navy.'[2]

For five days Ed convalesced impatiently in the grassy alp that had been the French base camp at 15,300ft. The weather was fine in the morning but snowing in the afternoon. They had a radio which picked up that the first assault party was on its way to Camp 4: 'Rather feel that Mike should have waited for better weather,' said Ed in his diary. Two days later, when the first assault had turned back from Camp 6½, Ed's anxieties were deepening:

> Radio communication hellish. We don't really know what's happening. I feel in my heart that the attack isn't going to be quite the same without me to direct and urge it. I hope I'm wrong but everything sounds rather disorganised.[3]

This was Ed and Jim's last day of communication with the camps on Makalu for a fortnight as they moved south-west over a snow-covered

Shipton Pass and across a series of forested gorges. Every day it rained, sometimes heavily, and with thunder and lightning. There were leeches everywhere but also masses of rhododendrons in flower and occasional big views back to Makalu. At Sedua they found fresh food – curd, potatoes, spinach and a roast chicken each. In the thicker air of 8000–12,000ft, Ed's old fitness was coming back.

But on 26 May when they at last made radio contact with both Silver Hut and Makalu Camp 2, they heard the first scraps of information that the expedition had gone awry:

> To my distress heard that Mike Ward had pneumonia, Tom Nevison had been ill and poor old Peter had frostbitten hands and feet plus a touch of what is probably pulmonary embolism. Have no idea how bad Peter is or where he is but hope to goodness he isn't too bad. Funnily enough I'd had a premonition about Peter for the last 3 or 4 days and been worried about it.[4]

On 29 May, the anniversary of Everest, Ed climbed the Namche hill and walked on to Changmatang where he found Desmond Doig in residence. It was he who passed on the news that Mulgrew, Ward and Ang Temba had been helicoptered to Kathmandu that morning. At least they were alive – though the severity of Peter's frostbite and general condition was still unknown.

Meanwhile, there was a school to be built from the prefabricated aluminium sections that had been flown into Mingbo and carried down to Khumjung. Wally Romanes, just arrived over the high route from Makalu, applied his building skills and within a week Khumjung had a school. A thin skin of aluminium was hardly warm in winter but it kept out the monsoon rains and the wind. It was a humble start to Ed's career running an expanding aid programme that continues to this day.

By mid-June the school had been opened by the reincarnate lama of Tengboche and was in daily use. The Silver Hut had been disassembled and its pieces stacked at Changmatang, awaiting the arrival of Tenzing Norgay, now director at the Mountaineering Institute in Darjeeling, to whom the hut had been donated for the institute's high training base in Sikkim. A few days after leaving

The Hillary family with garlands and Tasman Empire Airways Ltd bags set out for a year in Chicago working for World Book. HILLARY MUSEUM COLLECTION

Khumjung for Kathmandu, Ed met Tenzing on the trail.

> Reached Seti Gompa at 1.30pm and settled in when there
> was a shout and there was Tenzing looking as spick and span
> as ever and accompanied by a lovely Sherpa girl, who was his
> cousin. It was great to meet him. What a handsome, charming
> chap he is![5]

He arrived in Kathmandu on 23 June, and went immediately to
Shanta Bhawan Hospital. He was horrified by his first sight of a gaunt
Peter Mulgrew, lethargic from the pethidine injections required to
control the pain in his feet.[6] Ed sent a telegram to Louise, strongly
recommending that Peter's wife June come to Kathmandu as soon as
possible, and a week later she was there. He wrote to Louise:

> June arrived in at 4pm looking very bright and fresh ... Pete
> will be in hospital, or at least bedridden, for 3 or 4 months
> I would think. I think she'll find him both better and worse
> than she expected. I'm sure his feet will horrify her – they're
> pretty black and wizened up. But his lung is vastly improved
> and he has more energy and drive. He still has to have pain-
> killing drugs every couple of hours to subdue the pain.[7]

Ed was right that Peter had a long hard path ahead of him, a time
when he was immeasurably helped by June's nursing and emotional
support. In mid-July he was back in a New Zealand hospital being
told that his feet could not be saved and that bilateral below-knee
amputations were the only option. He soon mastered his new limbs.
He took up sailing, and very quickly became one of the country's top
skippers in the one-ton class. Peter was also highly successful in a new
career in business. Although he never again had quite the easy pre-
Makalu banter and wit, his abilities and determination never left him.
He wrote about his experiences in *No Place for Men*.

Careers with World Book and Sears
Ed's relationship with World Book was by no means over. During the
rest of 1961, he and Desmond Doig wrote the book of the Silver Hut
expedition, *High in the Thin Cold Air*. Then in January 1962 the whole

Hillary family moved to the USA for a year. World Book's payback for its considerable investment in the expedition was only partly the publicity associated with the yeti and the attempt on Makalu. The other half was an in-house public relations exercise which involved Ed travelling throughout North America and meeting the company's sales force, many of them teachers or housewives selling encyclopedias in their spare time.

At the beginning of each week, Ed would leave his rented house in Chicago to climb aboard a plane destined for cities where he would give lectures at banquets and meet the sales staff. They called themselves 'World Bookers' and he was told that he shook the hands of 17,000 of them. 'I was meeting some of the ordinary people of America and I found it easy to like their warmth, generosity and interest,' he wrote.[8] They were unassuming people, hard-working; in some ways they were like the people back home.

An outcome of the relationship with World Book was that Ed at last had offered to him a directorship in a large company, in this case the Australasian branch of World Book. With it for 10 years

Ed presents a set of World Book encyclopedias to a Hillary school in Nepal.
HILLARY MUSEUM COLLECTION

374

Ed in his Sears Advisory blazer. HILLARY MUSEUM COLLECTION

came an annual income of $10,000 before it tailed off as hard-copy encyclopedias began to be replaced by computer technology. World Book also became generous backers of Ed's development projects in Nepal. It was a good relationship.

Another career and important source of income materialised in January 1962 when the giant firm Sears Roebuck invited Ed to join its Ted Williams Sports Advisory staff as its representative for camping equipment and outdoor clothing. From now on, school-building expeditions would be fitted out with Sears tents and clothing bearing a label with a big tick and the name Hillary – an endorsement from the conqueror of Everest. The first one-year agreement was for a modest $1000, but this increased over the years to the useful sum of around $40,000 per annum.[9]

Neither Ed nor Louise were big spenders. Luxury goods had no

The family pose with their Mini for an alternative newspaper photo before leaving their home at 278a Remuera Road at the beginning of 1962.
HILLARY MUSEUM COLLECTION

appeal, and for the rest of his life Ed would live comfortably within his income without feeling he had to deprive himself of anything. Growing up as a beekeeper on Percy Hillary's payroll did not lead to conspicuous consumption. At the end of 1962, he and Louise had accumulated a surplus of US$20,000. He asked advice from a successful stockbroker he'd met. 'Give it to me and I'll double its value every seven years,' the broker said, and he did. It was a little piece of capitalism for which Ed developed an affection.[10]

Keep Calm If You Can

In the American midsummer the Hillary family went on a grand camping holiday in a Ford station wagon dragging a Sears camper-trailer. The distance was 16,000 kilometres and involved driving from Chicago to San Francisco, up the west coast to Alaska, then back through Canada. The book of the journey which launched Louise as an author was called *Keep Calm If You Can*. She had been married for nearly 10 years, most of them filled with the torrid business of raising three small children almost single-handed. The book opens with 'An Explanation' that sets the scene for her laid-back, self-deprecating good humour, and a view of Ed that displays irony as well as respect for his energy and imagination. She introduces their three children.

> I'm just a common 'garden variety' sort of wife. The cabbage kind, not the long-suffering pioneering type; there's not enough backbone for that. I just follow along with the ideas of my husband and because of his sometimes unusual interests I get led into many scrapes, strange situations and strange places.
>
> Why am I writing a book, and what is it all about? The answer is easy, I was bullied into writing it … As a family we are enthusiasts for adventure – the children have had this instilled into them almost from the day they were born …
>
> Peter, our eldest, loves all this. He's a capable young fellow and becomes unusually co-operative with the family packing as he whistles gaily in a nerve-shattering tireless manner. He is tall, bony and wiry, with sandy-coloured hair, grey eyes and a turned up nose. He always loves a good joke and rushes into every task like a large tractor tearing down a concrete wall …
>
> Sarah was five and a half years old when she left New Zealand. She had already been to school for four months and had in that short time absorbed a considerable amount of education, for she is a studious and determined young lady. She loves pretty things, especially clothes and flowers. She is always singing when there is a lull in the general family din, mercifully drowning some of her brother's whistling. Peter and Sarah look quite alike. They have the same colouring and the same turned up noses, but there the resemblance ends.
>
> The last member of the family is Belinda, age three. With great blue eyes and rosy cheeks she is the cuddliest of them all. She was too young to help very much or chat intelligently to people we met, but she is a very contented person who spends her days playing quietly or picking flowers. In our large untidy Auckland garden, arum lilies, nasturtiums, jasmine and morning glory grow in uninhibited profusion all the year round. Nobody cares how many flowers Belinda picks, so she picks a lot.

Peter, Sarah and Belinda boil the billy at a camp in Alaska.
HILLARY FAMILY COLLECTION

After this brief introduction we must start on our journey. As Peter said in a letter to a school friend – 'We left New Zealand in a plane and stayed up all night and woke up in Honolulu.'[11]

On the Worthington Glacier Sarah made a decision about her future.

'I like glacier climbing,' she said.

'That's good,' we replied absent-mindedly.

'If I get good at it,' said Sarah musingly, 'I'll be famous like Daddy.'[12]

At the end of the book, Louise reflects on their year of travel:

This had undoubtedly been the happiest experience of my life. Children are such wonderful ambassadors ... Through them we made friends with bus drivers, New York ballet dancers, London hotel housemaids, a Roman heiress, a Jesuit priest, an

Indian beggar, and hosts of others. In fact, I decided, travelling en famille was almost as easy, and certainly much more fun than travelling by oneself.

Peter had the last word: 'Mum, let's do a world trip again next year!'[13]

No career in fiction

An unexpected find in the Hillary archive was an unpublished novel,[14] or rather a 45,000-word novella, *Call Not to the Gods*, by Gary Sankar – a play on the majestic peak Gaurishankar in the Rolwaling Valley, still unclimbed in the 1960s. Ed's interest in developing his career as a writer was based on the financial success of the two books he had written prior to 1962: *High Adventure*, which provided him with three-quarters of his income between 1955 and 1958; and *No Latitude for Error*. Without these and later the salary/retainers from World Book and Sears, Ed would have had trouble supporting his family.

Call Not to the Gods is mentioned in a letter to Louise in April 1965:

> I showed my novel to Milton at the publisher's and he was very complimentary, said he would be happy to publish it based on just the first three chapters. So I may make a go of it after all. Anyway, I intend to see if I can finish it by September. I feel rather pleased about his reaction and don't think he's just trying to be friendly. He talks in his usual calm way about film rights and all that stuff...! Anyway he wants to show the chapters to others in the firm. It would be fun if I could make some money from novels and be nice and independent ...[15]

Here is a synopsis.

Himalayan explorer John Fenton is celebrating the end of an expedition when his Sherpa, Pemba, announces, 'I have a memsahib to see you ... and she won't go away!'

She is Dr Jennifer Wakefield, an anthropologist who during an interview with a venerated Tibetan Rinpoche learns that while escaping from Chinese soldiers he concealed the legendary Dzong treasure in the ruins of a derelict monastery. She asks Fenton to accompany her to recover the treasure.

At first he turns down her request but when he discovers that she has innocently hired a known villain by the name of Nami, he realises he must help her. He meets Tschering Rinpoche.

'I have seen my country overrun by an invader, its monasteries destroyed, its priests and leaders tortured and killed. These treasures represent a thousand years of Tibetan history. I have told the Doctor memsahib where to find this treasure.'

'As I have a habit of doing,' says Fenton to Jennifer, 'I made up my mind on the spot. I'll go with you but with one proviso. You'll have to agree that I'm in charge and be prepared to accept my final say-so when there's a decision to be made.' They set off, 'looking at ridge after ridge rising up to the jagged giants of the Himalayas, a dozen old adversaries. Jennifer's long legs carried her easily and well, and with a neatness of movement that promised endurance and toughness. Her black hair was swept behind her head in a severe fashion but she seemed more feminine than I had known her. Flushed and perspiring she flopped down beside me.'

They climb high into the mountains where a few Sherpas are driving their shaggy yaks down from the high pastures. They don Tibetan clothing and behind a train of fifty laden yaks cross the Nangpa La into Tibet, and pass unnoticed through the Chinese garrison.

They come to their destination, the village of Yirnak with its ruined monastery perched 2000 feet up a rock face. A narrow track winding up a cliff is the only access but in a line of steep cracks up the precipice behind, Fenton can see a climbers-only route up which they can escape with the treasure.

Jennifer takes them to the seventh carved stone in a mani wall facing the sunrise and here they find three black yak-hair bags filled with treasure. Fenton goes for one last look at the courtyard when suddenly he is face to face with Nami! 'I'm not really a great believer in violence but I do make a fair job of it when I get started. I clipped him under the chin and laid him out cold.' They sleep out on a ledge, Jennifer on Fenton's shoulder.

Next day, as they head for the Nangpa La, they see soldiers fanning out to cut them off. Fenton splits off to act as a decoy while Pemba and

Jennifer climb a concealed snow gully. 'She reached out in the dark and found my hand. "Come back, John," she said softly and I felt her lips on my cheek.'

Then the Chinese are shooting at them. In deteriorating weather Fenton creeps up on a soldier, lays him out with his ice-axe and takes his automatic weapon. In a gully he keeps his pursuers at bay by rolling rocks down on them. Catching up with Jennifer and Pemba he leads them into the concealment of the storm. They have escaped and successfully recovered the treasure.

The publisher's final assessment is not in the record and Ed wrote no more adventure stories for publication. Gary Sankar's story might have appealed to children but it would not have entered the feminist canon. Its chances would have been better in the early years of the last century.

CHAPTER 25

Repaying a debt

———⊰◈⊱———

Although Ed was kept busy throughout 1962 getting to know 17,000 World Bookers, his thoughts often turned to the school he'd built in Khumjung. There was no postal service out of Khumbu, but fragments of news found their way to civilised Kathmandu, and were passed on to Ed and Desmond. Khumjung was thriving and now other villages wanted schools. A request from the village of Thame read:

> Sir, Respected Burrah Sahib, Sir Edmund Hillary
> We the local people, the Sherpas of Thame, Khumbu, came to know that your honour, helping us in all respects, is going to open some more schools in Khumbu. So we Thame people are requesting your honour to open a school at Thame just like Khumjung.
> Though our children have eyes but still they are blind …[1]

Ten years earlier there would have been no such eagerness for schools, but the times were changing. The Chinese over the Nangpa La in Tibet were building schools where previously there had been none, and a few enlightened and well-off Sherpas had been sending their children to schools in Darjeeling or Kathmandu. But the biggest change had been the arrival of expeditions in the previously isolated villages of Khumbu. A new generation of Sherpas could ponder why these foreigners who employed them were so wealthy they could waste vast sums of money on something as useless as climbing a mountain. An outstanding point of difference was these people's ability to read and write. Europeans didn't have to hold everything in their heads; they could write it down, send it to others, learn from books, keep written records of their business dealings.

Requests for schools came from village headmen, expedition Sherpas and from children. Sardar Urkien was one of the most compelling advocates. He was exceptionally strong physically and of well above average intelligence. Yet he was illiterate, and when not on an expedition his frustrations surfaced as drinking and violence. He was not alone in this, and the effects were felt throughout their communities.

An important contributor to the early success of Khumjung School was its first teacher, who Desmond Doig had found through his extensive Himalayan network, in this case the Macdonald sisters who ran a hotel in Kalimpong. They had placed an advertisement in the *Himalayan Times* in Darjeeling which drew a response from a 42-year-old Sherpa schoolteacher, Tem Dorji.

> I beg to apply myself as one of the candidates for the aforesaid post if I get suitable salary. I am Sherpa by caste. I passed Master training in 1959. My dependants are my wife, 3 sons and 2 daughters. All my children are in school. If I get good salary I will go alone. I am not going to take anyone with me.
>
> For your act of kindness I shall ever pray.
>
> Yours faithfully, Tem Dorji Sherpa.[2]

He was a properly trained teacher, a rarity in the hill villages of Nepal. No one knew the personal circumstances that made him willing to leave his family behind, but it was common for Sherpas to leave home for months or even years when they found a good job.

A photo that hung in Ed's study for many years was of the first intake of pupils lined up on the verandah of the new aluminium school – another silver hut – with Tem Dorji standing behind. The children are dressed in yak-wool homespun garments, many ragged and patched. There is no surplus money here. One child is a hunchback from TB in his spine. Some look malnourished and hypothyroid; others are bright-eyed and alert. Ang Rita, son of the eminent religious

The first intake of pupils at the just-built Khumjung School in 1961. Head teacher Tem Dorji Sherpa is at the rear. HILLARY MUSEUM COLLECTION

painter Kapa Kalden, described the excitement of joining this school that had suddenly appeared in the little valley just beyond the big chorten at the entrance to the village:

> Classes began in the open grass field where the school was being installed. I have a vivid memory of how the teacher started. He introduced the Nepali alphabet to us by asking us to draw a Sherpa house pillar which is shaped like an English T. Then he asked us to draw around this pillar, thus completing the first letter of the Nepali alphabet, pronounced ka ... Those who could draw that ka felt very proud and excited. Day after day became more exciting as we kept learning more.[3]

By the end of the year the best pupils could read and write basic Nepali. The strokes and scrolls of the alphabet were a magic key that could open the door into a new world of opportunity.

Two more schools and a smallpox epidemic

Encouraged by petitions, Ed began planning a school-building expedition for 1963. World Book gave generously and by the end of the year had donated US$52,000, the easiest bit of expedition financing Ed had ever known. Schools would be built in the villages of Thame and Pangboche, and water pipelines laid for Khumjung and Khunde. These villages lie in the northernmost Khumbu region of the Solukhumbu district. Solu to the south is larger, lower (4000–8000ft) and more populated than Khumbu, and predominantly non-Sherpa. But Khumbu is better known because its six villages have traditionally been the home of the strongest Sherpa climbers. Their houses are built in the small hanging valleys that cling to steep mountainsides in view of the great peaks of the Everest region. Living at 12,000–13,000ft gives these Sherpas their altitude tolerance and familiarity with mountains. Ed's aid programmes began in Khumbu, though later extended down into Solu.

A small but important sub-region is Pharak, gateway to Khumbu, whose narrow strips of arable land follow the banks of the deeply

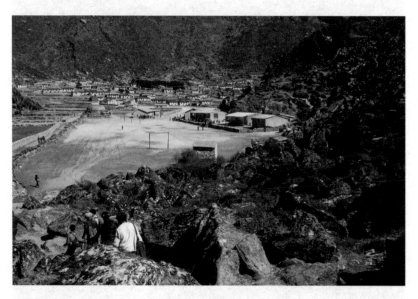

Ten years later four new schoolrooms have been added. In the background is Khumjung Village. HILLARY MUSEUM COLLECTION

entrenched Dudh Kosi Valley at 8000ft before the trail climbs
steeply to Namche. It was in Pharak in 1963 that Ed first realised
a health programme had to be added to his schools. His school-
building expedition had just arrived below the village of Lukla when
a frightened mother requested help for her daughter who was sick
with what the Sherpas called *hlendum*. This was smallpox, familiar
throughout Nepal because of recurring epidemics.

The disease had been brought in by a porter who five days earlier
had become ill with a fever before breaking out in the pus-filled
nodules and extreme prostration of smallpox. A day later he was dead.
Now the disease was spreading to all those who had been in the house
with him, including the girl whom Ed, Desmond and the expedition
doctor Phil Houghton had been summoned to help. In the corner of
an upstairs room they saw a bundle of rags beneath which lay a dying
child whose face was covered in the confluent sores of smallpox. There
was nothing they could do. There is no treatment for it, and it is highly
contagious. Expedition members had all been vaccinated, but there was

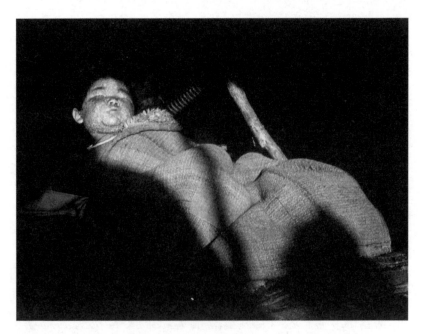

A Sherpa boy dying of smallpox in 1963. HILLARY MUSEUM COLLECTION

the frightening possibility that the vaccine might not have done its work – a vulnerability rarely felt by Westerners in modern times.

Next day the party continued up-valley towards Namche, hearing news as they went of contacts who had fallen ill. At the Namche checkpost Ed was able to radio a request to Kathmandu for an urgent airdrop of smallpox vaccine. Within days, crowds of Sherpas and Tibetans gathered to have the magic fluid scratched into their arms. It was too late for those already infected, but in less than a week more than 3000 people were vaccinated, limiting the outbreak to a few dozen people and about 20 deaths.

For Ed it was a compelling example of a life-saving procedure that was taken for granted in the West yet unavailable to the people of Khumbu despite its minimal cost: 'Of all the programmes we carried out on the expedition – schools, waterworks, medical clinics, and the like – the one most widely appreciated was undoubtedly the vaccinations, and this hadn't been part of my original plans.'[4]

It planted the idea that a health programme be added to education. Why not, Ed thought, provide the Sherpas with a simple hospital to meet basic needs, including immunisations against preventable disease? As it turned out, smallpox vaccination became unnecessary. Within 12 years a WHO programme had eradicated the disease, the only infection in history to have been eliminated by human intervention. But there was still plenty of scope for simple preventive health measures.

Getting to know each other

Ed was known to the Sherpas as the Burra Sahib, the Big Man, the Important Man, the one from whose largesse all might benefit, and he was welcomed in villages with the sort of veneration usually reserved for the most highly regarded Buddhist lamas. As he moved around Khumbu, Ed came to know the people and characteristics of the various villages. Khumjung and adjacent Khunde had achieved most-favoured status because so many of his expedition Sherpas had come from there, and it was the loan of their yeti scalp that had been conditional on building the school.

Ed and Desmond were ambivalent about Namche. There were warring political factions who made co-operation difficult. It had a school, recently funded by the government, but the teacher had absconded with funds. Trade with Tibet was in decline because of the Chinese presence across the border. Later it would become by far the largest and most important Khumbu village, with an excellent school supported by the community – but in 1963 it was in transition. Ed later saw it as a personal failure that he had not developed a better relationship with Namche.

Thame, with its fine monastery built into a cliff, was a more welcoming place. Desmond liked it too, and Ed's increasing rapport with Sherpas was helped immeasurably by having Desmond as interpreter, entertainer, and artistic and religious consultant. It was on his advice that the windows and other woodwork of the new Thame school were painted bright crimson and decorated with Buddhist motifs. A feature of Thame was the way its houses huddled facing south against an old moraine wall, and had heavy roofs of flat stone rather than the more usual wooden slabs held down loosely with stones. These preferences were explained when it was found that the aluminium roof of the school – which had been built on an exposed up-valley site – blew off each winter despite the best efforts of carpenters to fix it to the stone walls. The culprit was a fierce wind blowing down from Tibet during the bad months of January and February. Eventually the school was shifted to join the other houses in their more sheltered site under the moraine wall. Several of the most successful pupils to start their education in Ed's schools came from Thame.

Pangboche, two hours up-valley from Tengboche Monastery, was the last main village en route to Everest, but in 1963 was one of the poorest villages along with neighbouring Phortse. Ed had a soft spot for Phortse because it was home to some of the strongest Sherpas on Makalu, the ones who had been promoted from low- to high-altitude status by issuing them with socks. In 1963 Ed had no funds for a school at Phortse but a large house he rented in Pangboche became a hostel for pupils from that village.

Ed's focus in 1963 was on school-building, but climbing was not neglected. First ascents were achieved on Taweche and Kangtega, and a year later on the redoubtable Thamserku. These, along with Ama Dablam, are the dominant peaks that form an inner ring around the high villages of Khumbu. First ascents were made of all four by Ed's expeditions, though Ed himself did not climb on them.

The potato-growers and yak-herders of Lukla begin clearing land for an airstrip to enable building materials to be flown in, 1964. HILLARY FAMILY COLLECTION

Building an airstrip

In 1964 more schools were built, but it was the construction of the airfield at Lukla that was truly transformative in the years that followed. This was unanticipated, the original purpose having been simply to provide a strip for flying in materials for the hospital Ed was by now determined to build in 1966. Long trains of hundreds of porters carrying loads for 17 days from Kathmandu were just too cumbersome, and the Antarctic had taught Ed the value of small planes. He had already constructed – and closed – his kamikaze landing strip at 15,500ft in Mingbo. It presented altitude problems for pilots, passengers and planes, quite apart from its dangerous dog-

Phaplu airstrip rebuilt and extended in preparation for building Phaplu Hospital in 1975. HILLARY MUSEUM COLLECTION

leg approach and short length. Flat land anywhere below 12,000ft was in short supply and was used for growing potatoes where it existed. Nevertheless, Ed had noted a possible site at the village of Chaurikhakar, at 8600ft in Pharak. He asked his climbing friend Jim Wilson, at that time studying for a doctorate in Hindu philosophy at Varanasi in India, to trek in to Pharak pre-monsoon and write a report. Jim was joined by Ed's Sherpa sardar Mingma Tsering, and by Bernie Gunn, the Antarctic geologist and surveyor who had spotted the Skelton Glacier as the route to the Polar Plateau. As a survey team for an airstrip that would become the second busiest in Nepal they were light on engineering skills, but Ed was comfortable with that.

The Chaurikhakar option proved a disappointment. It was too broken, too short and too subject to cross-winds. But then a local survey team stepped forward with a new offer. They were local farmers from the village of Lukla, 800 feet higher than Chaurikhakar. 'We have a good place for aeroplanes to come to,' they said. 'It is quite long and there is never much wind.' None of this could be seen from below, and it was a mystery how these Sherpas could understand the technical requirements for landing a plane, but a quick climb showed they might be right. The village was a few houses and some terraced potato fields. Set at an angle of 12 degrees, it was far from flat, but when measured there was indeed room for a 400-metre airstrip. Bernie Gunn examined the approach for a plane coming from Kathmandu and declared there was room. The six land owners named their price, and for the equivalent of $835 the area became the property of the Government of Nepal.

Ed's expedition built the airstrip alongside 110 hard-working local Sherpas towards the end of 1964. The terrace walls were flattened, the rocks rolled aside or buried if too big to move, and the surface stamped down by dancing locals until it was hard enough for the first landing. Four weeks after work began, Swiss pilot Emil Wick circled low over the new airstrip in his Pilatus Porter before coming in for a perfect landing. 'The tricky bit is getting the height right,' he said. 'Come in too low and you hit the end of the runway and you die. Come in too high with a heavy load of passengers and you find yourself with the options of trying to pull out or maybe hitting the wall at the top of the strip.' There are videos of all three outcomes on Youtube, which is why it is always a contender for 'The Most Dangerous Airport in the World'.

Ed had always thought that Lukla would remain an infrequently used dirt strip for mountaineering expeditions and for aid projects such as his own. In the early 1960s trekker numbers were negligible, and even by the end of the decade there were fewer than a hundred a year, most of them starting from the end of the road out of Kathmandu. But then the number of trekking companies took off. Many were owned by Sherpas and they provided employment throughout the region. In 2016 more than 40,000 trekkers entered the Sagarmatha (Everest) National Park, most of them flying into Lukla with its smooth tarmac. As early as 1975 Ed was writing that at times he was 'racked by a sense of guilt',[5] but the Sherpas made no complaints about how their lives and environment were changed by so many visitors.

Khunde Hospital

Ed needed medical expertise to guide the building of his hospital. The doctor on the 1964 expedition was Max Pearl, a 40-year-old Auckland general practitioner who with his parents had fled Germany as a refugee in 1936. He was an excellent doctor – intelligent, knowledgeable, experienced, committed to his patients day and night – but his restless energy was not satisfied by general practice. A dream from his childhood days was to go to Tibet. When he read an article about the new Hillary hospital, he saw this might be his chance to find his own Tibet. He wrote to Ed who forthwith invited him to join the expedition. As Ed got to know him, he knew he had found in Max the ideal director for the medical aid work he saw ahead.

World Book and Sears again backed the project but this time Ed, assisted by Louise and Max, launched a public appeal in New Zealand. Louise became an expedition member and wrote about it in *A Yak for Christmas*.

> The raising of money for the Sherpa hospital dominated our lives for a year … It was a worrying time for all of us. What if we received no money? Or not enough? … Money started to trickle in – a few pounds from our local Member of Parliament, a few precious shillings from an old age pensioner. We organized a business appeal with me making the appointments and Ed doing the calls …[6]

Throughout 1965, they worked long hours to raise money. They approached individuals and companies, wrote articles, gave as many as five talks a day to service clubs and schools, and travelled thousands of kilometres up and down New Zealand. A breakthrough came at the end of the year, when the 40 Lions Clubs of the Auckland District agreed to raise £30,000 – over NZ$1 million in today's currency.

Ed, Louise and Max had their money for the post-monsoon season of 1966, but in which village would the hospital be built? Namche, crowded into its little amphitheatre on the flanks of the Bhote Kosi, didn't have room for a hospital. Thame, on the trail to Tibet, was not on the main track to Everest. Khumjung, adjacent to Khunde, already had the school. The deciding factor was that sardar Mingma Tsering came from Khunde, and the hospital would be the jewel in the crown of the village of which he was a headman.

Mingma had first come to Ed's notice in 1960–61 as 'the Sherpa who could be relied on to find the answer to any problem'.[7] From 1963 until his death in 1993, he was not only Ed's trusted sardar but also one

Mingma Tsering and Ed draped in welcome kata scarves.
HILLARY MUSEUM COLLECTION

of his closest friends. Mingma's parents were Tibetans who had crossed the Nangpa La to settle in Khumbu when they were young. Through hard work and application they raised themselves out of the poverty that was the lot of most immigrant Tibetans, but it was their sons, benefiting from the opportunities provided by expeditions and trekkers, who achieved status and became wealthy. Mingma was intelligent, hard-working, shrewd, loyal and tough. Like nearly all his contemporaries, he was illiterate, but he compensated for this with a memory that in some extraordinary way kept track of his responsibilities as a sardar: how many days each porter had worked, how much they had been paid, how many rafters or how many lengths of timber he had ordered from these wood-men, how much cut stone from those rock-men. He could be generous at times, but tough and unflinching at others.

As Ed's sardar he held a position of power in the local community. He could bestow jobs through his patronage, and was feared as well as respected – necessary attributes in a job that was complex and demanding. He was also Ed's interpreter, always a position of influence.

Like many expedition Sherpas, he was a linguist, fluent in Sherpa, Tibetan and Nepali, and his understanding of English was excellent, though when speaking he kept to the Sherpa pattern of using the present participle as an all-purpose verb form. Praise would come out as an approving nod and the words, 'This man I much liking. He very good work doing, plenty rock breaking.' The dreaded condemnation came with a scowl: 'This man I no liking. He no hard working. He too much money asking. I no job giving.'

For the building team, Ed called on an old mate from his beekeeping days. Nev Wooderson ran his own plumbing business but could turn his hand to building. He was the sort of person Ed liked – resourceful, competitive, conscientious, uncomplaining – and expert at his trade. In his youth, Nev had raced motorbikes, and of an evening, relaxed by a mug of Kukri rum, he would take up a crouching position behind the handlebars of an imaginary bike as he described the series of lethal corners that constitute the course on the Isle of Man. The main body of builders were Sherpas. The rock-men chipped and split boulders for the stone walls. The wood-men worked in the pine forests down-valley, felling selected trees and pit-sawing them into beams and planks. Carpenters, using adzes, made window frames, doors and furniture. Villagers, as their contribution, carried wood and rock to the building site.

When Louise joined the expedition, she brought Peter (11), Sarah (10) and Belinda (6) on their first visit to the Himalayas. She admitted to her fear of small planes when she described flying into Lukla:

> For days I had been steeling my shaky nerves for the flight … The expressive words 'operational' and 'un-operational' as applied to aircraft were new to my experience and I found them unnerving. I gained the impression that 'un-operational' was constantly being used when referring to the Twin Pioneers we were using … I have never quite understood how any aircraft remains in the air and my confidence hadn't been helped by the information that out of the original 'Twin Pins' only one was now 'operational'…
>
> We had been flying nearly an hour when we crossed into the tremendous chasm of the Dudh Kosi river to be tossed around by violent turbulence … We were now hemmed in by

The Hillarys in the grounds of the old Tengboche Monastery, 1966.
HILLARY FAMILY COLLECTION

great mountain walls and there seemed no possible place to make a landing …

Lukla! Yes, there it was! A tiny brown scar clinging to the side of the mountain. How could we possibly land on it? All the passengers except me yelled excitedly at one another. The brown scar became bigger and bigger until it finally took on the shape of a rather long tennis court with a wobbly looking 'Lukla' written in front of it.

'We'll never get down on the strip before that mountain wall comes up and hits us,' I said. So to be on the safe side I closed my eyes tightly.

'We've made it! We're down! There's Dad!' the children shrieked.

'We're alive!' I thought privately to myself.[8]

Arriving at Khunde three days later, Louise was able to look at the hospital for which she had worked so hard. It was a low building between the upper houses of the village and the steepening slopes of the holy mountain of Khumbila behind. To the south it looked up at the fine peak of Thamserku, while further east were Kangtega and Ama Dablam. At one end of the building were the doctors' quarters; in the middle was the kitchen, the warm heart of the hospital; and in the west was the clinic room, a two-bed short-stay ward for emergencies and a small long-stay ward for conditions like TB. The stone houses of the village sat amid potato fields of sandy soil, while to the north forested slopes led to cliffs and grass across which, for three mornings in a row, a huge white cat appeared, a snow leopard loping effortlessly from one boulder to another. Alarmed yak-herders raced up through rhododendron and juniper to retrieve their precious animals.

For five Hillarys a visit to Everest Base Camp was part of the plan. Ed led Louise and Peter up the 18,200ft peak of Kala Patar from which the Western Cwm and South Col route on Everest are visible. For Peter it was one of those remembered images that would inevitably lead him to climb the mountain himself.

Khunde Hospital opens for business

The first doctors were John and Diane McKinnon from Nelson, and they set the pattern for a total of 19 couples over 36 years to October 2002, when Dr Kami Temba Sherpa took charge.[9] For the volunteers, two years in Khunde was long enough to become deeply immersed in Sherpa culture. They were isolated, and their only communication with the outside world was through letters carried by runners. There were no other Westerners living in Khumbu. It was unlike anything they had imagined. The culture was permeated by Buddhism, and every village had its own monastery with its lamas. For the blessing and conduct of more important occasions there was the grandeur of Tengboche and its scores of red-robed monks. Sherpas could seem casual, but for the larger events of life, illness, danger or death, the presence of gods was real.

Illness was mediated by spirits, not bacteria, and the spirits were everywhere – in trees and springs, on the heights of the mountain Khumbila behind the village, and hovering over houses, hospital, and, thickest of all, over the area of rocks and forest where the dead were cremated. Convincing Sherpas that the hospital might be useful was not easy. It was dangerous to leave the protection of the deities in one's own house. The spirits outside were often less than benign.

Khunde Hospital in 1966 with the sacred mountain Khumbila behind.
HILLARY MUSEUM COLLECTION

The first healer to be called in was usually the local shaman or a lama, but slowly the villagers discovered that the doctors had medicines that miraculously cured a high fever in a child or the cough and wasting that was tuberculosis. Nearly every resident doctor had a terrifying encounter with a woman suffering an obstructed labour that required some sort of intervention. They might have had rudimentary instruction in how to do a Caesarian section back home, but it was different in the middle of the night in a grubby Sherpa house with snow on the ground outside. Over time, family planning in the form of depot hormones became accepted. The government-supported immunisation policy was implemented by the hospital and its Sherpa staff. Slowly the burden of disease in the community decreased.

A special situation was the high incidence of goitres and cretinism, a common problem in mountain peoples worldwide due to the lack of iodine in water. Goitres, sometimes growing to a grotesque size by middle age, were to be seen in the necks of nearly all Sherpas. Cretinism from lack of iodine in the pregnant mother affected up to 10 per cent of those born in Khumbu, causing mental retardation and stunting throughout their shortened lives. For expert advice, Max turned to endocrinologist Professor Kaye Ibbertson who had graduated with him from Otago Medical School. Kaye described how iodine deficiency in the New Guinea Highlands had been corrected by injecting iodised oil into a population as an intra-muscular depot of iodine which would be slowly released into the blood stream over a period of up to five years. A programme was started in which injections were given to everyone in Khumbu, starting with women of child-bearing age. The results were astonishing: after 1966 no more cretins were born, and huge disfiguring goitres became a thing of the past.

A philosophy of development aid
In *Schoolhouse in the Clouds*, published in 1964, Ed put down his thoughts on aid. He believed that 'wealthy nations have a responsibility to help undeveloped nations',[10] and he promoted this philosophy throughout his life. How does one approach delivering this 'help'? A first principle was that the local people must be partners in a project. Ideally they will have requested it themselves, as had the Sherpas of Khumjung with their school.

Another principle was that wherever possible work should be done by local people, not by visiting foreigners. Ed wrote, 'I am firmly convinced that one of the finest ways of helping an undeveloped community is to give the opportunity for worth-while and profitable employment.'[11] It followed from this that where non-traditional skills were required, locals should be trained either on the job, or through apprenticeships, or by way of training in Kathmandu.

Although Ed was proud of his hospital, he recognised that of all the assistance he gave, providing access to education was the most important. But when thinking about the question, 'What is the purpose of education?' Ed's answer was simple. Literacy: the three Rs, reading, writing, arithmetic.

> We had put much thought into the problem of how far we
> should take children along the path of education. Too much
> education could make them misfits in the simple life of their
> community. They'd drift to the towns, joining the growing
> band of the partly educated – those not well enough trained
> to get a good job but too proud to dirty their hands with

physical labour. In reviewing where Western knowledge could most profitably be used, I inevitably came back to the needs of public health and agriculture ...

It is not easy to teach people to adopt new methods and ways of living if they are unable to read and write so this seemed to us to be a first priority. Initially we didn't plan to take the children beyond sixth grade. Only those few pupils who made outstanding progress would be given more education with a view to filling the need for more teachers.[12]

An outcome that Ed did not foresee when he wrote this was that education would lead above all else to Sherpas entering the nascent trekking and guiding industries, bringing relative prosperity to many and wealth to a few. As it turned out, Sherpas weren't keen on the poorly paid teaching profession. One has to look no further than Kalden Sherpa, Ed's first young graduate teacher, who soon realised that teaching does not make use of the commercial instincts that are part of being a Sherpa. He settled in Kathmandu, worked in the tourist industry, started his own business and eventually became very wealthy indeed. There were many like him. Others took degrees in national park management – at Lincoln University in New Zealand – or environmental studies, and found jobs in international NGOs. One of them, from the first Khumjung School intake, was Mingma Norbu Sherpa who became a director in the World Wildlife Fund. Sherpas became pilots both in Nepal and for international airlines. And finally there were health workers, not least of them Dr Kami Temba who became Khunde Hospital's first Sherpa doctor and director.

Ed often said he had more pride in his aid work than in climbing Everest, but the one grew out of the other. Without his fame he could not have raised funds for development. Looking back, it is surprising that no one else had thought of such a simple project as building a school. An important reason why Ed was the first do to so was that he, greatly assisted by Desmond Doig in 1963, spent time listening to Sherpas and talking to them. It was an illustration of a piece of advice that Ed often gave to young people: 'Cultivate an energetic and roving eye for opportunity and grasp it when it comes.'

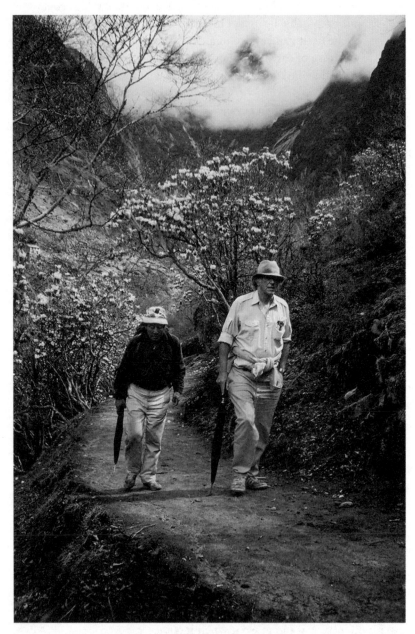

Mingma Tsering and Ed walking the Khumbu trails. HILLARY MUSEUM COLLECTION

CHAPTER 26

The best decade of Ed's life

⟫⟨◇⟩⟪

The years between 1964 and 1974 were as happy as Ed had ever known. The insecurities of his life before Everest were in the distant past. He had adapted comfortably to his fame and no longer had the old compulsion to prove himself against others. People loved to feel that he was the greatest climber on Earth, and nothing he could say would shake their belief. Standing in front of the North Face of the Eiger one day, someone he'd just met said with a chuckle, 'I suppose you could walk up that with your hands in your pockets,' to which Ed replied, 'I couldn't climb that if my life depended on it.' This was greeted with the usual indulgent smile and a companionable punch on the shoulder: 'This guy is just so modest.'[1] Ed was stating a fact, but it was interpreted as the sort of humility that added to his stature. He was not, of course, universally admired – some in England never forgave him for driving his tractors to the Pole – but in the wider world he bathed in admiration.

It was to Louise more than anyone that he owed this sense of fulfilment. She was the first woman he had loved, and when they were apart he missed her dreadfully. He might enthusiastically admire attractive women from afar, but Louise knew that he would never look elsewhere. This is not to say that there was no conflict. Ed said that 'Louise could be pretty fiery when she was provoked'.[2] When she felt she was right about something, she didn't give in easily, and nor did he. From time to time there were fierce rows, but underlying their relationship was the simple fact that he couldn't get by without her.

She always appeared grounded and confident, and Ed drew from her strength when his own reserves ran low.

Working for Sears and World Book

At a more prosaic level, Ed now had financial security through his arrangements with World Book and Sears. Each year as a paid director he would fly to Sydney for World Book board meetings. And each year he would attend gatherings of the Ted Williams Sears Sports Advisory Committee in Chicago. A non-American has to ask who Ted Williams is, but rudimentary baseball literacy reveals that he is one of the all-time greats, 'The Kid', 'The Thumper', 'The Greatest Hitter Who Ever Lived'. Around him Sears had gathered a group of luminaries who appear in publicity photos. Ted Williams is always in front, with Ed Hillary (camping) and Murray Crowder (guns) in the second row. The rest are further back: archery, basketball, boating, football, skiing and weightlifting, with golf, which one would have thought deserved better, bringing up the rear.

Before Ed's appointment, camping equipment was evaluated by examining tents pitched on the lawn of a comfortable hotel. Ted never went inside a tent, let alone slept in one. Ed had other ideas. 'We can do better than a lawn,' he said. 'What about a few days floating down a river with a bit of fishing, and camping?' Thus were born 27 years of Sears tent-testing expeditions. Bill Kelly, who wrote a book about them, recalled that 'Ed was always the focal point of these field test trips. He was what bound us, making hardships or mishaps seem like heroic adventures.' At least in the retelling, the events used to assume Olympian proportions. Not everyone loved them. Ted never went on even one. The gun-buyer in the midst of one ordeal named it 'The Bataan Death March', and the name stuck.[3]

But of all the stories, none was retold more often than 'The Middle Fork of the Salmon' in Idaho in 1970. As one member of the group said, 'We signed on for great adventure and I believe we achieved it.'[4] Ed had always been alarmingly intrepid in his dealings with the flooded rivers of New Zealand or the brown, monsoon-swollen rivers of Nepal, but even he found himself expressing doubts to the two young boatmen who were to take charge of their rafts in the Salmon in high flood. There was a warning of sorts in a local newspaper report that in two boating parties the previous week, 'several persons were

The Ted Williams Sports Advisory Committee of Sears Roebuck. Ed Hillary (camping – with tent) and Murray Crowder (guns) are second in importance only to Ted Williams himself. HILLARY MUSEUM COLLECTION

drowned in the same turbulent river'. The local expedition leader reassured the Sears executives by saying that he 'had seen the river this high six years ago'.

In the largest and least manageable raft were Ed and six others. The bottom was ripped out in the first of the bad rapids, but they completed the day to reach a camp at Elk Horn Creek. Thoughts were concentrated on the following day's rapids rather than tent design.

Sure enough, the next day, just above Sheepeater Hot Springs, a large rock in one of the rougher rapids tore off most of the raft's superstructure. Urgent repairs were needed, so when they passed close to shore, the two boatmen leapt over with a rope to secure the raft to a tree. Instead, the rope was torn from their hands and a reduced Sears team was swept once more into the main current. Another wild mile went by before they again came close to a bank. Ed and his companion Carl leapt overboard with a rope which Ed wrapped around a small tree before it snapped. The pontoon with the three most senior Sears executives aboard was once again swept out into the violence of the main current. Ed saw his happy relationship with Sears departing down the river with them.

Ed and Carl chased down the river bank, and eventually found their disabled raft and its bedraggled passengers caught in a backwater on the opposite bank. They swam across for a thankful reunion, then limped on to Black Hole where they could haul out to attempt repairs. There they made the decision 'to forego the rougher lower end of the river in the interests of safety'. From a small airstrip in the forest they were evacuated to civilisation.[5]

Mt Herschel and Cape Adare

In 1967 Ed made a special request to Sears for two snowmobiles (skidoos) and six Antarctic-style pyramid tents – a design that would not enter the general catalogue. He always had in mind potential expeditions, particularly those where a first ascent was a possibility. This one was the Antarctic continent's Mt Herschel, 10,942ft, an unclimbed peak which formed a mountain backdrop to the American base at Cape Hallett, some 650 kilometres north of Scott Base. A decade after the IGY, it was still an important point on the flight path between New Zealand and McMurdo, offering useful weather information and an emergency landing strip.

The penguin colony at Cape Hallett with Mt Herschel across the bay.
HILLARY MUSEUM COLLECTION

The one-month expedition's tiny budget of £2020 reflected
the generosity of the American Navy, which provided flights, and
New Zealand's Antarctic Division at Scott Base which helped with
equipment and food. Ed had invited three of his regulars to join the
expedition: Norm Hardie as deputy leader and surveyor, Murray Ellis
as snowmobile handler, and me as climber and photographer. Ed's
brother-in-law Larry Harrington, who had worked as a geologist in
the area the previous year, added science, and Bruce Jenkinson was a
professional guide. Climbers Peter Strang and Mike White completed
the team.

We left Christchurch on 18 October in a Super Constellation
ominously christened Phoenix because of an engine which had
recently caught fire. After nine hours in the air we landed on the ice at
McMurdo. It was Ed's first time in the Antarctic since 1958:

> We pulled on our warm clothes before stepping out of the
> aircraft and the cold was solid and tangible. We scrambled
> inside heated tracked vehicles and were driven over bulldozed

snow roads towards the familiar buildings of Scott Base on
Pram Point. It was nine years since I had left the Base and I
had a strange reluctance to return – even the warmth of our
welcome failed to eradicate this feeling. Late in the evening
I went for a stroll outside. The snow was hard frozen and
the light fading. To the west the mountains glowed pink
and blue in the midnight sun. I felt a deep sense of nostalgia
and sadness – a conglomeration of all the fears, hopes and
loneliness I'd experienced in my long stay many years before.
I was glad to go inside and lose my thoughts in the warm
activity of a well-run base.[6]

Three days later, a ski-equipped Hercules landed us on the ice near
Hallett Station, a scruffy assortment of orange and green huts sprawled
on a shingle spit jutting into the sea ice of Moubray Bay. We stepped
out into air that was noticeably warmer – 'It's called the Banana Belt,'
said Murray – and Mt Herschel was a spectacular presence, rising
abruptly to a summit pyramid of sharp rock. In the nesting season,
80,000 Adelie penguins share the spit, and already straggling black
lines of birds showed where they were coming in from the open sea,
some waddling upright, others tobogganing on their shirt fronts,
propelled by flippers and feet. At the station were 30 American sailors
under the charge of a tough little petty officer who immediately made
us welcome.

A day later, our two snowmobiles – tin dogs they were called –
were with difficulty dragging our four sledges across the bay to a line of
30-metre ice cliffs guarding access to the foot of Herschel. Beside them
we saw our first seals, huge, blubbery creatures lounging beside holes
in the ice which they kept open as access to food from the sea beneath.
Some had new pups, soft creatures with liquid black eyes. White snow
petrels fluttered overhead. The day was brilliantly fine, bright blue and
pure white, as it would be for the whole of the week of our climb.

As we drove across the ice we looked for routes on the mountain.
Back home we'd examined photos and talked easily of climbing a steep
east buttress leading direct to the summit. Faced with the reality, we
spoke no more of it. The obvious route now was to climb a steep, snow-
filled tributary valley to a campsite at 3000ft on a north-east ridge
which, higher up, swung left to the summit. The snow-filled valley

was harder than it looked because of its steepness, its soft snow and its thinly roofed crevasses, but eventually Ed was able to lead the carry of our camp on to the ridge. To Jenks and me he gave the first attempt on the summit. The plan had been to establish a second camp 4000ft higher on the mountain, but the more we looked at it, the less was the appeal of carrying more loads. Why not strike out for the summit from the present camp? We talked with Ed. 'Why not?' he agreed, and we decided to go for the top next day. At least there'd be no threat of spending a night out – the next night wasn't due for four months.

We woke early to the best day yet, perfectly still and clear. Our camp was still in shadow, but behind Cape Hallett was an orange glow where the sun was swinging northwards from below the horizon. Then the soft light of morning caught the towering east face of Herschel as we began to climb. For two hours we grappled with an ice wall astride the ridge. At midday, with the sun at its highest point on the northern horizon, we hauled ourselves on to a shoulder at 8000ft and lit the primus for coffee and biscuits. The ridge was never too difficult but nor was it easy. At 7 p.m., after we had spent two hours climbing the gullies, cracks and chimneys of the summit pyramid, the angle suddenly eased and we were on top. The patches of sunlight were shrinking and the shadows darkening. Stretching west and south were vast, anonymous ranges of mountains amid a tangle of icefalls and glaciers. It was beautiful in the soft light, but how inhospitable, how desolate those wastes of snow and ice. Shivering, we turned and fled. When we reached our camp after midnight, we had been climbing for 19 hours.

A couple of days later, after Pete Strang and Mike White had repeated the climb, we retreated off the mountain to start on the second half of the expedition, the crossing of Adare Saddle, 80 kilometres to our north, to reach Cape Adare. There were several reasons for making such an attempt. The first was that it had not been done before, but beyond this was Larry Harrington's interest in the geology of the area. Of particular interest to Larry was a comparison of the Cape Adare rocks with those of adjacent Australia which, according to Continental Drift theory, had once been joined.

There was history at Cape Adare too. In 1895 the Norwegian Carsten Borchgrevink landed there, the first person to set foot on the Antarctic continent. He returned in 1899 and sailed south to the Ross Ice Shelf, then east to a bay where the ice cliffs came down to sea level and a landing could be made. This was the Bay of Whales. Here in 1911 his Norwegian compatriot Roald Amundsen established the base Framheim from which he would set off to become the first man to reach the South Pole.

We were confident we'd soon be up the gently rising Moubray Glacier to Adare Saddle, from which we would have an easy descent to the cape. A reading of the US Sailing Directions for the region of the cape would have tempered our optimism: 'The weather is extremely variable with cycles of winds of great intensity alternating with periods of calm.' We'd had our period of calm. Ahead of us were the winds of great intensity. It was not until 7 November that we reached Adare Saddle and saw the view we had been waiting for. On our right the long black finger of Cape Adare pointed north, but we could see no easy route down to it and that was as close as we got to it.

During the night a southerly gale blew up, and the blizzard that followed for two more days was the worst Ed had ever encountered. At midnight on the third day the wind began to ease but time had run out. We ate briefly, crammed the wildly flapping tents into their long bags, lashed them to our two sledges and set off down the glacier, hoping that the wind would not break up the ice in Moubray Bay that was our route home. With fresh snow making conditions more difficult, Ed and Murray joined the two snowmobiles in tandem to one sledge, while the rest of us on skis began man-hauling the other.

The snowmobiles had a close encounter with a crevasse. Murray was in the lead machine when he felt the snow sinking. He knew what that meant – he hadn't travelled to the Pole and back for nothing – and opened the throttle. With a 'whoosh' a black hole appeared under the back end of the machine. Ed peered down into an ice-walled chasm, the floor of which was too far down to be seen. Had Murray gone in, Ed would have been dragged down to join him.

For the rest of us, man-hauling was the safer and more exhilarating option, but it was slower. At 9 p.m., two kilometres short of camp, a lone figure came towards us. It was Ed, worried that we might have fallen into a crevasse of our own. When he saw us dragging our sledge easily downhill, his face lit up.

Back in camp Murray watched sardonically as we swaggered in. 'All you lot need is a bloody standard-bearer out in front!' he said as he handed us some orange juice.

Next morning the sea ice was still there and we reached Hallett in time for a gala dinner, as much beer as we could drink, and four movies. For just a moment we had an inkling of how Ed might have felt when he reached the Pole.

Jet boats up the Sun Kosi River in Nepal

The Sun Kosi expedition of 1968 linked Ed's liking for flooded rivers with his interest in using mechanical vehicles: tractors, skidoos, and now jet boats. Bill Hamilton, inventor of the jet boat, was born a New Zealand back-country farmer but his creative brain turned him into a highly successful engineer. All farmers had a collection of tools and a workbench, but the Hamilton workshop was much larger and became a site of active research and development. A side-interest for Hamilton was how to navigate the local shingle rivers to reach better fishing spots. Tempestuous in flood, the rivers more usually ran swift but shallow in braids across a wide shingle valley. A propeller hanging off the bottom of a boat made movement impossible. An aeroplane propeller above deck was one solution but likely to decapitate the owner in the wild movements of a rapid. But planes had switched to jet engines – why not boats? Bill Hamilton saw the connection, and went on to develop a high-powered pump that sent a jet of water out the stern of a boat which could be steered by changing the direction of the jet. It worked brilliantly not only in shallow water but also in big white water where the boat's miraculous manoeuvrability allowed a skilful driver to pick a line up a rapid that at first sight looked impossible. An ascent of the Colorado River in 1961 was sensational.[7] Why not, Ed thought, try the Sun Kosi, the big river of East Nepal whose tributaries included the Arun draining Makalu and part of Southern Tibet, and the Dudh Kosi draining Everest? Perhaps jet boats on rivers would become the trucks of Nepal.

By 18 September Ed had raised funds for an expedition, bought two Hamilton jets to which he gave the names *Kiwi* and *Sherpa*, and assembled them on the banks of the Sun Kosi above its junction with the mighty Ganges. Besides Ed there were nine others, including four Sherpas. Lead driver was Jon Hamilton, son of the inventor, who had earned his reputation on the Colorado and had wide experience of white water in New Zealand. After Jon, and separated from him by a gap the size of the Grand Canyon in terms of driving experience, came the other five New Zealanders. Ed was leader but not keen to be

Jon Hamilton, world-class jet boat driver. HILLARY MUSEUM COLLECTION

a driver. I was the cameraman who perched safely on the banks of the more dangerous-looking rapids. Jim Wilson won – or lost, one might have said – the position of second driver. Jim had natural sporting skills, strength, balance, a good eye for the best route in a rapid, and reflexes that made the right decision in an emergency. He had everything except experience. Completing the party were doctors John McKinnon and Max Pearl.

Coming face to face with the monsoon-swollen Sun Kosi was a sobering experience. It was huge, brown and of immense power as it poured from between high banks on to the plain of the Terai before joining the Ganges in India. The surface was pressured into huge irregular waves, and there were big upwellings and whirlpools, though the gradient was as yet only modest. What would happen when the river steepened and narrowed?

Our first camp was at Tribeni, Nepali for confluence of three rivers – the Tamur from the east, the Arun from the north, and the continuation of the Sun Kosi from the west. A quick look at the smaller Tamur showed that within a short distance it had become too rough, so that afternoon we turned our attention to the much bigger Arun which, to begin with at least, looked benign. A local peasant tried earnestly to dissuade us from turning up the Arun.

'It is very bad,' he said, 'very, very bad,' and shook his head.

Well, it was only an afternoon reconnaissance. We'd turn back if it got difficult. And how could he understand the capabilities of the jet boat anyway?

The first four kilometres were easy, with tall forest on either side. Then the river narrowed into a gorge and steepened, and the water became progressively rougher, with big broken pressure waves filling most of the river's width. Jon led up the easier water against the bank, but always this ended at an impossibly rough corner, forcing the boat to cross to the other side through the pressure waves. Jim was coping with difficult water brilliantly, but the level of risk was rising.

Then difficulty turned into disaster. In the lead boat driven by Jon, Ed and I were watching the violent movements of Jim's boat behind

Jon drives his boat onto the tongue of one of the easier Sun Kosi rapids.
HILLARY MUSEUM COLLECTION

John McKinnon is rescued in calm water below the Arun rapid where one of the jet boats sank. HILLARY MUSEUM COLLECTION

us when suddenly its stern was vertical, blowing a jet of water into the sky. Then it disappeared beneath the waves. Jon turned his boat back to rescue the four occupants. There seemed to be only three of them until we realised that the submerging figure in mid-stream was Ang Pasang clinging tightly to John McKinnon. Sherpas weren't swimmers and his loose-fitting life jacket had been torn off during the sinking. By the time both men were hauled aboard Jon's boat, they were tiring fast.

A landing spot having been found, Ed called for volunteers to walk back. The response was overwhelming, particularly from the Sherpas. Ed changed the call to volunteers to return by boat. I was among the walkers, and as we made our way back we met the Nepali who had warned us of the dangers ahead. He was now happily carrying on his shoulder one of the padded seats from the sunken boat.

Back at Tribeni with our main objective, the Sun Kosi, still ahead, Ed was philosophical about losing a boat and thankful that no one had drowned. A re-write of the plan led to two Sherpas, along with John and Max, leaving the boats. Of the others, Ed would lead, Jon would drive, Jim would be back-up driver and I would film. Two Sherpas,

412

Sardar Mingma and strong man Siku, would portage loads around big rapids and do the cooking.

In the 400 kilometres of Sun Kosi that lay ahead of us between Tribeni and Dolalghat near Kathmandu, there were harder rapids than the Arun, but none was so buried in a gorge. We could anticipate the big rapids found wherever a large tributary joined the main river. We would hear the roaring of water, catch glimpses of tossing white waves. Jon would get out, make a careful inspection and plan a route. For the worst rapids, we emptied the boat of all passengers and freight. For a boat to be manoeuvrable it has to be planing – that is, moving fast on flat water, or poised on water moving fast beneath it in a rapid. Standing on the river bank, we marvelled at how easily Jon handled his lightened boat in tempestuous white water. His handling of a long succession of difficult rapids was a master-class in jet-boat driving.

Where the river met the road to Kathmandu, we hauled out and were met by waiting journalists.

'Are jet boats the transport of the future for Nepal?'

'Well, no, not really.'

'Could boat trips to Tribeni be recommended for tourists?'

'They'd need to be risk-tolerant and heavily insured.'

'Have you enjoyed your trip?'

That was easy. It had been amazing. And Ed was already thinking of a much bigger river to negotiate. The river was the Ganges.

Return to Mt Cook

Among his resolutions on his fiftieth birthday, Ed listed a Grand Traverse of Aoraki–Mt Cook. The opportunity came one fine day in February 1971. His party of six included his early mentor and guide Harry Ayres, now 59. The long ridge, with steep faces falling away on either side, is a magnificent arête of snow and ice, a long and exposed climb which is risky in icy conditions. A television crew filming from a helicopter exhausted their flying budget before they had even found the conqueror of Everest, but they touched a skid briefly on the summit. From the Low Peak, Ed looked down on the South Ridge, the first ascent of which 23 years earlier had brought him fame in the small world of New Zealand climbing. We climbed over the Middle Peak, the Tasman Sea visible to the west and the plains of Canterbury to the east. In the snow on the summit was a small rock with a piece

413

Ed celebrated his 50th birthday with a Grand Traverse of the summit ridge of Aoraki–Mt Cook. HILLARY MUSEUM COLLECTION

of thin line dropping down the east face. Attached to it was a half-bottle of red wine. We drank a toast to the Southern Alps, now spread around us, and to TV crews who deliver wine to fine summits. Continuing the traverse down the ice cap, we made the sad discovery that a black dot marked with a cross stamped in the snow of the Linda Glacier was the body of a young climber who had fallen to his death earlier in the day.

A day later, outside The Hermitage Hotel, an attractive middle-aged woman greeted Ed warmly. 'You remember me, Ed. James, from *The Times*.' By the time Ed had realised this was James Morris, now Jan, conversation had come to an end. Discomfited by his failure to recognise one of the Everest team, Ed watched the retreating figure, adding, reflectively, 'Old James has changed a bit, hasn't he.'

Commitment to the Himalayas

By the early 1970s, Ed's life had slipped into a more regular pattern. The months of October, November and December were taken up with business visits to Australia, Chicago, London and Nepal. His diary and letters from 1970 offer glimpses of his thoughts and experiences.[8] In Chicago he wrote to Louise:

> My salary for next year has been raised from $6,800 to $9,200 and I nearly fell over. It looks as though I'm appreciated here. I gave my lecture to 80 of the most important businessmen in Chicago – and it seemed to go extremely well even though I hammered them on the Affluent Society …
>
> … I'm a bit of a hero here because of my swim across the Middle Fork of the Salmon.

Nevertheless, when writing to senior management at Sears the image of the dauntless adventurer was not discarded entirely:

> Dear Bill, The last 3 weeks have been rather eventful. I've walked a couple of hundred miles and visited all our schools. The last week has been devoted to the Rolwaling Valley right on the Tibetan border. To save time getting into this isolated place I decided to use a pass that as far as I know had only been crossed once before. It proved higher (18,500ft) and more difficult than I had anticipated. Night was coming on as I finished lowering 14 porters and their loads down a 150 foot drop over the pass. Then there were crevasses and some steep slopes to negotiate before we could camp on flat snow at nearly 17,000 feet … I suffered quite a few altitude effects, including headache, nausea, and impairment of sight. I was relieved to get down to Beding village at 12,000ft and duly recovered … I agreed to try and build them a school.

A visit to London always included an excellent lunch with his publishers:

> London was foggy and grimy with all the piles of rubbish all around but for some reason I feel an affinity for the place … I had lunch with Hodders and they said I <u>must, must, must</u> do my autobiography. Maybe they're right! I want to anyway, even if I've lost a lot of the confidence in any writing ability I might have possessed. I always seem to be writing things on planes or in hotel rooms and I'm fed up with it … I think

Ed on a trail in the Himalayan foothills. HILLARY MUSEUM COLLECTION

more than anything I'd rather be doing a camping trip with the kids. It's funny how often I think of the views along the coast of Great Barrier Island when I was there with Peter.[9]

Nepal was the last stop before returning to New Zealand. Mingma would meet him as he stepped out of the plane at Lukla, and they would walk up to Khunde Hospital and Khumjung School. He wrote to Louise:

> In Khunde I woke with a rotten headache. You know I've always had a fear of really violent headaches ever since my altitude problem on Makalu in 1961. At the hospital [Dr] Selwyn Lang suggested I go down the hill and I did, finding the headache slowly eased until by the bottom of the Namche Hill it had pretty well gone. Selwyn is sure it was altitude compounded with wild Sherpa parties and I think he's right. Why I should think I can come back to Nepal after being away six months and dash crazily about I'm damned if I know. I really am about the stupidest person I know. You should have married the musician.

416

In a way this is a lonely sort of an existence. I have a few strange dreams at times – like last night I dreamt the whole family had crashed in a plane at Singapore – I felt quite depressed for a while and decided if something like that really did happen that life would scarcely be worth living.

I hate the sound of a helicopter – I always think they're bringing bad news.

In 1973 Louise published her third book, *High Time*, describing a month with Ed and the children in Nepal over the Christmas period 1971–72. They had been delayed briefly by the 13-day Indo-Pakistan War, during which Pakistan bombed Agra Airport and East Pakistan declared itself the independent new nation of Bangladesh.

The Solukhumbu development projects were now embedded in the lives of the Hillary family. Each year Ed was spending many weeks in Nepal, checking on building progress, talking to locals and government, listening for new ideas. But he was also spending six months of each year in Auckland and getting to know Peter, Sarah and Belinda – and Louise – more closely than had been possible in the frantic early years. Louise's parents, Phyl and Jim Rose, owned an isolated block of steep land on Auckland's wild west coast near Anawhata. They gave a part of it, perched on top of a 100-metre cliff, to Ed and Louise who built a small bach there. It became their tūrangawaewae, the Māori word for a place to stand, a spiritual home.

Fundraising was a constant commitment for both Ed and Louise, particularly in the US through World Book and Sears, but New Zealand was important too. Louise described the long hours put in by her, Ed and Max Pearl, and in *High Time* she showed on a map 34 completed projects, including 14 schools, one airstrip, one hospital with associated village clinics, six bridges, four water supplies, and two monastery repairs. By now Louise was visiting Nepal most years, as well as fundraising. A strikingly successful initiative was a bazaar in Auckland selling Nepali fabrics, carpets and handicraft, items largely unknown outside their own country. Stalls were set up in the city centre on a Sunday morning; the newspapers wrote headline stories. The result was a stampede, a sellout within two hours and a profit of $4400. In all, the New Zealand public donated $40,000 towards Ed's next project, a hospital at Phaplu in Solu.

417

Louise also put in long hours and gave public lectures in order to fundraise for building projects in Nepal. HILLARY FAMILY COLLECTION

On the legal side, Louise's father, Jim Rose, set up the Himalayan Trust as the vehicle for Ed's aid work. In January 1972, a first official agreement was signed with the Government of Nepal. Headlines in the Kathmandu papers read, 'HIS MAJESTY'S GOVERNMENT AND THE HIMALAYAN TRUST REACH AGREEMENT'. 'In some tangible way,' Louise wrote, 'we seemed to have been accepted fully into the great Nepalese brotherhood.'[10]

Ed's first full autobiography, *Nothing Venture, Nothing Win*, was released at the end of March 1975. The final three paragraphs portray a man whose life has been blessed:

> If my life finished tomorrow I would have little cause for complaint – I have gathered a few successes, a handful of honours and more love and laughter than I probably deserve. In a sense my life has been strung together by a series of

friendships – Harry Ayres, George Lowe, Peter Mulgrew, Mike Gill, Jim Wilson, Max Pearl, Mingma Tsering – and most of all Louise – the list goes on and on and I would have been nothing without them. I should be content I suppose. Yet, I look at myself and feel a vast dissatisfaction – there was so much more I could have done. And this is what really counts – not just achieving things … but the advantage you have taken of your opportunities and the opportunities you created.

Each of us has to discover his own path – of that I am sure. Some paths will be spectacular and others peaceful and quiet – who is to say which is the most important? For me the most rewarding moments have not always been the great moments – for what can surpass a tear on your departure, joy on your return, or a trusting hand in yours?

Most of all I am thankful for the tasks still left to do – for the adventures still lying ahead. I can see a mighty river to challenge; a hospital to build; a peaceful mountain valley with an unknown pass to cross; an untouched Himalayan summit and a shattered Southern glacier – yes, there is plenty left to do.[11]

CHAPTER 27

A plane crash ends two lives and blights another

———⊰◆⊱———

In 1974, with the Everest region having a school in each village, a hospital at Khunde, and an airstrip in the growing village of Lukla, Ed gave his full attention to the district of Solu. He had built a school and hostel in the attractive village of Junbesi on the trail to Kathmandu, and more recently had contributed to a high school in Salleri, administrative centre for the whole of Solukhumbu. Just north of Salleri was the wealthy little Sherpa village of Phaplu, where a neglected airstrip needed improvements.

One day Ed received an invitation to lunch at the home of Ang Kazi Lama, head of the wealthiest Sherpa family in Phaplu. The lavish scale of the banquet indicated that it would be the occasion for a very special request. Lengthening the airstrip was part of it, but more important was a petition to build a hospital in Phaplu on land the Lama family would donate. Ed looked south at the high school he had just built, west at the airstrip he would improve, east at a superb hospital site among pine forest, and north at the two magnificent peaks of Numbur and Karyolung filling the head of the valley. The invitation was irresistible.

Planning and fundraising were proceeding throughout 1974 when Ed's imagination lit on the idea that the whole family could base themselves in Kathmandu during the building of the hospital in 1975. He always missed Louise when he was on his own in Nepal. So at the beginning of 1975 the house in Remuera Road was let out and

Louise, Belinda, Julia Gresson and Sarah, early 1975. HILLARY FAMILY COLLECTION

another in Kathmandu rented for the year. Louise was soon proud of the abundance of veges and tropical flowers in her Nepali garden. The education of 16-year-old Belinda was a mix of Correspondence School from New Zealand; Nepali lessons, shared with Louise, from a Mrs Shresta; and attendance at a Kathmandu school. Sarah, age 18, was in Kathmandu before returning to Auckland University in March. Peter, age 20, having replicated his father's two-year university career, planned a year in Nepal mixed with travel in India. Ed's brother Rex was there to direct building of the new hospital throughout the year, as was mountaineer Murray Jones. Peter Mulgrew's wife June, running her first commercial trek into Solukhumbu, was one of the early visitors to the new Hillary home abroad. Ed was regularly flying back and forth between Phaplu and Kathmandu as building progressed.

Louise wrote animated letters about her new life. There was the Coronation of King Birendra on 24 February:

> At the airport huge jet after huge jet is landing bumpily on the unfamiliar strip. The whole valley is overrun with police

and soldiers bristling with weapons and completely untrained … What a marathon the day itself was … Lunch with PM … Palace reception for 3000 people … Mrs. Marcos of the Philippines is the bad lady of the Coronation and brought a party of 45 when she was told to bring 11 … Dinner at British Embassy at 9.30pm … I had Kirin opposite me and he was drunk and his huge row of medals fell off … Charles is really nice, so were all the Royals …[1]

Dealing with servants and their problems was a new experience:

> Had row with our bearer Surji who wanted 1000 RS advance to buy a radio!! I said No! and he got sulky and said why couldn't I help him when I spent 15 RS an hour on lessons in Nepali and yet I still couldn't speak it properly. I was very surprised and tried to leave the room with dignity …
>
> Came back later to find Surji's girlfriend up in the bedroom we've given to Belinda who seemed to think the girlfriend had come to stay. Pretty soon it became clear that she has eloped with Surji … Had a meeting to discuss Surji's problems, which are colossal, as he already has a wife and two daughters … we have summoned the girlfriend's parents …[2]

Then there were the numerous trips to the airport where a New Zealander, Peter Shand, had come on the scene a month earlier as a newly employed pilot with Royal Nepal Airlines. He had a reputation for being disorganised, as Louise's encounters attest:

> 22 March … Went to Peter Shand's for dinner. Nothing was ready and place a mess … a couple of odd young men and an RNAC mechanic and two girls – one NZ and the other Nepalese. Peter showed us some lovely slides …

> 23 March. A very busy day – Ed in a frenzy – everything is starting to happen madly now … Jim Rose wanted us to sign our wills and get them witnessed by June. They were signed and witnessed at the airport with pilots wondering a bit …

> 24 March … Ed and co to airport today but were sent back because the pilot – Peter Shand – was lost … It was not a

good day but finally they departed ... I feel as though we are operating an airline.[3]

On 31 March Louise and Belinda were scheduled to make one of their regular flights in to Phaplu so that Ed could show them progress on the hospital site. Ed offered to fly back from Phaplu so as to accompany them, but on 28 March Louise sent him a message: 'ALL IS GOING WELL. DON'T COME TO KATHMANDU.'

The flight was due to land in Phaplu at 8 a.m. Three hours later, Ed heard the chopping clatter of a helicopter, not the buzz of a plane. He had been uneasy about the flight's late arrival, but now he knew that something unexpected had happened. A grim Liz Hawley stepped out of the chopper. The news could not have been worse. Louise and Belinda were dead, lying in the burnt wreckage of the plane which had crashed soon after takeoff.

Pilot Peter Shand had arrived late, and without a pause had taxied into the takeoff. Almost immediately after leaving the ground, he was asking permission to land. One of the plane's ailerons remained fixed by a rod which should have been removed by ground staff; its presence would have been discovered if he had done pre-flight checks before take-off. Ailerons are used when banking into a turn. Without them, a plane is unflyable. Peter Shand got partway round a turn, but the plane slewed sideways into a sickening dive before bursting into flame in a paddy field beyond the north end of the runway.

At Phaplu a stunned Ed and Jim Rose climbed into the helicopter with Liz Hawley and flew back to Kathmandu. Ed told the pilot that he wanted to land at the crash site. Here he saw the burnt remains of his greatly loved wife and youngest daughter. He was told that it would be next to impossible to fly the bodies back to New Zealand for a funeral, so cremation was arranged on pyres at a Hindu non-caste site on the banks of the Bagmati River. The deaths, those burnt bodies, and the grief they evoked, were a descent into hell, a source of torment for years to come.

Ed wrote a letter to his friends five days later:

My dear and special friends,
It is now five days since Louise & Belinda died in the plane crash & I hope you will forgive me if I share some of my

pain with you. When the Pilatus failed to arrive at Phaplu I had a terrible premonition of disaster & when a helicopter approached I knew that something dreadful had occurred. We landed beside what little remained of the crashed plane – hardly more than a mile from the Kathmandu runway – as the bodies were being gathered from the wreck. Thank God it must at least have been sudden & immediately over.

People have been wonderfully kind and good & Phyl & Jim Rose have been unbelievably calm & strong. We've had messages from Kings & Prime Ministers & tears from our Sherpas and Nepalese friends. I think you know how much Louise has meant to me & Belinda was so kind & joyous. My one wish has been to join them if I could find a way without bringing further pain & suffering to my friends.

The arrival of Sarah with Peter Mulgrew has been a great blessing. She is a dear girl and stronger in spirit than I believed possible. I will stick around as long as she feels she needs me. Peter is somewhere in India – we haven't yet been able to locate him.

On Monday we go back into Phaplu for a while to start work going again on the hospital. Whatever else happens I feel the task must be finished. Sarah, Mingma & I will then walk up to Khumbu and cry a little with our friends.

What will happen then I don't quite know. Life must go on, I suppose, and Sarah says she will come with me to London & the USA to help do the tasks I have promised to do. I only hope I have the courage to carry through what has to be done.

Sometime I must return to NZ to give Sarah & Peter a home again – poor substitute though it may be – but it may take a little time before I can face that. It is so easy to die but God knows if I'll have the courage to go on living.

Love to you all. Your friendship has meant everything to Louise & me.

Ed.[4]

Peter Mulgrew had accompanied daughter Sarah from Auckland to Kathmandu, and Peter Hillary was tracked down in India. They joined Ed, Phyl and Jim in Kathmandu. Peter wrote:

Ed at the crash site, 31 March 1975. HILLARY MUSEUM COLLECTION

… our little green car came bumping along the road. Sarah was driving. Phyl was in the passenger seat and Dad and Jim were in the back. The car stopped and the three remnants of the Hillary family reached for each other. We stood there on the road and wept. For me that meeting was the final affirmation of our loss.[5]

As Sarah was to lament later, the two family members who might have held the survivors together were the ones who had died.

For Ed, it was the beginning of four years of deep depression. More than in most marriages, Louise had been his other half, and now he blamed himself for her death. 'I knew it was all my fault – Louise had hated flying in small planes, but I had ignored her fears. This feeling would hang over my head forever.'[6] To many of his friends he was never the same person, even after emerging from the worst of his depression. Di McKinnon, a Khunde volunteer in 1966–68 wrote, 'That was the beginning of the dark times when Louise and Belinda were killed. The joy went out of Ed. He carried on doing things, building Phaplu Hospital, but it wasn't the way it had been before. He was never again the person we had known before 1975.'[7]

A few days after the cremations, Ed flew back into Phaplu – what else was there to do? Sarah and Peter were there, and Max Pearl flew in from Auckland in the role of long-time friend and doctor. As a writer, Ed found letters an easier vehicle for expressing his emotions than talking. When Max returned to work a couple of weeks later, Ed thanked him:

> Dear Max, Your support has probably been far more valuable than you realize. I leaned on you rather heavily, but then I've been leaning on Louise for twenty years so it's not too much of a change … Sarah this morning said 'Dad, we still have a home you know and Phyl and Jim will be there.'[8]

By the beginning of May, the isolation of Phaplu was leaving too much empty time to think. Ed, Peter and Sarah packed their bags and embarked on a round-the-world trip to be with friends and family in Kathmandu, Delhi, Norwich, London and Chicago.

Norwich was the home of Ed's sister June and her husband Jimmy

Carlile, a GP in the city. Ed wrote to them after their visit there:

> Dear June and Jimmy, I read the huge pile of letters awaiting
> me. The kids very much enjoyed their visit but I regret that
> we never had the opportunity to have a peaceful talk without
> them being present. Everyone is always so kind and restrained
> that one gets the feeling that Louise died a generation
> ago. There is no doubt that most that is worthwhile in me
> died with Louise and Belinda. Although you both in your
> own professions hear such protestations with monotonous
> regularity I do not think it would be wise to brush aside too
> casually my feelings in this respect. My first thirty years were
> a rather strange and unhappy period and Louise brought
> me contentment and joy that I believe few people are lucky
> enough to experience. Fond as I am of Peter and Sarah, there
> is no doubt that Belinda had a special place in my affections
> (she had the same vitality and happiness as her mother) and
> to see her shattered body in the wreck of the aircraft was
> pretty hard to take.
>
> It's strange how the kids can see pictures of Louise and
> Belinda and thoroughly enjoy them while to me it is still a
> stab in the heart. Poor Belinda – she had such ambitions to
> help the world and so much potential. She never knew that
> she was the most successful student at Diocesan in her year
> at School Certificate with five A's and a B. I suppose that one
> must be thankful that in her 16 years she created far more joy
> and happiness than most people ever succeed in doing.
>
> But in the end it all comes down to Louise who had
> become the hub around which my life revolved. I think we
> had become rather a good team – she was contributing more
> than I could to the social scene in New Zealand. Few people
> realised the importance of her enthusiasm for our Sherpa
> projects. Even my old comrade Mingma Tsering said at
> Kathmandu Airport, 'Now the Burra Memsahib has gone,
> will you ever come back?' I frankly don't know.
>
> Sorry to be writing this way but I feel the need to unload
> to someone now and then. Maybe I'll dredge some motivation
> from somewhere – I certainly hope so. Sarah and Peter will have
> to work out their own futures somehow – they have reached

427

that stage anyway. Sarah no doubt will carry on as before but Peter will find it harder without his mother to fall back on.

Thank you both for your patience and kindness.

Love, Ed.[9]

After the Sears visit to Chicago, which included a canoe trip down the Buffalo River during which Peter displayed his developing rock-climbing skills, the three of them returned to 278a Remuera Road. As Ed had feared, it was an empty shell echoing with memories.

Painfully too, Ed's *Nothing Venture, Nothing Win* had been published at the end of March, and reviews were coming out within days of Louise's death:

> This is no classic tale of mountain adventure … It is rather an attempt to convey in everyman's language the belief of one man that life should be more than a succession of spirit-deadening routines, and that the excitement and harmony that comes from contact with the earth's wilderness areas is something that everyone should – and can – experience. This reader is left with the lasting impression that Edmund Hillary is, as a result of that experience, one of the sanest and perhaps happiest men he has come across in a long time.[10]

> The pride and joy he took in his family come out time and again … The tragic death of his wife and daughter in Nepal last week will call on reserves of moral courage to match his outstanding physical bravery. No reader of this autobiography will doubt those reserves … an over-mastering competitiveness and tremendous physical energy … his very readable story may inspire others to opt out from the dreary treadmill of materialism and follow his star. Meanwhile we can only offer him condolences and thanks.[11]

> 'I have been given more than my share of excitement, beauty, laughter and friendship.' Now, unhappily, Sir Edmund has been given more than his share of grief.[12]

In September *Nothing Venture, Nothing Win* won New Zealand's Wattie Book Award for the best book published in New Zealand during 1975.

Sarah accepted the prize on behalf of her father. In the UK it reached third place on the non-fiction bestseller list.

Ed had gone back to Nepal in mid-August. He arranged for friends such as Jim Wilson and Murray Jones to visit Phaplu during the rest of the year and to help Rex who was building the new hospital. Max Pearl came over again, and Ed wrote:

> Dear Max, I have left 165 Mogadon capsules which will keep me going for 55 nights and 274 of the Serepax 30mg tablets which I find I need quite a lot of so they will only last about 50 days ... I certainly have many periods of jollity with the gang but I also have some pretty grim nights when I tend to relive the whole ghastly accident. It will be good to see Sarah again but I find it difficult to imagine returning to Auckland or even New Zealand again ... I have come to accept that once the hospital and airfield are finished I can see little virtue in living ... but, who knows, I may still find some purpose that will keep me going. Kindest regards, Ed[13]

Before leaving Auckland, Ed and I had agreed to shoot a half-hour documentary film for New Zealand's TV2 channel. There were no funds for a professional crew to go to Nepal, but TV2 agreed to lend me an Arriflex camera, and Sarah was given brief training as a sound recordist. Ed liked making films. He needed the focus of a project, he enjoyed thinking up storylines, he thought about what he wanted to say, he liked having an audience.

At the site of the hospital, which included an outpatients' block, short- and long-stay wards, and staff quarters, Ed was putting in a full day's work. The local rum that we drank at evening meals allowed Ed to relax into something more like his old gregarious self, laughing and full of talk. But the insomniac nights were hard. After a few days in Phaplu, we trekked up the wild gorge of the Lumding Khola and in bad weather slept under a huge overhanging rock above the tree line. Murray Jones played his tape of *Dark Side of the Moon*. We continued to Khunde where Ed talked on camera about the past and about Louise and Belinda. There was among us a deep affection for Ed and a need to help him live through what we knew had been a grotesque act of violence against his innermost being.

429

Peter was not there but was writing letters.

> Dear Dad,
> Hope all is well. Just wondering what your future plans are.
> I was wondering if we could organize some sort of trip –
> camping, Great Barrier, etc, on your return – just the three of
> us or maybe a bigger crowd …
> … I just want to remind you that you are not alone in
> your feelings and depressions. The loss of Mum and Belinda
> is still unreal; I find the loss of the one person I used to talk
> with freely a terrible blow. Especially when that person is your
> mother and you only have one mother; I feel depleted when I
> think I must live on without her lively and enthusiastic nature,
> so filled with love and affection. I miss Lindy too, terribly. Her
> maturity and her astounding vitality and enthusiasm so like
> Mum's in many ways.
> The loss of people in whom you used to confide, plus a
> time of confusion and depression, is a time to reach out to
> others – to Phyl and Jim, and David Dove to mention a few
> and let them hear your moans and upsets. It's often hard to
> know the difference between genuine sorrow and being sorry
> for oneself. I think one needs friends for this. I have never
> been so open with my thoughts and feelings as I have recently
> with these people and I have been amazed and relieved to find
> their willingness to listen, to help and advise. There must be
> something in the old line, 'Seek and ye shall find'.
> Write soon,
> My best wishes and love, Peter.[14]

Postscript

Forty years later, an unexpected letter to Peter Hillary filled in some
back history:

> Dear Mr. Hillary
> … Peter Shand's father bought him a small plane when he
> was still a teenager. He told me he taught himself to fly but
> had a few lessons at a flight school in order to obtain his
> pilot's license. He clocked up a considerable number of hours
> flying this plane.

In about 1969 Peter came to Africa. He met with three pilots where I was living and heard about a job. He was a very outgoing person but very disorganized. He wasn't able to get the job as a pilot as he didn't have the correct license so he had to sort this out which he said would need flying lessons and take about 6 months and a lot of money.

Within a month he was back with a license – he had changed his log book to show he had night flying experience and other requirements.

I flew extensively to remote airstrips with Peter and ex-Air Force pilots and the difference was profound. Other pilots carried a proper case for documents and wore a uniform – white shirt / tie / cap – Peter was disheveled, a typical bush pilot. However that was not my main concern. All other pilots took care before takeoff, checking everything. I asked Peter many times why he never did this and he said 'they still think they're in the Air Force'. Peter was always in a hurry.

Two events led to Peter being told that his contract would not be renewed. He had a side business buying goats in remote places and flying them back on return journeys. This later led to his plane failing an inspection – the urine from the goats had damaged the rear control cables.

A more serious matter and one I had warned him about was that at remote air strips he would leave the engine running while loading passengers and freight. The inevitable happened when someone walked into the propeller killing him instantly.

When he was put on suspension he looked for another job and was accepted by Royal Nepal Airways. The moment I heard on the BBC that a plane carrying Edmund Hillary's wife had crashed in Nepal I knew it was Peter. Years later I learnt he had not done his pre-flight checks.

Mr Hillary, I was in a position to have stopped Peter flying on a commercial basis. This has been on my mind for over 40 years.

Please accept my apology. I was very young at that time.[15]

CHAPTER 28

Killing time making films

⟹•◆•⟸

The aching emptiness left by the death of Louise was filled, in part at least, by family and friends. Ed knew he was important to Peter and Sarah, and they to him, and they wrote to each other when they were apart. Ed was like a son to Louise's parents, Phyl and Jim Rose, and they were always there in the house next door when he returned from Chicago or Nepal to Auckland. His own parents had died a decade earlier, Gertrude at age 72 in March 1965, and Percy only four months later at age 80. They were a close-knit couple. It was as if Percy had simply lost the will to live.

In the years that followed the crash Ed seldom shared his grief with his friends, but he enjoyed their company when he went on trips. Making films added a new dimension. 'I get more pleasure out of these filming jaunts than anything else I do at present,'[1] Ed wrote. After 1975 this was not saying much, but filming seemed to be a lifeline, albeit frayed and likely to part under stress.

Television had come to New Zealand in 1960 and for more than a decade neither viewers nor the two TV stations were demanding as to the technical quality of the film they used. They – and even the BBC – had welcomed Ed's offer to shoot amateur footage of his schools, airstrips and hospitals. He had a primitive wind-up Bell and Howell movie camera which could be hung around the neck while climbing. Prior to setting out on an expedition, he would receive from NZTV 100-foot rolls of film on which to record events from time to time. On his return, the film would be edited, narrated and shown as

Ed looks into a bleak future after the plane crash. HILLARY MUSEUM COLLECTION

a half-hour documentary. I was a willing photographer, so assumed the jobs of cameraman, director and script writer. I had one hour of tuition on film-making in 1963 from a BBC producer in London who was buying, in advance, a copy of our footage for a weekly programme showing expeditions in distant parts of the world. His instructions were simple: 'You are not there to film landscapes. You are there to tell a story. There must be a climax, such as the summit of a mountain, the descent of a river, the finding of a rare bird; and on the way there will be side-stories. In part these can be anticipated but the best side-stories are often unplanned.' It was excellent advice and through it New Zealand TV viewers got to see Ed's expeditions.

The year 1973 had seen the dawning of a new day for Hillary films. An enterprising advertising executive by the name of Bob Harvey, later to become Sir Bob and mayor of Auckland's Waitakere City, had a dream in which he saw *The Adventure World of Sir Edmund Hillary* outshining *The Undersea World of Jacques Cousteau*, a hugely successful, long-running TV series that had begun in 1968. He put the idea to Ed, who called together the group that always accepted invitations to join his expeditions. There was Jim Wilson, climber, canoeist, jet-boat driver and expert on Hinduism; there was me, climber, amateur film-maker and occasional doctor; Graeme Dingle and Murray Jones, who were from a new generation of climbers and had climbed the six big north faces of the European Alps. Finally came two Hillarys, Ed who had no intention of climbing vertical walls but would be part of every expedition, and Peter who was described thus by his father:

> My son Peter is 21 years old – he's a ski instructor, has his amateur flying license and is working on his commercial license; has his deep diving scuba certificate; and has already done some alpine climbing as hard as I ever did. But although he is quite happy to work hard and raise money for his vigorous activities he dropped out from university after two years and has shown little interest in making a great career for himself in the business world. He is also rather reluctant to get jobs if there's any indication that they are influenced by his old man's name (he frequently calls himself Peter Hill). However on the whole he's quite kind to his decrepit father and methodically keeps a list of the money he owes me (although he'll never be able to afford to pay it back).[2]

As a pilot programme for the *Adventure World*, I was able to promote a script I'd dreamt of for 15 years. It was called *The Kaipo Wall* for the 4000 feet of sheer granite at the head of the Kaipo Valley, the entrance to which was guarded by a gorge so precipitous and remote that we could find no record of anyone having forced a passage up it. The wall was both unclimbed and undescribed, though given its seaward aspect in the Northern Darrans in the south-west corner of New Zealand, any passing ship could have seen it against its backdrop of glaciated granite peaks. Ed gave the script his approval; Bob Harvey's Daisy Films provided finance; and they employed as director and non-climbing cameraman Roger Donaldson, who later became one of New Zealand's best film-makers before making a career in Hollywood. I was the Darrans guide and climbing cameraman.

The Adventure World of Sir Edmund Hillary *made a film of the first ascent of the 4000ft Kaipo Wall in the Darran Mountains of the South Island's Fiordland.*
HILLARY MUSEUM COLLECTION

The weather turned on its usual mix of sunshine, floods and storm-force winds. We began by opportunistically rafting down the Cleddau River in high flood, then rafted and canoed down the Hollyford River with one fierce rapid at its centre. Graeme Dingle turned a tent fly into a spinnaker for the rubber dinghy's sail down Lake McKerrow. We walked down the deserted sandy beaches of the west coast, then turned inland up the Kaipo River – though we used a helicopter to avoid the gorge. Finally Dingle, Jones and I climbed the wall, while the two Hillarys and Wilson climbed their own route alongside the wall. The final shot was in a tent on top of the wall in a north-west storm with Ed, in a sleeping bag, saying, 'You know, Jim, some people wouldn't think this was fun.' It was light-hearted, set in an unblemished natural world, an escape from real life. As Ed put it later, 'The fact is I'm happiest with a bunch of my scruffy friends paddling down a river or walking over the hills.'[3]

But this was in the carefree times of 1974, and *The Adventure World of Sir Edmund Hillary* never achieved the multi-million-dollar future its backers had hoped for. Jacques Cousteau could breathe easily again. Nevertheless, Ed kept an eye open for the escape offered by his adventure films. There were two more during the summer of 1976, set in two of Ed's favourite haunts: Great Barrier Island in the Hauraki Gulf; and the Clutha River in the South Island's Central Otago.

At the northern tip of the Barrier a line of exposed basalt rock stacks rise out of a turbulent ocean. These are The Needles, and one of them, beautifully vertical, was worthy of a film. Ed landed his four climbers from a Sears rubber dinghy, timing the big ocean swells as they rose and fell against the wet foot of the rock. The sea was brilliantly blue, the foam white; ocean-going petrels flew past or dived among shoals of fish. The film was called *The Sea Pillars of Great Barrier.*

The second film, *Gold River,* used jet boats on New Zealand's most powerful river, the Clutha, which flows through an area of dry rocky hills and alluvial flats, the site of a gold rush during the 1860s but now better known for its apricot orchards and pinot noir wines. Rapids ranged from the easy on the upper Clutha to the seriously difficult in the gorge of its Kawarau tributary. A big rapid at the Clutha–Kawarau junction was marginal, with a steep tongue of smooth water recurving into a huge white stopper wave where it levelled off. The jet boats climbed it. Then it was the turn of Ed and three others to paddle down in a small rubber dinghy. It slid smoothly down the tongue before climbing into a somersault on the stopper, emptying the four life-jacketed occupants, including Ed, into a cauldron of boiling, air-filled white water. Murray Jones, lightest of the paddlers, was the first to surface, followed by two others. But where was Ed? He explained later that he'd been walking along the bottom looking for clear water with enough buoyancy to lift him to the surface. It certainly cleared the mind of other thoughts.

Ed kept a diary throughout 1976. On 17 October he records the death of his sister June's husband in England:

> Poor June. Her Jimmy has gone and died. But she's a redoubtable soul and she'll bear up. She's so different from me – it really helps her to have her family gathering around to talk about it all – while I just want to crawl away and die too. Rex has been his usual staunch self – he's had plenty of experience with family deaths in the last eighteen months, my family, his

family, and now June's. It almost sounds as though the Gods have put a big question mark against the Hillary family. Why don't they just gather **us** in and leave our families alone?[4]

Film topics come up from time to time:

> I've just had a week with Mike Gill, Jim Wilson and Murray Jones down the West Coast of the South Island doing a reconnaissance of the Buller River (which has one terrifying rapid and dozens of lively ones) and the Cook River and La Perouse Glacier. The weather was bad but I enjoyed the company and felt sure we could do a mighty film if I have the nerve to do everything I'm meant to. Blood curdling! – but if the project goes ahead I'll just have to float down everything and go to every unpleasant place I suppose.
>
> Peter, as a newly registered pilot, took me on my first flight yesterday – in bad weather out past Anawhata, over the Harbour Bridge and Rangitoto, and back to Ardmore. Very competently done too – maybe he could be quite good at the flying game?[5]

In November 1976 Ed was back in Nepal on a trek which he described as 'his last chance to get really fit'. He enjoyed the walk into Khumbu through a countryside that was green after the monsoon, with crops ready to harvest, and he was pampered by his three Sherpas. But the nights were as bad as ever. In a detached way he described a bizarre incident when a young American boy had been murdered in a teashop earlier in the year. 'Apparently they just whacked off his head with a kukri as he lay sleeping so at least the poor devil didn't feel anything.'[6]

In his diary Ed gives a bleak account of a crossing from Lukla into the Inkhu Valley and then further east to the Arun River. He was accompanied by Mingma and Murray Jones, who was hoping a reconnaissance of Peak 43 might lead to a first ascent. In late autumn the upper Inkhu Valley is an empty place, but Ed could still recognise its wild beauty:

> A windy night … had tea and biscuits, then moved off at 6.50am … a long stretch of exposed snow and ice … feet

were frozen ... plunged down through azalea, rhododendron and pine ... superb views of mountains but hard to identify in misty conditions ... a very beautiful valley, ideal for my Hidden Valley film. Plenty of juniper and azalea, so we camped here.[7]

In the mist and damp we lit our fires ... it was a fantastic scene and I kept thinking how Louise would have loved the expertise of the Sherpas as they turned damp branches into raging fires. Such a strange mixture of porters, Tamang, Kami, Sherpa. I'm so spoiled with all these people, capable of running 50 sahibs, all just looking after mournful me.[8]

But the nights were grim and the altitude was more of a problem than it had ever been:

A wild and ominous morning ... didn't sleep much, and some bad dreams – death of my family; disaster with Sarah; my conviction that nothing will come of the films ... a series of morbid and depressive topics ran through my brain related to the house, the kids, and my lack of purpose for living. I wrote letters, gave speeches, delivered advice – none of it very happy or constructive.

... A cold fine morning but I had a hellish night with headache and severe backache. I seem to be falling to pieces ... my age is beginning to tell on me and I'll probably never be particularly fit again ... Altitude worries me more. When I sleep above 14,000ft I have severe headaches.[9]

On 26 November, further east, they reached the Arun close to where Ed had joined Eric Shipton 25 years earlier for the Everest reconnaissance. 'What a beautiful river it is,' he wrote.

The problem of the benzodiazepines
As the second anniversary of Louise's and Belinda's death approached in 1977, Ed's continuing depression and insomnia were of concern to his friends and to Dr Max Pearl in particular. Ed had remained on benzodiazepines, a pharmaceutical family including Librium, Valium

and Halcion, which for many years were hailed as wonder-drugs in the alleviation of anxiety, depression and insomnia. During the first weeks of use their effects are miraculous. Initially benzodiazepines were described as being no more harmful than simple analgesics like paracetamol, but as the years went by it became apparent that they could be very harmful indeed and give rise to a tenacious dependency.

The brain's response during the weeks following the commencement of a benzodiazepine is to develop biochemical adaptations. As a result the drug becomes less effective in reducing anxiety. A more serious problem is that cessation of medication is followed by a withdrawal response. The patient caught in this dependency knows that without it they will be assaulted by intolerable withdrawal symptoms. For the benzodiazepines these could include anxiety, depression, sleep disturbance, depersonalisation, tremor, muscular pains and headache. In elderly people, other symptoms are confusion, fainting, ataxia and dementia. Of interest at high altitudes is 'respiratory depression when combined with other drugs'. The way out of dependency is gradual dose reduction over a period of months, a process which requires conviction and commitment from both patient and physician.

None of this was well understood in the 1970s, but in January 1977 Max Pearl had become concerned that Ed was still taking two benzodiazepines, Serepax and Mogadon. He consulted a psychiatrist colleague who recommended stopping the benzodiazepines while treating the withdrawal symptoms with a different medication.

During this trial regime Ed continued his diary: 'Max had me over to see Dr E about my insomnia and depression. Dr E says he will "help" me, which I resent!'

This was an inauspicious start. The patient's competitive instincts had been aroused and he didn't want to have any psychiatrist 'helping' him. Very quickly the withdrawal effects kicked in:

> [27th] A night of diarrhoea and fuzzy dreams. Got up in a daze and didn't improve all day … felt sick in the afternoon.

> [28th] Another dreamy night – sort of unreal. Got up 4–5 times to go to toilet. Drove out to Anawhata and had difficulty concentrating. Felt ghastly. Max said to persist.

[29th] Helluva night with almost continuous unpleasant dreams and frequent diarrhoea. Felt slightly desperate in morning. Started wondering what I was trying to prove so took a Serepax and after an hour felt much better. Reverted to old pills at night. Seven hours good sleep and woke feeling clear-headed … I can't stand being mentally fuzzy. I'm starting to feel like a medical experiment – and I have no idea what we are trying to achieve apart from making me miserable … Since the good doctor started to 'help' me I've felt worse, taken more pills and been more depressed than at any time I can remember. I suppose the next step will be shock treatment

… Met Dr E again and after a long chat we agreed that my problems are human ones and that I'll have to overcome them myself – or at least learn to live with them.[10]

No one knows whether Ed's life would have been different without the pills. After 1975 he lost some of the old dynamism and creativity. In later years he had the occasional fainting attack, and associates noted that his mental alertness could change from day to day. The benzodiazepines might also have contributed to his increasing sensitivity to altitude. Nevertheless he continued on with what he had always done – caring for the mountain people of Nepal, keeping a home for his children, working, always working hard, and conjuring up new expeditionary adventures – beneath a thinly veiled cloud of grief.

Mingma says 'Sherpas much liking'
Another preoccupation of Ed's Nepali friends was the idea that his spirits might be restored by a new wife. One fine morning in Nepal, on the route between Junbesi and Ringmo where the track climbs gently around a grassy ridge between two rivers, Ed recorded in his diary a discussion with Mingma, with whom he always felt comfortable:

Slept for about 6 hours and then lots of dreaming and sorrow. Somehow all the Sherpa stuff has brought Louise very keenly back into my thoughts. It was a beautiful morning and Mingma and I took the high route to Ringmo. We rested in the sun at the same place I remembered from the 1953

440

Everest expedition. Maybe it was the warmth or the view but Mingma and I started chatting in a very relaxed fashion. I told him that I had many problems – I had a beautiful house but it was no longer a home … that Sarah was gone and that Peter would soon be rushing off too … that without Louise I didn't find life very interesting. I'd become a sort of lonely drifter, wandering around the world.

Now everyone in Solukhumbu was wanting me to do things and perhaps this was the best thing for me. But I said it was a lonely sort of existence … everybody liking me when I money giving.

It wasn't a particularly negative discourse – just sort of musing along. And then I said jokingly to Mingma, 'If I stay on here in Nepal and work doing, maybe I get a nice Sherpani girl to look after me. What would the Sherpas think then?'

To my astonishment Mingma said 'Sherpas much liking.' I don't know whether he was talking about marrying a girl but he then said 'What Peter and Sarah thinking?' I assured him they wouldn't give a damn one way or the other – they were much too interested in their own affairs.

'Anyway,' I told him, 'I not long lasting and then girl rich getting and some young man marrying,' and we both laughed. As we walked on along I thought if I had any gumption it would be a good idea – but I wouldn't even know where to start. We crossed the Ringmo bridge, over Taksindu to Manedingma where we spent a cheerful evening and they asked me for a health clinic.[11]

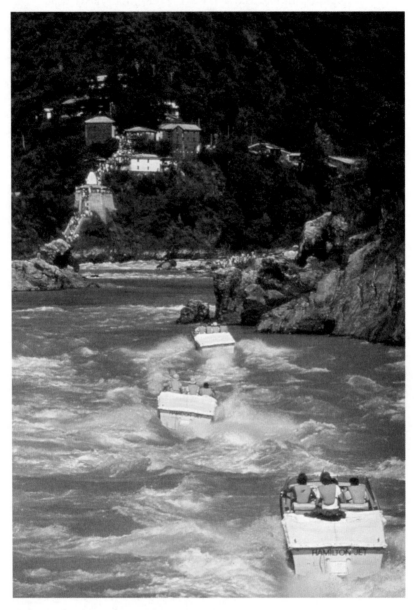

Three jet boats approach Deoprayag in the headwaters of Ganga.
HILLARY MUSEUM COLLECTION

CHAPTER 29

Ocean to Sky, the last big expedition

———⊰•◆•⊱———

I t was the 'Ocean to Sky' expedition of 1977 that lifted Ed's mood. The Sun Kosi jet-boat trip of 1968 had seemed ambitious at the time, but the conception of Ocean to Sky, and ascent of the whole 2500 kilometres of the Ganges River – Mother Ganga to Indians – was on an altogether grander scale. The river's vast and fertile plain had cradled the culture and civilisation of India for more than 3000 years. It was the birthplace of two great religions, Hinduism and Buddhism. At peak flow during the monsoon, the Ganges is the third-largest of the world's great rivers, and its water comes from the Himalayas, the greatest of Earth's mountain ranges. The Indian Ocean in the Bay of Bengal was where the expedition would start; the sky where it would finish was the Garhwal Himalaya, main source of the Ganga and by chance the place where Ed had begun his journey to Everest in 1951.

An early thought in 1973 had been for a small group to drive up the Ganges, casually exploring the lower reaches of its tributaries – but the plan grew because everyone wanted to be a part of it, not least the Government of India. On his way to and from Nepal between 1974 and early 1977, Ed would stop off in Delhi to talk with the Departments of Foreign Affairs and Tourism and receive encouragement, but he had no source of funds. Then one day in April 1977, a handwritten letter arrived unexpectedly in the letterboxes of Ed's friends in Christchurch and Auckland:

Mike, Jim and All, Life has been an appalling rush so I'm writing this to you at 6am in the morning. Sorry I haven't time to type it. Over the last few weeks I've had masses of discussions about the Ganges in Chicago, Toronto, London and Delhi. The results have been sufficiently encouraging that I feel we must press ahead.

Finances: I have signed a contract for a book with Hodder and Stoughton; Air India has confirmed that transport of 12 people plus 600kg of freight from Sydney to India and back and we'll get free shipment of the jet boats to India; Sears will supply the camping gear and air freight it to Sydney so we can take it to India as personal baggage. I had useful discussions in New York with major publishers and we confidently expect a contract to eventuate. Things look pretty good as far as magazine rights are concerned. Confirmation of these items will come in the next four weeks ... I am accepting the major task of bridging finance ... but the main thing is that we should press on with plans and worry about snags if and when they turn up.

Mike Gill – would you tell Peter and Max of the situation (and show them this letter) and give Graeme a call also? Jim – would you coordinate with Jon and with Murray.

The two major problems to be handled in New Zealand are the jet boats and the filming ... It is very important that we do a film as that has been one of my selling points. It is difficult organizing things at such short notice but so far things have gone rather well. I'm prepared to gamble a very large sum of money on the trip ... Would you have a conference about it all ... Please keep me informed. Regards, Ed.[1]

Jon Hamilton was the key person for the boats. He knew everything there was to know about the jet units and was arguably the most experienced driver in the world. Jon's son Michael had joined the family firm, and he too was a skilled driver and understood the mechanics of the boats. The third driver was Jim Wilson who was starting urgent training on the rivers of Canterbury.

Filming the expedition was more of a problem. We knew from experience that film projects can be fraught, subject to personality clashes, expensive to fund, difficult to see through to completion. As chance would have it, Ed received a letter from an unknown Australian:

> Dear Sir Edmund, I am writing to express my great interest in being involved in your Ganges Expedition film. Over the last four years I have participated in quite a number of film projects of this nature ... including four films in the Himalayas ... I have a great love of India ... having travelled on various sections of the Ganges, I know what a beautiful and fascinating river it is and I have a tremendous enthusiasm for portraying this to the very best of my ability on film.
> Yours sincerely, Michael Dillon.[2]

When Mike flew across from Sydney to meet us, we saw immediately that he was indeed motivated solely by a passion for filming India. He volunteered both his services as director-cameraman and his professional camera equipment at no cost, and offered to complete and market the film when the expedition was over. It was a gamble, but Ed could see that here was someone who fitted in with the low-key way he liked to do things. And it paid off. No one got rich, but the completed film was sold into every television market in the world and Mike Dillon went on to make more Hillary films over many years.

Sacred river of the plains
Four months after Ed had fired the starting gun for his expedition, his three boats arrived in the hold of the *Vishva Vikas* at the port of Haldia, 130 kilometres downstream from Calcutta – now Kolkata. The next day, 24 August, was the first of a 57-day journey which began at the temple of Ganga Sagar, the place where Ganga the river meets Sagar the ocean. It was a benign, sunny day with a fresh breeze blowing white caps off the waves on a blue sea. We drove along the shoreline of an island of flat silt until we found what we were looking for – a temple – and drove in through surf to beach our three boats. There at the temple pilgrims were sprinkling water and crimson petals on an image of the goddess Ganga in a simple act of devotion that we would see countless times on our journey up the river.

A blessing was needed, and soon Jim Wilson had found for us a priest, a small man who we liked immediately. Hastily he enlisted a few

Ganga Sagar on the shores of the Indian Ocean where the journey began.
HILLARY MUSEUM COLLECTION

small boys to carry offerings of coconuts and flowers. He showed no
surprise on seeing our three gleaming white boats but poured coconut
milk over their bows, garlanded them with red flowers, and pressed
crimson *tilak* marks on our foreheads and on theirs. Finally he filled a
small vessel with holy Ganga water to take with us to the sources of the
river in the mountains. We were on our way.

The combined Ganga and Brahmaputra rivers form the
Sundarbans, the largest river delta in the world, spreading over 60,000
square kilometres. Where it meets the ocean along its southern border
there are vast mangrove swamps in which tigers may still be found.
We had been offered the services of a guide who had said that if we
were exceptionally lucky we might see one. For three days we drove
our boats along muddy channels between tall mangroves. Why would a
tiger live here? They ate fish, we were told, and the occasional villager.

On the third day a miracle happened. Our guide was suddenly
pointing to where a big cat was leaving the mangroves, tail aloft, to slip
into the water and swim casually towards mid-channel. Seeing us, it
turned back to leap up the muddy bank in three immense loping bounds.

A few moments later, a second miracle happened: a big orange flank striped with black was moving inside the outer margin of the mangroves. Briefly he came into full view, powerful shoulders rippling under sleek tawny skin, big head held defiantly aloft as he looked us over. Turning, he walked slowly away, then glanced over his shoulder before gliding into the gloom of the swamp. A moment later a low, menacing growl reminded us who was in charge of this vast mangrove delta. That was a male, said our guide; the first one a female. We had indeed been exceptionally lucky.

Turning north from the Sundarbans we drove up the Hooghly River, one of the many distributaries into which the main Ganga divides as it encounters the flat lands of the delta. The great city of Calcutta, home to eight million people, lies on its banks.[3] Ed had many tasks there, including press interviews and the inevitable, and endless, requests for autographs. An important meeting was with Indian Oil which was not only donating fuel but also arranging its delivery at numerous towns along more than 3000 kilometres of river. It was a hectic two days, but the welcome had not been excessive and we assumed that from now on we would be on our own, apart from a few Indian Oil employees waiting on landing stages with drums of fuel.

We left Calcutta at 7 a.m. with a drizzling rain falling from a grey sky. Beneath the iron girders of the Howrah Bridge we heard the roar of traffic overhead, the sounds of a city on the move. People leaned over the rail high above and waved. Farewell Calcutta, we thought. But when we saw a crowd on the bank further up, we drove over to see what they were doing. To our surprise, the crowd leapt up in excitement, and began calling *Hillary, Hillary*. The morning became an unending triumphal procession. There was not a spare space on the banks. People were in the trees, on boats, swimming, leaning out of windows, on balconies. They would wave as we approached, and as we waved back there came an answering roar of welcome. We were first astounded, then exhilarated by their extraordinary warmth and enthusiasm.

At our first refuelling stop at Nabadwip, an excitable crowd packed the river banks. 'We will need to be careful here,' said Harish Sarin, a distinguished Indian Government officer from Delhi who had joined us at Calcutta. 'Bengalis are very emotional people.' As Ed was pressed towards a welcoming group, a policeman trying to restrain the crowd

A welcoming crowd on the banks of the great river. HILLARY MUSEUM COLLECTION

struck a large young man who became enraged. 'Go over and shake his hand,' said Harish urgently. Ed pushed his way through the surging crown and seized the hand of the young man, whose anger evaporated as he broke into a broad smile and shook Ed's hand vigorously in return.

Why were we seeing such crowds? We were told that the people had heard on the radio that one of the great heroes, about whom they had all been taught, was coming to ascend their river in magic boats. Some said he was a reincarnation of the god Vishnu. The boats could climb upriver against any current and could leap waterfalls. Hillary and their fellow Indian Tenzing had climbed a mountain that had been impossible to all men except these two. Perhaps Hillary was, like themselves, a Hindu. If they saw him in his magic boat on Ganga, they could receive his *darshan* – a glimpse that would give them spiritual strength.[4] They had travelled long distances and waited hours or even days.

How did Ed feel about his darshan? 'I wished I could dispense with my darshan. I could hardly explain my lack of faith in my own darshan or my feeling that it was too small a return for the warmth and generosity of the welcome given to me by these people and the thousands, or even millions, we passed on the banks of the river.'[5]

Next day we left the constricting banks of the Hooghly behind and found ourselves on the vast expanse of the main Ganga flowing west to east as it crosses the Gangetic plain. The far bank was so distant as to be hardly visible, yet we could feel in the brown water beneath us the currents, boils and eddies of a great river whose flow during the monsoon was 30 times greater than during its dry season. We passed through the Farakka Barrage by climbing a steep tongue of water pouring through Gate 92, which had been specially opened to let us through.

For a week we were almost alone on a broad river, encountering crowds only at our daily refuelling stations. The sky overhead was constantly changing, sometimes purest blue, sometimes filled with billowing white monsoon clouds higher than the Himalayas, sometimes inky black in pelting rain storms. Dolphins rose around us. Birds were everywhere: tall cranes, squat pelicans, storks, egrets, ibises, straggling ribbons of geese. The wide river parted around silt islands on which stood impermanent villages, some of them undermined and collapsing. We passed country boats driven upstream against the set of the current by multi-coloured, square-rigged sails, their black-timbered hulls carrying stone and sand for buildings in cities up-river from us.

After a week we came to the ancient and holy city of Varanasi. An array of old stone temples and palaces rose from the *ghats*, the broad steps dropping down to the river where throngs of pilgrims bathed as part of Hindu ritual. We spent three days here, which for Ed meant attending a round of social occasions arranged by civic authorities and social clubs. He wrote in his diary, 'Fed up with socialising and formalities. If I didn't get so rushed for autographs and photos I could enjoy the people so. But I find it impossible for me to turn people down – they smile and say urgently "please" as if their lives depended on it. How can I refuse? … I've become a sort of paper hero.'[6]

An exception was a late-afternoon *puja* performed as a blessing for the second half of the journey. Ed was joined by Harish and Jim Wilson, whose knowledge of Hinduism had come from two years of study in Varanasi. The *pujari* was a strikingly handsome, supple young man, dressed in a yellow robe. He was soon lost in the chanting of mantras; crimson petals and oil lamps floated at the river's edge; drums

Puja, a blessing for the second half of the journey, at Varanasi. Ed, Harish Sarin and Jim Wilson are standing behind the yellow-robed pujari. HILLARY MUSEUM COLLECTION

rose to a crescendo. At the conclusion, Ed knelt with the young priest and touched his forehead on Ganga's wet sands. The sanctity of the river was palpable.

We left Varanasi on 12 September. As the big tributary rivers from Nepal were left behind, the immensity of Ganga diminished. Allahabad at Prayag, the confluence of Ganga with Delhi's Jamuna River, was another place of great Hindu sanctity, host to the great Kumbh Mela gathering held every 12 years. We made a three-day diversion by road to Delhi, in part because Jon Hamilton needed expert medical care for a debilitating fever of unknown origin. We returned to the river whose bed was changing from silt to shingle as we approached the foothills of the Himalayas. We passed through Haridwar, the Gate of God, and on to Rishikesh where we stayed the night in a government forest bungalow, a modest building set among trees where a forested spur came down to the river. From here Ganga would start its climb into the mountains, and the increased gradient would change a swift but easy river into a series of steepening white-water rapids which must eventually become impossible cataracts. The unnerving question hanging over us was how we would identify that point. Perhaps by the sinking of the first boat? Or would we continue until the last boat had vanished beneath the waves?

Wild river of the mountains

The landmarks ahead of us were five confluences, called *prayags*, spread along 190 kilometres of river, each of them a site of pilgrimage. We would be camping from now on and Mingma had joined us from Khunde. Leaving in the afternoon of 24 September, we were soon confronted by a big rapid, but Jon led it easily. Beyond it we entered a gorge enclosed by steep rock walls in which two further rapids were handled without problems. The day was coming to an end and the gorge darkening when we heard the roar of big water and, turning the corner, found a rapid that was the most difficult yet. With not another human in sight, we camped on a beach of white sand at its foot. When the moon rose, it shone on big white waves. We called it Moonlight Rapid.

In the morning Jon showed the way by crossing to the far side in the trough between two huge standing waves. Then he was working his way up the far bank, disappearing from sight behind big waves, then reappearing before driving out into the centre of the river and on to the smooth steep tongue at the head of Moonlight.

Jim, with Ed beside him, followed, but while crossing the trough the boat moved so violently that he was thrown off the accelerator. The engine cut, the boat sank off the plane and in a moment was dropping two metres into the bottom of the trough. Back at the wheel, Jim pressed the starter button and in a moment the power of the jet was pushing them out of the waves. He had not driven water like this since the Sun Kosi nine years earlier. He was learning fast.

The next morning provided more encounters with large rapids but none caused serious problems before we arrived in Viyasi. Jon led, taking a load of five people and, as he so often did, made the moves through the waves and on to the tongue look easy. Having dropped his passengers, he returned to where others were waiting at the foot of the rapid. Again he led off, but this time something went wrong. He seemed to be right of his original line. The bow dropped and buried itself in the wave ahead. The boat seemed to skid sideways, drop into a hole, and then disappear from view in a welter of foam. We onlookers stared, certain that the boat had gone, incredulous that this had happened to the master. But slowly the boat rose to the surface, wallowing. Amazingly Jon got the motor started and limped out of the tail race on to the nearest beach. Our second day and we had nearly lost a boat. Part of the problem was that Jon was still tired from the fever he'd had since Varanasi. The best physician in Delhi had shrugged his shoulders as to the diagnosis, administered intravenous antibiotics and fluids, and assured Jon he was cured, but long days driving big rapids were not ideal for convalescence.

After an oil-change and repair of a lifting deck, we drove on, knowing that the first prayag, Devprayag, must be close. We came around a corner and there was a golden temple, some white houses and two rivers mingling their waters. We pitched a camp a few kilometres upstream and that night Mingma's prayers were said with a new fervour.

The next confluence was Rudraprayag, and we had seen from a photo on the wall of the Rishikesh bungalow that it looked down on a big rapid. We came to it in the afternoon. At the end of a gorge in which the water surged under our boats was a prayag with a narrow line of steep steps coming down the sharp ridge between the two rivers. The steps and the opposite bank were crowded with spectators waiting for the jet boats to attempt the rapid guarding the branch on our right. Jon threaded his way between big waves to the foot of an impressively steep tongue. For a long time he hovered, trying to get a grip on the slope ahead without slipping under the waves behind. Jet boats must be on the plane to be manoeuvrable but on fast steep water they can plane without moving forwards. Jon hovered, waiting for the changing level of water in front of him to swell up, then with full throttle he was surging forwards on to the tongue and up. Even to us who had been with them for five weeks, they seemed like magic boats that could leap at will.

Next day brought the boats to a pair of rapids that we had been warned might be impossible. They were The Deer's Leap and The Chute, a sequence of two rapids linked by a short narrow gorge. The Deer's Leap was so-called because Lord Siva in the form of a deer had been seen to leap across its six-metre gap. As a rapid it was not difficult, but The Chute at the upper end of the gorge was a different beast altogether. The river here was only a fraction of its size 1600 kilometres downstream, but it was still full of power as it funnelled through the

452

The white water becomes more treacherous as the jet boats advance up the mountain gorges. HILLARY MUSEUM COLLECTION

steep narrow entrance to The Chute. Jon handled it perfectly, hovering, waiting, timing his move on to the tongue to perfection.

Then Jim took his place on the boiling water. The crowd fell silent as he waited minute after minute, watching the movements of the water as it swelled or drained away. There seemed to be no recurring rhythm to the pattern. Suddenly Jim made his move, and at full throttle the boat leapt forwards, biting into the hard green water of the tongue. It knifed a little to the left, then right with the stern swinging hard across to miss by inches the narrowing rocks; then he was in the smooth water of the pool above. Mike Hamilton followed Jon's line exactly. All three boats were up The Chute – but it was hard on everyone's nerves.

That evening we camped beside Czech Hat Rapid, named for two Czech canoeists who had died only few days earlier when their boats capsized shortly after entering the river. The hat was a helmet we found on the river's edge – an unsettling reminder that even with a life-jacket one can drown in big rapids.

An unnavigable three-metre high waterfall brings the river journey to an end.
HILLARY MUSEUM COLLECTION

Next day a long sequence of rapids took us to Karnaprayag, where we turned north to the fifth and last prayag, Nandaprayag, quite close now but up an ever-steepening gradient. The river was continuously fast and was narrowing between banks of boulders on either side. Jon was in the lead, looking for a way up a big wave. He had crossed to the centre, then turned up-river and was easing forwards when suddenly the bow dipped and bit into the wave ahead. Hard green water poured over the bow, forcing it down, then flooded over the low windscreen as the boat disappeared in a chaos of white water. Surely it would sink! But then it was coming up, soggy and wallowing. Jon restarted the motor and brought the boat ashore with its gunwales awash. Sobered, we camped for the night.

We never reached Nandaprayag. We could see its houses but we could also hear a swelling roar ahead. We came around a corner to find ourselves confronted by a wall of water three metres high. We drove around the boiling pool at its foot, but it was clear that this was the end. The crowds dispersed, disappointed by the failure of our magic boats to leap the fall, but we were relieved to have reached such an end-point and still be alive. Our jet-boat journey was finished. From here we would continue on foot into the mountains.

On foot to the sky

Our destination was Badrinath, a walk of four days, but at the suggestion of Sikh expedition member Mohan Koli, and for the sake of fitness and acclimatisation, we spent three days walking into the Valley of Flowers and to the Sikh pilgrim destination known as Hem Kund, a mountain lake at 15,000ft. In the *gurdwara* at Ghangaria, the Sikh lodging at 10,300ft, Ed noted in his diary the return of the old bad dreams which he thought must be due to altitude. The night before our climb to the lake a storm blew up, with hail beating on the roof and fresh snow down low on the mountains. Even in these bleak conditions late in the season there were pilgrims of all ages on the trail. Under a grey sky some immersed themselves in the freezing lake before returning down-valley.

We read about ourselves in a local newspaper: 'GANGA BEATS HILLARY, EXPEDITION ABANDONED'. The people had expected that our boats would reach a true source, a cave perhaps in the side of a mountain, with a river flowing from deep in the earth.

On the seventh day we entered Badrinath with its temples and lodging houses. There was an autumnal air to the place. An icy wind whistled down the deserted streets and the few pilgrims left were wrapped miserably in shawls and balaclavas, their arms wrapped around themselves to keep out the cold.

Murray Jones and Peter Hillary had gone ahead for a first look at Narayan Parbat, the mountain we were expecting to climb. Their news was not good. It was too difficult for our minimally equipped group, and there was fresh snow everywhere. Repeating their climb next day we could only agree, but we needed a mountain. We looked east across the other side of the valley and liked what we saw. Grass and bluffs led to steep but easy rock and a site for a base camp at 15,000ft. Above this was an indolent glacier leading to a snow plateau at 18,000ft which could be the site for our top camp. A further thousand feet of snow-climbing led to an attractive snow summit which we named Akash Parbat, Sky Peak, and this became our objective.

It was hardly a major climb, but with 10 of us for a week and the usual film equipment we had 29 loads and needed porters. We tried the Bhotia village of Mana, where Ed had recruited porters in 1951. Then the guidebook had described Bhotias as 'few in number, powerfully built, both men and women, dirty in their habits and greatly addicted to drink'. In Mana we found that their number was very few indeed. A few old men came forward. Ed said that they looked like the same bunch he'd hired in 1951 and neither he nor they had grown younger during the intervening 26 years.

Ed appealed to the ever-helpful military, represented here by Major Bawa, a robust, noisy Sikh who lived in an unpretentious hut halfway between Mana and Badrinath. Thanks to an oil stove, the hut was cosy; the food he served was excellent; somewhere he had a case of rum; and at one elbow stood a telephone. It was a very functional headquarters.

'Don't worry,' he said, 'I will get you porters,' and he did. They were not eager, but by the evening of 10 October we had a snug base camp on a rock ledge at 15,000ft served by a small trickle of water. After a second night at base we set off for the top camp, but this time without porters. It was a tough day. Ed wrote in his diary, 'I found it a terrible struggle at the end and was greatly relieved to come on our camp site at over 18,000 feet. I had a warm but restless night with lots of dreams.'[7]

The 13th was a rest day, with Ed staying in his tent feeling subdued and without much energy. At 10 o'clock that night, while the rest of the camp slept, I was woken by an obviously worried Murray. 'Ed's been calling out for Jim,' he said. 'He's got a bad pain in his back. I thought maybe you'd better have a look at him.' I put on some clothes, grabbed a stethoscope and trudged through the new snow to Ed's tent. He had an acute pain in the small of his back; it had come on only in the last hour or so. I could find nothing wrong with Ed's lungs to suggest pulmonary edema. It left me puzzled and uneasy. Why this sudden, severe back pain? Was it due to the load he'd been carrying? He'd taken paracetamol tablets without relief. My only other painkiller was Omnopon which contains morphine. I decided to give him half an ampoule, the alternatives being this or nothing. Back in my own tent, I lay awake, questions turning over in my mind. Just before falling asleep I heard Murray calling out, 'How's it going, Ed?'

'Okay,' came the reply. 'The pain's going.' He sounded drowsy.

In the morning a worried Mingma, who had taken tea to Ed, came to see me. 'Burra Sahib some checking ...?'

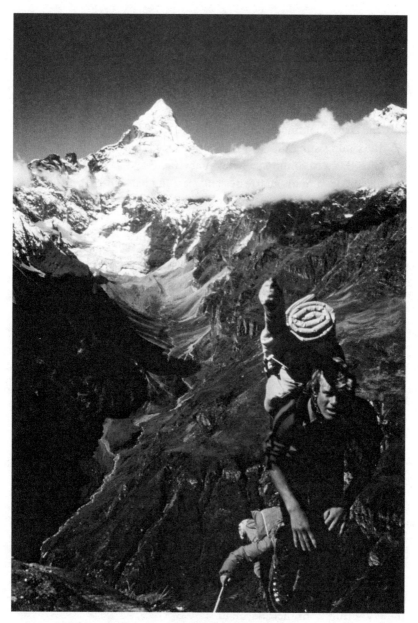

Peter Hillary climbing to reach the sky with Nilkhanta behind.
HILLARY MUSEUM COLLECTION

Finding Ed fast asleep, I gave him a hard shake, at which he opened his eyes slowly and said, 'I ... A-a-a-h ...' It was all I could get from him. Cerebral edema came immediately to mind and I felt a panicky sense of urgency. I was only too aware that my injection of Omnopon would have made the problem worse. There were only three treatments – a helicopter, oxygen, or a lower altitude – and of these only the last was immediately available.

The camp swung into action. Murray raced down the mountain to Major Bawa to summon a helicopter. The rest of us put together a sledge made of foam mattresses and sleeping bags all wrapped in a tent. We towed Ed down the gentle incline of the snow plateau to a suddenly steepening snow gully where he was lowered rather than dragged. In an hour we'd dropped 1500 feet and Ed was a better colour already.

'Where are we?' he said, his speech slurred but recognisable.

Lower down, the ice of the gully was broken by small crevasses but none of them too wide. Three hours and we were down to 16,000ft at the bottom of the snow gully. From now on we would be carrying Ed on broken rock. Graeme Dingle made a one-man carrying harness from a coil of rope, and for a while one of us tottered down the slabs, supported on each side and behind. Then we tried walking Ed down with support. By mid-afternoon we were within a few hundred feet of base camp, with Ed clearly on the mend. We heard the sound of a chopper but it couldn't find us in the mist, so we camped for the night.

Next morning Ed was so much better he could have walked down on his own, but soon soldiers with radios arrived to guide the helicopter to where we were. Ed and I piled aboard and dropped down to Major Bawa's headquarters where a helicopterful of newspaper men was waiting. 'I'm staying here,' said Ed, but he was no longer in control of the situation and in two hours we were in a military hospital at Bareilly down on the plains of the Ganga in Uttar Pradesh. They took x-rays but found nothing. Ed was oppressed by claustrophobia. He just wanted to get back, and eventually we persuaded the reluctant doctors to release him from their hospital.

On 19 October the group was reunited in Badrinath. While Ed and I had been in Bareilly, the climbers and film team had returned to the high camp, climbed Akash Parbat and poured the water from Ganga Sagar on the summit. Ocean to Sky was complete.

When he finished the book of the expedition, Ed wrote as his concluding sentence, 'It had been a unique experience for all of us – we would never be quite the same again …' without explaining what would not be the same again. Like so many of Ed's ideas, the concept of Ocean to Sky was at once brilliant and so simple that one wondered why it had not been done before. We had all known it would be a great trip, but the reality was beyond anything we had imagined: the extraordinary variety on the river, the brightness and radiance of the colours, the other-worldly intensity of the Hinduism informing every human contact, the adulation of the huge crowds lining the river banks, the dangers of the white water, the loneliness of the mountains. Perhaps Ed was thinking that never again would he conceive of or execute an adventure that could compare with Ocean to Sky.

CHAPTER 30

Reconciliation

⟹◆⟸

The trouble was the return to earth. Ocean to Sky was the last of the great adventures Ed had stored in his imagination and there was none to follow. There was the book of the expedition to be written but he lacked the urge to write with his usual vigour. Other expedition members contributed to it extensively. It was the nearest he ever came to using a ghost writer. The Ocean to Sky film was completed successfully but it was the end of the line. There were no more adventure films.

The work in Nepal could go on forever but that world was still haunted by the ghosts of Louise and Belinda. 'Oh Louise, my darling, my life and energy did indeed disappear with yours!' had been a diary entry in 1976, but the same sentiment was there in 1978.[1] There was no one Ed wanted to turn to for help. His sister June, usefully trained as a psychologist, was linked to Ed by strong family solidarity, and she shared with him a sense of adventure, but she lived in the UK, as did George Lowe. Rex was busy with his own family. The two people who were closer than anyone else were Peter and Sarah, but Ed was never able to share his troubles with them, even though they were locked in the same grief. Being the son and daughter of a famous father had been difficult enough even before the accident.

Peter and Sarah
Ed had raised his two children on a diet of adventure yet hoped they would acquire the sort of tertiary education he had walked away from.

On leaving school at the end of his sixteenth year, Peter had enrolled at Auckland University for a BSc majoring in geology, influenced by Louise's sister Shirley Anne, who was married to a geologist, and by Arnold Lillie, a good friend of Ed's who was Professor of Geology at Auckland University. But as Ed would say on more than one occasion, Peter was 'a chip off the old block', and at the end of two years he followed his father's example by abandoning university in favour of a factory job to earn money for a 750cc Kawasaki motorbike. In summer he began climbing in the Southern Alps and in winter joined the ski-racing circuit.

Sarah had left school after four rather than the usual five years, and in 1974 was enrolled at Otago University near the bottom end of the South Island, doing an arts degree while she thought about what she really wanted to do with her life. Ed was protective of his 17-year-old daughter but she was a long way from home. Louise easily accepted her children's decisions and was their confidante. She provided the matrix within which the family operated. Then came the crash. Peter and Sarah travelled intermittently with Ed during the rest of 1975, but he was too shattered to be easy to live with.

Thinking there might be a career in it, Peter took to flying, first for his basic pilot's licence, then six months training for his commercial licence, but he did not take the next step into a steady job. Skiing and climbing were more exciting by a long way. In January 1976 he met an Australian, Fred From, who Peter recalled 'had just completed an elementary climbing course and was fired with ambitious ideas that concurred admirably with my own'. They completed a couple of demanding training climbs together.

> Then came our moment of truth and we nervously headed
> off across the Grand Plateau to the East Face of Mount
> Cook. We surprised ourselves. We climbed more quickly than
> anticipated and were soon over halfway up the 4,500 foot face.
> Moving off the snow and ice face we climbed a narrow rock
> rib which proved more difficult and slowed our progress, but
> by late morning we pulled ourselves over the lip of the face
> and onto the summit icecap ... I called Dad in Auckland to
> tell him of my climbs. He is well known amongst his friends
> as one not overly disposed to spiels of superlatives, so his
> reaction seemed more an interested acknowledgment to me in
> my state of near euphoria.[2]

It had been a big climb, but it was always difficult for Peter to get praise from his father. Fred From and Peter would later climb to 27,000ft on Lhotse, the companion peak just south of Everest.

In 1979 Peter and three friends attempted what they considered to be one of the ultimate routes in the Himalayas: a direct line up the centre of the sheer west face of Ama Dablam that is seen by all trekkers as they walk past Tengboche Monastery on their way to Everest Base Camp. The party of four climbers was two-thirds of the way up the centre of the face when they were struck by a fall of ice from just above them. Three climbers were dislodged and went into free fall but the fourth, Merv English, had a strong belay and was able to hold Peter on the other end of his rope. Miraculously the rope of the other two climbers, who were falling through space, snagged on Peter like a hook on the end of a line. Merv was now holding two injured climbers and a third who had tragically been struck on the head by a large block of ice and was dead. On the normal route out to their right was an Austrian party, among whom was Europe's most famous climber, Reinhold Messner, who climbed up the lower face with Bully Oelz to help the remaining three on their descent. Peter had a broken forearm, ribs and ankle. It was a tough introduction to the world of extreme mountaineering. For the Hillarys, Ama Dablam had once again been a source of trouble.

In 1976 Sarah returned to Dunedin to continue her interrupted arts degree. Ed gave her a VW Beetle which she called Vic. 'It was my worst academic year,' she said. 'I was in a self-destructive space for a long time after the accident and I didn't go back to Dunedin in 1977. My partner Peter Boyer moved into 278a Remuera Road with me though Ed wasn't always comfortable with that.'[3]

Ed's first grandson, Arthur, was born in September while Ed and Peter were in India on the Ocean to Sky expedition. Sarah and Peter were married next door on the lawn of Phyl and Jim Rose's home, and for a while lived there rather than at 278a. 'Phyl was the most wonderful grandmother to me, so warm and loving,' said Sarah. Ed's diary notes, 'Sarah and Peter Boyer are now living here with little Arthur and I enjoy their company,'[4] but he had difficulty showing his pleasure. 'Just remember,' he wrote to Sarah, 'that although I am not very good at saying things, I am very fond of you and would like to help you in any way I can.'[5]

It was Arthur who turned the corner for Sarah. 'He jolted me back into real life. I realized I had to get a real job and I chose Art Conservation. When I talked to Jim Rose he told me to go down to the Auckland Art Gallery, knock on their door and ask them what I should do. They gave me good advice.' By 1980 she'd finished her degree majoring in Art History. Their daughter Anna Louise was born in September 1980. Ed was in London and wrote to say that he was 'delighted and liked the name too'. Sarah recalls:

> A degree in Art History doesn't get you a job and my next move was to Canberra in 1981–1982 doing a Masters in Art Conservation and working at the War Memorial Museum. Ed helped us with money but they were tough years. Both children were in nappies and I was breast-feeding Anna. We couldn't afford a car so it was all public transport. Peter had to go to Sydney to get a job. In 1983 I was back in Auckland doing an internship at the Art Gallery until finally getting a proper, paying job as Conservator in 1984.[6]

Everest without oxygen

On 8 May 1978 a new chapter was written into the history of Everest when Reinhold Messner and Peter Habeler reached the summit without oxygen. Both were climbers in their mid-thirties with records of extraordinary mountaineering accomplishments in the Alps, Andes and Himalayas over many years. Both believed in the simplicity of lightweight climbing without oxygen or cumbersome lines of camps. Because of the booking system on Everest – only one expedition each spring and autumn, and these booked years in advance – they joined an Austrian group in 1978. On their summit day, they left their tent in the Austrian camp on the South Col at 5.30 a.m. By noon they were on the South Summit. With the Hillary Step made easier this season by snow from top to bottom, they were on top by 1 p.m. Had it not been for their photographs and their reputations for endurance at extreme altitudes, such an achievement would have been deemed impossible. It was part of the new alpine-style approach to Himalayan mountaineering.

Three days later, Ed wrote to friend and archivist Liz Hawley in Kathmandu:

So Messner and Habeler did the job without oxygen. What is there to say? Although I have always thought that Everest could be climbed without oxygen I have also thought it would take someone remarkable to do it. Clearly Messner and Habeler are such men and they must have been operating at the limits of human endurance.[7]

Messner, however, was unhappy that he had taken the easy way by climbing with a companion and using the camps of another expedition. In 1980, having obtained permission from the Chinese for a monsoon attempt from Tibet, he trekked to the foot of the mountain with his girlfriend, who remained at Base Camp. Over three days he followed the old pre-war English route to the North Col, then up the north-east ridge to his first camp at 25,700ft. The second day saw him traverse the face and ascend the Norton Couloir which had turned back Norton and Smythe. Here at 27,000ft he made his second camp. At 3 p.m. on the third day he was on the summit, taking a photo of himself beside the tripod placed there by the Chinese expedition of 1975. It was an extraordinary feat, possible only to someone so accomplished that he could climb almost subconsciously in the twilight world of exhaustion at extreme altitude.

A new relationship begins a new life
Ed's gloom began to lift in 1979 after four long years of depression, and this was due not to a new adventure or project but to the warmth of a developing friendship with June Mulgrew. Ed wrote,

> I was living alone, so was she. So we started seeing rather more of each other. On occasions we pleasantly dined together and we did a few vigorous walks together along the wild Piha beach in company with her huge Afghan hound. We were developing a very comfortable companionship.[8]

Friends noted with relief that Ed looked less bleak and that his sense of humour was returning. Letters to June show ease in their relationship.

June was born in 1931 and grew up in Wellington where she was educated at St Mary's College. On leaving school she became a stenographer, and in 1952 she married 24-year-old Peter Mulgrew.

Temba Sherpa, June Mulgrew and Ed in Nepal, c.1984.
HILLARY MUSEUM COLLECTION

There were no privileges in Peter's background. After surviving the
First World War, his father Will had worked as a boiler-maker in
Glasgow before emigrating to New Zealand in 1922. His mother,
Edith Matthews, came to New Zealand that same year at the age of
20. She liked it so well that she persuaded her five sisters to follow her
from Huddersfield. She met and married Will Mulgrew while she was
working in the woollen industry, and with him had two sons, Peter
in 1927 and Ken in 1940. Peter did well at primary school but was
'unsettled at Hutt Valley Memorial Technical College and was asked to
leave at the end of 1942'.[9] In 1945 he joined the Royal New Zealand
Navy and trained as a radio mechanic. His intelligence and application
led to promotion to chief petty officer in 1952 and later sub-lieutenant
– a move from lower to upper deck that is not easy.

Peter was Ed's radio operator in the Antarctic and on Makalu, but
by the 1970s they were seeing less of each other, and in 1976 there
was a falling out. It followed the participation of Peter and his yacht
Tonnent in the film *The Sea Pillars of Great Barrier*. Peter felt he had

been excluded – a reflection, others felt, of his combative temperament rather than of the way he had been treated. June and Peter also had drifted apart in the 1970s, and by 1979 they were leading separate lives.

November 1979 brought a bizarre new tragedy to the saga of the Hillary and Mulgrew couples. Since 1977, Air New Zealand had been taking tourists south to Antarctica for an aerial view of McMurdo Sound, including Mt Erebus and Scott Base. During an 11-hour flight passengers were treated to wine and good food and a commentary from such Antarctic luminaries as Peter Mulgrew or Ed Hillary. The 28 November flight was Ed's turn, but because of another engagement he swapped with Peter.

The early flights had kept above the height of Mt Erebus, 12,440ft, but to give passengers a closer view they had more recently followed a flight path to the west of the mountain and 6000 feet lower than its summit – a height which, on a clear day, was low enough for passengers to see clearly the sea, the ice, the buildings of Scott Base and the mountains on either side, the closest being Erebus on their left. The day of the 28th was spoiled by whiteout conditions, a mistiness in the air which reduced the sky, the horizon and snow-covered Erebus to a featureless white void. In these conditions the flight path used is that which has been entered into the aircraft's computer. The cockpit recorder tells the story of the plane's last three minutes. The GPWS is the Ground Proximity Warning System.

> Commentator Mulgrew: This is Peter Mulgrew speaking
>   again folks. I still can't see very much at the moment.
>   Keep you informed soon as I see something that gives me
>   a clue as to where we are. We're going down in altitude
>   now and it won't be long before we get quite a good view.
> Flight Engineer: Where's Erebus in relation to us at the
>   moment?
> Mulgrew: Left, about 4 or 5 miles.
> Unidentified Crew: Left do you reckon?
> Unidentified Crew: Well I … no … I think.
> First Officer: I think it'll be …
> Flight Engineer: I'm just thinking about any high ground in
>   the area, that's all.
> Mulgrew: I think it'll be left.

Unidentified Crew: Yes, I reckon about here.

Mulgrew: Yes ... no, no, I don't really know.

Captain: Actually these conditions don't look very good at all do they?

Mulgrew: No, they don't. That looks like the edge of Ross Island there

Flight Engineer: I don't like this.

Captain: Have you got anything from him? [McMurdo Station radio]

First Officer: No.

Captain: We're 26 miles north. We'll have to climb out of this.

First Officer: It's clear on the right and ahead.

Captain: Is it?

First Officer: Yes.

Mulgrew: You can see Ross Island? Fine.

First Officer: Yes, you're clear to turn right ...

Captain: No ... negative.

First Officer: There's no high ground if you do a one-eighty.

GPWS: Whoop. Whoop. Pull up. Whoop. Whoop.

Flight Engineer: Five hundred feet.

GPWS: Pull up.

Flight Engineer: Four hundred feet.

GPWS: Whoop. Whoop. Pull up. Whoop. Whoop. Pull up.

Captain: Go-around power please.

GPWS: Whoop. Whoop. Pull-----[10]

All 257 people on board were killed as the plane ploughed into the slopes of Erebus. A royal commission inquiry headed by Justice Peter Mahon found that the accident was due to an alteration of the flight plan in the aircraft's navigation computer during the night before take-off. The flight crew had not been informed. They believed their computer was taking them on the usual flight path over the open water of McMurdo Sound to the right of Erebus, when in reality it had put them on a collision course with the mountain.

For Ed it was another loss: 'I felt great sadness at Peter's death. We had shared so much together in the Antarctic and the Himalayas ... For many years he had been a good and loyal friend. I knew he could never be replaced.'[11]

The Himalayan Trust works on

Only five months later, yet another freakish accident diminished the group of stalwarts underpinning the work of the Himalayan Trust. Max Pearl had been Ed's adviser on medical matters since his first visit to Nepal in 1964. He had been chair of the committee that planned Khunde and Phaplu hospitals, and found and supported their staff. On 27 April 1980 came the shattering news that he had been drowned in an extraordinary accident on the Waikato River. Max was only an occasional fly-fisherman. There wasn't much time in his crowded life for something as contemplative as flicking rod and line over a quiet stretch of water. As it turned out, his chosen fishing spot was anything but quiet, situated as it was on a rock that could be reached only by wading through a broad flow of swift water above the Huka Falls, an awesome 12-metre drop where the river thunders through a narrow gap. Standing in his waders on the rock, Max saw the river was rising around him. The control gates upstream had been opened to allow more water to reach the hydro-electric stations downriver, and the current through the gap separating him from safety was now too strong to wade through. On the bank, family, friends and onlookers frantically hunted, unsuccessfully, for a rope to throw to him, but the water level rose inexorably and he was carried away down a raging millrace and into the maelstrom of the falls. It seemed such an improbable way to die. Max was a truly good man, unfailingly generous with everything he had to offer: his time, his skills, his warmth.

By now, however, there was a group of ex-Khunde doctors, including John McKinnon and Lindsay Strang, providing medical support, and the work continued. Ed was finding new disciples overseas too. One of them was Zeke O'Connor who worked for Sears. On one of their backwoods camping trips in 1972, Ed had invited him to come to Nepal to meet the Sherpas, their mountains, their schools and their hospital. Zeke became a close friend and formed the Sir Edmund Hillary Foundation of Canada which from 1977 through to the present has funded Khunde Hospital. Another partner from Sears was Larry Witherbee who formed the American Hillary Foundation, raising funds in Chicago. The biggest American donor was Richard Blum of the American Himalayan Foundation who in 1981 began many years of generous donations. Later, in Germany in 1991, Ed invited Ingrid Versen from Bavaria to form a Sir Edmund Hillary Foundation of

Germany. For his part, Ed spent increasing amounts of his time in North America as guest speaker at fundraising banquets and lectures.

In Toronto at least, and perhaps the rest of Canada, Zeke O'Connor was a big name, famous for his career in professional football. Ed used to tell the story of being introduced to a fan who repeated the name Hillary thoughtfully, then lit up as he said, 'Yeah, I've heard of you. You're the guy who climbed Everest with Zeke O'Connor.'

The climax of Zeke's football career was a legendary touchdown in the final minutes of a close-fought contest for the Grey Cup of 1952 between the Toronto Argonauts and the Edmonton Eskimos. The key play was a spectacular 'long bomb', thrown with deadly accuracy by 'rifle-armed' quarterback Nobby Wirkowski to receiver Zeke O'Connor for the clinching touchdown. It was the last offensive touchdown by the Argonauts in a Grey Cup for 30 years. The fans never forgot it.

The annual visits to Nepal in the 1980s now were centred on Ed and June, Zeke and Larry, Ed's builder brother Rex, and of course the indispensable Mingma Tsering who advised on which schools should be extended, which bridge rebuilt, which monastery repaired.

The Kangshung Face of Everest, 1981

There was, however, one last mountain adventure for Ed, and it was initiated by Richard Blum of San Francisco. A philanthropist and merchant banker, Blum was also a mountaineer, and in 1979 while part of a trade delegation to China he requested permission for an expedition to attempt the untouched Kangshung Face, the great eastern flank of Everest in Tibet. After Blum's application was accepted, he began organising an expedition that would include not just top American climbers but also Ed Hillary who, as 'Chairman Emeritus', would help with fundraising and write press dispatches from a comfortable Base Camp with a grandstand view of climbers on the great face rearing 12,000ft above them. Ed would say later that he should have known 17,000ft was well above the limit he had defined for himself five years earlier – but maybe this time it would be different.

The journey began in Lhasa on 18 August 1981, followed by four days in vehicles to the road end at the village of Kharta. Ed kept his usual diary, and at lower altitudes he revelled in the Tibetan landscapes of brown hills and crops of green barley in the river valleys. The six-day

The Kangshung (east) face of Everest in Tibet, 1981. HILLARY MUSEUM COLLECTION

walk to the Kangshung Base Camp was higher, wetter and wilder.
There was mist and sometimes heavy monsoon rain. The trail ran west
across the grain of the land, crossing passes of up to 16,000ft. Thirty
years earlier Ed would have been racing along, first into camp, but at
the age of 62 every hill was exhausting: 'Fairly tired and glad to crawl
into sleeping bag ... up long hill feeling dead beat ... glad to stagger
down to camp at 14,400 feet ... reached terminal face of glacier, then
climb to camp at 15,000 feet ... 7 hours to reach Base Camp at 17,000
feet ... took plenty of aspirin ... didn't bother having dinner ...'[12]

They were now camped at the foot of the face. Their route lay up a
buttress that started with 4000 feet of highly technical rock leading to
a vast snow face crumpled into big folds of ice and snow that was prone
to avalanche after fresh falls. Advanced Base was set up at 18,500ft and
from there relays of climbers began to fix ropes up the rock. Snow fell
on most days.

Down in his tent Ed was feeling the altitude in the form of nausea,
headaches, and swelling around his temples and forehead. After three
days, Jim Morrissey, expedition physician as well as a lead climber,

470

realised he had to take Ed down to a lower altitude. Over a week Ed slowly improved, but not before climbing leader Lou Reichardt was suggesting that maybe Ed should retreat to the altitude of Lhasa at 12,000ft. This was tricky territory, and Ed's response was to improve and make his way back to Base Camp on 8 September.

He found that although the climbers had made good progress on the buttress, the expedition had stalled because of daily snowfalls blanketing the route and sending down avalanches. Clearly the steep snow above the rock buttress would be dangerous until it consolidated in fine weather. Snowbound in their tents, the climbers discussed the feasibility of the route and whether it might even be better to decamp around to the unclimbed North Face for which they also had permission. Reichardt called one of his team meetings at which all were invited to express their views. Ed wrote in his diary, 'I spoke at length. Pointed out my belief that we must concentrate on improvement of route up buttress.'[13]

Tabin, one of the climbers at the meeting, enlarged on this in his article for the *American Alpine Journal*:

> Sir Edmund Hillary made a very stirring speech, saying that it would be insignificant for the American team to reach the summit by the north, but that an attempt of any kind on the east face would be a triumph of the human spirit and a significant step forward in international mountaineering. His talk roused enthusiasm dampened by the late monsoon snow. The team voted on what to do. All but Roskelley and Eric Perlman voted to stay with the east face.[14]

Ed felt that it should be the leader who made decisions, not a team vote, but this was a younger generation of climbers and his was but one voice among them.

Over the next three weeks the team forced their way up to over 22,000ft, leaving the fearsome technical difficulties of the climb behind them. But though the angle of the snow above was easier, it remained soft, deep and avalanche-prone. Only five of the climbers were prepared to go higher, but their fitness to climb more than another 6000ft in reasonable safety without oxygen was uncertain. Lou Reichardt, who had been to the summit of K2 without oxygen, looked at what lay ahead and didn't like it. On 5 October, from their high camp, he announced his decision to abandon the climb.[15]

Long before this, Ed had been forced down from Base Camp by cerebral edema. On 13 September he began vomiting, and had double vision, a severe headache and hallucinations. After a night on oxygen, Jim Morrissey bundled him down to the more reasonable altitude of 14,000ft and then accompanied him over a high route to Kharta. Ed wrote a memorable description of their two-day shortcut to the road-head over the Langma La:

> Though I still had headaches and a tightness in my chest, I was moving reasonably well and recognized a long steep hill from the journey so my mind was clearing a little. Then we diverted to the left on a different route up a long traverse, entering a beautiful high valley with snow-tipped peaks all around, a sparkling stream running down the middle, a lovely clear blue lake, with nearby the remnants of an old monastery. Camped here were two handsome Tibetan children, a boy and a girl almost godlike in their looks. They had half a dozen yaks with them and willingly took some of the loads of our porters onto their yaks.
>
> The pass, the Langma La, rose steeply in front of us and and on we went. I was desperately tired and moving pretty slowly. Finally we came to the top at 17,660 ft, so we'd climbed 4000 feet that day. For quite a way we crossed a series of summits in deep snow and I noted how the Tibetan children almost danced along in their bare feet. Then we started descending by a steep zigzagging track, first over snow, and then on to slippery mud. We were entering a long steep gully, very narrow, with a small blue lake far below.
>
> I heard a shout from above and looked up to see a horrifying sight. Charging down the gully with widespread horns and a tent dragging behind was one of the yaks. I looked desperately for somewhere to escape but there was nowhere. I shrank into the right-hand wall and the desperate yak rushed by, knocking me headfirst onto some boulders. Groggily, I clambered to my feet, glad that I was still alive. Something wet was dripping down my neck and I realised it was blood.

472

Jim rushed up to join me and anxiously examined my skull. There was a two-inch split with the bone clearly to be seen. 'What next!' said Jim in despair, but he sat me down and went calmly and confidently to work, snipping off the hair, putting antibiotic in the wound and plastering it up. The yaks were reloaded and we continued down. First around the lake, then a plunging descent and finally a rocky traverse to a huge boulder which had been a campsite before. We pitched our torn tent and scrambled inside.

I had a rather uncomfortable night but next morning I felt stronger ... and at last reached the village of Kharta at the end of the road. I have rarely been more pleased to arrive anywhere.

Dick Blum and I travelled by Jeep and bus over the long road back to Lhasa. I was still experiencing headaches and slight difficulty in breathing and was eager to get to lower altitudes. After a reluctant wait of two days in Lhasa I caught a plane to Chengdu and the thicker air at lower altitude felt superb. I flew on to Canton, anxious to return home ... Hong Kong ... then for ten hours I flew south over the ocean to land in Auckland on a warm spring morning. For two weeks my head still troubled me but then the pain disappeared. The shaved hair grew back and my split scalp mended. It had been quite an adventure, but now I was back to normal ...[16]

I was amazed at how much I enjoyed being back with June Mulgrew again. It wasn't surprising really. Neither of us now had a partner and we'd known each other a long time. We had a great deal in common ...

... But one thing was clear – Chairman Emeritus or not, my big mountain days were now definitely over.[17]

High Commissioner in New Delhi

The 1980s began to have a settled and more comfortable look. With June to provide the emotional support Ed needed, life had become worth living again. There were annual trips to Solukhumbu with June, Rex, Zeke, Larry and various others who liked building additional classrooms, clinics or school hostels. There were trips to the States and Canada for Sears meetings and river trips, and there were lectures and fundraising dinners in Canada and San Francisco where Dick Blum's American Himalayan Foundation was raising large sums for the Himalayan Trust work.

It seemed there was nothing larger and more exciting on the horizon, but as always with Ed Hillary something turned up. This time it came from a politician, David Lange, New Zealand's just-elected left-of-centre Labour Party prime minister. Apart from in 1953, when Prime Minister Sid Holland basked in the windfall glory of the first ascent of Everest and had accepted the knighthood on Ed's behalf as though he had climbed the mountain himself, Ed's encounters with politicians, particularly those of the right-of-centre National Party, had been frosty. The tractors-to-the-Pole episode, and the British disapproval that followed, had caused Wellington to fear that Britain might renege on its duty to buy New Zealand butter and lamb and defect to the European Economic Community. The short-lived Labour prime minister of 1958, Walter Nash, had privately approved of Ed's trip to the Pole but shrank from saying so in public.

In 1967 there was a brief flare-up with the four-term National prime minister, Keith Holyoake. Ed had been invited by Rotary to inspire an assembly of school prefects in Auckland. 'Expediency and just plain dishonesty of utterance in Government and politics are recorded in our newspapers every day,' Ed told them. 'Let's have more honest-to-God morality in politics and government ...'[18]

'Substantiate or retract!' thundered the PM. Ed did neither, and the public was on his side.

A more formidable National Party opponent, PM-in-waiting Robert Muldoon, entered the fray in 1969 when Ed said that New Zealand should spend more of its GDP on aid for developing countries.

'I think Sir Edmund knows as much about the New Zealand economy as I know about mountain climbing,' said Muldoon, and stored in his capacious memory a note that Hillary was now an enemy.[19]

At the next election, Ed made his support for Labour explicit by joining a small group called Citizens for Rowling to help shore up the fortunes of the Labour leader, Bill Rowling. Muldoon won handsomely, leaving Ed in the political wilderness for another nine years.

During his last term of office, however, Muldoon made two

decisions that would directly affect Ed's future. The first was the closing of New Zealand's High Commission in Delhi, following Indian Prime Minister Indira Gandhi's outspoken criticism of Muldoon's support for South Africa's racial policies. The second was his decision to halt New Zealand's galloping inflation rate by imposing a wage and price freeze, a policy which brought the country to the brink of an economic precipice and gave Labour a landslide victory in the 1984 elections.

Within a month Prime Minister Lange, having reopened diplomatic relationships with India, was asking himself who should be offered the position of New Zealand High Commissioner in Delhi. Why not the one person who was seen as a living treasure in both New Zealand and India? Thus, in August 1984, Sir Edmund Hillary was invited to fill the sort of diplomatic position friends had been predicting for him since 1953.

But what about June Mulgrew? 'Why don't I come too?' she offered, and the decision was made that she would accompany Ed as his official companion.[20] So began four-and-a-half good years in a country for which Ed had much affection. June was an excellent hostess and ran the household. Ed's fame opened diplomatic doors for his trade commissioner, Tony Mildenhall: 'He and I made a number of calls on high officials to discuss problems in the importing of such things as coal, wool and timber which he had only been able to handle at a very low official level before. So slowly, but surely, our trade relations improved.'[21]

Ed was welcomed and revered at innumerable social occasions over all India, and participated in such diverse activities as addressing the World Wildlife Fund and Himalayan Mountaineering Institute, judging a mango competition, and launching a Rafting Association in Rishikesh. He had his stock stories and speeches but also an empathy and ease of manner, and an ability to improvise, which made each occasion seem special to his audience. From time to time he expressed personal doubts about whether he was achieving what a High Commissioner was expected to achieve, but letters from the Ministry of Foreign Affairs in Wellington reassured Ed of the esteem in which he was held: 'You continue to do an excellent job ... Everyone, but everyone, regards you as one of the best Heads of Mission we have abroad.'[22] 'NZ is never likely to have a higher profile in the subcontinent than it has now.'[23]

Ed and June on the steps of the High Commissioner's residence in New Delhi.
HILLARY MUSEUM COLLECTION

Further important recognition came from the Lange government in February 1987 with the conferring of the newly minted Order of New Zealand, an honour held by a maximum of 20 living members.

In 1986 Ed received news of the death of Tenzing at his home in Darjeeling. He was 74. He had been in declining health and had felt isolated in his last years, but his death was the breaking of a special bond formed on 29 May 1953. Ed wrote, 'It had been a sad occasion for us but June and I also felt it had been a great honour to be present at the farewelling of our old friend.'[24]

A sad event of a different sort was a devastating fire at Tengboche Monastery in 1989, thought to have been sparked by a fault in a recently installed hydro-electric system. It was mid-winter so there were few monks in residence, and the water supply that might have doused the fire was frozen. The first monastery built in 1916 had been destroyed by the great earthquake of 1934 but in its subsequent reincarnation it had acquired great sanctity. Ed and Dick Blum of the American Himalayan Foundation flew in to see the ruins and undertook to raise funds for the rebuild. This was completed four years later to a design which largely survived the next great 80-year earthquake, that of 2015.

Ed and June marry

Four months after their return from Delhi, June Mulgrew became June Lady Hillary.

> In November 1989 it was a superb sunny day when June and I were married on the deck of my home in Auckland … It was a very happy event with all our children, grandchildren, relations and friends gathered around. I was now seventy years old and June was twelve years younger. My life would have been very empty without Louise and June. For the twenty-two years after Everest Louise was responsible for the happiest and most productive period of my middle years. After her death I had five years of depression and misery. When my long friendship with June blossomed into a much warmer relationship, I learned to live and love again. Louise and June are different in many ways, but they have each given me a feeling of unchanging security and happiness. They both have had sound judgment and their advice has been kind and prudent. What a fortunate person I have been!
>
> Being married didn't seem to make a lot of difference to our lives. June and I had already established a strong supportive friendship that we knew would last. But now we had become respectable – and all the old squares in the community must have nodded their heads in approval.[25]

CHAPTER 31

The last two decades

In 1989 Ed turned 70. During the years in Delhi he and June had taken time off from diplomatic work to continue Himalayan Trust work in Nepal. He had been able to walk from the lower altitudes of Phaplu or Lukla up to the main Sherpa villages such as Khunde at 12,500ft, and could work and sleep comfortably at the heights at which his Sherpa friends lived. But by 1990 that freedom had been eroded by his increasing susceptibility to the effects of altitude.

Doctors had long been puzzled by the paradox of an Ed Hillary who was stronger than anyone else at altitude in 1953, yet from 1954 onwards had experienced serious altitude sickness at progressively lower altitudes. In 1991, he suffered yet another life-threatening episode, this time in Khunde. He had become breathless even when walking downhill, and that night was deeply cyanosed and confused. His oxygen saturation was a perilously low 34 per cent, indicating severe pulmonary edema compounded by cerebral edema. After resuscitation with oxygen he was flown to Kathmandu where he was seen by Dr David Shlim, a physician with wide experience of altitude sickness who made suggestions about the underlying abnormal processes.[1] After this episode, Ed's visits to Khumjung and Khunde were by helicopter, and from 2000 he carried a bottle of supplementary oxygen. He regretted the loss of the good times when he could wander and sleep at will in the villages and among the people he loved so much, but he still returned each year to see his friends and the familiar landscape.

June and Ed in Nepal, c.1995. HILLARY MUSEUM COLLECTION

Settling in at 278a Remuera Road

From 1975 to 1984 the house at Remuera Road had been more like a student flat than the family home it had been during the 20 years when Louise was there. Sarah and her husband Peter Boyer were living there from time to time with their son Arthur and later their daughter Anna; Peter Hillary had various friends passing through. During the years when Ed and June were in Delhi, Ed helped Sarah and Peter Boyer with the purchase of a house in the suburb of Mt Eden, and Peter Hillary married Ann Moorhead in Melbourne, where their two children, Amelia and George, were born.

Back in New Zealand in 1989, Ed and June settled into 278a Remuera Road. June had previously worked as an interior decorator, and she applied her skills to redesigning their Auckland home. The annual trips to Solukhumbu continued, though now from a base in Phaplu or Lukla rather than higher up. There were still the business and fundraising visits to Chicago, San Francisco, Toronto and London, and around New Zealand Ed accepted a wide range of speaking engagements. For relaxation there were holidays in tropical Fiji or the summer warmth of the South of France. June said that India gave them their best times, but Auckland was good too. Sarah had by now risen to the position of senior conservator at the Auckland Art Gallery and in 1997 would become principal conservator.

Throughout the 1980s Peter had remained attracted to extreme climbing, and on two west ridges, one on Makalu and the other on Everest, companions had died. These were lightweight expeditions lacking the safety margins of fixed ropes, oxygen or Sherpas. And they could be deadly if you slipped and fell on steep terrain. In May he reached the summit of Everest by the route first climbed in 1953 by his father and thus became the first of the second generation to climb the world's highest mountain. He rang Ed in Auckland from the summit on his satellite phone. 'How did you find the Hillary Step?' Ed asked. 'I was pretty impressed,' said Peter – a reply which pleased his father.[2] Two years later Peter's marriage to Ann ended.

In 1995 Peter was attempting the notoriously risky K2, 28,250ft, the second-highest summit in the world. A diverse group of eight climbers from five countries had come together by chance on 13 August. They were close to the summit when ominous cloud could be seen rapidly advancing from Tibet. Peter chose to retreat and although the storm, which was of extreme violence, had struck by 5 p.m., within two-and-a-half hours he was in the shelter of his Camp 2. All seven climbers who had continued on were killed by the storm. He gave the title *In the Name of the Father* to the account he wrote of the climb.

Peter still had a second ascent of the South Col route on Everest ahead of him, but K2 was his last climb involving exceptional risk. In March 1996 he married Yvonne Oomen on the lawn at 278a Remuera Road. They have two children, Alexander and Lily, and Peter now makes his living as a speaker and a guide on trips to the Antarctic and Himalayas.

Handing over to the Sherpas
Ed used the early years of the 1990s to plan for a future when he would no longer be here. The aim of any NGO in a developing country is not to do their work for them but to find and develop local staff to take over. In 1987 Ed had appointed a Sherpa to the position of administrative officer at the Himalayan Trust office at Dilli Bazaar in Kathmandu. This was Ang Rita, born in Khumjung, and one of a trio of exceptionally bright pupils from the school's early intakes who were

given full scholarships for their secondary education in Kathmandu and tertiary education outside Nepal. Ang Rita had wanted to become a doctor, but the only medical school with a place available was in politically volatile Myanmar, where strikes forced him to return to Nepal and into jobs working in tourist hotels. During the early years, the Kathmandu administration of the Himalayan Trust had been handled by American Liz Hawley, famous among other things for her database in which she enters the names of climbers in Nepal and the peaks they have climbed. In 1987 Ang Rita became a full-time employee of the Trust and over a period of years took over from Liz all the work in Kathmandu.

But Kathmandu and Solukhumbu were different places, and for his link to the grass roots of what was happening in the villages Ed relied on Mingma Tsering, his sardar since 1963, the commander-in-chief of his operations in the villages, the foreman on his building sites, and

Mingma Tsering, Ed's sardar since 1963, died in October 1993.
HILLARY MUSEUM COLLECTION

his adviser on the work he did there. Mingma was endlessly capable, hard-working and loyal, and despite his illiteracy was the best partner Ed could have had. He lived in Khunde, not Kathmandu, so knew what was happening at ground level. Ed had a deep affection for him. When Mingma died in 1993, Ed lost not only an adviser but an essential friend and a connection to the people and villages of the area where they worked.

Mingma's death brought home to Ed the need for planning to continue the work of his Trust. So in 1994 he organised in Auckland a plenary meeting of the principal donors, senior Sherpas and Trust members to discuss what projects should be planned for the next decade and how to fund them. Richard Blum, chair of his American Himalayan Foundation, came from San Francisco; Zeke O'Connor of

Key international donors and Sherpa leaders in Ed's Himalayan Trust, 1994 (L to R): Ang Rita, Chief Administrative Officer; Dr Kami Temba, Khunde Hospital; George Lowe, UK Himalayan Trust; Dr Mingmar Gyelzen, Phaplu Hospital; Larry Witherbee, Hillary Foundation, Chicago; Ed Hillary; Mingma Norbu, Director World Wildlife Fund Nepal and Bhutan; Zeke O'Connor, Sir Edmund Hillary Foundation, Canada; Richard Blum, American Himalayan Foundation, San Francisco; Ingrid Versen, Sir Edmund Hillary Stiftung, Germany.
HILLARY MUSEUM COLLECTION

the Sir Edmund Hillary Foundation came from Toronto, George and Mary Lowe from the Himalayan Trust UK, Ingrid Versen from the Sir Edmund Hillary Stiftung in Bavaria, and Larry Witherbee from the Hillary Foundation of Chicago. All gave generous pledges of support for the next eight years, and in 2002 would promise funds for a further 10 years. During the 40 years from 1974 to 2014, this group would contribute US$12 million. Together with US$6 million from New Zealand, donations to the Trust totalled $18 million over that period. It was a tribute to the unique impact of Ed's development programmes since the first school was built in Khumjung in 1961.

Education had been strikingly successful in the way it had helped Sherpas prosper in the trekking business. They became guides, sardars, managers and owners of trekking companies, even of helicopters and small planes. Others built tea houses, small lodges and comfortable hotels with en suite bathrooms. The schools were less successful, however, in inspiring local people to take up teaching, a profession that was more part of the upbringing of the Brahmin caste of Hindu Nepal. The better teachers of whatever caste preferred to live in the big city, leaving the less well trained to work in the hills. Recognising the need for better training of teachers in his schools, Ed asked Christchurch educationist Jim Strang to set up a teacher training programme. Jim established a Nepali NGO, REED, which currently employs more than 30 trainers working in Solukhumbu and Taplejung, with financial support from Australian and UK NGOs as well as the Himalayan Trust. The schools grew bigger. Secondary classes were added, with hostels for pupils from more distant villages. Scholarships were provided for the best students to go to university in Kathmandu. Trekkers often helped by funding individual students they had met, some of whom were accepted into Western universities. A significant Sherpa diaspora developed, particularly in the United States.

By the 1970s the first alarm bells were ringing about the environmental damage being caused by the influx of trekkers and mountaineers who at night liked to sit around a fire fuelled by slow-growing sub-alpine juniper bushes. Working alongside the Nepal Government, Ed encouraged the establishment of the Sagarmatha National Park which created and enforced rules about cutting firewood. For six years, from 1975 to 1981, New Zealand funded a succession of full-time Head Wardens based in Namche as advisers until Nepalis took over in 1982.[3] These included Mingma Norbu and Lhakpa Norbu who were educated at Khumjung School and subsequently Lincoln University in New Zealand. Although the emphasis was on preservation of existing forest cover, forest nurseries funded by Canada were set up for reforestation by planting out fir, pine, juniper and rhododendron seedlings.

An important environmental project was the Austrian hydro-electric installation at Thame, which generated 620kw when it came online in 1994, and has been recently upgraded. It supplies power to Thame, Namche, Khunde and Khumjung, where food is cooked by electricity; cafes, restaurants and school homework continue after dark; and local trees can grow undisturbed.

Ed's medical projects were placed completely in the hands of Sherpas after being run for many years by volunteers from New Zealand and Canada. Of his two hospitals, Khunde was taken over by Dr Kami Temba of Thame in 2002, while Dr Mingmar Gyelzen had become medical superintendent of Phaplu Hospital in 1982. They treated the simple infections that might otherwise kill young people; they provided an obstetric service and family planning; they set broken bones and implemented the national immunisation programme. Health-care expenditure follows the law of diminishing returns. Care at Khunde and Phaplu is at the most basic end of the spectrum, where remarkable results can be achieved with a small budget. Before 1970, florid, untreated disease was visible throughout the hill country of Nepal, but by the turn of the century a well-run Health Department had achieved many of its goals, assisted by programmes such as those of the Himalayan Trust.

Mingmar Gyelzen left Phaplu in 2006 to work in the Government of Nepal's Health Department and went on to become its director-general – a remarkable achievement. In 2014 Mingmar's nephew Dr Mingma Chhiring followed in his uncle's footsteps to become the resident surgeon at Phaplu on a salary funded by the Sir Edmund Hillary Foundation of Germany.

Fame and more honours
These development projects received further widespread recognition for Ed in the unexpected form of honorary doctorates – a source of amusement as well as pleasure for someone who had not bonded with

Ed receives one of his nine honorary doctorates. HILLARY MUSEUM COLLECTION

academia during his two years at Auckland University. He also became the first living New Zealander to have his image on a banknote, the five-dollar note, first issued in 1992 with a 1950s profile photo of a tousled Hillary in the mountains. During his remaining 16 years Ed would sign many thousands of these notes, and some Sherpas would interpret this as evidence of his wealth.

Another important recognition of his achievements came in April 1995 when Ed and June were at the Sherpa village of Junbesi, located in pine forest three hours' walk above Phaplu. Modern facilities were limited, but they had a telephone link which one day came to life with a request to speak to Sir Edmund Hillary. It was the British Ambassador on behalf of Queen Elizabeth, asking that Ed accept the Knightly Order of the Garter. It was not the sort of thing one expects in Junbesi. Of the 19 other Knights of the Garter, one was John Hunt, who had been inducted into the order in 1979. Resolute republicans sometimes claim that Ed disliked his knighthoods, but his son and daughter both give evidence that he was fond of his KBE and just

Assembly of Knights of the Garter. HILLARY MUSEUM COLLECTION

Hillary Coat of Arms, first version. HILLARY MUSEUM COLLECTION

loved being a Knight of the Garter – it was a final recognition not only of the aura of the Everest expedition but also of his continuing efforts to help the people of his much-loved Nepal. Ed wore the regalia well. His craggy features were framed by the wide-brimmed, black velvet hat with its ostrich plume; his large frame swathed in the dark-blue mantle with its rich edgings and decorations and the outsize insignia of the Garter with its Cross of Saint George.

He now required a Coat of Arms. The first version, drawn by a New Zealand designer, was wry and affectionate: a modest, somewhat harassed kiwi with an ice-axe in his half-raised claw stands atop a helmeted knight whose elbow is draped nonchalantly over a shield displaying three mountain peaks and Sherpa prayer wheels. The shield is held by the extended flippers of two flanking emperor penguins, and the motto on the flowing scroll on which the penguins stand states the strongest of Ed's personal beliefs, *Nothing Venture, Nothing Win.*

The final version was lighter on humour. The kiwi had become larger and lost some of his proletarian personality; the nonchalant knight had been deleted; the noble emperor penguins had been replaced by two dumpy Fiordland crested penguins; *Nothing Venture, Nothing Win* had lost its flowing ribbon to enter a linear rectangle; and the Garter motto, *Honi soit qui mal y pense*,[4] had been added to its ribbon. The prayer wheels on the escutcheon were now smaller than the mountain, which was, after all, Mt Everest. The honour was, nevertheless, something Ed had reason to be proud of. He was only the second New Zealander, after Sir Keith Holyoake, to become a Knight of the Garter.

Now into his seventies, Ed might have thought he would be less in the public eye. But if anything the adulation increased as the realisation dawned that he, a living treasure, would not live forever. In 1991 NZTV had made its first foray into the heights of Solukhumbu to photograph Sir Ed on his Himalayan home territory. The project was abbreviated when Ed suffered from a severe bout of altitude sickness, but not before three TV programmes had been completed and scriptwriter Tom Scott was introduced to the Hillary story. Tom was back in 1996 directing a more extended treatment of Ed's life. The result was a four-part television series with the title *View from the Top*. There was some synergy here between the TV series and Ed's last autobiography, *View from the Summit*, published in 1999, which was partly a collaboration with Tom Scott. Ed acknowledged him in the book as 'a friend of long-standing whose research has ensured that many anecdotes and stories I might have overlooked or never seen are incorporated in this narrative'.

Ed also paid generous tribute to June: 'Perhaps most important of all has been my wife, June, who read every word and made sure the story was correctly presented, as nobody knows more about my life than she does.'

A third acknowledgment went to George Greenfield, Ed's literary agent for more than 40 years, who had once again secured excellent contracts from English, American and German publishers. On this occasion George, now over 80 but still as sharp as ever, included a proviso in his will that his share of the earnings from *View from the Summit* should revert to Ed on his death, of which he seemed to feel a premonition. 'A new and rather sombre point has struck me,' he wrote in April 2000. 'I've just been reading Andre Deutsch's obituary and, dammit, he is – or was – eight months younger than me!'[5] Less than a month later George died of a heart attack, and Ed had lost another old and valued friend.

View from the Summit rose quickly up the bestseller lists in the UK, USA and New Zealand, and the German rights were sold for NZ$130,000. Reviews were favourable, though some regretted a lost opportunity for more reflection and more about the people in his life. 'Few women feature, Louise Hillary [being] the most significant Character in Absentia ... The splendid June Mulgrew [is] another woman whose stature is established by implication rather than indication ...'[6] Letters show that editors Maggie Body and Joanna Goldsworthy tried to persuade Ed to be more discursive, but he admitted that 'my creative instinct is fading fast'. He was feeling old, and at times it showed. Only UK reviewers commented specifically on the Antarctic chapters, to which Ed gave much space. The *Spectator* quoted Ed's belief that Tenzing should have been knighted as 'endearing proof that at the age of 80 the New Zealander still does not understand the British caste system'.[7] And Jan Morris, who preferred the younger Hillary she knew in 1953, 'wishes that just occasionally the old hero would lose a dispute, or a New Zealander would prove less resilient, adaptable and informal than a Briton ...'[8] But overall the book came out with a strong recommendation.

The last years

Ed entered his ninth and last decade in less than perfect health, but he got by. Important people died: the much-loved John Hunt in 1998 at the age of 88, and Bunny Fuchs, tough to the end, a year later at 91.

Ed accepted invitations to record the narrations for two symphonic works: Vaughan Williams' *Sinfonia Antarctica*, which has optional lines of spoken words; and Douglas Lilburn's *Landfall in Unknown Seas* whose words, written by Allen Curnow, applied equally to twelfth-century Māori, the seventeenth-century Abel Tasman and eighteenth-century James Cook:

> Simply by sailing in a new direction
> You could enlarge the world.
> You picked your captain,
> Keen on discoveries, tough enough to make them.

They were words Ed could identify with and he spoke them well.

In 2004 Ed's brother Rex died at 83, victim of a lifetime of cigarette-smoking. He had always been Ed's hardest-working and most loyal helper on building projects in Nepal. At home, Betty Joplin, Ed's personal secretary and a close friend of Louise, retired after nearly 50 years' service. She recalls:

> By the time I resigned in 2006 he couldn't remember anything recent though his memories of Everest and the Antarctic were very clear when people called. When I'd ask him about something he'd just say, 'I can't remember. You work it out Betty.' If you put a cheque in front of him he'd just sign it without question. But there came a time when his memory was so faded I couldn't do anything for him.[9]

Ed's visits to Canada, the US and UK tailed off as the years went by but he remained in demand as a speaker. He had always had a remarkable ability to rise to occasions and it was a skill he never lost. His agent said that though he no longer spent time on speeches, it hardly mattered. In New Zealand at least, people just wanted to spend time in the same room with him. This was *darshan* in a southern hemisphere setting.

In 2006 Ed was awarded his fifth honorary doctorate, this one from the University of Waikato for his work in education, the environment and humanitarian causes. A year later he was flown again to the Antarctic, this time for the fiftieth anniversary of the founding of Scott Base, accompanied by Prime Minister Helen Clark who had become a personal friend.

His brief visits to Khunde Hospital and Khumjung School, with Everest in view, continued each May. Early in 2007 he said, 'I would hate to think I would never see Khumbu again,' but in Kathmandu that year it was decided the now-usual trip was too much of a risk, and the helicopter took off without him. It seemed an odd inversion that after a lifetime of risk-taking, this was no longer acceptable as the end approached.

As 2007 wore on, he spent more and more time in his bed. Visits to Auckland Hospital became more frequent, and by the end of the year local TV producers were assembling commemorative film from their archives.

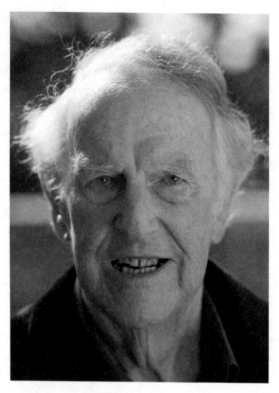

Ed in his late eighties. JANE USSHER/LISTENER MAGAZINE

The end came on the morning of 11 January 2008 when he died suddenly just before he was due to leave hospital. For the 11 days leading up to the State Funeral on 22 January, the people of New Zealand remembered their greatest, most-loved and most-admired fellow citizen with a mixture of affection, grief and pride. The media was filled with stories and images of the life of Sir Edmund Hillary. Tributes flowed in from around the globe. For 24 hours prior to the funeral, the casket lay in state in Auckland's Holy Trinity Cathedral to allow people to pay their last respects. The bright sun of a fine summer day gave way to mist and a drizzling rain. 'Rangi is weeping,' Māori said. All that day a queue of people filed into the cathedral to touch the casket and think of the man who so many felt they had known since 29 May 1953. Long after midnight, people old and young were still arriving to join the line stretching down the road. The *New Zealand Herald* noted, 'As they stood in the damp night, with the pale street lighting blurred by the misty rain, the mood was anything but sombre. There was an abiding sense of community among complete strangers who chatted while they waited.'[10]

During the funeral service, the drizzle swelled to a tropical downpour, beating on the roof as the traditional words of the Anglican funeral service and the speeches of close family and friends were spoken at the last farewell.

Among overseas speakers at the New Zealand Alpine Club's memorial gathering after the funeral, none had known Ed longer than Jan Morris. She said of the famous climb:

> Almost the moment the news reached the world at large it entered the realm of allegory.
>
> It was allegorical in many senses. It was symbolically a last earthly adventure before humanity's explorers went off into space. It was a final flourish of the British Empire. The news arrived in London on the morning when the new queen, Elizabeth II, was being crowned …
>
> In the end Ed repaid a debt to the country that made him famous by all those things he did in Nepal.
>
> You in New Zealand are lucky that your greatest hero is great because he is good.[11]

Sir Edward Halliday's oil portrait of Ed in 1955. AUCKLAND WAR MEMORIAL MUSEUM

Epilogue

———✦———

The mystery in Ed's life is not just how he came to achieve fame as one of the two men to make the first ascent of the world's highest mountain, but also how he retained that fame and even increased it. No one who knew Ed Hillary during the first 30 years of his life would have predicted that great fame lay ahead, yet those years were a necessary part of his story. Ed inherited a powerful work ethic and stubborn determination from his father. Percy's war experience at Gallipoli and the economic destructiveness of the 1930s had left him with uncompromising ideological certainties. The purpose of life was to work with diligence and ingenuity. And in hard times – and they didn't get much harder than the Great Depression of 1930–35 – it was one's duty to help those more in need than oneself. In the event of war, an evil in itself, Percy was equally certain that one had a moral duty to be a conscientious objector. Percy's strict code of ethics was difficult for others to live by, but Ed admired his father's 'moral courage – he would battle fiercely against society or the powers-that-be on a matter of principle'.[1] The Labour politicians of 1935–40 were heroes in the pre-war Hillary household and Ed remained, by upbringing and instinct, on the political left.

Gertrude Hillary filled her traditional role as the mother who provided a warm and emotionally secure home. As a teacher she added her belief in salvation through education while softening her husband's severity. There were books in the family and she encouraged her children to write stories. On trips to nearby Auckland, June, Ed and Rex mixed with their unmarried aunts and saw something of city life, small though it was. In Tuakau they had streams, fields, trees, animals and birds, and the great Waikato River nearby. These were the ingredients of a happy childhood and they had each other. June did well at school and went on to succeed at university. Rex, the youngest, was less interested in study but moved easily into the outdoor pleasures of tending 1600 beehives.

That left Ed, who was regarded as the cleverest of the family. He was tall, with strong features, a good voice – yet by the age of 20 he had found no occupation that caught his interest beyond the family business of beekeeping. The closest he came to standing out from the crowd was to be a fine speaker at meetings of the Radiant Living faithful, an involvement that did little to abate his restless insecurity. He lacked confidence and found girls so unapproachable that in his first 30 years he had only one brief and tentative relationship, and this with the help of Rex who had grown up with fewer inhibitions. Some of his insecurity stemmed from the fact that he never had enough money to assert his independence. Percy might have believed that one should help one's less fortunate neighbours, but he also believed that sons should help their father by working for next to nothing. For a whole decade after leaving school Ed was controlled by his father's strength of will and stubbornness.

The declaration of war in 1939 offered no escape to the wider world. Percy's convictions meant conscientious objection was the only path for his sons, but it brought disapprobation from the outside world. Ed was granted exemption from military service but younger brother Rex was incarcerated for four years. Finally in 1944 Ed decided he had to join the armed forces. At the age of 25 he was at last starting to loosen the bonds that held him in the closed circle of his family. From his training camp in the South Island he spent weekends in the mountains and confirmed a passion for mountaineering that would become the lodestone of his life for the next 10 years.

Why did Ed Hillary want to climb? At the age of 16 he'd been excited by his first contact with snow on the broad dome of Mt Ruapehu. Four years later, he 'felt so weighed down by mental turmoil' that he decided to escape briefly from his father and the bees.[2] The place he chose to escape to was the Hermitage–Mt Cook region, where he saw at first hand the adulation bestowed on two climbers who had

496

just climbed New Zealand's highest mountain. He had long dreamed of performing heroic exploits but found no outlet. Now he recognised an arena in which he might excel. His first Air Force camp gave him access to the South Island's Kaikōura mountains. His climbs on Mt Taranaki from his second camp led to his acceptance into the New Zealand Alpine Club. He was a proper climber at last.

After the war he made annual trips to the Mt Cook area, developing his skills on the heavily glaciated peaks of the central alps. He had wanted a challenge and now he had peak after peak on which he could prove himself. The finesse of rock climbing had no appeal. It was the long days on the biggest ice routes that were the challenge, hewing steps on frozen snow and hard ice. He had boundless energy and loved the remote and sublimely beautiful mountain environment, a world away from the insecurities he felt in suburban Auckland.

The year when everything changed was 1951, and the Garhwal expedition which led to the Everest reconnaissance with Eric Shipton later in the same year. Ed would say of his first 32 years that they were unhappy, lost ones, but in many ways they were a perfect preparation for the expeditions of 1951, '52 and '53. Each was perfectly scripted for Ed's unfolding abilities. Shipton took a liking to Ed who coped easily with altitude and was always eager for work. He was good company too. To the end of his life Ed could charm people with his yarns and enthusiasms, the twinkle in his eye and his readiness to laugh.

Neither Shipton nor Ed had a university degree. They did not hold to the Victorian belief that science was a necessary justification for an expedition. For both, travelling in the wild parts of the Earth was an end in itself, to be shared with others who liked to adventure by proxy. It was through Eric Shipton that Ed found a place on the Cho Oyu expedition of 1952; and when John Hunt took over the leadership of Everest '53, Shipton gave Ed so strong a recommendation that Hunt made him a member of his planning group alongside deputy leader Charles Evans. Hunt was generous to a fault. His fellow Englishmen might have preferred that two of them be selected for the favoured second Everest assault team, but he put climbing strength first. Hillary and Tenzing were the chosen pair in position at the highest camp on 28 May. The following day the weather and snow conditions on the untrodden summit ridge were perfect. At 11.30 a.m. the ridge gave way to a rounded summit. Two men, a lanky, unknown beekeeper from New

Ed on the Khumbu Glacier, 1953. GEORGE LOWE

Zealand and a Tibetan Sherpa who had been born and raised in the shadow of the mountain, were realising their ambitions.

Thus began the 22 happy years of fame – and marriage to Louise Rose. Ed had till then led an austere life of work, leavened, up to a point, by mountaineering. Suddenly, within three months of climbing Everest, he was engaged and then married. Louise was vivacious, intelligent, confident, unflappable, ironic – the perfect foil for his energy, restlessness, ambition, depressions. She was the only person to whom he could easily turn for help with life's problems and the only person who would give him no-nonsense advice.

There were other changes in his new life. Through lack of exercise he became less fit. The rangy 80 kilograms of sinew and muscle that had been the pre-Everest Hillary gave way to 100 kilograms of softer flesh thanks to banquets and cocktail parties. On the other hand, a range of more sophisticated skills developed: formal and informal speech-making, media interviews, writing, interacting socially with an endless array of people, learning to entertain with his stories. He fulfilled his own and his mother's ambition to be a writer when *High Adventure* was published in 1955 and became a critical and financial success. His eight books between 1955 and 1999 generated not only a substantial income but also the stories of his life as he wanted them to be remembered.

The Antarctic expedition of 1957–58 sustained Ed's reputation as an adventurer. He saw from the beginning that a trip to the Pole could be an option if timing allowed. Fuchs was late and Ed had discovered that three farm tractors supplied to drag loads around Scott Base could be upgraded to reach the Pole. It wasn't in the contract but it happened. Ed's English literary agent, George Greenfield, who knew both Ed and the London Committee of Management, wrote, 'Some of the best brains in the City and the higher reaches of academe were part of the committee but it was collectively naïve of them to think that the first man on top of Everest would forgo the double of reaching the South Pole.'[3]

Ed's journey raised questions about whether the challenge of an adventure is a valid reason for going to the Pole – or to a mountain, for that matter. In the long term, the controversy was largely forgotten, especially in New Zealand where 'driving farm tractors to the South Pole' became part of the Hillary legend. When asked in 1960 whether Everest was 'his greatest thrill', Ed said, 'No. My greatest thrill came in Antarctica when we took three tractors to the Pole, when everybody said it couldn't be done. You get a great deal of satisfaction out of doing something people say is impossible.'[4]

Another major change of direction came in 1961 when Ed responded to a request from the Sherpas of of Khumjung village to build a school. Nothing could have suited him better. Using the simplest of means he was bringing education and employment to people who were eager for what was on offer. There was never an element of sacrifice or duty. He loved living amid the spectacular mountains of the Khumbu, and he became more and more fond of the Sherpas as he worked with them. Raising funds could be a labour, but he knew it was worth it. He was now working for World Book and Sears, and increasingly in demand on a lecture circuit where American generosity could be relied on.

With the building of Lukla airstrip, the trekking industry was born. Sherpas working as guides, porters or cooks improved their English – or Japanese, German or French. Some were invited back to their clients' country; some married them. The people of Khumbu prospered. Health initiatives were the next step with the building of two hospitals and provision of simple interventions including immunisations, mother and child care, and family planning. Encouragement of environmental protection followed to prevent the cutting of slow-growing high-altitude trees and juniper scrub. Ed strongly promoted the development of the Sagarmatha/Everest National Park and in collaboration with Canadian funding developed forest nurseries growing fir, pine, juniper and rhododendron seedlings for re-afforestation.

Ed went out of his way to encourage young people. John and Di McKinnon were the first doctor couple at Khunde Hospital in 1966–68. 'He gave us an enormous amount of responsibility,' Di said. 'Just get on with it, he said, and that was incredible for us. He unleashed the potential inside so many different people.'[5]

Back in New Zealand Ed became the President of Volunteer Service Abroad (VSA), the New Zealand version of America's Peace Corps. He was in constant demand as speaker at school prizegivings, and business or academic conferences, and he seldom refused what he saw as his obligations. For many young people growing up after 1953, Ed Hillary was a hero: 'He made me attempt things I would not otherwise have tried,' they said.

Here is the sort of story which must have been repeated many times. Marilyn Eales was a medical laboratory scientist passing through Canterbury University in 1967 when she saw a notice that Ed Hillary would be talking to a student gathering at 7 p.m. She slipped in at the back of the room and listened as he began with his usual understated account of climbing Everest.

> But it was his work on behalf of the Sherpas that made a great impression on me. He had recently been elected president of VSA, and after the lecture I plucked up courage to approach the great man himself. I asked him about working for VSA and he took my name and address, promising to send further information. True to his word a sheaf of papers arrived a few days later. I applied, was accepted, and found myself working in a medical laboratory in Fiji. This was truly a turning point in my life. I was working with people from other cultures, Fijian and Indian, and came to realise that I was learning more from them than I was able to give. Later I took positions elsewhere in the Pacific. Thanks to Ed Hillary my life became more rewarding than I ever imagined it would be.[6]

The crash happened on 31 March 1975. It was Ed's Gallipoli. The loss of 16-year-old Belinda was terrible enough, but it was the death of Louise that was so unmanageable and so destructive. A minute of uncontrolled flight in a small plane and his life had changed irrevocably. He felt a numb regret that he had not died with them. He seemed to retreat into some inner sanctum where there was no one but himself. Many who had known Ed since the early 1950s felt that he was never the same again. It was like some Faustian compact that he would enjoy unparalleled success starting with Eric Shipton on the Everest reconnaissance in 1951, continuing through the climb of 1953, the South Pole in 1958, the new life with the Sherpas in Nepal where Louise had shared what he was doing. Everything fell into place until 1975; and then everything fell apart. 'He was always exciting in the old days,' Sarah remembers. 'But in those years after the crash you couldn't get through to him. He no longer engaged with anything. So far as support was concerned he just wasn't there.'[7]

Peter remembered during his childhood that his father was often away – but what a lift it was when he returned. 'He was always active and he used to whistle cowboy songs. He had this strength and confidence that I felt could never be challenged. Then came the crash, and that was the end of the marvellous times. That was the end of Ed Hillary as we'd known him. I never heard him whistle cowboy songs again.'[8]

The Ocean to Sky expedition, originally conceived in collaboration with Louise in 1974, filled most of 1977 with activity, but the lifting of the main weight of grief came through Ed's developing relationship with June Mulgrew in 1979. Their move to India where Ed had been appointed High Commissioner cemented their ties, and in November 1989, on their return to Auckland, they were married.

Ed had just turned 70, and the last two decades of his life were settled years. Honours, including honorary doctorates, flowed in from around the world. Most prestigious of all was his appointment Knight of the Order of the Garter in 1975, but there were many others including, in 2003, honorary citizenship of Nepal on the fiftieth anniversary of the climbing of Everest.

He remained in demand as a speaker around the world. His notes were a small sheaf of A5 slips of paper.[9] He would begin with an anecdote: a favourite was about the attractive hotel receptionist who sees his name, looks up in apparent admiration but adds in surprise, 'I thought you died years ago.' He established a link to his audience by noting shared interests, and then told stories to illustrate a theme. Growing up in Tuakau in the Depression with few educational achievements, for example, did not preclude later success. 'Life must remain a challenge and it must force you to your limit. Fear is a stimulus to be welcomed.' He was never short of ideas and an address to an important audience was an opportunity to explore them.

In the years before 1975 he made more of an effort to develop ideas for each audience. During the latter years, his speeches were selections from earlier material, but people still loved them, even at such distinguished venues as the Smithsonian Institute or major universities. Retelling the story of the climbing of Everest never failed to hold his audience. He was living history and a memorable presence with his big frame, familiar long face and strong jaw with a ready smile, and a full head of hair even in his eighties. His voice was strong with an accent which was not English but not entirely New Zealand either.

In New Zealand he remained in the public eye for 55 years. He became the nearest we had to royalty. He had won fame through a sporting achievement but of such an unusual and unrepeatable sort that it seemed more like a coronation, even beatification. Yet his beginnings were simple and he had retained those characteristics we like to admire in ourselves. He was egalitarian, without conceit or showiness, and transparently honest. He was neither rich nor wanting to be, but not poor either. His humility about his fame was genuine, though overlaid, ironically, by the realisation that modesty was a useful part of the Hillary persona created jointly by himself and his public. He never wanted to live anywhere except New Zealand whose inland mountains and long coastline he loved equally.

He was not of course without fault. He could be overly stubborn and sensitive to criticism. He was not always magnanimous in recognising people who had helped him. In his 1999 autobiography he is a less tolerant and generous person than he was in 1955 and 1975. He was prone to depression and what he called 'our civilized curse of self-pity'.[10] He was not as supportive a father as he might have been in his later years. He shared the insecurities of the people of a small country with a short history, but he had their strengths too, their independence.

John Mulgan was a New Zealand writer who had been at Oxford in the 1930s and then joined the war and fought in North Africa with an English battalion. In 1942 he encountered a New Zealand division who had been fighting in the desert for over a year and 'it was like coming home':

> They were mature men, these New Zealanders of the desert, quiet and shrewd and skeptical ... Moving in a body, detached from their homeland, they remained quiet and aloof and self-contained. They had confidence in themselves, such as New Zealanders rarely have, knowing themselves as good as the best the world could bring against them, like a football team in a more deadly game ... they marched into history.[11]

These were men of Ed's generation. His own march into history was in a different place, and around it grew a different sort of myth. He

Ed on the deck at 278a Remuera Road, 2007. JANE USSHER/LISTENER MAGAZINE

was the man from humble beginnings who with Tenzing was the first person to look down on Earth from the highest point on its surface. Because they were not important figures from the great nations of our planet, anyone might identify with them. They had gone where no one had gone before. Peasants on the plains of the Ganges crowded to the banks of the river to glimpse someone they saw as a reincarnation of the great Hindu warrior Arjuna. In the West, too, there was the legend of the person who devoted half a lifetime to working in the heart of the world's highest mountains, helping the people who had made him famous. He was an ordinary person, he always said. 'I should be content,' he wrote in 1975, 'yet I look at myself and feel a vast dissatisfaction – there was so much more I could have done.'[12] He was always striving. What is apparent is that out of what he claimed was his ordinariness, he created, during eighty-eight years, an extraordinary life.

Acknowledgements

My first thanks go to Ed Hillary for bequeathing such an archive of papers and photos to the Auckland Museum; and to Peter and Sarah Hillary who gave me permission to use these papers and their own files of personal letters; they have also made valuable comments on the manuscript. Amongst other members of the extended Hillary family I particularly thank Hilary Carlile, John Hillary, and Yvonne Oomen. After the Hillary Collection, the Royal Geographic Society has been my most important source of photos and I extend my grateful thanks for their efficient and expert help. Sue Gregory has kindly supplied the important cover photo, which was taken by her husband Alf at the Everest Base Camp in 1953.

As have so many readers before me I have been fascinated by stories of mountaineering – and of Everest in particular – as told and photographed by so many individual writers. I have often quoted their own words and I particularly thank: Jan Morris and Faber and Faber for quotations from *Coronation Everest*; Mary Lowe for allowing me to quote from George Lowe's writings and use his photos; Arthaud publishers for quotations from Raymond Lambert and René Dittert in *Forerunners to Everest*; The Swiss Foundation for Alpine Research for photos of the 1952 Swiss expedition; Jim Perrin for his observations on yeti tracks in his *Shipton and Tilman*; Tap Richards and Dave Hahn of the Mallory and Irvine Research Expedition for photos of Mallory and the Second Step; Tony Astill of Mountaineering Books in Southampton for sharing with me his wide range of contacts; Anna Riddiford for quotations and photos from her father Earle Riddiford; Derek Gunn for the memoir of his father Bernard Gunn; Tom Nevison for his Makalu diary, 1961; Irene Ortenburger/Beardsley for the Makalu diary of her husband Leigh; Brian Wilkins for his photo from the Barun 1954; Norman Hardie for his 1954 photo of Makalu and his comments on the manuscript; Francis Russell and George Rodway for the photo of George Finch; Colin Monteath of Hedgehouse House for photos of Aoraki/Mount Cook, Footstall and Cho Oyu; Julian Godwin for his memoir of Ed in 1945.

Potton & Burton as publishers have been of central importance and I particularly thank Robbie Burton. From the time I mentioned that the Museum archive contained the material for a new biography he has been unfailingly encouraging, supportive and reassuring. Geoff Walker wrote a most useful manuscript assessment of my first draft and Jane Parkin has been endlessly patient with me as she has worked through the detailed editing of the second draft. Others who have made valuable suggestions on the manuscript include: Jonathan Baskett for his medical and editing input; Pat Baskett; David Ellis; Claire Scholes; Diane McKinnon; Ruth Bonita; Robert Beaglehole; and Oliver Mitchell.

The staff of the Auckland Museum have always been most helpful making material available during several months spent working in their research area. Particular thanks go to Shaun Higgins, Pictorial Curator, for providing me with high-quality digitised versions of images from the Hillary Collection.

My wife Linda has lived with the Hillary project for as many years as I have. As a writer herself she has been tolerant of the intrusions of the book's demands into our shared life. She has been my resident editor and advisor and for all these reasons has my gratitude and warmest thanks.

– Michael Gill

Notes

Sources

The most important source of information and images has been the archive Ed Hillary bequeathed to the Auckland Museum where its reference is: Sir Edmund Hillary Archive, Auckland War Memorial Museum Tāmaki Paenga Hira, PH-2010-4. The documents are contained in 50 boxes with a total of 809 folders. My personal shorthand to source such a reference from these Museum Hillary Folders is MHF, box 1, fdr 1. The photos are in a separate file. I have credited these as Museum Hillary Collection. Photos or documents held privately by Peter or Sarah Hillary are attributed to Hillary Family Collection. Copies of interviews from which quotations have been taken are referenced in the endnotes.

Note on units of measurement

Because nearly all the books I have quoted were published before 1980 and gave altitudes in feet, I have followed their practice. The factor for converting metres to feet is 3.281. Otherwise I have used metric units: metres and kilometres for distance; grams and kilograms for weight.

Spelling of names of people and places

Because these can vary quite widely I have chosen a single spelling for each person and place. The most famous of Khumbu monasteries is Tengboche rather than the Thyangboche which used to be common. Tenzing of Everest always spelt his name with a z even though other Sherpas of the same name often call themselves Tensing. The village of Khunde has an h because the k is aspirated and is transliterated from Tibetan/Sherpa into Nepali script as such. And so on.

Endnotes

Chapter 1 A pioneering heritage

1. Gertrude Hillary, 1957, MHF, box 7, fdr 153.
2. Undated letter, MHF box 6, fdr 140.
3. Hillary, *Nothing Venture*, 1975, p. 18, and Hillary, *View from the Summit*, 1999, p. 38.

Chapter 2 Percy goes to Gallipoli

1. David Green, quoting Richard Stowers, ww100.govt.nz/how-many-new-zealanders-served-on-gallipoli; NZ History at www.nzhistory.net.nz/media/interactive/gallipoli-casualities-country (accessed 27 March 2017).
2. MHF, box 7, fdr 154.
3. Liddell Hart, *History of the First World War*, 1970, p. 188.

Chapter 3 Growing up in Tuakau and Auckland

1. MHF, box 7, fdr 157.
2. Peter Hillary interviews with Rex Hillary, 2003.
3. Hillary, *Nothing Venture*, 1975, p. 18.
4. Hillary and Hillary, *Two Generations*, 1984, p. 19.
5. Ibid.
6. Letter to Tom Scott, MHF, box 33, fdr 518.
7. Peter Hillary interviews with Rex Hillary, 2003.
8. Hillary and Hillary, *Two Generations*, 1984, p. 19.

9. June Carlile, personal communication.

10. MHF, box 6, fdr 134.

11. Hillary, in a talk at the Tuakau 150th Jubilee, 1992.

12. Hillary, *View from the Summit*, 1999, p. 39.

13. Hillary, *Nothing Venture*, 1975, p. 19.

14. Peter Hillary interviews with Rex Hillary, 2003.

15. Hillary, *Nothing Venture*, 1975, p. 22.

16. Ibid.

17. Haggard, *King Solomon's Mines*, 1907, Kindle location 2261/73%

18. Burroughs, *A Princess of Mars*, 2013, Kindle location 694/24%

19. Hillary, *Nothing Venture*, 1975, p. 23.

20. Ibid.

21. Ibid., p. 26.

22. Auckland Grammar School Magazine, 2003, pp. 19–20.

23. Hillary, *Nothing Venture*, 1975, p. 24.

Chapter 4 'The most uncertain and miserable years of my life'

1. The author was a member of the AUC Tramping Club in 1955.

2. MHF, box 7, fdr 158.

3. MHF, box 40, fdr 619.

4. Hillary, *Nothing Venture*, 1975, pp. 25–26.

5. www.nzhistory.net.nz/culture/radiant-living/edmund-hillary (accessed 27 March 2017).

6. MHF, box 48, fdr 749.

7. MHF, box 7, fdr 157.

8. MHF, box 6, fdr 137.

9. MHF, box 6, fdr 136.

10. Hillary, *Nothing Venture*, 1975, p. 28.

11. Ibid., pp. 30–31.

12. MHF, box 22, fdr 360.

13. MHF, box 22, fdr 350.

14. MHF, box 40, fdr 617.

15. MHF, box 40, fdr 619.

16. Hillary, *View from the Summit*, 1999, pp. 46–47.

17. Hillary, *Nothing Venture*, 1975, p. 32.

Chapter 5 Escape into the Air Force

1. 'Mt Tapu-o-uenuku', www.theprow.org.nz, 31 October 2013 (accessed 27 March 2017).

2. Hillary, *Nothing Venture*, 1975, pp. 33–36.

3. MHF, box 22, fdr 350.

4. Ibid.

5. Mike Gill interview with Julian Godwin, 2015.

6. Memoir from Julian Godwin, May 2014, Hillary Family Collection.

7. MHF, box 45, fdr 698.

8. Ibid.

9. Ibid.

10. MHF, box 21, fdr 331.

11. MHF, box 6, fdr 135.

12. MHF, box 21, fdr 332.

13. Ibid.

14. Letter, MHF, box 21, fdr 330.

15. 'Airman remembers Sir Ed', *Hawke's Bay Today*, 15 June 2008.

Chapter 6 Harry Ayres teaches Ed the craft of mountaineering

1. MHF, box 7, fdr 157.
2. MHF, box 40, fdr 619.
3. Peter Hillary interview with Rex Hillary, 2003.
4. Hillary, *Nothing Venture*, 1975, p. 77.
5. Hillary, Foreword in Mahoney, *Harry Ayres*, 1982.
6. MHF, box 21, fdr 340.
7. Langton, Graham, 'Ayres, Horace Henry', in Dictionary of New Zealand Biography, www.teara.govt.nz/en/biographies/5a28/ayres-horace-henry (accessed 28 February 2017).
8. Mahoney, *Harry Ayres*, 1982, p. 45.

Chapter 7 The New Zealand Garhwal expedition and the Shipton cable

1. Edmund Hillary, 2007, Foreword in Lowe and Lewis-Jones, *The Conquest of Everest*, 2013, pp. 23–25.
2. Lowe, *Because It Is There*, 1959, p. 10.
3. Mary Lowe, personal communication, January 2017.
4. Hillary, *Nothing Venture*, 1975, pp. 97–98.
5. Hillary, *High Adventure*, 1955, p. 17.
6. McKinnon, *Only Two for Everest*, 2016, Ch. 8. McKinnon has written the definitive account of the Garhwal expedition.
7. Lowe to Riddiford, 31 May 1950, in ibid., p. 28.
8. Ibid, p. 28.
9. Hillary, *Nothing Venture*, 1975, p. 115.
10. Lowe, 1951. Reproduced in a special George Lowe edition of *Pohokura*, Journal of the Heretaunga Tramping Club, 2003, p. 13.
11. Riddiford, *NZ Alpine Journal*, 38, 1951, p. 28.
12. Hillary diary, 1951, MHF, box 23, fdr 379.
13. Ed Cotter, personal communication, 2011.
14. The older spelling was sirdar. The sardar is the leader of an expedition's porters and the interface between expedition members and the local people.
15. Hillary diary, 22 June 1951, MHF, box 23, fdr 379.
16. Riddiford, *NZ Alpine Journal*, 39, 1952, p. 179.
17. Hillary diary, 4 June 1951, MHF, box 23, fdr 379.
18. Lowe, 1951, in *Pohokura*, 2003, p. 17.
19. Riddiford, *NZ Alpine Journal*, 39, 1952, pp. 181–82.
20. Lowe, 1951, in *Pohokura*, 2003, p. 17.
21. MHF, box 23, fdr 379.
22. Ed Cotter, personal communication, 2011.
23. Hocken Collection, Dunedin, MS1164 1/11/18.
24. Shipton, *That Untravelled World*, 1969, p. 187.
25. Ibid., p. 96.
26. Ibid., p. 187.
27. McKinnon, *Only Two for Everest*, 2016, p. 102.
28. Ibid., p. 289.
29. MHF, box 39, fdr 596.

Chapter 8 Everest Reconnaissance 1951

1. Telegram, 31 August 1951, MHF, box 42, fdr 648.
2. Hillary, *High Adventure*, 1955, p. 20.
3. Ibid., p. 33.
4. Hillary, *View from the Summit*, 1999, p. 81.
5. Hillary, *High Adventure*, 1955, pp. 32–33.

6. Ward, *In This Short Span*, 1972, p. 70.
7. Tilman, *The Alpine Journal*, Vol. 58, May 1951.
8. Steele, *Eric Shipton*, 1998, p. 9.
9. Alpine Club Archives, D 103 Bourdillon diaries, quoted in Tuckey, *Everest, the First Ascent*, 2013, p. 20.
10. Shipton, *The Mount Everest Reconnaissance Expedition 1951*, 1952, chapter 2.
11. Hillary diary, MHF, box 39, fdr 596.
12. Shipton in *The Geographical Journal*, Vol. 118, No. 2, 1952, p. 133.

Chapter 9 Everest from Tibet, 1921 and 1922

1. The traditional instrument over 300 years for measuring atmospheric pressure has been the mercury (Hg) barometer consisting of a tall glass tube filled with Hg and sealed at its top end. The lower open end sits in a bowl of Hg whose surface is pressed down by the weight of air in the surrounding atmosphere. The upper level in the tube falls until the weight of the column of Hg is counterbalanced by the atmospheric pressure.

   The standardised barometric pressure at sea level is 760mm Hg. Twenty-one per cent of this air is oxygen, the other 79% being inert nitrogen. Twenty-one per cent of 760mm is 160mm: this is the pO_2 (pressure of oxygen) available for the brain to think and muscles to move. On the summit of Everest the atmospheric pressure is around 250mm. As at sea level, 21% of this is oxygen, so the pO_2 available to the climber is around 53mm which is barely enough to support even the most basic functions of brain, heart and lungs.
2. Bert, 1878, quoted in West, *High Life*, 1998, p. 71. The italicisation of *Alpine Club* is Bert's indication of two foreign words in his French text.
3. Norton, *The Fight for Everest 1924*, 1925, p. 111.
4. Robertson, *George Mallory*, 1969, p. 17.
5. Wainwright, *The Maverick Mountaineer*, 2015.
6. J.B. West, *Journal of Applied Physiology*, Vol. 94, No. 5, 2003, p. 1705.
7. Wainwright, *The Maverick Mountaineer*, 2015, Ch. 16.
8. RGS Everest Archives, box 12.
9. Kellas, 1912, quoted in Douglas, *Tenzing*, 2003, p. 9.
10. Davis, *Into the Silence*, 2011, p. 291.
11. Ibid., p. 206.
12. MHF, box 13, fdr 220.
13. RGS Everest Archives, box 18.
14. Somervell, *After Everest*, 1936, Ch 10.
15. Finch, *The Making of a Mountaineer*, 1924, pp. 318–19.
16. Ibid., pp. 322–23.
17. Somervell, *After Everest*, 1936, Ch 10.
18. Bruce, *The Assault on Mount Everest 1922*, 1923, p. 264.

Chapter 10 Mallory and Irvine, 1924

1. Norton, *The Fight for Everest 1924*, 2002, pp. 222–23.
2. Ibid., pp. 236, 238.
3. Robertson, *George Mallory*, 1969, p. 225.
4. Hemmleb, Johnson and Simonson, *Ghosts of Everest*, 1999, p. 118.
5. Ibid., p. 119.
6. An equivalent achievement on the South Col route would be to climb twice, in three days, from Camp 6 on the Lhotse Face to a height of 1200ft above the South Col – without oxygen.
7. Odell in Norton, *The Fight for Everest 1924*, 2002, pp. 127, 128.
8. Quoted in Davis, *Into the Silence*, 2011, p. 544.
9. Ibid.

10. Ruttledge, *Everest, The Unfinished Adventure*, 1933, p. 152.
11. Hemmleb et al., *Ghosts of Everest*, 1999, p. 173.

Chapter 11 The 1930s, a decade of disillusion
1. Noel, *Through Tibet to Everest*, 1927, p. 279.
2. Ibid., p. 294.
3. Shipton, *Upon that Mountain*, 1943, p. 126.
4. Ruttledge, *Everest 1933*, 1934, p. 163.
5. Ibid., p. 119.
6. Tilman, *Mount Everest 1933*, 2004, p. 107.
7. Shipton, *Upon that Mountain*, 1943, p. 95.
8. Unsworth, *Everest*, 1989, Ch. 15.

Chapter 12 Lessons on Cho Oyu, 1952
1. Tuckey, *Everest, The First Ascent*, 2013, p. 317. This is an authoritative biography of Griff Pugh and his scientific work written by his daughter Harriet Tuckey.
2. Hardie, *On My Own Two Feet*, 2006, p. 93. Hillary also paid tribute to Riddiford in his article for the *NZ Alpine Journal*, 1952, p. 4: '… due very largely to fine organization by H.E. Riddiford … this [Cho Oyu] expedition was arranged, equipped and transported to India according to schedule.'
3. For a description of open and closed systems, see chapter 14, page 186.
4. Hillary, *High Adventure*, 1955, p. 81.
5. MHF, box 24, fdr 382.
6. Dittert, Chevalley and Lambert, *Forerunners to Everest*, 1954, p. 176.
7. MHF, box 6, fdr 135.
8. MHF, box 39, fdr 596.

Chapter 13 The Swiss get close, 1952
1. Douglas, *Tenzing*, 2003, pp. 40–52.
2. Dr Kami Temba, personal communication, 2009.
3. Tilman, *Mount Everest 1938*, 1948.
4. Dittert, Chevalley and Lambert, *Forerunners to Everest*, 1954, pp. 114–16.
5. The earliest Swiss apparatus did not use oxygen in a metal cylinder as did all later sets. Oxygen was generated by passing humid breath through the chemical potassium tetroxide. Extreme hyperventilation is a feature of climbing at very high altitudes and designing valves with acceptably low resistance to air flow was not achieved until 1953.
6. Lambert in Dittert, Chevalley et al., *Forerunners to Everest*, 1954, pp. 143–46.
7. Lambert in ibid., p. 147.
8. Lambert in ibid., p. 151.
9. Chevalley in ibid., p. 196.
10. Chevalley in ibid., p.237.
11. Lambert in ibid., p. 252.

Chapter 14 Organising Everest, 1953
1. MHF, box 24, fdr 382.
2. MHF, box 39, fdr 596.
3. MHF, box 40, fdr 620.
4. Hillary, *View from the Summit*, 1999, p. 107.
5. Shipton, *That Untravelled World*, 1969, p. 213.
6. MHF, box 40, fdr 620.
7. Hillary, *High Adventure*, 1955, p. 114.
8. Letter Hunt to Hillary, 12 December 1952, MHF, box 40, fdr 620.

9. Ibid.

10. Letter to Hunt, 25 December 1952, MHF, box 40, fdr 620.

11. Hunt, *The Ascent of Everest*, 1953, pp. 241–50.

12. Further evidence came in 1944 from *Operation Everest 1*, a remarkable month-long study held in a decompression chamber at the US Naval School of Aviation Medicine. Over 32 days four volunteers were progressively acclimatised by being decompressed to a height of 22,500ft. By now the subjects no longer had headaches but were lethargic and eating and sleeping poorly. On Day 29 they commenced their 'climb' of Everest at a rate of 1000ft per hour. By 27,500ft, two subjects had requested oxygen masks but the remaining two were placed on the summit for 21 minutes. An observer noted that these two 'were well coordinated at all times, and in full command of their mental faculties, though on the verge of passing out ...They did not wish to go any higher'. West, *High Life*, 1998, p. 239.

13. Hillary, *Nothing Venture*, 1975, p. 145.

14. Ibid.

15. Stobart, *Adventurer's Eye*, 1958, p. 195.

16. Ibid., p. 190.

17. Morris, *Coronation Everest*, 1958, p. 21.

Chapter 15 'We were on top of Everest!'

1. Hillary diary, 29 May 1953, MHF, box 44. The full text reads, 'Finally I cut around the back of an extra large hump and then on a tight rope to its top. Immediately it was obvious that we had reached our objective. We were on top of Everest!'

2. Hunt, *The Ascent of Everest*, 1953, p. 74.

3. Bourdillon, T., *Proceedings of the Royal Society* B, Vol. 143, 1954, p. 28.

4. Closed-circuit systems have never been effectively developed for high-altitude climbing. The oxygen used by climbers on modern commercial expeditions is always delivered by an open-circuit apparatus.

5. Noyce, *South Col*, 1954, p. 25.

6. Everest diary, 7 May 1953, MHF, box 44.

7. Morris, *Coronation Everest*, 1958, p. 84.

8. On his second visit to the Himalayas two years later, Band made the first ascent of Kangchenjunga, the world's third-highest mountain.

9. Ward, *In This Short Span*, 1972, p. 133. The reason was probably that 23,000–24,000ft was Mike's altitude ceiling. In 1961 he led the first ascent of Ama Dablam, a much more difficult peak but also, at 22,500ft, significantly lower. At 24,400ft on Makalu Col in 1961, he lapsed into a coma with cerebral edema.

10. Hillary, *Nothing Venture*, 1975, pp. 154–55.

11. Michael Ward diary, quoted in Conefrey, *Everest 1953*, 2012, p. 169.

12. Ward, *In This Short Span*, 1972, p. 133.

13. Noyce, *South Col*, 1954, p. 185.

14. Ibid., p. 195.

15. Lowe, *Because It Is There*, 1949, p. 35.

16. Ward, *In This Short Span*, 1972, p. 124.

17. Hillary, *High Adventure*, 1955, p. 210.

18. Stobart, *Adventurer's Eye*, 1958, pp. 236–37.

19. Ibid.

20. Morris, *Coronation Everest*, 1958, pp. 135–36.

21. Ullman, *Man of Everest*, 1955, p. 268.

22. Ward, *In This Short Span*, 1972, p. 95.

23. Hunt, *The Ascent of Everest*, 1953, p. 228.

24. Ward, *In This Short Span*, 1972, p. 91.

25. Tuckey, *Everest, The First Ascent*, 2013, p. xix.
26. Ibid., p. xx.
27. Tilman, H.W., review in *Time and Tide*, quoted in Tuckey, *Everest, The First Ascent*, 2013, p. 155.
28. Ward, *Everest, A Thousand Years of Exploration*, 2013, p. 229.
29. Letter Ward to Unsworth, 30 July 1978, quoted in Unsworth, *Everest*, 1989, p. 297.
30. Pugh, *British Expedition to Cho Oyu*, 1952.

Chapter 16 'The most sensible action I've ever taken'

1. Booth, *Edmund Hillary*, 1993, pp. 14–16.
2. Little, *After Everest*, 2012, p. 36.
3. MHF, box 40, fdr 620.
4. Hillary, *Nothing Venture, 1975*, p. 164.
5. Hillary, *View from the Summit*, 1999, p. 28.
6. MHF, box 3, fdr 65.
7. MHF, box 2, fdr 38.
8. Gummer, in *Tribute to Louise Rose, December 1990*, Hillary Family Collection.
9. Ibid.
10. MHF, box 1, fdr 17.
11. Ibid.
12. Three letters in MHF, box 35, fdr 559.
13. Hillary, *View from the Summit*, 1999, p. 29.
14. MHF, box 35, fdr 559.
15. Ibid.
16. Ibid.
17. MHF, box 40, fdr 620.
18. MHF, box 35, fdr 559.
19. Ibid.
20. MHF, box 40, fdr 620.
21. MHF, box 35, fdr 559.
22. Hillary, 1975, *Nothing Venture*, p. 167.
23. Hillary, *View from the Summit*, 1999, p. 31.
24. MHF, box 35, fdr 559.
25. Hillary, *View from the Summit*, 1999, p. 32.
26. Ibid.
27. Hillary Family Collection.
28. Lowe, *Because It Is There*, 1959, p. 42.

Chapter 17 'A somewhat disastrous journey' into the Barun Valley

1. Hillary, *View from the Summit*, 1999, p. 118.
2. Letter Charles Evans to Louise Hillary, 6 April 1954, MHF, box 23, fdr 369.
3. Hillary, *View from the Summit*, 1999, p. 119.
4. Ibid., p. 121.
5. Ibid.
6. Most people will develop symptoms of high-altitude sickness if they go too high too quickly. Symptoms include headache, insomnia and loss of appetite, and in the benign form, termed AMS (Acute Mountain Sickness), these symptoms resolve as the individual acclimatises. The malignant forms, which are often fatal if untreated, are termed HACE (High Altitude Cerebral Edema) and HAPE (High Altitude Pulmonary Edema). There are wide and unpredictable individual variations among those going to altitude. West et al., *High Altitude Medicine and Physiology*, 2013, is a recommended reference work.
7. Wilkins, *Among Secret Beauties*, 2013, p. 82.

Chapter 18 Employment opportunity in the Antarctic

1. Hillary Family Collection.
2. Ibid.
3. Wilkins, *Among Secret Beauties*, 2013, p. 69.
4. Quoted in Douglas, *Tenzing, Hero of Everest*, 2003, p. 245.
5. Hillary in Hunt, *The Ascent of Everest*, 1953, p. 204.
6. Tenzing in Ullman, *Man of Everest*, 1955, p. 265.
7. MHF, box 40, fdr 619.
8. Ibid.
9. Lowe, *Because It Is There*, 1959, p. 3. Lowe claims that he first introduced Ed to Fuchs in November 1954, whereas Ed puts the meeting in 1953. I have accepted 1953, though there is no mention of Fuchs or the Antarctic in his correspondence before late 1954. In *The Crossing of Antarctica*, Fuchs makes no mention of Hillary until he is appointed leader of the Ross Sea party in June 1955.
10. Ibid.
11. Hillary, *No Latitude for Error*, 1961, p. 13.
12. This outline is taken from Fuchs's 1990 autobiography, *A Time to Speak*.
13. Quoted in Haddelsey, *Shackleton's Dream*, 2012, p. 15.
14. Copy of Minutes of Polar Committee meeting, September 1953, Falla Papers, Alexander Turnbull Library.
15. MHF, box 45, fdr 689.
16. Ibid.

Chapter 19 Scott Base

1. Lowe, *Because It Is There*, 1959, p. 113.
2. Ibid., pp. 159–60.
3. Fuchs, *A Time to Speak*, 1990, p. 221.
4. During 1957–58 there were four stations along this coast: the British Royal Society IGY station at Halley Bay supported by the vessel *Tottan*; Fuchs's TAE station at Vahsel Bay; the Argentinian General Belgrano station on the Filchner Ice Shelf supported by the *San Martin*; and the American IGY station Ellsworth, also on the Filchner.
5. Fuchs's journal quoted in Stephenson, *Crevasse Roulette*, 2009, p. 26.
6. Hillary, *View from the Summit*, 1999, p. 129.
7. MHF, box 21, fdr 338.
8. McKenzie, *Opposite Poles*, 1963, p. 103.
9. 10 January 1957, MHF, box 2, fdr 56.
10. In the Antarctic chapters, distances are given in miles because they were the units of distance in 1957–58, and the naming of depots reflected this. Depots were called D280, D480 and D700 to indicate their distance in miles from Scott Base.
11. Gunn, *Land of the Long Day*, 2007, Ch. 2.
12. MHF, box 21, fdr 336.
13. Ibid.
14. Ibid.
15. Gunn, *Land of the Long Day*, 2007, Ch. 15. Bernie Gunn had a good four months on the Northern Survey, but when he returned to the Antarctic a year later he had an accident of the kind that illustrates the potentially lethal nature of Antarctic crevasses. Three of the party were in a Sno-Cat on what seemed to be safe snow when suddenly they were falling into an immensely deep crevasse. The driver was killed immediately but Bernie and his fellow geologist Jim Loweri survived, though with injuries and frostbite that kept them in hospital for months.
16. Ibid., Ch. 5.
17. Hillary diary, 31 October 1957, MHF, box 21, fdr 327.

Chapter 20 'Hellbent for the Pole'

1. Lister's diary, 22 November 1957, quoted in Haddelsey, *Shackleton's Dream*, 2012, p. 129.
2. Lowe, *Because It Is There*, 1959, pp. 105–06.
3. Hillary, *No Latitude for Error*, 1961, p. 122.
4. Ibid., p. 137.
5. Letter, 8 November 1957, MHF, box 21, fdr 336.
6. Ibid., 7 November 1957.
7. Ibid., 2 November 1957.
8. Letter Bowden to Hillary, 22 May 1957.
9. Hillary, *No Latitude for Error*, 1961, p. 156.
10. Hillary, *View from the Summit*, 1999, p. 162.
11. Letter, 1 December 1957, MHF, box 21, fdr 336.
12. Hillary, *No Latitude for Error*, 1961, p. 171.
13. Ibid, p. 172.
14. Ibid, p. 186.
15. Hillary, *View from the Summit*, 1999, p. 173.
16. Barber, *The White Desert*, 1958, p. 90.
17. Diary, 18 December 1957, MHF, box 21, fdr 336.
18. Hillary, *No Latitude for Error*, 1961, p. 191.
19. Fuchs, *The Crossing of Antarctica*, 1958, p. 239.
20. Stephenson, *Crevasse Roulette*, 2009, p. 104.
21. Fuchs diary, 19 December 1957, quoted in Haddelsey, *Shackleton's Dream*, 2012, p. 204.
22. Personal communication, 1963.
23. Hillary, *Nothing Venture*, 1975, p. 211.
24. Hillary, *No Latitude for Error*, 1961, p. 194.
25. Ibid., p. 195.
26. Fuchs, *The Crossing of Antarctica*, 1958, p. 239.
27. Hillary, *View from the Summit*, 1999, p. 176.
28. Diary, 23 December 1957, MHF, box 21, fdr 336.
29. Hillary, *View from the Summit*, 1999, p. 177.
30. Hillary, *No Latitude for Error*, 1961, p. 205.
31. '... of fifty drums of fuel the New Zealand party placed in the depots, only twenty drums were actually used by Bunny', Hillary, *View from the Summit*, 1999, p. 179.
32. Quoted in Haddelsey, *Shackleton's Dream*, 2012, p. 204.
33. Hillary, *No Latitude for Error*, 1961, p. 206.
34. McKenzie, *Opposite Poles*, 1963, p. 103.
35. Hillary, *Nothing Venture*, 1975, p. 231.
36. Stephenson, *Crevasse Roulette*, 2009, p. 124.
37. Hillary, *View from the Summit*, 1999, p. 177.
38. Fuchs, *The Crossing of Antarctica*, 1958, p. 248.
39. Ibid.
40. MHF, box 2, fdr 56.
41. Ibid.
42. MHF, box 21, fdr 336.
43. Hillary, *View from the Summit*, 1999, p. 182.

Chapter 21 Beekeeper in search of a better-paying occupation

1. Letter Parry to Hillary, MHF, box 45, fdr 696.
2. Greenfield, *A Smattering of Monsters*, 1995, p. 145.
3. Hillary, *Nothing Venture*, 1975, p. 235.
4. Hillary, *Two Generations*, 1984, p. 19.
5. McKenzie, *Opposite Poles*, 1963, p. 176.

6. MHF, box 31, fdr 490.
7. Thomson, *Climbing the Pole*, 2010, p. 210.
8. Mac Vincent in the *Auckland Star*, 27 May 1961.
9. MHF, box 1, fdr 22.
10. *Zealandia*, 1 June 1961 in ibid.
11. Diary, 6 July 1958, MHF, box 24, fdr 383.
12. MHF, box 40, fdr 619.
13. Diary, 26 January 1958, MHF, box 21, fdr 328.
14. Letter, 25 June 1958, MHF, box 45, fdr 696.
15. Letter, 16 February 1959, MHF, box 43, fdr 667.
16. Ibid.
17. Ibid.
18. Ibid.
19. Ibid.
20. This letter has been abbreviated.
21. Hillary to Dienhart, 19 September 1959, MHF, box 5, fdr 104.
22. MHF, box 5, fdr 104.
23. Letter, 14 October 1959, Sarah Hillary archive, box 4, fdr 83.
24. MHF, box 43, fdr 668.

Chapter 22 The Silver Hut expedition
1. Doig and Bhagat, *Look Back in Wonder*, 1995, pp. 259, 273.
2. Letter to Pugh, 18 August 1960, MHF, box 42, fdr 651.
3. Letter to Pugh, 14 September 1960, in ibid.
4. Hillary and Doig, *High in the Thin Cold Air*, 1962, p. 109.
5. Ibid., p. 120.
6. 13 September 1960, MHF, box 1, fdr 6.
7. Unattributed newspaper clipping, June 1961, MHF, box 1, fdr 12.
8. Perrin, *Shipton and Tilman*, 2013, pp. 379–87.
9. Ibid., p. 386.
10. Ibid., p. 387.
11. Snellgrove, *Buddhist Himalaya*, 1957, p. 294.
12. Morris, *Coronation Everest*, 1958, p. 116.
13. Stobart, *Adventurer's Eye*, 1958, p. 213.
14. MHF, box 42, fdr 651.
15. Ibid.
16. Hillary diary, MHF, box 3, fdr 74.
17. Tuckey, *Everest, The First Ascent*, 2013, p. 352.
18. Hillary diary, 12 November 1960, MHF, box 3, fdr 74.

Chapter 23 Makalu unravels
1. MHF, box 42, fdr 651.
2. Letter, 29 December 1960, Hillary Family Collection.
3. Letter, 27 February 1961, in ibid.
4. MHF, box 1, fdr 4.
5. MHF, box 5, fdr 104.
6. Ibid.
7. Doig and Bhagat, *Look Back in Wonder*, 1995, p. 304.
8. MHF, box 5, fdr 130. Eight hundred rupees was the equivalent of US$80.
9. Undated letter, MHF, box 42, fdr 651.
10. Letter, 8 April 1961, Hillary Family Collection.
11. Letter, 25 April 1961, in ibid.

12. Franco, *Makalu*, 1957, p. 41.
13. Hillary diary, 4 May 1961, MHF, box 3, fdr 74.
14. Hillary diary, 7 May 1961, in ibid. In 1961 when altitude sickness was not well understood these symptoms were attributed to a stroke/cardiovascular accident. In retrospect, it can be seen that the symptoms and their time-course are consistent with cerebral hypoxia due to the cerebral and/or pulmonary edema that Ed had become prone to.
15. Franco, *Makalu*, 1957, p. 234.
16. Nevison diary, MHF, box 6, fdr 126.
17. Ibid.
18. Ibid.
19. Ortenburger diary, MHF, box 3, fdr 81.
20. Ibid.
21. West, *High Life*, 1998.

Chapter 24 Three new careers
1. Diary, 9 May 1951, MHF, box 22, fdr 358.
2. Ibid.
3. Ibid., 14 May 1961.
4. Ibid., 26 May 1961.
5. Ibid., 16 June 1961.
6. Ed to Louise, 29 June 1961, Hillary Family Collection.
7. Ed to Louise, 30 June 1961, Hillary Family Collection.
8. Hillary, *Nothing Venture*, 1975, p. 253.
9. MHF, boxes 13–17, 35–38.
10. Hillary, *View from the Summit*, 1999, p. 215.
11. Hillary, Louise, *Keep Calm If You Can*, 1963, pp. 9–11.
12. Ibid., p. 91.
13. Ibid., p. 159.
14. MHF, box 24, fdr 387.
15. Ed to Louise, 26 April 1965, Hillary Family Collection.

Chapter 25 Repaying a debt
1. Hillary, *Schoolhouse in the Clouds*, 1964, p. 3.
2. MHF, box 43, fdr 666.
3. Fisher, *Sherpas*, 1990, p. 100.
4. Hillary, *Schoolhouse in the Clouds*, 1964, p. 49.
5. Hillary, *Nothing Venture*, 1975, p. 263.
6. Hillary, Louise, *A Yak for Christmas*, 1968, p. 47.
7. Hillary, *Nothing Venture*, 1975, p. 295.
8. Hillary, Louise, *A Yak for Christmas*, 1968, pp. 28–33.
9. Their experiences are described in Gill and Cook, *Himalayan Hospitals*, 2011, based on letters written by the volunteers.
10. Hillary, *Schoolhouse in the Clouds*, 1964, p. 5.
11. Ibid., p. 135.
12. Ibid., pp. 23–24.

Chapter 26 The best decade of Ed's life
1. Ed to author, personal communication.
2. Hillary, *Nothing Venture*, 1975, p. 252.
3. MHF, box 10, fdrs 194–198.
4. Ibid.
5. MHF, box 20, fdr 315.

6. Hillary, *Nothing Venture*, 1975, p. 285.
7. Hamilton, *White Water*, 1963.
8. Following quotations from MHF, box 23, fdr 370.
9. Great Barrier is a large island at the outer edge of Auckland's Hauraki Gulf.
10. Hillary, Louise, *High Time*, 1973, pp. 185–86.
11. Hillary, *Nothing Venture*, 1975, p. 308.

Chapter 27 A plane crash ends two lives and blights another
1. Letter, 20 February 1975, Hillary Family Collection.
2. Letter, 12 March 1975, Hillary Family Collection.
3. Letters, 22–24 March 1975, Hillary Family Collection.
4. Letter, 5 April 1975, MHF, box 41, fdr 636.
5. Hillary and Hillary, *Two Generations*, 1984, p. 140.
6. Hillary, *View from the Summit*, 1999, p. 240.
7. Gill and Cook, *Himalayan Hospitals*, 2011, p. 120.
8. Letter, 21 April 75, MHF, box 41, fdr 636.
9. Letter, 29 May 1975, in ibid.
10. Andrew Pollak in the *Irish Times*, 3 April 1975, MHF, box 24, fdr 385.
11. Maurice Wiggin in the *Sunday Times*, MHF, box 24, fdr 385.
12. *Burnley Evening Star*, MHF, box 24, fdr 385.
13. Letter, 9 October 1975, MHF, fdr 638.
14. Letter, 12 September 1975, MHF, fdr 638.
15. Hillary Family Collection.

Chapter 28 Killing time making films
1. Letter Ed to Jim, Murray, Graeme and Mike, 2 April 1976, MHF, box 40, fdr 626.
2. Ibid.
3. MHF, box 41, fdr 637.
4. Hillary diary, 1 October 1976, in ibid.
5. Ibid.
6. Hillary diary, 2 October 1976, in ibid.
7. Hillary diary, 1 November 1976, in ibid.
8. Hillary diary, 2 November 1976, in ibid.
9. Hillary diary, 1 November 1976, in ibid.
10. MHF, box 41, fdr 637.
11. Hillary diary, 2 April 1976, MHF, box 41, fdr 637.

Chapter 29 Ocean to Sky, the last big expedition
1. MHF, box 46, fdr 708.
2. Hillary, *From the Ocean to the Sky*, 1979, p. 43.
3. Calcutta is the anglicisation of Kolkata, the name of the original village where the city was built. In 2001 the city returned to its original name. Since 1977 the population of Greater Kolkata has grown from 8 million to 15 million.
4. Darshan is to acquire merit by being in the presence of a holy person or someone who is making a great pilgrimage.
5. Hillary, *From the Ocean to the Sky*, 1979, p. 89.
6. Diary, 1 September 1977, MHF, box 47, fdr 717.
7. Diary, 1 October 1977, MHF, box 47, fdr 718.

Chapter 30 Reconciliation
1. MHF, box 46, fdr 707.
2. Hillary and Hillary, *Two Generations*, 1984, pp. 144–45.

3. Personal communication, 2016.
4. Hillary diary, 22 February 1978, MHF, box 41, fdr 637.
5. Letter to Sarah, 4 February 1977, MHF, box 41, fdr 638.
6. Personal communication, 2016.
7. Letter to Liz Hawley, 11 May 1978, MHF, box 46, fdr 710.
8. Hillary, *View from the Summit*, 1999, p. 256.
9. Graham Langton, 'Mulgrew, Peter David', from the Dictionary of New Zealand Biography. Te Ara – the Encyclopedia of New Zealand, www.teara.govt.nz/en/biographies/5m61/mulgrew-peter-david (accessed 27 February 2017).
10. www.stuff.co.nz/national/erebus/3030756/flight-transcript (accessed 27 February 2017).
11. Hillary, *View from the Summit*, 1999, p. 257.
12. Hillary diary, 23–28 August 1981, MHF, box 47, fdr 719.
13. Hillary diary, 10 September 1981, in ibid.
14. Tabin, Geoffrey C., 'The Kangshung Face of Everest', *American Alpine Journal*, 1982.
15. In 1983 an American expedition led by Jim Morrissey, and including Lou Reichardt and many of the 1981 team, returned to the Kangshung Face. Climbing the buttress in 28 days, they found better snow conditions and weather on the face above. On 8 October three climbers reached the summit, followed next day by three more.
16. Hillary and Hillary, *Two Generations*, 1984, pp. 106–11.
17. Hillary, *View from the Summit*, 1999, p. 268.
18. *Auckland Star*, 27 June 1967.
19. *New Zealand Herald*, 14 April 1969.
20. Hillary, *View from the Summit*, 1999, p. 272.
21. Ibid., p. 276.
22. Merv Norrish to Ed Hillary, 7 April 1986, MHF, box 34, fdr 541.
23. Merv Norrish to Ed Hillary, 23 June 1986, MHF, box 35, fdr 557.
24. Hillary, *View from the Summit*, 1999, p. 280.
25. Ibid., p. 285.

Chapter 31 The last two decades

1. David Shlim interpreted this episode in the light of what was known about high altitude sickness (HAS) and his description helped explain Ed's later health problems.

   The hypoxia of high altitude is known to cause changes in the small blood vessels in the lungs and brain. In the lungs hypoxia causes constriction of small blood vessels (arterioles) leading to pulmonary hypertension: an increase in the blood pressure on the right side of the heart. In most people this is of little consequence but in a few where hypertension is more severe, high altitude pulmonary edema (HAPE) develops. Uniform arteriolar constriction throughout both lungs would cause hypertension but not edema. In HAPE, constriction is patchy, not uniform, so in an area of lung where there is no constriction the capillaries, which are the smallest vessels and the site where absorption of oxygen into blood cells takes place, are subjected to a damagingly high pressure. As a result the capillaries leak fluid into the alveoli, the air spaces of the lung. This is pulmonary edema. Oxygen cannot be absorbed from these fluid-filled alveoli, and the oxygen saturation/content of the blood feeding brain, muscles and heart falls. Breathlessness and cyanosis are major symptoms of HAPE. On a chest x-ray the edema shows as patches of increased opacity. If untreated, severe HAPE will follow a downward spiral to death.

   In high altitude cerebral edema (HACE) the cerebral vessels do not constrict but are damaged by hypoxia. Damaged capillaries leak fluid into the brain, causing an increase in intracranial pressure and a range of symptoms depending on which areas of the brain are most affected. Because HAPE reduces the oxygen supply to all tissues, including the brain, it makes HACE worse. As with HAPE, untreated severe HACE typically follows a downward spiral to death.

Ed suffered from both HACE and HAPE at various times. His cerebral symptoms included severe headache, unilateral facial pain, dysarthria, diplopia, anorexia, nausea, vomiting, backache, fever, ataxia, insomnia, nightmares, confusion and coma.

Why do some people suffer from HACE and HAPE and not others? The answer is that it is an idiosyncratic response unrelated to the individual's fitness or climbing ability. It just happens. An analogy is the way some individuals develop asthma when exposed to an allergen like grass pollen.

Ed became increasingly susceptible to HAPE and HACE each time he returned to the Himalayas from 1954 onwards. From 1960 he was spending weeks or months of each year at high altitude while managing his projects, and by 1991 there was evidence of permanent lung damage, as shown by an oxygen saturation of 90% at sea level when a normal value is 97–100%. By 2001 he was taking digoxin for heart failure and in his last year he had ascites secondary to right heart failure. See West et al., *High Altitude Medicine and Physiology*, 2012 for a more detailed account of the pathophysiology of HAPE and HACE.

2. Hillary, *View from the Summit*, 1999, p. 287.
3. Jefferies, *Sagarmatha*, 1986, p. 20.
4. The Most Noble Order of the Garter was founded by Edward lll in 1348 and is England's highest order of chivalry. An explanation of the motto is that when Edward was dancing with Joan of Kent, her garter slipped to her ankle. The King, having reached for her garter, silenced sniggering courtiers with the words *Honi soit qui mal y pense* – Shame be to him who thinks evil of it.
5. MHF, box 49, fdr 775.
6. David Hill, in *New Zealand Listener*, 31 July 1999.
7. Antony Rouse, in *London Evening Standard*, 14 July 1999.
8. Jan Morris, in *Literary Review*, July 1999.
9. Betty Joplin interview with the author, 2008.
10. *New Zealand Herald*, 14 January 2008.
11. Jan Morris speaking at the New Zealand Alpine Club commemorative gathering in the Auckland Domain, 23 January 2008.

Epilogue

1. Hillary and Hillary, *Two Generations*, 1984, p. 19.
2. Hillary, *Nothing Venture*, 1975, p. 28.
3. Greenfield, *A Smattering of Monsters*, 1995, p. 152.
4. Interview in the *Washington Post*, 24 July 1970.
5. Di McKinnon, personal communication, 2011.
6. Marilyn Eales, personal communication, 2014.
7. Sarah Hillary, personal interview, 2009.
8. Peter Hillary, personal interview, 2011.
9. The museum files have many sets of speech notes.
10. Hillary, *Schoolhouse in the Clouds*, 1964, p. 1.
11. Mulgan, John, *Report on Experience*, Oxford University Press, 1947, p. 14.
12. Hillary, *Nothing Venture*, 1975, p. 308.

Bibliography

Arnold, Anthea, *Eight Men in a Crate: The Ordeal of the Advance Party of the Trans-Antarctic Expedition 1955–1957. Based on the diary of Rainer Goldsmith*, Erskine Press, Norwich, 2007.

Astill, Tony, *Mount Everest: The Reconnaissance 1935. 'The Forgotten Adventure'*, Published by author, London, 2005.

Barber, Noel, *The White Desert*, Hodder & Stoughton, London, 1958.

Bert, P., *La Pression Barométrique*, Masson, Paris, 1878.

Booth, Pat, *Edmund Hillary: The Life of a Legend*, Moa Beckett, Auckland, 1993.

Bruce, C.G., *The Assault on Mount Everest 1922*, Edward Arnold & Co., London, 1923.

Conefrey, Mick, *Everest 1953, The Epic Story of the First Ascent*, Oneworld, Oxford, 2012.

Davis, Wade, *Into the Silence: The Great War, Mallory and the Conquest of Everest*, Vintage, London, 2011.

Dittert, René, Chevalley, Gabriel and Raymond Lambert, *Forerunners to Everest: The Story of the Swiss Expeditions of 1952*, George Allen & Unwin, London, 1954.

Doig, Desmond and Dubby Bhagat, *Look Back in Wonder*, Indus-Harper Collins, New Delhi, 1995.

Douglas, Ed, *Tenzing: A Biography of Tenzing Norgay*, National Geographic, Washington, 2003.

Fisher, James, *Sherpas: Reflections on Change in Himalayan Nepal*, University of California Press, Berkeley, 1990.

Franco, Jean, *Makalu*, Jonathan Cape, London, 1957.

Fuchs, Sir Vivian and Sir Edmund Hillary, *The Crossing of Antarctica*, Cassell, London, 1958.

Fuchs, Sir Vivian, *A Time to Speak*, Anthony Nelson, London, 1990.

Gill, Michael, *Mountain Midsummer*, Hodder & Stoughton, London, 1969.

Gill, Michael and Lynley Cook, *Himalayan Hospitals*, Craig Potton Publishing, Nelson, 2011.

Greenfield, George, *A Smattering of Monsters: A Kind of Memoir*, Little Brown & Co., London, 1995.

Gunn, Bernard, *Land of the Long Day*, unpublished memoir, 2007.

Haddelsey, Stephen, *Shackleton's Dream: Fuchs, Hillary and the Crossing of Antarctica*, The History Press, Brimscombe Port, Stroud, 2012.

Hamilton, Joyce, *White Water: The Colorado Jet Boat Expedition*, Caxton Press, Christchurch, 1963.

Hardie, Norman, *On My Own Two Feet*, Canterbury University Press, Christchurch, 2006.

Hatherton, Trevor (ed.), *Antarctica*, Methuen, London, 1965.

Hemmleb J., Johnson L.A. and E.R. Simonson, as told to W.E. Nothdurft, *Ghosts of Everest: The Search for Mallory and Irvine, from the expedition that discovered Mallory's body*, The Mountaineers Books, Seattle, 1999.

Hillary, Edmund, *High Adventure*, Hodder & Stoughton, London, 1955.

Hillary, Edmund, *No Latitude for Error*, Hodder & Stoughton, London, 1961.

Hillary, Edmund, *Schoolhouse in the Clouds*, Hodder & Stoughton, London, 1964.

Hillary, Edmund, *Nothing Venture, Nothing Win*, Hodder & Stoughton, London, 1975.

Hillary, Edmund, *From the Ocean to the Sky*, Viking, New York, 1979.

Hillary, Edmund, *View From the Summit*, Doubleday, London, 1999.

Hillary, Edmund and Desmond Doig, *High in the Thin Cold Air*, Hodder & Stoughton, London, 1962.

Hillary, Edmund and Peter Hillary, *Two Generations*, Hodder & Stoughton, London, 1984.

Hillary, Louise, *Keep Calm If You Can*, Hodder & Stoughton, London, 1963.

Hillary, Louise, *A Yak for Christmas*, Hodder & Stoughton, London, 1968.

Hillary, Louise, *High Time*, Hodder & Stoughton, London, 1973.

Hunt, John, *The Ascent of Everest*, Hodder & Stoughton, London, 1953.

Hunt, John, *Life is Meeting*, Hodder & Stoughton, London, 1978.

Jefferies, Margaret, *Sagarmatha, Mother of the Universe*, David Bateman, Auckland, 1986.

Johnston, Alexa, *Sir Edmund Hillary. An Extraordinary Life*, Viking, Auckland, 2005.

Kurz, Marcel, *The Mountain World 1953*, George Allen & Unwin, London, 1953.

Kurz, Marcel, *The Mountain World 1954*, George Allen & Unwin, London, 1954.

Liddell Hart, B.H., *History of the First World War*, Cassell, London, 1970.

Little, Paul, *After Everest: Inside the Private World of Edmund Hillary*, Allen & Unwin, London, 2012.

Lowe, George, *Because It Is There*, Cassell, London, 1959.

Lowe, George, *Letters from Everest*, Silverbear, an imprint of Polarworld, UK, 2013.

Lowe, George and Huw Lewis-Jones, *The Conquest of Everest*, Thames & Hudson, London, 2013.

Mahoney, Michael, *Harry Ayres: Mountain Guide*, Whitcoulls, Christchurch, 1982.

McKinnon, Lyn, *Only Two for Everest: How a First Ascent by Riddiford and Cotter Shaped Climbing History*, Otago University Press, Dunedin, 2016.

McKenzie, Douglas, *Opposite Poles*, Robert Hale, London, and Whitcombe & Tombs, Christchurch, 1963.

Morris, James, *Coronation Everest*, Faber & Faber, London, 1958.

Mulgrew, Peter, *No Place For Men*, A.H. & A.W. Reed, Wellington, 1964.

Noel, John, *Through Tibet to Everest*, Hodder & Stoughton, London, 1927.

Norton, E.F., *The Fight for Everest 1924*, first published Arnold, London, 1925; Pilgrims Publishing, Kathmandu, 2002.

Noyce, Wilfrid, *South Col: One Man's Adventure on the Ascent of Everest, 1953*, William Heinemann, London, 1954.

Perrin, Jim, *Shipton and Tilman: The Great Decade of Himalayan Exploration*, Arrow Books, London, 2013.

Pugh, L.G.C.E., *British Expedition to Cho Oyu. Report to the Medical Research Council*, unpublished paper (66 pp.), 1952, in Pugh Papers, Mandeville Collection, University of California, San Diego.

Robertson, D., *George Mallory*, Faber & Faber, London, 1969.

Ruttledge, Hugh, *Everest 1933*, Hodder & Stoughton, London, 1934.

Ruttledge, Hugh, *Everest, The Unfinished Adventure*, Hodder & Stoughton, London, 1937.

Shipton, Eric, *Upon that Mountain*, Hodder & Stoughton, London, 1943.

Shipton, Eric, *The Mount Everest Reconnaissance Expedition 1951*, Hodder & Stoughton, London, 1952.

Shipton, Eric, *That Untravelled World, An Autobiography*, Hodder & Stoughton, London, 1969.

Snellgrove, D.L., *Buddhist Himalaya: Travels and Studies in Quest of the Origins and Nature of Tibetan Religion*, Bruno Cassirer, Oxford, 1957.

Somervell, T.H., *After Everest*, Hodder & Stoughton, London, 1936.

Steele, Peter, *Eric Shipton. Everest and Beyond*, Constable, London, 1998.

Stephenson, Jon, *Crevasse Roulette. The First Trans-Antarctic Crossing 1957–58*, Rosenberg Publishing, Kenthurst NSW, 2009.

Stobart, Tom, *Adventurer's Eye: The Autobiography of the Everest Film-man*, Odhams, Watford, 1958.

Tenzing, Norgay, with James Ramsay Ullman, *Man of Everest: The Autobiography of Tenzing of Everest*, George Harrap, London, 1955.

Thomson, John, *Climbing the Pole. Edmund Hillary and The Trans-Antarctic Expedition 1955–1958*, Erskine Press, Norwich, 2010.

Tilman, H.W., *Mount Everest 1938*, first published Cambridge University Press, Cambridge, 1948; Pilgrims Publishing, Kathmandu, 2004.

Tuckey, Harriet, *Everest, The First Ascent, The Untold Story of Griffith Pugh, The Man Who Made It Possible*, Rider, London, 2013.

Unsworth, Walt, *Everest*, Oxford University Press, Oxford, 1989.

Wainwright, Robert, *The Maverick Mountaineer: The Remarkable Life of George Ingle Finch: Climber, Scientist, Inventor*, HarperCollins, Sydney, 2015.

Ward, Michael, *In This Short Span: A Mountaineering Memoir*, Victor Gollancz, London, 1972.

Ward, Michael, *Mountain Medicine: A Clinical Study of Cold and High Altitude*, Crosby Lockwood Staples, London, 1975.

Ward, Michael, *Everest, A Thousand Years of Exploration: A Record of Mountaineering Geographical Exploration Medical Research and Mapping*, Hayloft Publishing, UK, 2013.

West, John, *High Life: A History of High-Altitude Physiology and Medicine*, Oxford University Press, New York and Oxford, 1998.

West, John B., Schoene, Robert B., Luks, Andrew M. and James S. Milledge, *High Altitude Medicine and Physiology, 5th edition*, CRC Press, Boca Raton, Florida, 2012.

Wilkins, Brian, *Among Secret Beauties: A Memoir of Mountaineering in New Zealand and the Himalayas*, Otago University Press, Dunedin, 2013.

New Zealand & Antarctica

Bay of Islands

Dargaville • Whakahara
Wairoa River
Kaipara Harbour   Great Barrier Is.
Helensville   Rangitoto Is.
                                    Waitematā Harbour
Anawhata • AUCKLAND

                                    TAURANGA
HAMILTON

NEW PLYMOUTH
        • Mt Taranaki   • Mt Ruapehu

                    Cook Strait

NELSON   WELLINGTON
BLENHEIM

Mt Tapuaeunuku •

        KAIKŌURA MTNS

Mt Elie de Beaumont
Aoraki-Mount Cook
Mt Footstool   • Malte Brun
SEALY RANGE   Hooker Valley   CHRISTCHURCH
                 The Hermitage

QUEENSTOWN

        DUNEDIN

INVERCARGILL

0   100   200 km

South Georgia

Drake Passage

WEDDELL SEA

Cape Norvegia

Antarctic Circle

Graham Land

Ronne Ice Shelf

Shackleton Base

Filchner Ice Shelf

South Ice

East Antarctic Icesheet

West Antarctic Icesheet

TRANS-ANTARCTIC MOUNTAINS

South Pole

Polar Plateau

D700

D480

Skelton Gl.

Ross Ice Shelf

Scott Base

Ross Is.

McMurdo Sound

ROSS SEA

Cape Hallett · Mt Herschel

Cape Adare

SOUTHERN OCEAN

Tasmania

Melbourne

Christchurch

NEW ZEALAND

AUSTRALIA

0   500   1000 km

Index

373–75, **374**, 379, 402 (*see also* Silver Hut expedition (Himalayan Scientific and Mountaineering Expedition), 1961–62)

film-making: *The Adventure World of Sir Edmund Hillary* 433–36; documentaries 429, 432–33; *Gold River* 436; Ocean to Sky expedition, 1977 444–45, 460; plans for Hidden Valley film, Nepal 438; *The Sea Pillars of Great Barrier* 436, 465–66; West Coast reconnaissance 437

health: altitude sickness 248–51, 343–44, 355, 357, 364, 415, 416, 438, 456–58, 470–73, 478, 489, 512n6 (chap. 17), 516n14 (chap. 23), 518n1; benzodiazapine use 429, 438–40; depression 499, 503; depression after deaths of Louise and Belinda 426–28, 429, 430, 438–40, 464, 477, 501–02; final illness and death 491–92

leisure activities: boxing, wrestling and ju-jitsu 47, 48; Ōrewa bach 48, **64**; reading 46, 68, 75–76; rugby 40, 49, 52, 66, 67–68; skiing 49, 229–30; table tennis 69; tramping 51

marriages and family: bach near Anawhata 417, 439; camping holiday, United States and Canada 376–79, **378**; car 253; correspondence with Louise after marriage 276–77, 288–89, 292, 294, 305–06, 322, 348–49, 355, 373, 415–17; courtship and marriage to Louise 225–41, **239**, **240**, 242, 283, 401–02, 419, 426, 427, 477, 490, 499; and deaths of Louise and Belinda 423–24, **425**, 426–30, **433**, 438–41, 460, 461, 477, 501–02; family in Chicago **372**, 373–74; family photos **308**, **372**, **376**, **395**; financial assistance to children 434, 463, 479; grandchildren 462, 463, 479; house, Remuera 241, 253–54, 314, 428, 462, 479, 480; relationship with, and marriage to June 464, **465**, 473, 477, 479–80, 489, 490, 502; *see also* Hillary, Belinda; Hillary, Peter; Hillary, Sarah

non-mountain expeditions: Commonwealth Trans-Antarctic Expedition, 1955–58 89, 259–61, 264–66, 268–79, **278**, 281–307, **297**, **300**, **303**, **307**, 401, 474, 499–500; Nepal trek, 1976 437–38, 440–41; Ocean to Sky expedition,

1977 **442**, 443–60, **450**, 502; Sun Kosi jet boat expedition 409–13

personal attributes and beliefs: affability 68; ambition 96, 499; characteristics inherited from father 495; conscientious objector 59. 61, 62; determination 79, 495; egalitarianism 69, 503; feeling of inferiority about physique 45, 53; humility 503; loneliness 40, 44, 71; political left 495; Radiant Living 56–58, **58**, 61, 65, 496; restlessness 499; ruggedness 79, 95; shyness 53, 496; stubbornness 503

portraits **50**, **492**, **494**, **504**

public speaking 491, 499, 500–01, 502–03; acceptance speech, *Argosy* Explorer of the Year award 319; Dominion Reconstruction Conference, youth speaker 62–63; Everest lectures 83, 237, 238, 241, 242; fundraising for development aid projects in Nepal 417, 469, 473–74, 479, 500; lectures for World Book and Sears Roebuck 374, 415, 500; narrations for *Landfall in Unknown Seas* and *Sinfonia Antarctica* 490–91; national radio programme 62, 233; Radiant Living speaker 57, 496; speech, at Rotary's invitation, to school prefects in Auckland 474

social life and friendships: Air Force 68; on board *Orion,* 1951 98, **99**; dinner with George Lowe and friends, 1951 228–29; first girlfriend 63–65; friendships 419, 467; George Lowe **90**, 91–93, 96, 210, 228–29, 256, 268, 310, 419, 460; social interactions 499; *see also* names of individual friends

writing: account of summit day in Hunt's *The Ascent of Everest* 241, 254, 257–58; autobiographies 21, 307, 415, 499 (*see also High Adventure; Nothing Venture Nothing Win; View from the Summit*); *Call Not to the Gods* (unpublished novel) 379–81; correspondence with Tenzing 257–60; *The Crossing of Antarctica* **309**; *High Adventure* (1955) 59–61, 208, 237, 239, 253–55, **255**, **256**, 256–57, 306, 379, 499, 503; *High in the Thin Cold Air* (1961) 373; income from writing 254–55, 314, 379, 499; influence of School of Radiant

533

538